A PRINCELY BRAVE WOMAN

This book is dedicated to two princely brave women:
Leah and Lauren

A Princely Brave Woman

Essays on Margaret Cavendish, Duchess of Newcastle

Edited with an Introduction by
STEPHEN CLUCAS

Routledge
Taylor & Francis Group
LONDON AND NEW YORK

First published 2003 by Ashgate Publishing

Reissued 2018 by Routledge
2 Park Square, Milton Park, Abingdon, Oxon OX14 4RN
711 Third Avenue, New York, NY 10017, USA

Routledge is an imprint of the Taylor & Francis Group, an informa business

Publisher's Note
The publisher has gone to great lengths to ensure the quality of this reprint but points out that some imperfections in the original copies may be apparent.

A Library of Congress record exists under LC control number: 2001099657

ISBN 13: 978-1-138-72416-7 (hbk)
ISBN 13: 978-1-138-72414-3 (pbk)
ISBN 13: 978-1-315-19263-5 (ebk)

Contents

List of Illustrations

Notes on Contributors

Neil Ankers is currently completing a PhD thesis on Margaret Cavendish's natural philosophy and its political and cultural contexts at the University of London. He has, for the past five years taught at Liverpool John Moores University, and has a number of articles dealing with aspects of Cavendish's writings awaiting publication.

Stephen Clucas is Senior Lecturer in English and Humanities at Birkbeck College, University of London. He organised the first Margaret Cavendish Colloquium at Birkbeck in December 1993, and contributed to a special issue of *The Seventeenth Century* on the Cavendish Circle edited by Timothy J. Raylor. Recent publications include a translation of Paolo Rossi's *Clavis Universalis* jointly published by the Chicago University Press and the Athlone Press as *Logic and the Art of Memory: The Quest for a Universal Language* (2000) and a facsimile edition of manuscript treatises by Henry Percy, ninth Earl of Northumberland for the Roxburghe Club (co-edited with Professor Gordon R. Batho) *The Wizard Earl's Advices to his Son* (2002).

Rebecca D'Monté is Lecturer at the University of the West of England, Bristol. She has written on the plays of Margaret Cavendish and Aphra Behn, and with Nicole Pohl has co-edited *Female Communities 1600-1800: Literary Visions and Cultural Realities* (Basingstoke: Macmillan, 2000). She is currently researching women's drama in the twentieth century.

James Fitzmaurice is Professor and Coordinator of Graduate Studies in English at Northern Arizona University. He holds a BA in comparative literature from Occidental College, an MA in English from California State University at Long Beach, and a PhD in English from the University of Iowa. He has been a postdoctoral fellow at Yale University and a senior visiting research fellow at Gonville and Caius College, Cambridge. He has published articles on Aphra Behn, Thomas Carew, Margaret Cavendish, Ben Jonson, Jane Barker and others. He was general editor for *Major Women Writers of Seventeenth-Century England*, and edited Margaret Cavendish's *Sociable Letters* as well as *The Humorous Lovers* by William Cavendish.

Susan Fitzmaurice (formerly Wright) is Associate Professor of Applied Linguistics and Associate Chair of the English Department at Northern Arizona University, Flagstaff, Arizona. Her PhD is in English from Cambridge University, England. She has taught at universities in South Africa, Britain and the United States. She has published extensively on the history of the English language, and specifically on the structure and history of literary discourse.

Sarah Hutton is Reader in Renaissance and Seventeenth-Century Studies at Middlesex University. Her publications include *New Perspectives on Renaissance Thought* (edited with John Henry, Duckworth 1990), *Henry More (1614-1687), Tercentenary Studies* (Kluwer Academic Publishers, 1992) and a revised edition of Marjorie Nicolson's *Conway Letters* (Clarendon Press, 1992). Her edition of Cudworth's *Treatise Concerning Eternal and Immutable Morality* was published by Cambridge University Press in 1996. Most recently she has edited, with Lynette Hunter, *Women, Science and Medicine, 1500-1700* (Alan Sutton, 1997). She is currently working on a book-length study of Anne Conway

Kate Lilley teaches literary history and theory in the Department of English at the University of Sydney. She is the editor of *The Blazing World and Other Writings* (Penguin Classics), and has contributed to a number of collections on early modern women's writing, most recently *Women's Poetry in the Enlightenment* (Macmillan, 1999), *Women's Writing 1550-1750* (Meridian, 2000), *Who's Who in Gay and Lesbian History* (Routledge 2000) and *Renaissance Women Online.*

Judith Peacock has participated in a number of conferences on Margaret Cavendish due to her work in the professional theatre. She researched and staged a rehearsed reading of *The Sociable Companions; or The Female Wits* for the Theatre Museum in Covent Garden in 1993. This led to the first ever professional production of a Cavendish play – *The Female Wits*, directed by George Pensotti – which enjoyed a successful month-long run at the Canal Café Theatre, Maida Vale, London, in February 1994.

Nicole Pohl is Lecturer at University College Northampton. Her research and publications concern early modern women's utopias and utopian architecture. She has co-edited *Female Communities 1600-1800: Literary Visions and Cultural Realities* (Macmillan, 2000), with Rebecca D'Monté.

Emma L. E. Rees is Lecturer in English at Chester College. In 1996 she organised an International Margaret Cavendish Conference at the University of East Anglia in 1996, and edited a special issue of *Women's Writing* shortly afterwards. Elected President of the International Margaret Cavendish Society in Paris in 1999, her main research has as its focus Cavendish's exilic writings, and the essay in this collection is part of a forthcoming book called *A Glorious Resurrection: Margaret Cavendish's Writings of the 1650s* (Manchester University Press, 2002). Other interests include Shakespeare studies; early-modern literature and culture; film theory, and gender studies. Further Cavendish publications are: *Heaven's Library* and *Nature's Pictures*: Platonic Paradigms and Trial by Genre', *Women's Writing* 4 (3), 1997, and '"Sweet honey of the Muses": Lucretian resonance in *Poems, and Fancies*', *In-Between: Essays and Studies in Literary Criticism* 9:1 (2000), 3-16. Emma also wrote the introduction to *Nature's Pictures* for Brown University's Women Writers Electronic Publications project, *Renaissance Women Online*.

Julie Sanders is Reader in English at Keele University. She is the author of *Ben Jonson's Theatrical Republics* (Macmillan, 1998) and *Caroline Drama* (Northcote House, 1999), as well as being co-editor of *Refashioning Ben Jonson* with Kate Chedgzoy and Susan Wiseman (Macmillan, 1998). She is currently working on an edition of Jonson's *The New Inn* for The Cambridge Edition of the 'Works of Ben Jonson'.

B. J. Sokol lectures at Goldsmiths College, University of London. His recent publications include several essays on Shakespeare, essays on Rochester, Robert Frost (and science), *Shakespeare's Legal Language* (with Mary Sokol), and *Art and Illusion in The Winter's Tale*. He is currently busy with biographies of several poets for the new *Dictionary of National Biography*, and with research on Shakespeare and early modern epistemologies.

Jay Stevenson is a freelance writer. He completed a doctoral thesis on Margaret Cavendish 'Physical Fictions: Margaret Cavendish and her Material Soul' at Rutgers University in 1997. His article 'The Mechanist–Vitalist Soul of Margaret Cavendish' was published in *Studies in English Literature 1500–1900* in 1996.

Marion Wynne-Davies is Reader in English at the University of Dundee. Her published works include *Women and Arthurian Literature* (1996) and *Renaissance Women Poets* (1998). With S. P. Cerasano she has edited *Renaissance Drama by Women: Texts and Documents* (1996) and *Readings in Renaissance Women's Drama* (1998).

Abbreviations

Glorious Fame	Kathleen Jones, *A Glorious Fame: The Life of Margaret Cavendish, Duchess of Newcastle, 1623–1673* (London: Bloomsbury, 1988).
Grounds (1668)	*Grounds of Natural Philosophy: Divided into thirteen parts: with an Appendix containing five parts. The Second Edition, much altered from the First, which went under the Name of Philosophical and Physical Opinions. Written by the Thrice Noble, Illustrious, and Excellent Princess, the Duchess of Newcastle* (London: A. Maxwell, 1668).
Letters and Poems (1676)	*Letters and Poems In Honour of the Incomparable Princess, Margaret, Dutchess of Newcastle* (London: Thomas Newcombe, 1676).
Life (1667)	*The Life of the Thrice Noble, High and Puissant Prince William Cavendishe, Duke, Marquess, and Earl of Newcastle; Earl of Ogle; Viscount Mansfield; and Baron of Bolsover, of Ogle, Bothal and Hepple: Gentleman of His Majesties Bed-chamber; one of His Majesties most Honourable Privy-Councel; Knight of the most Noble Order of the Garter; His Majesties Justice in Ayre Trent-North: Who had the honour to be Governour to our most Glorious King, and Gracious Soveraign, in his Youth, when He was Prince of Wales; and soon after was made Captain General of all the Provinces beyond the River of Trent, and other Parts of the Kingdom of England, with Power, by a Special Commission, to make Knights. Written by the Thrice Noble, Illustrious, and Excellent Princess, Margaret, Duchess of Newcastle, His Wife* (London: A. Maxwell, 1667).
Life (1906)	*The Life of William Cavendish, Duke of Newcastle*, To which is added *The True Relation of my Birth Breeding and Life By Margaret, Duchess of Newcastle*, ed. by C. H. Firth (London: Routledge & Sons Ltd., 1906).

Margaret the First	Douglas Grant, *Margaret the First: A Biography of Margaret Cavendish, Duchess of Newcastle* (London: Rupert Hart-Davis, 1957).
Natures Pictures (1656)	*Natures Pictures drawn by Fancies Pencil to the Life. Written by the thrice Noble, Illustrious, and Excellent Princess, the Lady Marchioness of Newcastle. In this Volume there are several feigned Stories of Natural Descriptions, as Comical, Tragical, and Tragi-Comical, Poetical, Romancical, Philosophical, and Historical, both in Prose and Verse, some all Verse, some all Prose, some mixt, partly Prose, and partly Verse. Also, there are some Morals, and some Dialogues; but they are as the Advantage Loaves of Bread to a Bakers dozen; and a true Story at the latter end, wherein there is no Feignings* (London: J. Martin and T. Allestrye, 1656).
Natures Picture (1671)	*Natures Picture Drawn by Fancies Pencil To the Life. Being several Feigned Stories, Comical, Tragical, Tragi-comical, Poetical, Romancical, Philosophical, Historical, and Moral: some in Verse, some in Prose; some Mixt, and some by Dialogues. Written by the Thrice Noble, Illustrious, and most Excellent Princess, The Duchess of Newcastle.* The Second Edition. (London: A. Maxwell, 1671).
Observations (1666)	*Observations upon Experimental Philosophy. To which is added, the Description of a New Blazing World. Written By the Thrice Noble, Illustrious, and Excellent Princesse, the Duchess of Newcastle* (London: A. Maxwell, 1666).
Observations (1668)	*Observations upon Experimental Philosophy: to which is added, The Description of a New Blazing World. Written by the Thrice Noble, Illustrious, and Excellent Princesse, the Duchess of Newcastle. The second Edition.* (London: A. Maxwell, 1668).
Orations (1662)	*Orations of Divers Sorts, Accommodated to Divers Places. Written by the thrice Noble, Illustrious and*

	excelent Princess, the Lady Marchioness of Newcastle (London: [n.pub.], 1662).
Philosophicall Fancies (1653)	*Philosophicall Fancies. Written By the Right Honourable, The Lady Newcastle* (London: Printed by Tho[mas] Roycroft, for J. Martin, and J. Allestrye, at the Bell in St Pauls Churchyard, 1653).
Philosophical Letters (1664)	*Philosophical Letters: or Modest Reflections Upon some Opinions in Natural Philosophy, maintained By several Famous and Learned Authors of this Age, Expressed by way of Letters: By the Thrice Noble, Illustrious, and Excellent Princess, The Lady Marchioness of Newcastle* (London: [no pub.], 1664).
Physical Opinions (1655)	*The Philosophical and Physical Opinions, Written by her Excellency, the Lady Marchionesse of Newcastle* (London: Printed for J. Martin and J. Allestrye at the Bell in St Pauls Church-Yard, 1655).
Physical Opinions (1663)	*Philosophical and Physical Opinions. Written By the Thrice Noble, Illustrious, and Excellent Princess, the Lady Marchioness of Newcastle* (London: William Wilson, 1663).
Playes (1662)	*Playes Written by the Thrice Noble, Illustrious and Excellent Princess, the Lady Marchioness of Newcastle* (London: Printed by A. Warren for John Martyn, James Allestry and Tho[mas] Dicas, at the Bell in Saint Pauls Church Yard, 1662).
Plays (1668)	*Plays, Never Before Printed. Written by the Thrice Noble, Illustrious, and Excellent Princesse, the Duchess of Newcastle* (London: A. Maxwell, 1668).
Poems (1668)	*Poems, or, Several Fancies in Verse: With the Animal Parliament, in Prose. Written By the Thrice Noble, Illustrious, and Excellent Princess, The Duchess of Newcastle. The Third Edition* (London: A. Maxwell, 1668).

Poems and Fancies (1653)	*Poems, and Fancies: Written by the Right Honourable, the Lady Margaret Countesse of Newcastle*, (London: Printed by T[homas] R[oycroft] for J. Martin and J. Allestrye at the Bell in Saint Pauls Church Yard , 1653).
Sociable Letters (1664)	*CCXI Sociable Letters, Written by the Thrice Noble, Illustrious and Excellent Princess, the Lady Marchioness of Newcastle* (London: William Wilson, 1664).
Sociable Letters (1997)	*Margaret Cavendish: Sociable Letters*, ed. by James Fitzmaurice (New York: Garland, 1997).
True Relation (1814)	*A True Relation of the Birth, Breeding, and Life, of Margaret Cavendish, Duchess of Newcastle, ed. by Sir Egerton Brydges* (Kent: Private Press of Lee Priory, 1814).
Women, Texts and Histories	*Clare Brant and Diane Purkiss (eds.) Women, Texts and Histories 1575–1760*, (London: Routledge, 1992).
Women, Writing, History	*Susan Wiseman and Isobel Grundy (ed.) Women, Writing, History 1640–1740* (London: B. T. Batsford Ltd., 1992).
Worlds Olio (1655)	*The Worlds Olio. Written By the Right Honorable, the Lady Margaret Newcastle* (London: J. Martin and J. Allestrye at the Bell in St Pauls Church-Yard, 1655).
Writings (1994)	*The Description of a New World Called the Blazing World and Other Writings*, ed. by Kate Lilley, (London: Pickering and Chatto, 1992, repr. Penguin Books, 1994).

1

Introduction

Stephen Clucas

After nearly three decades of feminist literary criticism, decades which have seen the recovery of a wide-ranging canon of women's writing, from the middle ages through to the twentieth century a collection of essays on Margaret Cavendish, Duchess of Newcastle hardly needs an apology. Cavendish was arguably the first Englishwoman to fashion herself as an author – a woman who desired, and achieved, publication on an unprecedented scale, and in a wide variety of literary genres. Her pursuit of literary fame and reputation was vigorous and startlingly self-conscious. She wrote an epistolary dedication addressed 'To all the Universities in Europe,'[1] and presented the handsome folio volumes of her works to the universities of Oxford and Cambridge, and to prominent members of the nobility.[2] She maintained an argumentative philosophical correspondence with Joseph Glanvill and openly criticised the 'experimental philosophy' of the Royal Society and the philosophical writings of Thomas Hobbes and Henry More.[3] And yet – as Kate Lilley has noted – Cavendish's works have frequently been interpreted as 'deformed in various ways: chaotic, old-fashioned, uneven, contradictory and insane.'[4] Perhaps more than any other early modern woman writer Cavendish has prompted critical disclaimers, qualifications, and apologies. The necessity for these apologetics is not entirely clear. The unimpeachably canonical Sir Thomas Browne, whose style was condemned by his contemporary Sir Kenelm Digby for its 'wilde fantasticke qualities and moods,'[5] does not require elaborate contemporary apologetics – there is no 'Sir Tom o' Bedlam' label to negotiate, as 'Mad Madge' must be repeatedly negotiated by Cavendish scholars. It is as if at some unconscious level of modern apologetics, beneath the principled complaints of women's unequal access to education, and consequent 'lack' of literary and philosophical mastery, we are still negotiating Margaret Cavendish's writings as transgressive, and thus in need of justification.

The uneasiness that has marked Cavendish's scholarly reception in the past is currently being revised in the light of re-emergent contexts for her 'lack' of order and method. As Anna Battigelli has recently argued in her book, *Margaret Cavendish: Exile of the Mind*, when viewed in the light of particular philosophical and literary concerns:

> The very characteristics that have caused scholars to dismiss Cavendish – her lack of method, her willingness to embrace contradictions, her confidence in deductive thinking, her eccentricity and self-absorption – become historically significant.[6]

Margaret Cavendish, like many other early-modern figures, benefits from being located in appropriate discursive contexts. 'Discourse' itself, in fact, in the sense of speech, or conversation, is a neglected, but vitally important key to understanding Cavendish's work, which she often talks of in connection with familiar (and familial) conversation. In her *Philosophical and Physical Opinions* of 1655, for example, Cavendish defended her familiarity with the 'names and terms of art' as a natural attainment for a member of a 'family of quality', who are accustomed to use such language in ordinary discourse. Her family she says, were 'rational, learned, understanding and wittie' and so was their discourse (see illustration 1.1).[7] She has learnt her discursive skills, she says, from 'my neerest and dearest friends as from my own brothers, my Lord brother, and my Lord,' and listening to their discourse, she says, has taught her more than others have gained from a formal education because of her natural wit:

> For truly I have gathered more by piece-meals, then from a full relation, or a methodical education for knowledge; but my fancy will build thereupon, and make discourse therefrom, and so of every thing they discourse of [.][8]

Charges of plagiarism lead her, however, to distinguish between the knowledge she acquired through 'intimate acquaintance and familiar conversation' and the more specialised knowledge that she might have gleaned from 'visiting and entertaining discourse' with 'professed Philosophers' (such as Descartes and Hobbes). Her exchanges with the philosophers in their circle she says was largely made up of 'cautionary, frivolous, vain, idle, or at least but common and ordinary matter'. She has, however, discoursed intimately with her 'husband, brothers, and the rest of my family' who although they neither 'Philosophers nor Scholars' are 'learned therein.'[9] This point about the emergence of her philosophical talents in the context of familial discourse is re-iterated by William in his apologetic preface, where he defends her philosophical literacy from charges of unseemliness and plagiarism:

> I assure you her conversation with her Brother, and Brother-in-law, were enough without a miracle or an impossibility to get the language of the arts, and learned professions, which are their terms, without taking any degrees in Schooles [...] but truly she did never Impe her high-flying Phancies, with any old broken Fethers out of any university[...].[10]

Ultimately, of course, it is these 'high-flying Phancies' of her own, that are the self-legitimating grounds of Margaret's discourse, especially in the arena of natural philosophy, which she saw as a realm of particular philosophical liberty:

> in natural things my natural reason will concieve them without being any wayes instructed; and so working a brain I have that many times on small objects or subjects will raise up many several phancies, and opinions therein, from which my

Illustration 1.1 Familiar Conversation in the Cavendish Household: Engraved frontispiece from *Natures Pictures* (1656), by permission of The British Library, 8407hll

> discourse betwixt reason and the opinions will be produced [...] [so that] my head is fully populated with divers opinions, and so many phancies are therein, as sometimes they lie like a swarme of bees in a round heap, and sometimes they flie abroad to gather honey from the sweet flowry rhetorick of my Lords discourse, and wax from his wise judgement which they work into a comb making chapters therein.[11]

It is in this collapsing of the distinction between philosophical and civil discourse, and the privileging of 'natural' wit, reason and fancy that Cavendish's unique claims to female authorship reside – claiming her right to discourse, first as a noblewoman, and then as an author and philosopher.

In his 1995 novel *Slowness*, Milan Kundera suggested that conversation is no trivial occupation. 'Conversation', he said, 'is not a pastime; on the contrary, conversation is what organises time, governs it, and imposes its own laws [...].'[12] Cavendish's 'conversation' of the intellect (an intellect whose identity is fractured in discourse), her discursive productivity, organises her time (displacing the structures of 'domestic time' allotted to her sex – 'such Works as Ladies use to pass their time withall') and imposes its own discursive laws (see illustration 1.2). 'I understand the [...] Ordering of a grange, indifferently well' she says in the prefatory epistle to her husband in her *Sociable Letters*, although she does not 'Busie' herself with it 'by reason my Scribling takes away the most part of my Time.'[13] In this collection the contributors seek to understand the self-proclaimed 'laws' of Cavendish's discourse and, in their different ways, make various aspects of Cavendish's work historically legible.

Hero Chalmers in her 1997 article on Cavendish's 'authorial self-representation' argued that 'Cavendish's marital circumstances and her figuration of their links with her publication [...] assist her to reconcile an unusually self-promoting authorial voice with the dictates of wifely obedience.'[14] In the first essay of this volume Kate Lilley also focuses on Cavendish's discursive dependence on the 'particular economy of the [aristocratic] married couple', and the way she uses it to legitimate the 'linked activities of writing, reading, conversing and publishing.'[15] In this nuanced tropological analysis of Cavendish's strategies, Lilley argues that Cavendish constantly presents her writing as a 'conjugal effect' of her marriage to William and uses 'Emulation towards Men' (with her husband as an exemplary masculine type), and the reciprocal rhetoric of the marriage contract, to legitimate her own intellectual independence. 'Cavendish's sexualised and hierarchical poetics', Lilley suggests, and

> the scene of marriage and its textual instantiations offer a complex venue for negotiating relations between author and reader, discourses of gender, and hierarchies of knowledge and value.[16]

Drawing sustenance from the unquestioned 'law of [aristocratic] privilege as self-reproducing and self-authorising', Cavendish validates herself as simultaneously

Illustration 1.2 'Studious she is and all alone': Cavendish and the 'time of composition': Engraved portrait from the frontispiece of *The Worlds Olio* (1655), by permission of The British Library, G. 11599 fp

a 'singular or catechrestic woman' and as 'the fixed and chaste term' of a noble, companionate marriage.

Marion Wynne-Davies also sets Cavendish's literary productivity within the context of a familial structure, but in this case not the limited sphere of the 'couple', but the broader, dynastic milieu of the aristocratic family as a social unit. While it is important, Wynne-Davies argues:

> to recognise the importance of a female tradition of writing within the early modern period, at the same time we have moved beyond the need to link all women writers simply because of their sex. Rather, and perhaps not unsurprisingly, family bonds emerge as a powerful way of uniting female literary productivity, and these familial discourses simultaneously encompass and deflect male influence, resonating about certain fixed locational points.[17]

It was the 'combination of wealth, a secure space, together with male complicity', she argues, that allowed a few Early Modern women dramatists to evade the prohibitions on women's writing, and begin to find a voice. Like Susan Wiseman, who also suggests that the disruption of the social hierarchy during the Civil War and the Protectorate was a motor of Cavendish's literary production,[18] Wynne-Davies maintains that the exiled situation of the Cavendish family, which was 'representative of the widespread disruption experienced in many Royalist households' was a stimulus to literary productivity amongst the women of the Cavendish family.

Cavendish's prose fictions, ranging from orations to epistles, from utopian fantasy to aphorism, are amongst her most generically plastic or fluid literary forms of expression. Nicole Pohl's essay on Cavendish's *Blazing World* focuses on what she calls the 'transgressive hermaphroditism' of Cavendish's 'new utopian discourse'. Using Gilles Deleuze's concept of the 'Baroque', as it was developed in *The Fold: Leibniz and the Baroque*, Pohl argues that Cavendish concept of the 'hermaphroditical' text is baroque in the Deleuzian sense – that is 'a multiplicity that makes for inclusion' – and that Cavendish's 'singularity' by constantly gesturing towards 'a larger multiplicity', subverts and 'deconstructs contemporary notions of binary opposition in gender politics, science and literature'.[19] Like Mihoko Suzuki, who in her recent essay on Cavendish's *Worlds Olio* has noted the strategic advantages which Cavendish gains from her choice of genres which allow her to 'express divergent and at times contradictory perspectives,'[20] Pohl argues that Cavendish's generic (or 'transgeneric') hybridity enables her to 'present a range of speculative prospects which do not reduce discourses of gender, knowledge and power to crude either/or choices.'[21]

James Fitzmaurice's essay on the *Sociable Letters* examines the 'biographical or autobiographical import' of the work, and shows how the figures of Margaret and William Cavendish lurk under the cryptic sobriquets of characters such as 'Lady M.L.' and 'Mr N.N.' In particular Fitzmaurice shows how Cavendish was able to deal with anxieties about her husband's womanising activities, and respond to contemporary gossip about her writing through gentle satire and parody. Presenting new manuscript evidence relating to William Newcastle's dalliance with one Elizabeth Darcye and his epistolary dalliance with Christiana, Countess of Devonshire, Fitzmaurice reflects upon the role of flirtation and the keeping of mistresses in Stuart Court politics.

Margaret Cavendish's plays are amongst her most adventurous and paradoxical literary endeavours, adventurous because of their potentially conspicuously public nature, and paradoxical because of Cavendish's (possibly disingenuous) insistence that her works were designed for publication rather than performance: written for the 'Brain' rather than the 'Stage'. In an age where the texts of plays usually followed successful public performances, Cavendish's pre-emptive publication (as she herself acknowledges) seemed to preclude the possibility of publishing:

> The printing of my Playes spoils them for ever to be Acted; for what men are acquainted with is despised, at lest neglected; for the newness of Playes, most commonly, takes the Spectators [...].[22]

Her choice of publication rather than performance seems to have been deliberate. Making a pointed contrast with her husband's plays, which were performed, Cavendish insists that she would rather 'send them forth to be printed [...] than keep them concealed in hopes to have them first Acted.'[23] And yet, in spite of this apparent eschewing of performance, Cavendish insists on the inherently theatrical nature of her literary texts:

> Having pleased my Fancy in writing many Dialogues upon several Subjects, and having afterwards order'd them into Acts and Scenes, I will venture in Spight of the Criticks, to call them Plays.[24]

Cavendish's theatrical writings, as Susan Wiseman has argued, are radicalised by her collapsing of the boundaries between theatre and social action (conceived as a kind of performance):

> In Margaret Cavendish's writings, contradictions emerge around the issues of the court, power, gender, sexual desire and representation as they converge on the signifier 'theatre'. Her dramatic and non-dramatic writing plays with and redefines the marginalised position of women in relation to the 'theatre' of public affairs, on the one hand, and the theatre of representation on the other.[25]

In her essay in the present volume Judith Peacock argues that it was precisely Cavendish's radical approach to the position of women in public affairs that would have made her plays ideologically 'unperformable' in the Restoration theatre. Comparing Cavendish with her younger contemporary Aphra Behn whose plays were performed in the public theatres, Peacock argues that it is not the inherently 'untheatrical' nature of Cavendish's plays which prevented them being performed (as has often been suggested), but their unorthodox handling of women's autonomy and independent action. Cavendish's reputation as a dramatist, as Peacock shows, whether in the seventeenth century or the present has less to do with the inherent worth or producibility of her plays than with the fact that no attempt was ever made to subject them to the collective editorial re-shaping which production and performance necessarily entail.

Rebecca D'Monté's essay considers the complexities of what Wiseman calls the 'theatre of representation'. D'Monté argues that Cavendish's theatre is underpinned by the contemporary understanding of subjectivity as performance. 'The idea of staging or recreating oneself through performance,' she suggests, 'was one that was endemic to seventeenth-century culture', and this essay shows how Cavendish was able to exploit the spectacular presentation of the self on the stage so as to empower both her heroines and herself. Just as the ladies of the Caroline court empowered themselves through conspicuous display, Cavendish's characters deliberately display themselves 'as potential objects of desire to an audience of male admirers' but are staged in such a way that they are controlling the spectacle, and 'retain ocular freedom'. Not only do Cavendish's characters (such as the orators in *The Female Academy*) flagrantly display their 'eloquent loquaciousness', but they also maintain control of their visibility to the men. When female characters are displayed openly on the stage they often do so transgressively, like Lady Victoria in *Bell in Campo*, whose military bearing, as D'Monté notes, brings together 'the figure of courtly lady, the Amazon, and the writer.' Cavendish thus controls the spectacle of 'femininity' in order to problematise it.

Julie Sanders's essay also considers Cavendish's plays as a form of self-performance, although her analysis focuses on space rather than spectacle. Interrogating the linked seventeenth century notions of 'closet' and 'closet drama', Sanders argues that the 'closets or cabinets' of Cavendish's *Convent of Pleasure* and *Lady Contemplation* were not 'compensatory places of play, but rather areas of genuine self-staging'. The 'closet' of closet drama, far from being a 'negative and diminishing adjective', signals the 'shift of power centres' in the seventeenth-century household, a 'relocating' of power where the margin was becoming central. The supposed 'privacy' of the closet was, Sanders argues, becoming 'overtly performative' and thus 'public', both in prose fictions and dramas by women, but also in actual households. The closet and the cabinet were 'sites [...] of theatre, actual and political, but also of literary productivity', and Cavendish used the theatrical space of the closet to 'empower' the 'private space of her mind' and 'empower it from within'.

Cavendish's conception of her 'Brain' as a 'Stage' is also addressed by Jay Stevenson, who sees Cavendish's representation of the mind as a kind of collective entity (which was often in dialogue with itself) in her poetry, prose fiction, philosophy and drama, as a characteristic trope of Cavendish's discourse. Stevenson sees this not only as a strategy for legitimating her writing 'in physiological as well as rhetorical terms', but also as a 'process of playful mental and social ordering'. Cavendish's materialist theories of mind (which sees thought as simply an effect of particular self-moving 'rational parts' of matter), are – Stevenson argues – both atheist and radically relativist. 'Cavendish's writings about the mind,' he says, 'suggest that *everything* is thought and that all thought is the tangible figment of its own imagination.' In the process of defending her claims to authority by stressing the 'imagined and self-realising success of female discourse', Stevenson argues, Cavendish undermines the absolute claims of religion and politics, which are also revealed to be 'self-produced and imaginary'. Cavendish's astonishing flights of paradoxical fancy are not, Stevenson argues, 'evidence of her lack of training as a writer' but rather 'part of her elliptical strategy of self-display', which deserves a 'complex and approving response'.

In two very different approaches to Cavendish's generically polymorphous *Poems and Fancies*, Jerry Sokol and Emma Rees also belie critical commonplaces concerning the untutored nature of Cavendish's literary output. Sokol argues that while she has often been portrayed as philosophically and scientifically ignorant or inept, *Poems and Fancies* provides evidence that Cavendish was, in fact, abreast of some of the most advanced mathematics of her time. Previous critics, Sokol suggests, have found Cavendish wanting by measuring her against a mistaken conception of seventeenth century science, a 'prevailing Baconian paradigm' that grossly simplifies the complex intellectual currents of the 1650s and 60s. Examining a number of poems in the light of some transcriptions by Charles Cavendish of the unpublished manuscripts on the mathematical doctrine of infinites by the Elizabethan mathematician and natural philosopher Thomas Harriot, Sokol shows that Cavendish 'appreciated the huge importance of abstruse mathematical theoretical thinking to modern science.'

Emma Rees's essay on Cavendish's poetry focuses on her rhetorical ingenuity. Cavendish's 'adroit manipulation of domestic images,' (and the subversive potential of the Homeric figure of Penelope in particular) are used, Rees argues, to 'negotiate her position as woman writer'. Although Penelope was a conventional trope of female obedience and chastity, Cavendish uses her as a representation of the inventive ingenuity of the woman writer who 'weaves' herself an endless text. Cavendish's claim that her verses in *Poems and Fancies* are 'like *Chast Penelope's Work*, for I wrote them in my *Husbands* absence, to delude *Melancholy Thoughts*, and avoid *Idle Time*'[26] is, Rees suggests, not simply to present herself as a 'paragon of passive female domesticity', an exilic Royalist heroine of the hearth, but is also 'a motif of ingenuity and initiative' which simultaneously vaunts her literary productivity and avoids 'public impugnment of her reputation' as a writing woman.[27]

If Cavendish's literary productivity wasn't unsettling enough for her contemporaries, her unprecedented philosophical output was truly astounding, and judging by the defensive nature of some of her prefatory epistles (where Cavendish vehemently insists on her authorship against charges of plagiarism) the idea of a woman who produced philosophical treatises was virtually unthinkable. As with her literary works, it is Cavendish's determined intellectual self-creation which causes problems for contemporary scholars seeking to place her within an intellectual landscape from which she has (until relatively recently) been excluded. Susan James, reappraising Cavendish's natural philosophy in the *British Journal for the History of Philosophy* in 1999, observed that while Cavendish's theories on matter, perception and generation, can be placed within the context of a number of other 'English vitalists' writing in the latter half of the seventeenth century, her work was nonetheless highly unorthodox in a number of ways. Cavendish's works, James wrote:

> Bear the marks of her autodidacticism, intellectual confidence, powerful imagination and drive to overall consistency, features which in some ways make her work hard to place in the exotic and crowded landscape of late seventeenth-century explanations of nature.[28]

Whilst Cavendish was 'theologically unorthodox' and espoused the idea of self-moving and sentient matter more readily than some of her contemporaries, James sees Cavendish's philosophical works as a 'reasonably coherent programme designed to improve on mechanism,' and one which, in certain respects, anticipated those of Ralph Cudworth, Anne Conway, Gottfried Wilhelm Leibniz and Baruch Spinoza later in the century.[29] One cannot escape, however, the 'singularity' of Cavendish's thought and expression, and – as James acknowledges – the 'playful fantasies' and 'artfully undisciplined style' of Cavendish's writing are difficult to judge by contemporary yardsticks.[30]

There is no question that Cavendish was extremely fortunate in her proximity to a particularly fertile philosophical milieu. The initial conditions for taking advantage of this philosophical moment, were her unusually supportive philosophical relationships with both her husband William and her brother-in-law Charles Cavendish (to whom she warmly dedicates a number of her works). In her biography of her husband she characterised William as having 'not so much of Scholarship and learning as his Brother Sir *Charles Cavendish* [...] [yet] he is both a good Natural and Moral Philosopher, not by reading Philosophical Books, but by his own Natural Understanding and Observation [...].'[31] Cavendish was indeed fortunate in her choice of husband, as he does not seem to have shared some of the objections of his contemporaries to intellectual engagement with the opposite sex. Cavendish records, for example 'some Discourse I held with him one time, concerning that famous Chymist Van Helmont, who in his Writings is very invective against the School-men [...].'[32] It is clear from allusions scattered throughout her writings that such discourses do not appear to have been isolated incidents. Not only did Margaret appear to have a husband who encouraged his wife in her philosophical interests, but she was also privy to philosophical discussions which took place in their household, as when she records an occasion 'when my Lord was at *Paris*, in his Exile', when she witnessed William 'discoursing with some of his Friends, amongst whom was also that Learned Philosopher Hobbes' (although at times she took pains to deny having participated in these discussions).[33] Cavendish's involvement in the Parisian discussions, and particularly in the philosophical discussions between her husband and his philosophically-inclined client Thomas Hobbes, and his occasional visitor, René Descartes, clearly played an important role in her intellectual development.[34] Cavendish took full advantage of her direct access to some of the most advanced philosophical thinking of her age, and this is reflected in her works, where she grapples with some of the most important issues of the day. Cavendish's claims to have been uninfluenced by the writings of her contemporaries have too often perhaps been taken at face value, in spite of the openly responsive character of her *Philosophical Letters* (1664), which systematically engages with the differences between Cavendish's own philosophical system and those of her more celebrated contemporaries.

Sarah Hutton – who has previously elucidated the connections between Cavendish's philosophy and those of Thomas Hobbes and Anne Conway – turns her attention in the present volume to Cavendish's critique of Henry More in the *Philosophical Letters*, which, Hutton argues, also gives us 'important clues about several figures whom she subjects to critique in *Blazing World*.'[35] Hutton stresses that while Cavendish's works lack 'philosophical formality', the 'devastating common sense' of her polemical attacks on Henry More are nonetheless highly effective. Through a close comparison of More's 'Spirit of Nature' and Cavendish's concept of nature as an 'infinite, self-moving body', Hutton shows that Cavendish's natural philosophy 'turns Cambridge Platonism upside down'. Her radically materialist philosophy, whilst maintaining a place for God as the overall 'Master' of nature was vehemently opposed to the idea of 'incorporeal substances,' which she considered to be a contradiction in terms. Hutton shows that not only was More an explicit target in the *Philosophical Letters* but also that he plays a more prominent role in the satire of the *Blazing World* than has hitherto been suspected. Although More is not explicitly invoked in those sections of the work where the Empress expresses a desire to construct a 'philosophical Cabala', Hutton shows that Cavendish is satirising More's *Conjectura Cabbalistica* (1653), and the implied philosophical critique of these passages, Hutton argues, have much in common with Cavendish's critique of More in the *Philosophical Letters*. For Hutton Cavendish had a 'gadfly' rather than a 'butterfly' mind, and although her attacks on her contemporaries were as much to do with establishing her philosophical 'singularity' as they were straightforward critique, they betray a mind which was keenly attuned to some of the most the philosophical problems of the day.

In my contribution to this volume I place Cavendish's works in the context of a rising epistemological tendency in mid-seventeenth-century natural philosophy toward probabilism and provisionality. Comparing her protestations of artlessness and lack of method to similar prefatory disclaimers by Robert Boyle in the 1660s, and comparing her insistence on the probable (and non-veridical) status of her philosophical ideas to the probablism of her contemporaries and correspondents Walter Charleton and Joseph Glanvill, I argue that Cavendish's caveats are not a product of diffidence and insecurity, but a sophisticated engagement with contemporary epistemological debates. Cavendish's appeal to a nature whose infinite motions and figures always exceed the individual philosopher's ability to describe them, becomes I argue, an 'inexhaustible occasion for discourse [...] the pretext for an interminable series of descriptive acts, it becomes, in fact, the foundation of a copious rhetorical discourse, in the Erasmian sense.'[36] This rhetorical superabundance, I argue is the foundation for a philosophical libertinism, which eschews the 'strickt rules' of dogmatic, veridical discourse for an infinite expression of probabilities.

In his essay Neil Ankers takes up the question of Hobbes's influence on Cavendish's philosophy from a new perspective. Whereas the focus on the Cavendish–Hobbes connection in the past has tended to focus on the similarities in their matter thories, Ankers argues that Cavendish was also tacitly engaging with Hobbes's political philosophy. Unlike Anna Battigelli, who has also stressed Cavendish's debt to Hobbes and the interconnectedness of Cavendish's natural philosophy and political beliefs, Ankers sees her philosophy as a 'counterthrust' to Hobbesian political thought rather than its culmination.[37] For Ankers the philosophies of Hobbes and Cavendish represent distinct paradigms, and while they were both materialists and had a 'shared approach to philosophical method', their worldviews are in pointed opposition when it comes to their understanding of nature and human nature. Cavendish, Ankers argues, 'offers an alternative [to the Hobbesian paradigm] where willing compliance replaces competitive struggle as the fundamental "motivation" in nature.'[38]

Not only do Cavendish's works show that she was familiar with the latest philosophical ideas, they also reveal a theoretical and practical knowledge of medicine. Susan Fitzmaurice's essay – which uses an linguistic approach derived from literary stylistics and pragmatics, compares the functions and effects of the medical passages in Cavendish's *Sociable Letters* with contemporary medical advices offered by professional physicians. In this work – a compendium of opinion, advice and gossip' – Cavendish, Fitzmaurice argues, 'seems to borrow as much from the convention of the medical counsel as from the familiar letter'.[39] Although a woman offering medical advice to a friend was socially acceptable in the mid-seventeenth century, Cavendish's *Sociable Letters* 'turns a sociable but essentially private practice [...] into a public one through the publication of her opinions.'[40] Negotiating the characteristic paradox of the published 'familiar letter' (that of a public intimacy), the printing of Cavendish's medical advice or opinions involves another level of difficulty: her implicit claim to authorial and/or authoritative expertise. One of the effects of casting doubt on physicians's advice in some of the letters, for example, is to 'compare the authority of her stance with the authority commanded by doctors'. Unlike the anthologies of women's medical recipes which were published in the second half of the seventeenth century, such as Elizabeth Grey's, *A Choice Manuall, Or Rare and Select Secrets in Physick and Chyrurgery* (1653) Lady Alethea Talbot's *Natura Exenterata* (1655), or Hannah Woolley's, *The Ladies Delight: or a Rich Closet of Choice Experiments & Curiosities* (1672), Cavendish's work advances opinions, rather than practical remedies, and in her address to Mrs T's physician, in which she argues with his diagnosis and prescription, Cavendish 'assumes the position of opponent or disputant rather than colleague'.[41] While Cavendish 'plays with the figure giving counsel', and sometimes couches her advice in 'non-factive assertion[s] that will not admit contradiction', ultimately her advices in the *Sociable Letters* are of necessity neither purely familiar nor completely professional. The conventions of the medical casebook are 'too narrow to fulfill the function of [familiar] advice,' and the 'sociability of advice' is too personal to be relevant to a general readership. What the medical advice of the *Letters* do provide, however, is a further generic pretext for Cavendish's discursive volubility.

The broad scope of this volume – which deliberately seeks to cover as much of Cavendish's oeuvre as possible – is to reveal the precariousness, but also the courage of Cavendish's authorship. In seeking contexts for her literary and philosophical productivity, we are not seeking to reduce her to an instance in a normative cultural milieu. Cavendish's 'generic *copia*' (her deliberate attempt to elegantly vary her generic expressions), which sought a 'perpetual motion, with continual changes and varieties,'[42] and her championing of 'a generous discoursitive Wit'[43] need to be set in the context of contemporary literary and philosophical norms, but we should be wary of allowing this to diminish her exuberant, philosophically libertine singularity. 'Wit is wilde and fantastical', Cavendish proclaimed, 'and therefore must have no set Rules; for Rules Curb, and Shackle it, and in that Bondage it dies.'[44] Cavendish's 'conversation' with her age, for all of its witty strategies of self-parody and seeming ambivalence and apology, amounts to a courageous refusal to be silenced:

> In Common and ordinary Conversations, the most Wittiest, Learnedest, and Eloquentest Men, are forced to speak according to the Wit, Learning, Language, and Capacities of those they are in Company and Conversation with, unless they will speak all themselves, which will be no Conversation: for in Conversation every particular person must have his turn and time of speaking as well as hearing; yet such is the folly of the World, as to despise the Authors of Witty, Learned and Eloquent Writings, if their Conversations be as other mens, and yet would laugh at them, or account them mad, if they should speak otherwise, as out of this ordinary way; but the greatest talkers are not the greatest writers, which is the cause women cannot be good Writers; for we fear of being thought Fools, make our selves Fools, in striving to express some Wit, whereas if we had but that power over our selves as to keep silence, we perchance might be thought Wits, although we were Fools, but to keep silence is impossible for us to do, so long as we have Speech we shall talk, although to no purpose, for nothing but Death can force us to silence [....].[45]

Notes

[1] *Grounds* (1668), sig. A2 recto–A3 recto. She also presented at least one of her books to a European university, as can be seen from a letter from the Rector of the University of Leiden dated 28 November 1658 in *Letters and Poems* (1676), p. 2.

[2] On her presentation of works to Oxford and Cambridge see the letters of thanks in *Letters and Poems* (1676), pp. 3–38. Shirley Stacey's bibliographical work on extant copies of Cavendish's works promise to shed further light on Cavendish's presentations.

[3] For evidence of Cavendish's correspondence with Glanvill see *Letters and Poems* (1676), pp. 102–5, 123–7, 137–142. Her critique of the experimental philosophy appears in *Observations* (1668), and her criticisms of Hobbes and More appear in *Philosophical Letters* (1664). For evidence that Cavendish presented More with a copy of *Philosophical Letters*, and that More was aware of her criticisms of his work see Hutton, infra, pp. 177–8.

[4] *Writings* (1994), p. xiii.

[5] Kenelm Digby, *Observations vpon Religio Medici* (London, 1643), pp. 14–16.

[6] Anna Battigelli, *Margaret Cavendish and the Exiles of the Mind* (Lexington: The University Press of Kentucky, 1998), p. 10.

[7] *Physical Opinions* (1655), sig. A4 recto–verso.

[8] *Physical Opinions* (1655), sig. B recto.

[9] *Physical Opinions* (1655), sig. A4 verso.

[10] *Physical Opinions* (1655), 'An Epistle to justifie the Lady Newcastle, and Truth against falshood, laying those false, and malicious aspersions of her, that she was not Authour of her Books', sig. A1 recto–A2 recto.

[11] *Physical Opinions* (1655), sig. B verso.

[12] Milan Kundera, *Slowness*, trans. Linda Ash (New York: Harper Collins, 1996), p. 32

[13] *Sociable Letters* (1997), p. 4. This other 'Time' is what Kate Lilley calls 'the time of composition', see Lilley, infra, p. 23.

[14] Hero Chalmers, 'Dismantling the Myth of "Mad Madge": the cultural context of Margaret Cavendish's authorial self-presentation', *Women's Writing*, 4:3 (1997), 323–339 (p. 326).

[15] See Lilley, infra, p. 30.

[16] See Lilley, infra, p. 20.

[17] See Wynne-Davies, infra, p. 48.

[18] Susan Wiseman, *Drama and Politics in the English Civil War* (Cambridge: Cambridge University Press, 1998), p. 91.

[19] See Pohl, infra, p. 54.

[20] Mihoko Suzuki, 'The Essay Form as Critique: Reading Cavendish's *The World's Olio* through Montaigne and Bacon (and Adorno)', in *Prose Studies*, 22:3 (1999), 1–16 (p. 3).

[21] Pohl, infra, p. 52.

[22] *Playes* (1662), 'To the Readers', unsigned page between sig. A3 and A4 (sig. χ verso).

[23] *Playes* (1662), 'The Epistle Dedicatory', sig. A3 recto.

[24] *Plays* (1668), 'To the Readers', sig. [A] recto–verso.

[25] Wiseman, *Drama and Politics in the English Civil War*, p. 97.

[26] *Poems and Fancies* (1653), p.122.

[27] See Rees, infra, pp. 174, 178.

[28] Susan James, 'The Philosophical Innovations of Margaret Cavendish', *British Journal for the History of Philosophy*, 7:2 (1999), 219–244 (p. 219).

[29] James, 'Philosophical Innovations', 229, 243.

[30] James, 'Philosophical Innovations', p. 243.

[31] *Life* (1667), pp. 142–3.

[32] Margaret Cavendish, *Life* (1667), p.145.

[33] *Life* (1667), p. 143.

[34] On Hobbes, and his position in the Cavendish household see Battigelli, *Exiles of the Mind*, pp. 62–73 and Lisa T. Sarasohn, 'Thomas Hobbes and the Duke of Newcastle: A Study in the Mutuality of Patronage before the Establishment of the Royal Society', *Isis*, 90 (1999), 715–737.

[35] Hutton, infra, p. 186. For Hutton's previous studies of Cavendish's philosophy see 'In Dialogue with Thomas Hobbes: Margaret Cavendish's natural philosophy', *Women's Writing*, 4 (1997), 421–432 and 'Anne Conway, Margaret Cavendish and Seventeenth-Century Scientific Thought', in Lynette Hunter and Sarah Hutton (eds.) *Women, Science and Medicine 1500–1700. Mothers and Sisters of the Royal Society* (Stroud: Alan Sutton, 1997), pp. 218–234.

[36] Clucas, infra, p. 206.

[37] Ankers, infra, p. 242. Battigelli argues that while Cavendish 'disagreed with Hobbes's mechanistic view of human nature, she absorbed his political thought, taking it to its logical extreme.' (Battigelli, *Exiles of the Mind*, p. 83).

[38] Ankers, infra, pp. 245.

[39] Fitzmaurice, infra, p. 212.

[40] Fitzmaurice, infra, p. 212.

[41] Fitzmaurice, infra, p. 227. On the medical anthologies of seventeenth-century women see Lynette Hunter, 'Women and Domestic Medicine: Lady Experimenters 1570–1620' in Lynette Hunter and Sarah Hutton (eds.) *Women, Science and Medicine 1500–1700. Mothers and Sisters of the Royal Society* (Stroud: Alan Sutton, 1997), pp. 89–107.

[42] *Worlds Olio* (1655), p. 11.

[43] *Playes* (1662), 'To the Readers', sig. A5 recto.

[44] *Worlds Olio* (1655), 'Epistle' preceding Lib. II, sig. O3 verso.

[45] *Playes* (1662), sig. A5 recto–verso.

PART I

PROSE FICTIONS

2

Contracting Readers: 'Margaret Newcastle' and the Rhetoric of Conjugality*

Kate Lilley

> In some respects the better a book is, the less it demands from binding. Fielding, Smollet, Sterne, and all that class of perpetually self-reproductive volumes – Great Nature's Stereotypes – we see them individually perish with less regret, because we know the copies of them to be 'eterne'. But where a book is at once both good and rare – where the individual is almost the species, and when *that* perishes [...] such a book, for instance, as the Life of the Duke of Newcastle, by his Duchess – no casket is rich enough, no casing sufficiently durable, to honour and keep safe such a jewel. (Charles Lamb)[1]

Cavendish construed her life's work as the prudent management and disposition of a singular oeuvre materialised through the benefits of marriage. Claiming much more than husbandly permission she strategically represented her writing as a conjugal effect, framing the emulation of her husband's greatness as the synecdochical marker of a permitted 'Emulation towards Men' in general 'for their Courage, Prudence, Wit, and Eloquence.'[2] Offering herself – and her signature – as the fixed and chaste term which circumscribes and completes a richly various textual catalogue, she defends the legitimate paternity of her books, figuring Newcastle as a domesticated metonym for the potential grandeur and tragedy of masculinity under duress. Marriage to him gives her access to an heroic line of great men; but, as befits the ambitious protégé, Cavendish's emulation extends far beyond an expected deference to her husband; it becomes the ambivalent ground of her own practices of reading, writing and publishing:

> I fear Women are not Capable [...], and the Despair thereof makes me Envy or Emulate Men [...]. And of all the Men I read of, I Emulate Julius Caesar most [...] insomuch as when I read of Julius Caesar, I cannot but wish that Nature and Fate had made me such a one as he was; and sometimes I have that Courage, as to think I should not be afraid of his Destiny, so I might have as great a Fame. But these

---

* This essay had its beginning as a paper presented at the Cavendish Conference in Oxford in June 1997. For talk at and around that event I thank especially Ros Ballaster, Hero Chalmers, James Fitzmaurice, Lorna Hutson, Lee Khanna, Paul Salzman and Susan Wiseman. Melissa Hardie's close reading of subsequent drafts helped immeasurably.

> wishes discover my Aspiring Desires, and all those Desires are but Vain that cannot be Attained to.[3]

Cavendish bypasses Newcastle for Caesar to open a discourse of masculine desire and self-love which casuistically confuses the terms she sometimes holds apart and sometimes collapses: emulation and envy, masculine and feminine, husband and wife. She explores the gendered possibilities of *chiasmus* (mirror inversion) as a means of rhetorically displacing or usurping the priority of the husband through a tropological engagement of the reciprocal rhetoric of the marriage contract. Reading and writing are offered as dynamic conduits of both masculine and feminine affect, especially for married noblewomen whose circumstances facilitate – indeed, in Cavendish's terms, proscribe – a retired and contemplative life sequestered from 'the itch of Talk, Luxury, Wantonness and Vanity.'[4] Within the chaste circle of the home and the closet, Cavendish trades envy for emulation, even as she renders acute – and acutely desirable – the chiastic cross-coupling of these supposed antitheses within the marital home.

Foreshadowing a rebuttal of the fixed 'nature' of sex, Cavendish warns in *Sociable Letters*: 'There are more Effeminate Men than Masculine Women, that is, there are few Women so wise as Men should be, and many Men as Foolish as Women can be.'[5] This kind of pre-emptive strike gives her leave to suggest that a wife's emulation – or envy – of her husband entails a critique or at least supervention of gender ideology in the service of female singularity and contingency. The claims of the wife as non-pareil threaten to far exceed the terms of marital synecdoche or imitation, producing a hyperbolic, copious and self-contradictory discourse of capacity and lack, purity and hybridity, fixity and mobility.

In Cavendish's sexualised and hierarchical poetics, the scene of marriage and its textual instantiations offer a complex venue for negotiating relations between author and reader, discourses of gender, and hierarchies of knowledge and value. The copious prefatory materials, framing devices and free-floating orations of Cavendish's catalogue of published works, compulsively stage the excess and anxiety invested in the signature of the married woman of letters.[6] This anxiety, precisely because it can never be satisfactorily recuperated or allayed, becomes the efficient engine of Cavendish's catachrestic writing career. She returns again and again to the problematic of classification and genealogy with a defensive and transparently self-serving agenda: to license certain kinds of novelty and experiment – especially herself and her books – as fortuitous category errors, rejecting others as pernicious.

Using the Civil War as exemplar of unlawful trespass and unnatural usurpation, Cavendish situates herself as multiple witness and victim, implicated through the desecration of her original family and its property, her employment in the service of Henrietta Maria, and her marriage to the banished Newcastle.[7] In *Sociable Letters* she writes:

> Vices Increase in a Civil War, by reason Civil Government is in Disorder, Civil Magistrates Corrupted, Civil Laws Abolished, Civil Manners, and Decent Customs

Banished, and in all their Places is Rapine, Robbing, Stabbing, Treachery, and Falshood, all the Evil Passions and Debauch'd Appetites are let Loose, to take their Liberty; But this is so commonly Known to those that have seen a Civil War, as I should not have needed to Mention it, although those that have Liv'd alwayes in Peace will not Believe it, but I have Suffered so much in it, as the Loss of some of my Nearest, and Dearest Friends, and the Ruin of those that did Remain, that I may desire to Forget it.[8]

Unsurprisingly, Cavendish locates herself and her writing exclusively through elegiac aristocratic precedent and the demonstration of husbandly consent. But Cavendish's materialist, atomist project of self-authorisation is, in fact, far more audacious, active and rhetorically complex than the feminised tropes of witness or permission might suggest. Claiming a symmetrical, even indivisible, relationship between conjoint, conjugal pleasure and responsibility and singular textual ambition, Cavendish suggests that, through writing and publishing, she can simultaneously prove her loyalty to herself and her husband.[9] By reiterating the law of privilege as self-reproducing and self-authorising, Cavendish's enunciation of inclusion and exclusion represses her fear of being wrongly or punitively classified. At the same time, however, she displays an acute awareness of the difficulty of defending her claim to *authorised* singularity from censure or misrecognition.[10]

Fear of anonymity and oblivion – of being mistaken for, or judged less worthy than, a past or future wife of Newcastle; of being charged with plagiarism or of being plagiarised; of being forgotten or lost to the historical record – are everywhere thematised in Cavendish's writing and ameliorated through her strenuous attention to publication, distribution and prefatory instruction. As Laura Rosenthal argues, 'Authorship signifies and remains a position of ownership for Cavendish, not in the proprietary sense that concerns professionals, but in a Hobbesian sense of property as both an extension and realisation of the self and at the same time as something deeply and bitterly contested.'[11] Despite her best efforts, the prestigious proper name 'Margaret Newcastle', deployed as a token of authorship, acquires a taint of impropriety, novelty and instability which cannot be expunged, only endlessly defended and dilated.

In Letter 143 of *Sociable Letters*, Cavendish describes the loss of the scribal copies of her plays en route from Antwerp to be published in London:

I heard the Ship was Drown'd [...], and if I had not had the Original of them by me, truly I should have been much Afflicted, and accounted the Loss of my Twenty Playes, as the loss of Twenty Lives, for in my Mind I should have Died Twenty Deaths, which would have been a great Torment, or I should have been near the Fate of those Playes, and almost Drown'd in Salt Tears, as they in the Salt Sea; but they are Destinated to Live, and I hope, I in them, when my Body is Dead, and Turned to Dust; But I am so Prudent, and Careful of my Poor Labours, which are my Writing Works, as I alwayes keep the Copies of them safely with me, until they are Printed, and then I Commit the Originals to the Fire, like Parents which are willing to Die, whenas they are sure of their Childrens Lives, knowing when they are Old, and past Breeding, they are but Useless in this World.[12]

Here, mechanical reproduction effectively renders the manuscript obsolete, but it is hard at first to say which is more fetishised, manuscript or printed book, in the competitive thematics of 'Paper Bodies' versus bound volumes. Cavendish introduces an insoluble and constitutive confusion between 'labours' and 'works', 'originals' and 'copies', 'parents' and 'children'. Figuring the intimacy, privacy and vulnerable singularity of manuscript culture – 'I alwayes keep the Copies of them safely with me' – Cavendish elides herself with these threatened 'originals', mapping their 'Fate' onto her own through the metonymy of 'Salt Tears' and 'Salt Sea'. Both are 'Parents which are willing to die,' but in this allegorised narrative, the singular must yield to the multiple, the particular to the general, the hand to the machine. In this scenario of transference between bodies and technologies, the birth of the book does not directly cause the death of the manuscript, but it is the precondition for a complex set of exchanges which entail both profit and loss, and keep in play both positive and negative affects. As the proximate text passes from hand to machine, closet to marketplace, distance ensues. If printed books in some sense vampirise their authors and preserve them in another form, once published they are not at risk of being killed by their 'parents'. Instead, a different set of relations is instituted based on the generalised and threatening proximity of the overcrowded marketplace and the reproducibility of intimate ownership. Cavendish allegorises the *telos* of the printed book as the origin of the manuscript as fetish: she 'commit[s] the originals to the fire' in a gesture which simultaneously memorialises and scotomises their – and her – archaic singularity. Other reversals follow from Cavendish's agonistic reading of print culture, leading her to prioritise reproduction (print) over production (writing) to such an extent that, in the 'Epistle to the Reader', which introduces the first edition of *The Worlds Olio* (1655), she asserts that an unpublished manuscript is as if dead: 'This Book, most of it was written five years since, and was lockt up in a Trunk as if it had been buried in a Grave, but, when I came out of England, I gave it a Resurrection.'[13]

In the service of managing and authorising her own will to publish, her desire to become memorable and be remembered specifically through the medium of print, Cavendish institutes a diverse and yet repetitive series of discursive campaigns and generic manoeuvres. These are designed not just to keep her before the public, but to inculcate a certain orientation towards her career; a view of her oeuvre as panoramic, polemical, experimental and encyclopaedic. Apart from producing new and substantial texts at regular intervals, Cavendish never neglects the entrepreneurial and editorial aspects of maintaining her profile. Through a second tier of metadiscursive supplementation and management, she introduces, divides and distributes, revising, annotating and reissuing in a process that represents the contingencies of a textually engrossed everyday life. Cavendish's pedagogical practice focuses attention, above all, on the diversified labour of the 'authoress' as 'creator' and steward of an internally coherent and yet various, self-sustaining textual estate. Her attentions are turned especially to the protection and nurture of the book as simultaneously material and abstract commodity, at the expense of the grammatical or stylistic correctness of the text as writing. In the 'Preface to Noble Readers' in *Sociable Letters*, Cavendish defends herself against 'former Readers' who have made 'the Mistake of a Word a Crime in my Wit':

> I was not Bred in an University, or a Free-School to Learn the Art of Words; neither do I take it for a Disparagemente of my Works, to have the Forms, Terms, Words, Numbers, or Rhymes found Fault with, so they do not find Fault with the Variety of the Subjects, or the Sense and Reason, Wit, and Fancy, for I leave the Formal, or Wordative part, to Fools, and the Material or Sensitive part to Wise men.[14]

On this account, even the text's errors become an authenticating gesture, preserving the trace of singular authorship and the time of composition.[15] But the process of writing remains, for Cavendish, necessarily subordinated to the imperatives of publication as the crucible of fame.

No reader can fail to be struck by the exponential character, rhetorical interest and serious pedagogical purpose of prefatory matter in Cavendish's work, even to the extent that it threatens to alienate the text-proper from its proper share of attention. However, that potential indecorum or imbalance is itself interpreted in advance as successive books conceptualise the returning reader. Cavendish's textual habits over time are naturalised as authenticating gestures, and the putative division between paratext and proper text is reordered. As the printed catalogue grows, so too does the author's expectation of persuasive influence over her readers; and indeed it is impossible to imagine a reading of Cavendish's oeuvre indifferent to the dispersed poetics of her expressly authorial inscriptions. Cavendish undertakes the care of her printed name and texts as at once generic and inimitable, sovereign and contingent, on the understanding that any and every thing in nature must be understood as both irreducibly particular and an instance of a type or species. By analogy, the kinds of relations she wants to enter into with readers are construed in cognate terms, according to a ratio of sameness and difference, fixity and mobility, which must be strenuously interpreted and ordered.

If, for her, it seems productive or amenable relations can only be conceived via the analogy of typological purity and specificity, she also recognises the necessity of conceptualising the interrelations of reading, writing and publishing as mutually dependant modes of what Marta Straznicky calls 'civic engagement'.[16] The question of how to initiate and strategically govern such contact between 'self' and 'other' forms the problematic of Cavendish's emphatically public writing, in the sense that no matter how often it is thematised, theorised and enacted, its troubling productivity cannot be exhausted or contained. This passage from *Sociable Letters* may stand as emblematic:

> in my Opinion, Societies should be apart by themselves, like several Commonwealths, Courtiers should only Converse with Courtiers, or Courtly Persons, and Country Gentlemen with Country Gentlemen, Citizens with Citizens, Farmers with Farmers, and I think they do so, at least, are most pleased with the Conversation of their own likeness: Also Statesmen should only Converse with Statesmen,

> Learned Men with Learned men, Wits with Wits, or else their Wit will be Lost; indeed, Societies should be Chosen, and not Mix'd, and every Society should Move in its own Sphere, for the truth is, in Mix'd Societies is Confusion of Tongues, of Wits, of Capacities, and the like.[17]

Replete with telling slippages in the movement between ungendered and masculine categories, such a catalogue – with its conspicuous omission of any direct adjudication of women – inevitably begs the question: where would either Cavendish or her books – or the 'species' which they might be thought to represent – be placed in such a scheme? In this context, marriage and friendship become the mediating tropes that allow some profitable rhetorical negotiation of the impasse between self-sufficient singularities, and some recuperation, specifically, of the singular or catachrestic woman. Whereas the unitary rhetoric of the marriage contract in principle alleviates the difficulty of negotiation, other forms of intimacy and sociality remain intrinsically suspect. 'Friendship,' Cavendish asserts in one of the allegorical axioms of *The Worlds Olio*, 'is like to two Convex Glasses, where the Species come forth and meet each other.'[18]

The desire to distinguish herself among other *femmes couvertes* – and particularly as a childless second wife – is paramount and explicit in Cavendish's books. The concern and expense lavished on her books, both before and after first publication, confirms her acute awareness of the need to defend the circulation of her signature as both authorising and authorised, singular and implicitly plural. In a counterintuitive strategy that is as audacious as it is canny, Cavendish claims that her ministrations on behalf of the work collected and circulated under her married name, far from conflicting with wifely duty and love, are the best proof of her fitness for that position.[19] What makes this plausible is the confirmation supplied in the form of the signed testimony of her husband. Cavendish's expensively produced and rhetorically elaborate editions, all but one in folio, are offered as a public rehearsal and dividend of companionate marriage; a dividend which, despite the law of coverture, she is able to claim as effectively her own. In the public space of Cavendish's books, husband and wife alibi one another in a complex textual modelling of the ideological conjoining of reciprocity and inequality, consent and appropriation, in the married estate.[20]

Cavendish's desire for fame through writing, both in the present and posthumously, is figured in explicitly genealogical terms. Her uniquely textual productivity marks her potentially monstrous difference from the child-bearing first wife, but also renders inalienably hers the textual products of her own marital labour. No matter what rhetorical recuperation or *politesse* is put into place, Cavendish's books finally belong most to her and signify her; and if she has her way, they will be read not only as hers, but as her. So long as she can prove her claim to authorship, the benefits accrue to her, in excess of – but not in breach of – the patriarchal prerogatives of the marriage contract. Equally, if she can demonstrate her husband's consent, as it is clear she can, then she is able to preserve – and read as chiastic – the benefits of both elite authorship and noble marriage.

Certainly, Cavendish takes pains to do both, through her own efforts and with Newcastle's co-operation. At the same time, she is careful to distance herself from the stigma of too much labour:

> There is more Pleasure and Delight in making than in mending; and I verily believe my Neighbours, which are my Readers, would have found fault with it if I had done it as I could [...], but I am so well armed with carelessness, that their several Censures can never enter to vex me with Wounds of Discontent; However, I have my delight in Writing and having it printed; and if any take a Delight to read it, I will not thank them for it; for if anything please therein, they are to thank me for so much pleasure; and if it be naught, I had rather they had left it unread: But those that do not like my Book, which is my House, I pray them to pass by, for I have not any entertainment fit for their Palats.[21]

This aggressive epistle immediately precedes the long and often cited 'Preface to the Reader' in which Cavendish avers the ineluctable inferiority of the 'Effeminate Sex' and argues that Women will 'be against [her] out of partiality to themselves,' and men out of fear of 'Womens Tongues'. In a characteristically ironic and convoluted argument, she produces an extended *occupatio* on the danger of women 'bring[ing] forth Branches from a wrong Stock, by which every man would come to lose the property of their own Children,' only to conclude that, although 'generally all Women are weaker than Men, both in Body and Understanding,' 'some [women] are far wiser than some men,' just as 'some Ground, though it be Barren by Nature, yet, being well mucked and well manured, may bear plentifull Crops, and sprout forth divers sorts of Flowers, when the fertiller and richer round shall grow rank and corrupt, bringing nothing but gross and stinking Weeds, for want of Tillage.' Here, as so often in Cavendish's writing, a chiastic scheme of gender and sexual difference is overlaid with the ratio of general to particular, in such a way as to suggest that the *a priori* superiority of men must be measured against the qualities of particular women. Particular women may rise where the generality of men will fall.[22]

Far from indicating any lack of confidence in the value of her texts, Cavendish stresses the pleasurable and 'negligent' genealogy of her books in order to inscribe herself in the annals of feminised Sidneian 'unelected vocation'. Pointedly alluding to Denny's infamous attack on Lady Mary Sidney Wroth's publication of *The Countesse of Montgomery's Urania*, Cavendish claims an alliance:

> It may be said to me, as one said to a Lady, Work Lady Work, let writing Books alone, For surely Wiser Women ne'er writ one; But your Lordship never bid me to Work, nor leave Writing [...] the truth is, My Lord, I cannot Work, I mean such Works as Ladies use to pass their time withall [...].[23]

Cavendish makes clear that, under the protection of her husband, she will not desist from publishing, promising herself the ongoing and lavish career in print which the widowed Lady Wroth, besieged by debt and sexual scandal, could not afford. At the same time, she is anxious to finesse the distinction between her own textual productions and whatever meagre expectations might attach to women's writing in general. Although she always published under variants of the full and improving dignity of her married name –'the Right Honourable, the Lady Margaret Countesse of Newcastle', 'the Right Honourable, the Lady Newcastle', 'the Most Excellent Lady the Lady M. of Newcastle', 'her Excellency, The Lady Marchioness of Newcastle', 'the thrice Noble, Illustrious and Excellent Princess, the lady Marchioness of Newcastle', 'the thrice Noble, Illustrious and Excellent Princesse, the Duchess of Newcastle'[24] – she will not tolerate the assimilation of 'writing Books' to the demeaning category of 'work' fit for 'a Lady'. As Victoria Kahn has convincingly argued, against Catherine Gallagher's influential reading of the abyssal interiority of the absolutist woman, 'Cavendish uses the royalists' own analogy of the marriage contract to political contract not to withdraw into a domain of subjectivity but rather to comment on parliamentary as well as sexual politics.'[25]

Whilst Cavendish often warns of the contaminations and defects of groups of women together, she consistently argues for the affective and ethical benefits of intimate pairs when properly managed – husbands and wives, same-sex friends, writers and readers – and associates techniques of management with the mediations of textuality. Cavendish prefers to deal in pairs, but when she does figure the potential benefits of collectivity they tend to be represented figurally and metaphysically. She especially relies on personification and allegory to animate the pastoral scene of willing marital sequestration.[26] One might also find in this internalised or theoretical multiplication of personifications an oblique formal response to the reification and homosocial fungibility of women. The metonymic exchange of readers presents a series of openings which ratify the singularity of the author's name, whilst the creation of a library's worth of authored books suggests the possibility of profitable iteration of a singular female nature in a way that subverts the patriarchal, dynastic incorporation of women. 'Daughters,' Cavendish argues, 'are but Branches which by Marriage are Broken off from the Root from whence they Sprang, & Ingrafted into the Stock of an other Family, so that Daughters are to be accounted but as Moveable Goods or Furnitures that wear out; [...] the Line, Name and Life of a Family ends with the Male issue'. The fact that Cavendish consistently averred the benefits of her own upwardly mobile and childless marital incorporation, only strengthened her ability to critique the institution of marriage in general, for 'a Bad Husband is far worse than No Husband [...] where One Husband proves Good, as Loving and Prudent, a Thousand prove Bad.'[27]

The force of Cavendish's polemical defences and critiques notwithstanding, her campaign relies on a compelling rhetoric of unconstrained conjugality and the romance of consensual domesticity. Newcastle's husbandly permission and patronage, his generous public owning of his wife's books and her, sought to guarantee a certain profitable reading of Margaret's conduct in general and her publishing in particular as chaste, illustrious and prodigal. Against all the odds of her own public notoriety, Cavendish offers her circulation as author as a paradoxical sign of her modest and willing withdrawal from social life to the licensed intimacy of the marital home. In a striking and often cited passage she insists: 'I could most willingly exclude myself, so as Never to see the face of any creature, but my Lord, as long as I live, inclosing my self like an Anchoret.'[28] On the logic of her own argument, it is because she announces her willingness to be enclosed at home that her writing may circulate unsupervised without bringing either herself or her husband into disrepute. As the words printed under her signature multiply – and in the very prefaces to her published books – Cavendish insists on the absolute difference between speaking and writing, appearing and inscribing, idle talk and productive thought, figuring herself as studying to correct the 'natural' errors and improve the virtues of femininity. By cultivating the 'disease' of writing she will become a 'monster for silence', insofar as such a transformation is possible: 'it is very Improbable, if not Impossible, for a Woman to be Silent; indeed it is against the Nature of Women, so that a Silent Woman would be as a Monster in Nature; but howsoever, my Desire is rather to be a Monster for Silence, than a Natural in Talk.'[29]

Here Cavendish's readiness to deploy misogynist figurations of femininity to her own advantage betrays the anxiety attaching – in general and particular – to the spectacular woman. Cavendish's rhetoric of inversion and transvaluation, fraught with affect and contradiction, acutely mobilises the transitivity and historical contingency of discourses of gender, value and propriety in order to stage a recuperation of herself and her writing as 'improbable, if not impossible'. In this context, marriage functions as the exemplary space of permission, correction and naturalisation; the endorsement of conjugality itself subtends the praises which flow to and from it. Newcastle's endorsement of Cavendish's value, productivity and chastity, like his wife's praise of him as the type of the loyal husband and courtier, emblematises their marriage as Royalist romance. Whatever their real relations, they conducted a rhetorically subtle discourse of conjugality in the margins of Cavendish's books, designed to defend and promote the durability of conservative discourses of epicurean nostalgia, extravagance and natural hierarchy in a post-revolutionary context.

Letter 78 of *Sociable Letters* raises the abstract and diffuse possibility of finding or writing for a perceived market of readers with shared tastes and interests, but the negativity of Cavendish's account suggests the caprice of any reader motivated simply by 'delight': 'if any will present their Works to Persons of their Own Nation, they must present them to such as are Known to Delight in such Subjects their Books treat of, and then perchance they may read a leaf or two, and by that Censure all the Book.'[30] Cavendish frequently asserts the recursive pleasure of reading one's own writing – 'I delight my self with Self'[31] – but the question of how to read, or to be read by, a stranger is troubling. The cipher-like, anonymous and silent addressee–auditor of the bulk of *Sociable Letters* represents one response to this problem: her supposed replies are excluded and paraphrased, while her unseen text is dismissed on the grounds that particular skills of writing cannot excuse the general deficiency of 'an Ill-chosen Subject': 'give me leave to tell you, the Poem is good in that kind, but I do not like such kind of Poems.'[32] The texts and the subjects she likes are her own, or like her own. Cavendish is so far from imagining the iterability of ideal readers – who, it follows, must either be her or as inimitable as she is if they are to warrant the compliment – that she repeatedly dilates on the dangers of choosing a friend or a husband, or of losing them once found. For the loss or failure of an ideal other not only breaches the contract of shared solitude but buries the solitary's texts. The unwavering solicitude of self-love underwrites all intimacy and affect in Cavendish's poetics, but the will to fame requires the solicitation and seduction of others: 'so many Friends as Remember me, so many Lives I have.'[33] The ideal married female friend framed by *Sociable Letters* operates as a kind of *prosopopoeia* of Margaret Cavendish herself in a structure close to the scribal contract of the Empress and 'Margaret Newcastle' in *The Blazing World*. Thus the text imagines what Eve Keller calls 'the forward progression of selves'[34] as a one-sided dialogue between the death of the author and the death of the reader in order to broach the possibility of its own extinction:

> I desire to Live in every Heart, especially in your Ladiships, wherein I believe I do already, and wish I may live Long. Wherefore for my own sake, as well as yours, let me entreat you to Remove out of that Plaguy City, for if you Die, all those Friends you Leave, or Think of, or Remember, partly Die with you, nay, some perchance for Ever, if they were Personally Dead before, and onely Live in your Memory.[35]

Against the potentially democratic effects of print, Cavendish mobilises an epideictic model of carefully vetted textual hospitality, distinguishing between welcome and uninvited readers, 'neighbours' and strangers, in order to reproduce an already understood set of hierarchical relations: 'those that do not like my Book, which is my House, I pray them to pass by.' Emerging from the bastion of the marital home, and the *otium* of her closet, Cavendish addresses her books to neighbourly simulacra whilst warning off others. She figures publication through a ramifying model of proprietary interest, as an extension of territory already staked out and an investment in the ideological reproduction of credit. In this sense, she does not so much want to gain readers by publishing as demonstrate in perpetuity what she already knows herself to be. As Walter Charleton, one of Cavendish's invited readers, observed in 1667, the Duchess of Newcastle did not need or want to make money by publishing, but rather to conspicuously spend it: 'whereas [others] employ only their wit, labour and time in composing books, you bestow also great sums of money in printing yours; and not content to enrich our heads alone with your rare notions, you go higher and adorn our libraries with your elegant volumes'.[36]

Cavendish figures writing as a natural avocation, finessed and matured through the improving effects of marriage as a kind of apprenticeship. In the *Worlds Olio,* Cavendish styles herself as apprentice to her husband–master[37] and, to a lesser extent, the student of other near male relations such as her brother-in-law, Charles Cavendish:

> Not any hath a more able master to learn from, then I have, for if I had never married the person I have, I do beleeve I should never have writ so, as to have adventured to divulge my works, for I have learned more of the world from my Lords discourse, since I have been his wife, then I am confident I should have done all my life, should I have lived to an old age.[38]

But she also insists on the pedagogical importance of nature as the tutor of intrinsic rational capacities: 'every straw, or grain of dust, is a natural tutor, to instruct my sense and reason, and every particular rational creature, is a sufficient School to study in.'[39] These complementary discourses of instruction suggest the self-sufficiency of the marital estate and its status as harmonious sequel to the maternal education of Cavendish's country childhood:

> I am not a Dunce in all Imployments, for I Understand the Keeping of Sheep, and Ordering of a grange, indifferently well, although I do not Busie my self much with it, by reason my Scribling takes away the most part of my Time.[40]

Writing is offered as prophylaxis against feminised expense and time wasting, and as readable within a discourse of husbandry rather than inimical to it. Cavendish insists that aristocratic married life at best not only supplies retirement and contemplation consistent with proper female conduct and desire, but also facilitates certain kinds of public engagement. Cavendish offers herself as prime example of feminised georgic improvement, narrating her own marital instruction in 'masculine understandings' as proof of women's ability to acquire 'fortitude':

> Women that are bred, tender, idle and ignorant (as I have been) are not likely to have much Wit; nor is it fit they should be bred up to Masculine Actions, yet it were very fit and requisit they should be bred up to Masculine Understandings; it is not fit for Women to practice the behaviour of Men, yet it is fit that Women should practice the Fortitude of Men;[...] I beseech my Readers to believe I speak not out of Envy or Spight, for I am guilty of neither, but out of a grieved love to my own Sex [...].[41]

For obvious reasons, Cavendish chooses not to interpret writing and publishing books as 'practic[ing] the behaviour of Men,' always striving to maintain the association of writing with the legitimately forceful public witnessing of the productivity of marriage and the rational capacities of women.

In *Sociable Letters*, Cavendish pointedly distinguishes the copious manuscript writings of her pre-married life from her subsequent catalogue of publications, in order to narrate the transition from an illegible natural propensity or singular predisposition to viable public authorship. Not only does it behove the aristocratic wife, as a woman withdrawn from the market, to situate herself in the home, willingly sequestered and immobilised, but it is fitting that she employ herself in the home in a way that marks her freedom from the more menial demands of housewifery. Although Cavendish represents herself as equipped with certain practical skills and responsibilities, she insists that her chief desire and occupation is to place herself through the linked activities of writing, reading, contemplating, conversing, and publishing, in the particular economy of the married couple and its analogue, the reciprocity of ideal writer and reader. In this sense, whatever the temporal relation of any particular text to the narrative exigency of effecting a good marriage, the signature of the author *qua* wife not only explicitly frames the text but is understood as its perennial occasion. By extension, the benefits of wifely prerogative, with its concomitant acknowledgement of husbandly authority, provide a dialectical key to the proper and improper reading of a married woman's oeuvre, for 'A Writer hath a double desire, the one that he may write well, the other, that he may be read well.'[42]

Newcastle's 'Hearty Commendations' in 'To The Lady Marchioness Of Newcastle On her Book of Epistles' opens *Sociable Letters* by defending his wife's reputation from possible attack ('Your Fames of Wit, this Age may think a Sin') and charging her with exceeding all precedent:

> Y' have Spoil'd Commerce, Intelligencers, Trade,
> None now dares write a Letter, so Afraid
> To be thought Fools, and is the Carriers Curse,
> To find his Empty Budget, and Lank Purse,
> Nay all the Post-house's Ruin'd, and will Complain,
> From their Vast Gettings now they have no Gain.[43]

Newcastle specifically figures his wife's letters as anti-economic and anti-social; the fear they engender in men shuts down all circulation: 'why would you Undo/Yourself at once thus and the whole World Too.' And yet, his own response, figuring the husband as ideal reader and patron, averts the disaster it imagines. Followed by Margaret's reply, 'To His Excellency The Lord Marquis Of Newcastle', the reciprocity of marital address offers an alternative economy and an alternative reading of the meaning of *Sociable Letters* – and all Cavendish's books – as the product of the legal union between an incomparable woman and 'one of the Best of men.' Newcastle's intimate and yet public patronage, paired with Margaret's praise of him as exemplifying those virtues both he and she share with 'Beasts' ('Temperate, Sociable, Laborious, Patient, Prudent, Provident, Brotherly-loving and Neighbourly-kind'), 'but most Men [do] not,' combines critique of the competitive masculine marketplace ('Pride, Vanity, Ambition, Covetousness, Faction, Treachery, and Treason') with hyperbolic praise of 'natural', 'noble' virtues. As a pedagogical emblem, Margaret –'Honest Wife and Humble Servant' and 'a Friend to Virtue'[44] – assumes the role of exhibiting in the marketplace those qualities claimed as inimical to it, thus reforming 'letters' in favour of an ideal correspondence between husband and wife, nature and virtue.[45]

The correct sequence of husband to wife, then wife to husband, paves the way for Cavendish to address in turn a specifically masculine professoriat, the 'Most Famously Learned', and then the generalised company of ungendered 'Noble Readers', whom she cautions to understand her method as impartial and dialogic:

> my Orations for the most part are Declamations, wherein I speak Pro and Con, and Determine nothing' in the form of the Correspondence of two Ladies, living at some Short Distance from each other, which make it not only their Chief Delight and Pastime, but their Tye in Friendship, to Discourse by Letters, as they would do if they were Personally together, so that these Letters are an Imitation of a Personal Visitation and Conversation.[46]

The anonymous poem which follows, 'Upon Her Excellency The Authoress', I take to be Cavendish's unsigned dedication to herself. In it she glosses the autotelic structure of the collection's 'conversation', and explains the absence of any replies:

> This Lady only to her self she Writes
> And all her Letters to her self Indites;
> For in her self so many Creatures be,
> Like many Commonwealths, yet all Agree [...].
> But in her brain doth Reason Govern well,
> Not any Thought 'gainst Reason doth Rebell [...].
> They bring Intelligence from every State,
> Their Peace, their Wars, their Factions, and their Hate [...].
> And thus Her thoughts, the Creatures of Her Mind,
> Do Travel through the World amongst mankind,
> And then Return, and to the Mind do bring
> All the Relations of each several thing [...],
> Then Contemplation calls the Senses straight,
> Which Ready are, and Diligently Wait,
> Commanding Two these Letters for to Write,
> Touch in the hand, as also the Eye-sight,
> These Two the Soul's Clerks are which do Inscribe,
> And Write all Truly down, having no Bribe.[47]

In this allegory of the scene of writing as supernaturally omniscient, singular feminine authority ('This Lady') is atomised through personification, so that the secluded 'Mind' of 'Her Excellency The Authoress' may be pluralised and invisibly dispersed to 'Travel through the World amongst mankind, / And then Return.'[48] What begins as a reassurance against authentic dialogue or partisan opinion, as a promise of the narcissistic circularity of a woman's correspondence, opens into a politicised model of writing as a process of intelligence-gathering and a technology of surveillance. The panoptic threat of the woman who, without seeming to leave home, is everywhere at once from confessional to 'Privy-Counsel', is only partly mitigated by installing 'Reason' as 'Great King', a Newcastle-style lieutenant-husband to feminised 'Contemplation'. Both are internal functions of the 'Authoress', and the multitude of wandering thoughts remain 'Creatures of her Mind'. If 'Upon Her Excellency The Authoress' is offered as a paradigm of the various ways in which Cavendish structures and ameliorates her claim to singular authority, it is also clear that the personified couples – Reason and Contemplation, Touch and Sight – who integrate the work of the multitude of subject-thoughts, represent a congenial division of labour and resist any easy hierarchisation: together they serve 'Her Excellency' and disseminate her powers 'through the World amongst Mankind'.

The text of *Sociable Letters*, with its frankly imaginary 'correspondence of two Ladies [...] Tye[d] in Friendship,' deploys feminised retirement as the ground of meta-commentary – 'under the Cover of Letters' – on 'the Actions of a Man's Life' ('The Preface'). Despite earlier reassurances of impartiality, the final prefatory piece, directed 'To The Censorious Reader' (as distinct from Newcastle as ideal reader, and the 'Noble Readers' already addressed), makes plain the project of female 'Satyr' of the 'Errours, Vanities, and Idle Times' of men, 'lest they should Forget':

> [...]take Heed, Beware, and have a Care,
> For there are Stumps of Trees, or a Deep Pit,
> Or Dangerous Passages where Thieves do sit
> And Wait, or Ravenous Beasts do lye for Prey.[49]

Given that Cavendish had several pages earlier extolled the virtues of 'harmless' beasts, and likened herself and her husband to them, their reappearance as 'ravenous' in a rebuke to 'censors' sounds an ominous note.

In exile and then in retirement, Cavendish undertook with great versatility and ambition a maverick wifely career as author of a copious polemical and experimental oeuvre under the express protection of her husband's name and title. It can be no accident that after so many speculative and fantastic texts in which she remarked her profound debt to Newcastle whilst advancing her own powerful claims to notice, Cavendish ended her career with a biography of her husband, sealing their textual romance with a work offered as a devoted wife's testimony to his wronged greatness. Even in this apparently selfless enterprise, however, Cavendish speaks categorically in her own person.[50]

Cavendish's textual recycling and repetition represents a necessarily open-ended negotiation of the fecundity of feminised error and speculation under masculine protection. She works the problematic of gender and genre in the hope that the infamy and momentum of her signature will survive both her literal death and the multitude of 'ignorant dolts' who can be guaranteed not to 'esteem or admire [...] rare Qualities, Learned Sciences, Curious Arts, and Divine Fancies.'[51] If her own singularity and the correlative uniqueness of her texts constitute Cavendish's perpetual boast, that is partly a function of her pessimism and paranoia about fit readers outside the mutual endorsements of marriage, and her vulnerability with respect to the vicissitudes of the life of books in the public sphere. The fact that she cannot compel those who will not or cannot read her to enter into this circuit of exchange threatens to undo the narcissistic motivation of writing in the first place, for, although she sometimes claims to write chiefly for her own pleasure, she is far more tenacious and convincing in her desire to be remembered in perpetuity by and for her writing. If Cavendish writes in order to become famous, she also aligns herself with the Sidneian rhetoric of writing as recuperative political praxis for self-styled noble exiles.

The fact that Cavendish frames all her writing in terms of the necessarily speculative enterprise of natural philosophy allows her to recuperate hostility as disciplinary authentication. In 'An Epistle to the Unbelieving Readers in Natural Philosophy', she appeals again to a calculated 'negligence':

> I, and those that write, must arm ourselves with Negligence against Censure; for my part, I do: for I verily believe, that Ignorance, and present Envy, will slight my Book; yet I make no question, when Envy is worn out by Time, but Understanding will remember me in after Ages, when I am changed from this Life: But I had rather live in a General Remembrance, than in a Particular Life.[52]

Meaningful remembrance and lasting reputation require the relocation of the private pleasure of writing to the treacherous public economy of print and ownership of books. The commodities issued in her name must compete for notice in the market against all other books currently circulating or archived, and even against those books that will be published in the future. Not just reading but re-reading, the ratio of owners to readers, and the preferred manner of reading – aloud rather than silent – all feature as vital contingencies in Cavendish's discourses on the fate of (her) books. In the *Animal Parliament*, for instance, the fear of an unpublished manuscript or unread printed book is displaced by a more insidious critique of novelty:

> Books have the worst Fate; when they once are read,
> They're laid aside, forgotten like the Dead.
> Under a Heap of Dust, they buried lye,
> Within a Vault of some small *Library*.[53]

No matter how substantial, various and curious, how inimitable and ambitious her textual legacy, the futurity of Cavendish's name, and the names of her books, cannot be guaranteed, thus rendering the desire for fame exponential and incommensurable. In Letter 79 of *Sociable Letters*, she writes:

> I wish, whereas I have One Friend to Praise my Works, although Partially, I had a Thousand, or rather Ten thousand Millions, nay, that their number were Infinite, that the Issue of my Brain, Fame, and Name, might live to Eternity if it were possible.[54]

Textual singularity, difficulty and eccentricity, as a strategic claiming, is thus perpetually at risk of falling into complete obscurity and illegibility, an unwitnessed and unrecorded solitude. So it is that Cavendish is led into the indignity of supplicating for readers or subjects of her textual empire, now and in the future, all the while insisting that her texts have been generated in advance by a pre-existing demand or regard. From book to book she uses the surrounding matter to inscribe an ongoing audience and market for her work, allocating praise and blame to them even when they will not return her challenge.

Suspicious though she is of the anonymising effects of collectivity in general, her particular fear is the metropolis, 'spred broad with Vanity, and almost smother'd with Crowds of Creditors for Debts,' characteristically structured in terms of a defensive *chiasmus*: 'But, Madam, as you Condemn my Life, so I Condemn Yours, for the Nobles that live in a Metrapolitan City, live but as Citizens, and Citizens that live in the Country, live like Noble Men.'[55] As a remedy in advance for the dangers and rigours of that market to which she repeatedly submits, Cavendish offers the solicitude of the favoured couple, located in the 'Liberty' and 'Extension' of the 'Country', whose mutual fitness and regard promises to pair and bind singularities together. Beyond the confirmation of Cavendish's own self-love and acknowledged ambition, Newcastle is figured and also represents himself in her books as the master–patron who alone is free to authorise the circulation of his wife's name as the author of a library's worth of substantial volumes. Finally, then, one of the most arresting aspects of the matter of Cavendish's books is their inscription of reciprocal marital obligation and credit as a collusion on behalf of the potentially errant noble wife, in anticipation of the unregulated aggression of the public sphere. As spectacularised author–wife, 'Margaret Newcastle' becomes, in her own texts and on her husband's authority, a surprising figure for the public sphere's capacity to threaten or misread the privileges and innate difference of nobility as such.

Notes

[1] Charles Lamb, 'Detached Thoughts on Books and Reading', *The Last Essays of Elia* (1833), in Charles Lamb, *Elia and the Last Essays of Elia*, ed. by E. V. Lucas (London: Methuen, 1912), p. 197.

[2] *Sociable Letters* (1997), Letter 27, p. 37.

[3] *Sociable Letters* (1997), Letter 28, p. 38.

[4] *Sociable Letters* (1997), Letter 29, p. 42.

[5] *Sociable Letters* (1997), Letter 158, p. 170.

[6] I follow current convention in referring to the Duchess of Newcastle as 'Margaret Cavendish', itself a catachrestic modernisation, but my reading focuses on the witting invention of the authorial signature 'Margaret Newcastle' as figuratively and ideologically catachrestic.

[7] Margaret was first separated from her family when she fled to France in Henrietta Maria's party in 1644. She married Newcastle in Paris in 1645. In 1647, her mother, Elizabeth Leighton Lucas, and one of her sisters, Mary Lucas Killigrew, died of natural causes; in the same year, her brother, Sir Charles Lucas, was executed with Sir George Lisle, and the family tomb desecrated. Newcastle was formally banished in March 1649, in the immediate aftermath of the regicide. See *Margaret the First*, pp. 98–103. Cavendish published a group of familial elegies in her first book, *Poems and Fancies* (1653): 'On a Mother dyed for griefe of her only daughter which dyed', 'On a beautifull

young maid dyed daughter to the grieved Mother', and 'An Elegy on my Brother, kill'd in these unhappy Warres', as well as a number of poems suggesting the epistemological violence of revolution, such as 'Of the death and buriall of Truth'. See Kate Lilley, 'True State Within: Women's Elegy 1640–1700', in ***Women, Writing, History***, pp. 72-92. See also N. H. Keeble, 'Obedient subjects? The loyal self in some later seventeenth-century Royalist women's memoirs', in Gerald Maclean (ed.), ***Culture and Society in the Stuart Restoration: Literature, Drama, History***, (Cambridge: Cambridge University Press, 1995), pp. 201-218.

[8] *Sociable Letters* (1997), Letter 120, p. 128.

[9] 'From Nicholas Hill to Thomas Carew, the atom and its qualities are compared with the royal and noble persons of the nation. Both sides of the analogy, the natural and the political, pose the pure and fundamental "principle" against the mixed and derivative dross of the world.', Reid Barbour, 'The Early Stuart Epicure', ***English Literary Renaissance***, 23 (1993), 170–100 (p. 172). Barbour offers a cogent elaboration of the ambivalent political, intellectual and aesthetic force of Epicurean atomism in the court of Charles I. Although he does not treat Margaret Cavendish in any detail, Barbour convincingly suggests that '[f]or Cavendish, Epicurean atomism was the impetus for the freedom of authorship' which she justified 'as fidelity to her husband's property and to her King.' (p. 195n). Barbour analyses the radical conservatism of the 'cult revival' of atomist discourses in the court culture of the 1630s (p. 180), but he also stresses that 'both conservative and subversive positions are almost inextricable from one another.' (p. 195). John Rogers, *The Matter of Revolution: Science, Poetry and Politics in the Age of Milton*, (Ithaca: Cornell University Press, 1996), interestingly complicates the question of nostalgia in Cavendish's natural philosophy and utopian speculation by investigating its affinities with 'the defeated cause of the vitalist revolutionaries' (p. 211). He devotes a chapter to an intriguingly counter-intuitive reading of Cavendish's post-Restoration 'engagement of a political radicalism inescapably tied to an earlier epoch' (p. 211n), finding in her work a compromised vision of 'a utopia of female volition – like the true commonwealth Milton foresaw, like the communist state of the Diggers, like the green age of Marvell's idle pastorals – [which] might never materialise.' (p. 211). Jay Stevenson, 'The Mechanist–Vitalist Soul of Margaret Cavendish', ***Studies in English Literature***, 36 (1996), 527–543, stresses the heretical aspect of her interest in 'acentric' and atheistic 'atomic determinism'. For an account of the rhetorical cathexis of textual mixing, hybridity and utopian speculation in Cavendish's writing, see my 'Introduction' in ***Writings*** (1994) and Kate Lilley, 'Blazing Worlds: Seventeenth-Century Women's Utopian Writing', in ***Women, Texts and Histories***, pp. 102-133.

[10] As Susan Wiseman argues: 'What is at stake throughout Cavendish's writing is the intransigent interrelationship between patriarchal or monarchist ideals and the desire to disrupt gender ideology.' See Wiseman, 'Gender and Status in Dramatic Discourse: Margaret Cavendish, Duchess of Newcastle', in ***Women, Writing, History***, pp. 159-77 (p. 177).

[11] Laura J. Rosenthal, *Playwrights and Plagiarists in Early Modern England*, (Ithaca: Cornell University Press, 1996), p. 104. See also Jeffrey Masten's chapter on Cavendish in his *Textual Intercourse: Collaboration, Authorship, and Sexualities in Renaissance Drama* (Cambridge: Cambridge University Press, 1997) p. 162: 'Her writing both draws on emergent paradigms of authorship – the nascent policing of textual theft and borrowing –

and inscribes discourses that have become more familiar in the author's subsequent domain and reign: the self-sufficient, "natural" organicism of the home-grown genius; authorship as cottage industry.' Rosenthal suggests that 'charges of plagiarism against Cavendish must have been frequent, particularly disturbing, or both, for she defends herself vehemently'(p. 58). She notes, amongst many other instances, Cavendish's claim, in the dedication to the second edition of the *Life of William Cavendishe*: 'my attending servants are witness that I have had none but my own Thoughts, Fancies, and Speculations to assist me.'(p. 59). If Cavendish frequently offers Newcastle as star witness, clearly servants in this equation represent a kind of mute hearsay which is purely derived, always available to the citation of the mistress–author, and always alienated from its source. This example offers a telling instance of Cavendish's reliance for her own limited and uneven critique of gender inequality on the unchangingly instrumental status of those who serve, for those who are served. As Wiseman comments: 'At every juncture the assertion of class stability and of fixed lowerness stands surety for the noble ladies' liberation from gender constraints and entry into the theatre of the world' (*Women, Writing, History*, p. 177). The dynamics of power are altogether less schematic, however, when service between elite subjects is at issue, as for instance in the representation of the 'Duchess of Newcastle' as 'scribe' to the Empress in *The Blazing World*. On the constitutive and erotic ambiguity of the Elizabethan (male) 'secretary' see Alan Stewart, *Close Readers: Humanism and Sodomy in Early Modern England* (Princeton: Princeton University Press, 1997), 'Epistemologies of the Early Modern Closet', pp. 161-187. Cavendish employed a number of secretaries during her career and also detailed her reliance on Newcastle's longstanding secretary, John Rolleston, in gathering information for her biography of Newcastle. Rolleston also contributed a prefatory epistle to the completed *Life*. Noting Cavendish's untutored hand and spelling, Grant comments: 'one can only sympathise deeply with her succession of secretaries, one of whom died at his post.' *Margaret the First*, p. 115.

[12] *Sociable Letters* (1997), Letter 143, pp. 153–154.

[13] 'Epistle to the Reader', *Worlds Olio* (1655), sig. A1. *Sociable Letters* also offers an alternative account of the infantilised economy of manuscript in its commentary on the circulation between friends of 'the Sixteen Books I Writ in my Childhood' composed of 'Unknown Letters' and rendered still more 'Unlegible' by 'huge Blots' and 'Hard Scratches'. See *Sociable Letters* (1997), Letter 131, pp. 140–141. Cavendish returns to these disproportionately large and impenetrable 'Baby-books' in Letter 134, calling them her 'Paper Book' in a move which again confuses the singular and the plural. This manuscript collection has been souvenired because it is destined never to be printed, and thus may remain in the care of the author.

[14] 'Preface', *Sociable Letters* (1997), pp. 7–8.

[15] Cavendish is concerned about scribal and printer's errors, only to the extent that they may change the intended sense and leave her open to attack for the wrong reasons.

[16] Marta Straznicky, 'Reading the stage: Margaret Cavendish and Commonwealth closet drama', *Criticism*, 37 (1995), 355–390 (p. 360). Straznicky offers a very suggestive reading of Cavendish in terms of her contribution to the 'unprecedented conflation of public and private' in Commonwealth closet drama (p. 362).

[17] *Sociable Letters* (1997), Letter 142, p. 153.

[18] 'Allegory 50', *Worlds Olio* (1655), p. 106.

[19] Rosenthal similarly stresses the sense in which 'Margaret's upwardly mobile marriage to William enabled her to understand herself as at least potentially an owner of literary property' (*Playwrights*, p. 62), suggesting that 'Cavendish's significance lies not so much in originality itself [...] as it does in her claim to it as a strategy of entitlement.' (*Playwrights*, p. 64). For a subtle overview of female authorship, literacy and coverture see Margaret W. Ferguson, 'Renaissance Concepts of the Woman Writer', in Helen Wilcox (ed.) *Women and Literature in Britain, 1500–1700* (Cambridge: Cambridge University Press, 1996), pp. 146–152.

[20] See Victoria Kahn, 'Margaret Cavendish and the Romance of Contract', *Renaissance Quarterly*, 50 (1997), 526–566. My thinking about Cavendish has been greatly enriched by this remarkable essay.

[21] *Worlds Olio* (1655), 'An Epistle to the Reader', sig. A1.

[22] *Worlds Olio* (1655), 'The Preface to the Reader', sig. A3.

[23] 'To His Excellency The Lord Marquis of Newcastle', *Sociable Letters* (1997), p. 4.

[24] Adapted from the check-list of Cavendish's published work in *Margaret the First*, pp. 240–242.

[25] Kahn, 'Romance of Contract', p. 558n. Catherine Gallagher's, 'Embracing the Absolute: the Politics of the Female Subject in Seventeenth-Century England', *Genders*, 1 (1988) 24–89, remains a polemical cornerstone of critical work on Cavendish. Anna Battigelli, 'Between the Glass and the Hand: the Eye in Margaret Cavendish's Blazing World, 1650–1850', *Ideas, Aesthetics, and Inquiries in the Early Modern Era*, 2 (1996), 25–38, usefully contextualises Gallagher's characterisation of 'a process of infinite regression' (p. 31) in Cavendish's textual modelling of the self in *The Blazing World* as 'a micrographia of the mind' which offers 'a series of magnifications of the self' (p. 37). This observation is congruent with the argument I am developing here for the significance of chiastic rhetorical ratios of scale and value in Cavendish's writing. See also Eve Keller, 'Producing Petty Gods: Margaret Cavendish's Critique of Experimental Science', *English Literary History*, 64 (1997), 447–471, for a nuanced reading of the 'asymmetry' of Cavendish's critique of 'discrete self and stable object.'

[26] Barbour argues that 'the Stuarts imagined themselves in a garden of tranquility – the very essence of Epicurean pleasure – where they could rest like gods free from the tumult of the vulgar world' (p. 180). Cavendish employs this topos throughout her writing.

[27] *Sociable Letters* (1997), Letter 93, p. 101.

[28] 'A True Relation of my Birth, Breeding, and Life', in *Natures Picture* (1656), p. 390.

[29] *Sociable Letters* (1997), Letter 147, p. 158.

[30] *Sociable Letters* (1997), Letter 78, p. 90.

[31] *Sociable Letters* (1997), Letter 29, p. 41.

[32] *Sociable Letters* (1997), Letter 72, p. 85.

[33] *Sociable Letters* (1997), Letter 90, p. 98.

[34] Keller, 'Producing Petty Gods', p. 463.

[35] *Sociable Letters* (1997), Letter 90, pp. 98–99. Rosenthal – drawing on Traub and Butler – argues that 'the inscription of women's erotic desire for other women' in some Cavendish plays such as *The Presence* and *The Convent of Pleasure* 'permits the disruption of bipolar gender oppositions that regulate reproduction, ownership, and authorship' (*Playwrights*, pp. 87, 92–101). *The Presence* shares with *Assaulted and Pursued Chastity*, though in diluted form, the plot device of a Queen's unrequited and

unwitting love for a cross-dressed female courtier which continues unabated even after the truth of the courtier's sex is unveiled. On *Assaulted and Pursued Chastity* see Karen R. Lawrence, *Penelope Voyages: women and travel in the British literary tradition*, (Ithaca: Cornell University Press, 1992), pp. 30–51; and Lilley, 'Introduction' in *Writings* (1994).

[36] Cit. *Margaret the First*, p. 219. Collected by Newcastle in *Letters and Poems* (1676), p. 109. The fact that the Newcastles in exile were able to live in appropriate style and with many servants largely on credit indicates the pragmatic benefits of such a posture. The Duke expended great effort in maintaining his lavish credit, and was able to use his rank as surety even when his estates were confiscated and his person banished, thus converting purely ideological value into goods, services and personnel. According to Grant, 'When the creditors' patience was finally exhausted [...] he fell back on persuasion [...]. They always found his charm and his arguments irresistible.' (*Margaret the First*, p. 90). In *Sociable Letters*, Cavendish writes: 'in these needy times Tradesmen must venture to Trust, or else they will hardly put off their Commodities, for where one payes ready Mony, five, nay twenty, run on the Score; the reason is, there is not so much Mony *in Specie*, not in all Europe, nay, in the World, as to pay readily for all that is Bought, for there are more Commodities than Mony, I may say, more Paper than Mony.' *Sociable Letters* (1997), Letter 41, p. 54.

[37] 'Epistle', *Worlds Olio* (1655), p. 27.

[38] 'Epistle', *Worlds Olio* (1655), pp. 30–31.

[39] 'Epistle', *Worlds Olio* (1655), p. 27. For an interesting account of Cavendish's strategic figurations of nature see Rebecca Merrens, 'A nature of "infinite sense and reason": Margaret Cavendish's natural philosophy and the "noise" of a feminised nature', *Women's Studies*, 25 (1996) 421–439.

[40] *Sociable Letters* (1997), p. 4.

[41] 'Noble Souls and Strong Bodies', *Worlds Olio* (1655), p. 215.

[42] *Worlds Olio* (1655), 'To the Reader', sig. A3.

[43] *Sociable Letters* (1997), p. 3.

[44] *Sociable Letters* (1997), p. 8.

[45] On Cavendish's emblematic self-fashioning and frontispieces see James Fitzmaurice, 'Fancy and the Family: Self-characterisations of Margaret Cavendish', *Huntingdon Library Quarterly*, 53 (1990), 198–209. He suggests that Cavendish 'pictured herself as more reclusive than she actually was in order to reinforce the characterisation she was forming of herself as melancholic.'(p. 201).

[46] 'Preface', *Sociable Letters* (1997), pp. 8–9.

[47] 'Upon Her Excellency The Authoress', *Sociable Letters* (1997), pp. 10–11.

[48] For valuable related explorations see Sophie Tomlinson, '"My Brain the Stage" : Margaret Cavendish and the Fantasy of Female Performance', in *Women, Texts and Histories*, pp. 134-63; and Lee Cullen Khanna, 'The Subject of Utopia: Margaret Cavendish and Her Blazing World', in Jane L. Donawerth and Carol A. Kolmerten (eds.), *Utopian and Science Fiction by Women: Worlds of Difference*, (New York: Syracuse University Press, 1994), pp. 15-34.

[49] 'To The Censorious Reader', *Sociable Letters* (1997), p. 12.

[50] For another reading which draws out the theoretical consequences of this aspect of Cavendish's textual production see Sandra Sherman, 'Trembling Texts: Margaret Cavendish and the Dialectic of Authorship', *English Literary Renaissance*, 24 (1994), 184–210.

[51] *Sociable Letters* (1997), Letter 109, p. 117.

[52] *Worlds Olio* (1655), p. 173.

[53] 'The Common Fate of Books' in *Poems* (1668), p. 350.

[54] *Sociable Letters* (1997), p. 91.

[55] *Sociable Letters* (1997), Letter 82, p. 93.

3

'How Great is Thy Change': Familial Discourses in the Cavendish Family

Marion Wynne-Davies

In *A Room of One's Own* (1929), Virginia Woolf created an Early Modern woman dramatist called Judith Shakespeare, but lamented that no real counterpart existed for Judith since,

> [...] it is unthinkable that any woman in Shakespeare's day should have had Shakespeare's genius. For genius like Shakespeare's is not born among labouring, uneducated, servile people [...] how, then, could it have been born among women whose work began [...] almost before they were out of the nursery.[1]

Of course, Woolf was perfectly accurate in identifying a female author's need for security, both economic and environmental, but the seeming lack of actual texts led her to assume that women of the early modern period had experienced neither, instead being trapped within a domestic vortex of familial responsibilities. Indeed, Woolf was not alone in her assumptions, for many readers and critics over the centuries were unaware of the works of Early Modern women authors such as Mary Wroth, Elizabeth Cary and Aemilia Lanyer (the list could easily run into triple figures), as their books and manuscripts were neglected, lost or ignored. However, with the emergence of feminist criticism in the early 1970s and the subsequent commitment to rediscover neglected women writers, female authors were reinstated in our literary awareness. Their works are now published in modern editions and are increasingly a focus of scholarly research, literary conferences and undergraduate courses. Woolf's suppositions have therefore been superseded, and the function of her text has metamorphosed from its original polemical defence of women writers into an uninformed, but benign, salvo which is rehearsed mainly as a prelude to contradiction by the radicalised feminism of the late-twentieth century. But Woolf's lengthy description of Judith's 'career' deserves more attention than as a pretty vignette since it serves to identify several important elements in the development of female dramatic authorship in the late sixteenth and early seventeenth centuries.

To begin with, the necessity of economic security cannot be questioned: by far the majority of women writing drama in the English Renaissance belong to, or are firmly associated with, the nobility. Thus, it is essential to recognise that as the patterns of literary productivity are traced they encompass a very small section of the population; the bonds of kinship and class are tightly woven about the women discussed in this essay. Indeed, the few criticisms which refer to the three Cavendish women comment upon their 'family' or 'coterie' bonds: Margaret J. M. Ezell comments that 'for readership, "family" is the obvious answer';[2] Sophie Tomlinson argues that 'the fact that the sisters also authored a pastoral suggests that their dramatic writing, like that of their stepmother, was in part an effect of the culture set in motion by Henrietta Maria';[3] and Susan Wiseman concludes that 'in their private entertainments the women of this family shift from mere actors to authors.'[4] However, the economic security mentioned above should not be confused with economic freedom, since the women discussed here were all dependent upon male relatives or associates for their status and wealth, and any infringement of the implicit regulations governing their behaviour could lead to ostracism and destitution. Judith Shakespeare's indiscretions lead to just such an end: 'at last Nick Greene the actor–manager took pity on her: she found herself with child by that gentleman and so [...] killed herself one winter's night,'[5] and her fictional narrative may be authenticated with the history of a real Renaissance woman dramatist, Elizabeth Cary, whose conversion to Catholicism led to the breakdown of her marriage and to a life of poverty and isolation.[6] Cash, as Woolf so succinctly determined, was an essential ingredient in the background of women writers, but their access to such monetary stability was achieved only through an apparent acquiescence with and conformity to the unwritten rules of patriarchy. Moreover, Woolf's central idea of a 'room of one's own' is not totally inappropriate for the early modern period, although the constraints on privacy during this time suggest a shared space rather than a single occupancy. (Although Margaret Cavendish's 'closet', her private space, was renowned during her own lifetime, indeed, perhaps because of its unusual nature.) The large castles and houses that surrounded London and were scattered across the British Isles seemed to provide the secure environment in which women could nurture their creative talents. Indeed, it was precisely this combination of wealth, a secure space, together with male complicity, that allowed a few Early Modern women dramatists to evade the fate of Judith Shakespeare and to experience an environment suited to literary productivity.

Nevertheless, while earlier families such as the Sidneys and Herberts remained secure within their economic and locational stations, the Cavendish family experienced the destabilisation of the very framework that had served to liberate female voices into the dramatic arena. The houses that had been deemed 'safe' during the late-sixteenth and early-seventeenth centuries became, during the period of the Civil War and the Interregnum, sites of conflict and destruction.[7] The Cavendish family is here representative of the widespread disruption experienced by many Royalist households. Welbeck and Bolsover, the two houses supervised by Jane Cavendish in the absence of William Cavendish, her father, were respectively commandeered and plundered by the Puritan troops during the Northern campaign, while St John's Abbey, the childhood home of Margaret Cavendish, William's second wife, was utterly destroyed during the siege of Colchester.[8] Moreover, although their status was never in question, all three women suffered from economic hardship in relation to their previous expectations; Jane records how she managed to take two pairs of sheets with her from Welbeck, while Margaret's account of her life with her penniless husband in Antwerp recorded in *The Life of William Cavendish* (1667) can leave little doubt as to the precarious nature of their budget.[9] On the other hand, it must be acknowledged that none of the Cavendish family suffered the hardships experienced by the majority of the British populace during the same period; for example, Jane was able to raise £1,000 to send to her father, and Margaret always kept her own maid, Elizabeth Chaplain, although the new Duchess did ask her servant to pawn the gifts given to her in more prosperous times. Within their own premises, however, Jane, Elizabeth and Margaret Cavendish, together with William Cavendish, all confronted an overwhelming reversal in their fortunes which not only undermined their material security, financial and locational alike, but which also challenged the very ideological foundations of their lives. What is, perhaps, most remarkable, is that these adverse conditions provided the environment necessary for literary productivity; Jane and Elizabeth wrote two dramatic entertainments while besieged in Welbeck, and Margaret began 'to conceive' her extensive canon while in the chilly exile of the Rubenhuis in the Netherlands.

The difference between pre- and post-War expectations is dealt with by Margaret Cavendish in a poem concerning her return to England in 1651 in an attempt to recover her husband's property from the Sequestration Committee. In '*A Dialogue* between a *Bountifull Knight*, and a *Castle* ruin'd in *War*' she provides a conversation between the knight, Charles Cavendish (William's brother) and Bolsover Castle, which is personified as a distressed lady:

KNIGHT: Alas, poor Castle, how great is thy change
From thy first form! To me thou dost seem strange.
I left thee comely, and in perfect health;
Now thou art withered, and decayed in wealth.

CASTLE: O noble Sir, I from your stock was raised,
Flourished in plenty, and by all men was praised:
For your most valiant father did me build,
Your brother furnished me, my neck did gild;
Towers upon my head like crowns were placed;
Walls, like a girdle, went about my waist;
And on this pleasant hill he set me high,
To view the vales below, as they do lie,
Where like a garden is each field and close,
Where fresh green grass, and yellow cowslip grows;
There did I see fat sheep in pastures go,
And hear the cows, whose bags were full, to low.
By wars I'm now destroyed, all right's o'erpowered:
Beauty and innocency are devoured.
Before these wars I was in my full prime,
And held the greatest beauty in my time;
But, noble Sir, since I did see you last,
Within me hath a garrison been placed:

Their guns and pistols all about me hung,
And in despite their bullets at me flung;
Which through me sides those passages you see
Made, and destroyed the walls that circled me,
And let my rubbish on huge heaps to lie.
With dust I'm choked, for want of water, dry;
From those small leaden pipes, which winding lay
Under the ground, the water to convey,
Were all cut off; the water murmuring
Run back with grief to tell it to the spring.
My windows broke, the winds blow in, and make
That I with cold like shivering agues shake:
Oh pity me, dear Sir, release my band,
Or let me die by your most noble hand.[10]

The details in the poem are sharply realistic, referring to the initial building of the castle by Charles Cavendish senior (father to William and Charles junior) and to the improvements made by William, whose lavish extensions were undertaken – including the instalment of running water – in the 1630s when Charles I twice visited his estates and was on each occasion entertained lavishly. The Cavendish crest of a 'crown' and the building of the Terrace Range, which does indeed go about the 'waist' of the hill, are also referred to. The castle then continues with a self-pastoralisation, which evokes the country-house idealism epitomised in Ben Jonson's 'To Penshurst',[11] and although Jonson's poem might initially appear a far distant antecedent, the allusion becomes more apt when considered alongside his two masques which were written for those expensive visits paid by Charles I to the Cavendish houses: 'The King's Entertainment at Welbeck' (1633) and 'Love's Welcome. The King and Queenes Entertainment at Bolsover' (1634).[12] In the former a similar pastoral vision is presented:

The joy of plants, the spirit of flowers,
The smell, and verdure of the bowers,
The waters murmure; with the showers
Distilling on the new-fresh howers.[13]

Margaret Cavendish was, of course, familiar with Jonson's work for her husband, even though the entertainments took place twenty years before they met, and she cites both the author and the cost of the events in her *Life of the Duke of Newcastle*: '*Ben Johnson* he employed in fitting such Scenes and Speeches as he could best devise [...] [and made] This Entertainment at *Bolsover*-Castle in Derbyshire, some five miles distant from *Welbeck* [...] it cost him in all between Fourteen and Fifteen thousand pounds.'[14]

Cavendish's presentation of Bolsover as a pre-war pastoral retreat is therefore perfectly commensurate with the location's prior literary identity, and she might well have drawn upon Jonson's actual text or her husband's account of it. What is doubtful, given the date of 1651, is that she could easily refer to other pastoral visions of the Cavendish houses, ones which were also influenced by Jonson, but which were written while the family still resided in their ancestral home. There is some evidence, however, that a version of Jane and Elizabeth's work was sent to their father in France, and therefore could have been seen by their stepmother.[15] In any case, sometime between Jonson's 1634 masque and 1637 (the following text in the MS is dated 'Christmas Day 1637'), William Cavendish wrote 'a country masque, a Christmas toy'[16] specifically for his daughters, who were subsequently, between 1644 and 1645, to use similar material in their own *A Pastorall*.[17] This latter drama written by Jane and Elizabeth evokes the same setting as Jonson's work, but the lamentations of its shepherds and shepherdesses are a prelude to the complaint of Margaret's personified Bolsover, for the country has already been divided by war and many royalists were by then exiled in France. The three shepherdesses, representing Jane, Elizabeth and their sister Frances, sing of their sadness now 'He' (that is, their father William Cavendish) is no longer with them:

> His absence makes a Chaos sure of me,
> And when each one doth looking look to see
> They speaking say, That I'm not I,
> Alas do not name me for I desire to die.[18]

These sentiments are not far removed from the Knight's address to the castle in Margaret's 'A Dialogue', where he begins, 'Alas, poor Castle, how great is thy change [...] To me thou dost seem strange', and where the Castle concludes by wishing for death: 'or let me die by your most noble hand.'

Yet, the loss of pastoral bounty in Margaret Cavendish's poem is undercut by Jane and Elizabeth's comic antemasque where two country wives bewail their losses:

> *Hen*: I have lost my melch cow.
> *Pratt*: And I have lost my sow.
> *Hen*: And for my corn I cannot keep,
> *Pratt*: Neither can I my pretty sheep.
> *Hen*: And I have lost four dozen of eggs.
> *Pratt*: My pigs are gone and all their heads.[19]

The drama affords the possibility of laughter in a way the poem clearly evades. There are several possible explanations for this, apart from the difference in personal style between the three authors. First, the dramatic form is able to offer sufficient time for a variation in tone, and the hybrid structure of comedy/masque allows for a shift between the romantic shepherds and shepherdesses (the nobility) and the humorous rustic characters (the lower classes). Indeed, the Cavendish sisters employ a similar variation of tempo through class in their more formal play, *The Concealed Fancies*.[20]

In this pre-Restoration Restoration Comedy, three female cousins (who represent the three Cavendish sisters) are besieged and then captured by the Parliamentarian forces; they enter discussing their imprisonment:

SH	O cousins, our neighbouring peasants
CICILLEY	Or our pedantical servants, have given us up for a prey to the Enemy.
SH	Pray, how did I look in the posture of a delinquent?
CICILLEY	You mean how did you behave yourself in the posture of a Delinquent? Faith, as though you thought the scene would change Again, and you would be happy though you suffered misery for a Time. And how did I look?
SH	As yourself; that's great, though in misfortune.
CICILLEY	So did you.
SH	How could I do otherwise, for I practised Cleopatra when she was in her captivity, and they could have thought me worthy to have adorned their triumphs. I would have performed his gallant tragedy and so have made myself glorious for time to come.[21]

The women appear to treat the war as merely a game that affords them the opportunity to 'act' their favourite dramatic parts and indulge in lavish self-dramatisation. Yet, these lines are prefaced with the darker recognition of betrayal, either by 'peasants' or 'servants', a common event during the Civil War and one which was experienced by the Lucas family.[22] Moreover, placed within the context of 'Cavalier' writing the lines present the audience with a female version of light-hearted gallantry. Indeed, Brackley and Cavendish also include in the play the responses of two men from the royalist party, allowing the audience to contrast the differing male and female experiences. Action and Moderate are two prisoners in the same besieged castle, Ballamo:

ACTION	Sir, brought as a prisoner?
MODERATE	Yes, sir.
ACTION	Pray, what news?
MODERATE	Alas, sir, I wish there were no news, but that my cow had newly calved, or how much cream makes a pound of butter. I'm only brought in by reason they have a thought I am rich.
ACTION	They would have money of me too. A pox take them all and the devil go with them, for they are a company of knaves.
MODERATE	Aye, sir, but pray take heed, for since you are of our party, I must give you counsel, and desire you not to be so liberal of your tongue. It may do you hurt, and our party no good.
ACTION	'T is true, for I was put into such a room for talking, as I had no bigger a window to take breath at than the bigness of my little finger, and no more to piss at.
MODERATE	Sure your imprisonment hath made you mad!
ACTION	Faith, so it has, to them in hatred. Come let's go drink a health to the good success of our party and to the rogues' condemnation.
MODERATE	This would be a very good health, but not in this garrison, and thus much known may hang you.[23]

The scene neatly parodies two groups of Royalist supporters: the penniless 'Cavaliers' who swear and drink, and the careful landowners who have been involved in the conflict against their wishes. The women dramatists appear to support neither type, directing their attacks equally in this scene as in the whole play. Indeed, perhaps it is the very freedom they enjoyed in satirising their own troops, their lovers, and even their father, that is most surprising considering their own confined position while writing the play. Moreover, their sharp wit is expounded in language which might well have been deemed inappropriate for female authorship, even though voiced in the play by Action. As in their pastoral drama, Brackley and Cavendish seem at ease with comic voices drawn from a wide social spectrum, once again invoking the influence of Ben Jonson.

It is important to remember that although Margaret Cavendish might have had access to the texts of Jonson's masques she did not see them being performed, whereas on the other hand it is highly likely that Jane and perhaps Elizabeth (they would have been 11 and 6 in 1633, and 12 and 7 in 1634, the years of the two Jonson entertainments) would have been present to see the low comedy of the antemasques, where at Welbeck a '*May Lady* [...] and Sixe Maids [...] drest after the cleanliest Countrey guise' appeared, and at Bolsover there is a whole processsion of '*Mechanickes*'.[24] Finally and most importantly, the earlier work is set at that precise moment of change when it is impossible to know whether or not the pastoral ideal will once more be realisable. As such, the Knight in Margaret's poem can offer very little hope: 'Alas, poor Castle, I small help can bring', whereas in Jane and Elizabeth's drama a character aptly entitled 'Freedom' calls for the last dance: 'Come Music, lets now have a round/To prove my country wenches rightly sound.'[25] However, the most striking change occurs in the sexual references, for in the earlier work the women may remain chaste, refusing the advances of their swains since:

> Our vow will admit no such toy,
> For absent friends give us no joy.[26]

The allusion being to the exile of their father and brothers in France, whereas in the later poem the Castle presents her conquest in terms of a rape, describing how her 'rights [have been] o'erpowered', how her 'Beauty and innocency are devoured', and how the penetration of her walls, earlier described as a 'girdle', by the male garrison, with their 'guns [...] pistols [...and] bullets', have 'made passages' and left her 'destroyed'. Although these two works are separated by only seven years, the Civil War discourse has for the Cavendish women shifted from a melancholy linked with hope to a bleak and desolate vision. The castles of Welbeck and Bolsover, which serve as the site for this ideological shift, move from the ideal pastoralism of Jonson and William Cavendish in the 1630s, through the besieged threats experienced by Jane and Elizabeth in the 1640s, to the plunder and destruction that Margaret witnessed in 1651. As the Knight so aptly comments 'how great is thy change.'

Margaret Cavendish, however, was not quite accurate in her tracing of Bolsover's beginnings, for it was bought along with Welbeck and numerous other houses by Bess of Hardwick. The 'stock' alluded to should therefore be traced to

William Cavendish's formidable grandmother rather than to his father.[27] This seems to me a significant shift, for the property's provenance moves out of the male lineal descent to a broader female range. It is thus possible to rewrite, 'Sir [...] all men [...] valiant father [...] brother' (which may be understood as 'Charles junior coming to see the castle which all men had admired, and which had been built by Charles senior and embellished by William'), with: 'Madam [...] all women [...] grandmother [...] step daughters.' In this instance Bolsover/Welbeck greets Margaret Cavendish (who went with Charles to see William's lands and is, after all, writing the poem), pointing out that the property had always been admired by other women (the Countess of Rutland for example), that it had been founded by Bess of Hardwick and that it had been cared for during the Civil War by Jane and Elizabeth. This is not, of course, the poem that Margaret Cavendish chose to write; she was caught within her own period's ideology as much as we are trapped within our own late-twentieth century expectations, and the association of property with an inheritance governed by primogeniture would have been as 'natural' to her as the questioning of gender roles has become familiar to academic discourse today. But it requires a very small shift in perspective to allow a familial discourse to become regendered, or at least to open out the possibilities of a joint contribution by women to a family's literary productivity. By looking at the Cavendish family tree, and beginning with Bess of Hardwick, it becomes possible to trace patterns of female authorship: her grandchildren included William Duke of Newcastle, whose second wife was, of course, Margaret Cavendish, but they also include Arbella Stuart, who wrote numerous letters which have since been published, and Elizabeth Grey, Countess of Kent, who wrote an influential treatise on medicine, *A Choice Manual of Rare and Select Secrets in Physic and Surgery* (1653). Of Bess's great grandchildren (in the Newcastle line) Jane and Elizabeth were both accomplished authors. Sara Jane Steen, in her recent edition of Arbella Stuart's letters, comments that 'Stuart belonged to an extraordinary and extended family of women writers', and she goes on to list those whom I have already mentioned; she adds, however, Mary Sidney and Mary Wroth.[28] The connection here is via another of Bess's granddaughters, Mary Talbot, Elizabeth Grey's sister; Mary married William Herbert, the son of Mary Sidney and cousin to Mary Wroth. But here the connections are being taken too far, for the Mary Talbot who is depicted as strolling and conversing so eloquently with Arbella about court intrigues in the latter's letter (1602–3), is the same Mary Talbot who is partly pilloried as the ignorant, vain and dull Antissia by Mary Wroth in her *Urania*.[29] The immediate cause of such a discrepancy is that Mary Talbot married the man with whom Mary Wroth was in love, that is William Herbert. But these intimate family rivalries coincide with significant differences in familial discourses, both political and literary. On a very basic level, the *roman à clef* identifications in Wroth's oeuvre betray the covert and hazardous manoeuvrings within Jacobean court politics, while the clear identifications in the Cavendish works uncover a world in which the nobility has been destabilised and danger constantly threatens from beyond the closeted aristocratic frame. Thus it is possible to deduce the linking Cavendish family discourses to be: pastoral, masque, civil war, medicine and science, clothes, unstructured writing, equality of men and women in marriage, references to Shakespeare, access to one another's manuscripts, and 'fancy' and imagination, although, of course, it has not been possible to allude to all of them within the space of this essay. While, therefore, it is essential to recognise the importance of a female tradition of writing within the early modern period, at the same time we have moved beyond the need to link all women writers simply because of their sex. Rather, and perhaps not unsurprisingly, family bonds emerge as a powerful way of uniting female literary productivity, and these familial discourses simultaneously encompass and deflect male influence, resonating about certain fixed locational points.

Even if the safe houses of the early 1600s had by the middle of the century been besieged, plundered and 'raped', they still represented a strong attachment for the noble women who had once lived in them and hoped to occupy them again. While Jane Cavendish could only take her sheets from Welbeck in 1646, after the Restoration Richard Flecknoe was able to celebrate the reinstatement of the Cavendish family into their ancestral home in his poem 'On the Duchess of Newcastle's Closet' (1664/5–6).[30] The civil war writing of the Cavendish sisters had negotiated the discourses of dispossession and alienation, but Flecknoe's verse, as much as Margaret Cavendish's own works, is able to operate once again within the protective ramparts of wealth and locational security. As such, the 'sacred cell' in Flecknoe's verse[31] re-opens the economic and spatial possibilities of 'a room of one's own', ensuring, as Woolf herself concluded, that the 'stately retreat at Welbeck' had once more become a 'safe house' for the Cavendish women writers.[32]

Notes

[1] Virginia Woolf, *A Room of One's Own* (London: Hogarth Press, 1929, repr. St Albans: Triad Books, 1977), pp. 47–8.

[2] Margaret Ezell, '"To Be Your Daughter in Your Pen" : The Social Functions of Literature in the Writing of Lady Elizabeth Brackley and Lady Jane Cavendish', *Huntingdon Library Quarterly*, 51 (1988), 281–296 (p. 284).

[3] Sophie Tomlinson, '"My Brain the Stage": Margaret Cavendish and the Fantasy of Female Performance', in *Women, Texts & Histories*, pp. 134-63 (p. 138).

[4] Susan Wiseman, 'Gender and status in dramatic discourse: Margaret Cavendish, Duchess of Newcastle', in *Women, Writing, History*, pp. 159-77 (p. 161).

[5] Woolf, *A Room of One's Own*, p. 47.

[6] Barry Weller and Margaret W. Ferguson (eds.), *The Tragedy of Mariam The Fair Queen of Jewry with The Lady Falkland: Her Life by One of Her Daughters* (Berkeley: University of California Press, 1994), pp. 1–17 and 183–275.

[7] The concept of the 'safe house' and its role in the liberation of female authorship is the subject of more extended research which covers several family groups (the Sidneys, Carys and Cavendishes among others). See my forthcoming book, *Literary Families in Early Modern England* (Oxford: Oxford University Press, 2001).

[8] Geoffrey Trease, *Portrait of a Cavalier: William Cavendish, First Duke of Newcastle* (London: Macmillan, 1979), pp. 114–43, and *Glorious Fame*, p. 68.

[9] *Life* (1906), 'The Second Book', pp. 43–81; and *Glorious Fame*, pp. 53–129.

[10] 'A *Dialogue* between a *Bountifull Knight*, and a *Castle* ruin'd in *War*', *Poems and Fancies* (1653), pp. 89-90, cit. Alastair Fowler, *The Country House Poem: A Cabinet of Seventeenth-Century Estate Poems and Related Items* (Edinburgh: Edinburgh University Press, 1994), pp. 315–316.

[11] Ben Jonson, *Ben Jonson*, ed. C. H. Herford and Percy Simpson, 11 vols (Oxford: Clarendon Press, 1925–52), VIII, pp. 93–6.

[12] *Ben Jonson*, VII, pp. 787–803 and 804–14.

[13] *Ben Jonson*, VII, p. 792.

[14] *Life* (1906), p. 103.

[15] *Ben Jonson*, XII, p. 703, and *Glorious Fame*, pp. 114 and 128.

[16] Trease, *Portrait of a Cavalier*, pp. 72–3.

[17] University of Oxford, Bodleian Library, MS Rawlinson Poet 16.

[18] Germaine Greer (ed.), *Kissing The Rod: An Anthology of Seventeenth-Century Women's Verse* (London: Virago, 1988), p. 111.

[19] Greer, *Kissing the Rod*, p. 110.

[20] Jane Cavendish and Elizabeth Brackley, *The Concealed Fancies* in S. P. Cerasano and Marion Wynne-Davies (eds.) *Renaissance Drama by Women: Texts and Documents* (London: Routledge, 1996), pp. 127–54.

[21] Cavendish and Brackley, *Concealed Fancies*, p. 143.

[22] *Glorious Fame*, pp. 18–20.

[23] Cavendish and Brackley, *Concealed Fancies*, pp. 144–5.

[24] *Ben Jonson*, VII, pp. 800 and 809.

[25] Greer, *Kissing the Rod*, p. 109.

[26] Greer, *Kissing the Rod*, pp. 114–5.

[27] Fowler, *Country House Poem*, pp. 163–5.

[28] Sara Jayne Steen (ed.), *The Letters of Lady Arbella Stuart* (Oxford: Oxford University Press, 1994), p. 7.

[29] Steen, *Letters*, p. 151, and Josephine A. Roberts (ed.), *The First Part of the Countess of Montgomery's Urania* (Binghampton, New York: Medieval and Renaissance Texts and Studies, 1995), pp. lxxxviii and 29.

[30] Fowler, *Country House Poem*, pp. 169–70.

[31] Fowler, *Country House Poem*, p. 179.

[32] Virginia Woolf, 'The Duchess of Newcastle', in *The Common Reader. First Series* (London: Hogarth Press, 1925), p. 84.

4

'Of Mixt Natures': Questions of Genre in Margaret Cavendish's *The Blazing World*

Nicole Pohl

In her essay, 'A Room of One's Own', Virginia Woolf celebrates the creative wit and intelligence of the 'harebrained, fantastical' Margaret Cavendish, Duchess of Newcastle. She laments the fact that the Duchess was unfairly depreciated by her contemporaries like Dorothy Osborne or Samuel Pepys as 'the crazy Duchess [who] became a bogey to frighten away clever girls with' and was never acknowledged for her wit and intelligence.[1] Virginia Woolf herself though has only limited esteem for the actual literary accomplishment of Cavendish and writes:

> Margaret too might have been a poet: in our day all that activity would have turned a wheel of some sort. As it was, what could bind, tame or civilise for human use that wild, generous, untutored intelligence? It poured itself out, higgledy-piggledy, in torrents of rhyme and prose, poetry and philosophy which stand congealed in quartos and folios that nobody ever reads. [...] What a vision of loneliness and riot the thought of Margaret Cavendish brings to mind! as if some giant cucumber had spread itself over all the roses and carnations in the garden and choked them to death.[2]

Times have changed. More and more scholars, feminists and literary critics are proving Woolf wrong by cherishing those 'quartos and folios that nobody ever reads', paying tribute to the oeuvre of Margaret Cavendish, who was one of the first women who wrote specifically for publication.

In this essay, I want to question Woolf's judgement and investigate Margaret Cavendish's *Observations upon Experimental Philosophy. To which is added, The Description of a New World Called The Blazing World* of 1666 in terms of its apparent 'higgledy-piggledy' forms of writing. I propose that this unique blend of fiction, philosophy and fantasy is not a result of Cavendish's wild and untamed wit, but rather a 'hermaphroditic' text, as Cavendish herself classifies the book. With a critical exploration of literary genres, including the traditionally male domain of political utopian and scientific writing, Cavendish challenges seventeenth-century concepts of identity and gender. Whilst she is thoroughly dedicated to questions of gender throughout her oeuvre, Cavendish goes even further in her theory of writing and rhetoric. In her work, Cavendish develops a consequential philosophy that goes beyond the vindication of women's writing. She elevates the (female) subject to a new non-gendered and singular status and thus finally creates a truly emancipatory poetic space.[3] In developing, in the terminology of Gilles Deleuze, a Baroque narrative based on a celebration of singularities, of perspectivism and ultimately suppression of the imperative of closure, Cavendish not only creates a new poetics but ultimately a new utopian discourse.[4] As Deleuze notes, 'Utopia designates absolute deterritorialisation, yet always at the critical point where the latter is attached to the relatively present milieu, and especially with forces that are the fabric of this milieu.'[5] The concept of transgressive hermaphroditism as presented by Cavendish encompasses precisely this 'deterritorialisation'. Her poetic creation of a 'heterocosmos' is not the simplistic blue-print of an alternative better world, but presents a range of speculative prospects which do not reduce discourses of gender, knowledge and power to crude either/or choices.[6]

In his book, *The Fold: Leibniz and the Baroque*, Gilles Deleuze investigates the philosophy of Gottfried Wilhelm Leibniz (1646–1716) in the context of seventeenth-century intellectual and artistic movements. Leibniz developed the notion of the 'fold' in his philosophy, which, according to Deleuze, is in fact the founding principle of the Baroque:

> The Baroque refers not to an essence but rather to an operative function, to a trait. It endlessly produces folds. [...] Yet the Baroque trait twists and turns its folds, pushing them to infinity, fold over fold, one upon the other. The Baroque fold unfurls all the way to infinity.[7]

The basic premise of the Baroque is thus continuity, multiplicity, variation and inclusion. This becomes particularly apparent in fashion, which Cavendish herself appreciated very much, and art:

> It radiates everywhere, at all times, in the thousand folds of garments that tend to become one with their respective wearers [...]. We find it in painting, where the autonomy conquered through the folds of clothing that invade the entire surface becomes a simple but sure sign of a rupture with Renaissance space.[8]

The ideal fold is the *Zweifalt*, 'a fold that differentiates and is differentiated. When Heidegger calls upon the *Zweifalt* to be the differentiator of difference, he means above all that differentiation does not refer to a pre-given undifferentiated, but to a Difference that endlessly unfolds and folds over from each of its two sides.'[9] This focus on the differentiated and differentiating process introduces another important aspect of the Baroque: the singular. Multiplicity does not only involve the 'unity of the multiple, in the objective sense,' but 'a multiplicity "of" one and a unity "of" the multiple, but now in a subjective sense.'[10] This reconciliation between continuity and multiplicity with singularity and individuality constitutes the 'new harmony' of the Baroque. It also revises the position of the subject:

> Harmony is twice preestablished: by virtue of each expression, of each expressant

> that owes only to its own spontaneity or interiority, and by virtue of the common expression that establishes the concert of all these expressive spontaneities.[11]

Whilst Deleuze's book investigates Leibniz's notion of the monad, its interaction with infinity and the possible application of the Baroque as a theoretical device to examine the 'modern' condition, I suggest that Margaret Cavendish develops her own Baroque concept of the hermaphroditical which is 'a multiplicity that makes for inclusion.'[12]

It is not possible to trace in detail the history and the changing importance of the figure and myth of the hermaphrodite. It must suffice at this point to sketch some important moments in the distinct discourses on hermaphroditism in the context of Margaret Cavendish's writing. Eternalised in Ovid's *Metamorphoses*, the mythical fusion of the nymph Salmacis with the son of Hermes and Aphrodite has always been of great fascination to artists and sculptors throughout centuries and in different cultures.[13] The symbolic impact of this union of complementary opposites was not confined to the arts. Although Judeo–Christian traditions were based on a fundamentally dichotomic framework, they allowed for the celebration of the spiritual marriage between male and female in the iconography of Adam, Christ and numerous examples of saints. Further, the Neo-Platonic notion of love and marriage prevalent in the Renaissance re-united the two separated halves of the former hermaphroditic self.[14] The hermetic school of science in the Renaissance used the image of the hermaphrodite to depict the conjunction of two chemical elements, the *rebis*, to conclusively discover the *prima materia*.[15] Whilst these discourses represent, as Ruth Gilbert suggests, 'an illusory quest for wholeness', based on the belief 'that the creation of sexual difference had broken an original condition of plenitude,' early modern legal and medical discourses displayed a strong anxiety of precisely this spiritual and somatic 'plenitude'.[16] Although biological hermaphrodites have existed since Antiquity, Renaissance medicine was particularly fascinated with this phenomenon. A multitude of pamphlets, legal and medical texts were published on this subject, analysing and studying the prospect of sex change.[17] Biological hermaphroditism was though more than an interesting somatic phenomenon to be studied by professionals. Its appearance, as Maryanne Celine Horowitz, Ruth Gilbert and Deborah Taylor Bazeley suggest, contested gender classifications at large:

> Hermaphrodites challenge not only gender construction but also the classification by sex fundamental to the patriarchal functioning of the Renaissance family, church, and state. They appear to corroborate the accidental nature of sex designation asserted in Aristotelian and Galenic biological theories, which view female and male as polar opposites on a continuum from weakness to strength and which accept that monstrosities occur in nature.[18]

This challenge is reflected in early modern drama where cross-dressing and gender confusion is a recurrent topic. But this playful negotiation of anxieties and fears caused by the possibility of somatic sex changes and reversal of traditional gender roles was already producing disquiet. Horowitz suggests that 'the growing opposition to theatre in the Seventeenth Century may reflect a fear that men effeminising themselves on stage will infect the audience with similar transformations.'[19] A similar reaction was caused by the 'chic of *Hic Mulier*' at the beginning of the seventeenth century, which promoted a masculine style for women's fashion and general appearance.[20] The manifestation of biological and cultural hermaphrodites thus confused and challenged rigid gender stereotypes, which were the foundation of an exclusive system of division of labour, and social and political identities. Whilst seventeenth-century theories see the phenomenon as a union of male and female somatic and psychological characteristics, Margaret Cavendish developed a notion of hermaphroditism which goes beyond the 'sexual dimorphism'.[21] Her concept of hermaphroditism in fact contains three elements: the male, the female and the individual, developing a triangular discourse. Cavendish associates the triangular with multiplicity, transgression and transcendence when she writes that 'the triangular points being odd, multiplie and subtract by reflections, as we [...] see by triangular glasses, that from one face millions are made by subdividings.'[22] By advocating the discourse of multiplicity, Cavendish consciously deconstructs contemporary notions of binary opposition in gender politics, science and literature. The importance of the gendered body is rejected in favour of a transgressive but singular mind, which as singularity is part of a larger multiplicity.[23]

Cavendish delivers three aspects of hermaphroditism in her oeuvre. In her *Observations on Experimental Philosophy*, Cavendish defines hermaphroditism in a scientific–philosophical context as something 'of mixt natures', or more precisely, the composite of the natural and the artificial.[24] Another context is that of historical/cultural hermaphroditism, which is a prevalent theme in Cavendish's work. In the *Female Orations* (1662), five women discuss the role of women in society, investigating all distinct aspects of the subject dialectically. Despite the obvious result of the discussion that women are the oppressed sex, the emulation of male characteristics is not the solution. They conclude thus: 'to have Female Bodies, and yet to Act Masculine Parts, will be very Preposterous and Unnatural.' The women reflect further that to imitate men signifies 'neither to be Perfect Women, nor Perfect Men, but Corrupt and Imperfect Creatures.'[25]

A third context is strictly literary, when Cavendish discusses the pluralistic writing modes of Shakespeare. In Letter 123 of the *CCXI Sociable Letters*, she writes:

> [...] so Well he hath Express'd in his Playes all Sorts of Persons, as one would think he had been Transformed into every one of those Persons he hath Described; and as sometimes one would think he was Really himself the Clown or Jester he Feigns, so one would think, he was also the King, and Privy Counsellor; [...] nay, one would think that he had been Metamorphosed from a Man to a woman, for who could describe *Cleopatra* better than he hath done, and many other Females of his own Creating [...].[26]

What seems to be the underlying assumption of the latter two notions of 'hermaphroditism' is a concept of gender that surpasses the plain biological character of the sexes. For Cavendish this gendered subjectivity applies to all forms of cultural representation. In the following I show how she deconstructs these notions of gendered subjectivity by creating a transgressive literary form in her utopia, *The Blazing World*. Her text corresponds in an exemplary fashion to the criteria of Baroque narrative: 'stories enclosed one in the other, and the variation of the relation of narrator-and-narration' and, further, the 'concertation' of genres.[27] According to Cavendish's definition of the hermaphroditical as 'of mixt Natures', the 1666 and 1668 editions of *The Blazing World* are doubly hermaphroditical, since the text has been published within a scientific treatise, *Observations Upon Experimental Philosophy*, and is itself 'of mixt Natures', combining a fantastic travel account, scientific didactic prose and fairy tale. The scientific project in the *Observations* is taken up several times in the fictional *Blazing World*. In fact, the two parts frequently cross-reference details and incidents. In the same editions, Cavendish originally planned to complement these two works with a play, now called 'A Piece of a Play', published in the 1668 edition of *Plays Never Before Printed*.

The main protagonist, Lady Phoenix, is a dramatic version of the Empress of *The Blazing World*, 'clothed all with light', travelling in a 'Chariot [...] made of air, and that airy ship is gilded with the Sun.'[28] Further, she 'is of a studious nature', 'civil to Strangers', 'charitable to the poor' and finally 'humble to those that are respectful, but severe to those that are rude.'[29] The final work of the *Observations* together with the *The Blazing World* and the 'Piece of a Play' would therefore have consisted of three different but complementary genres with analogies and cross-references throughout the book. Unfortunately, Cavendish abandoned this exciting project, as she explains in 'Advertisement to the Reader':

> THe [*sic*] Reader is desir'd to take notice, That the following Fragments are part of a Play which I did intend for my Blazing World, and had been Printed with it, if I had finish'd it; but before I had ended the Second Act finding that my Genius did not tend that way, I left that design [...].[30]

The *Observations upon Experimental Philosophy* is a treatise on natural and experimental philosophy which belongs to a whole series of philosophical and natural science works by Margaret Cavendish in which she addresses a number of subjects such as mathematics, physics, chemistry, biology and philosophy. Further, Cavendish not only voices her opinion about the changing discourse of science in the mid-seventeenth century, symbolised by the establishment of the Royal Society, but she also contextualises this paradigmatic shift in cultural and proto-feminist terms. Cavendish vindicates the philosophers and scientists of Antiquity, valuing their methodology and insight into natural sciences. Moreover, she recognises that with the paradigmatic shift from Old to New Science, it is not only women who have been strictly excluded from the domain of science and natural philosophy. Modern scholars like Wolfgang van de Daele, Londa Schiebinger and Deborah

Taylor Bazeley among others have confirmed this slow elimination of the general public and traditional professionals, including women, from the scientific discourse of the mid-seventeenth century.[31] With only the support of a handful of similar-minded women–scientists, Margaret Cavendish zealously tried to reclaim this territory for women. By eagerly publishing her scientific works, Margaret Cavendish openly opposed the principle that women should not publish at all in the seventeenth century and also challenged the exclusive circle of the 'new science', which consciously barred women. She wrote numerous treatises on natural and experimental philosophy, partially dedicating them to the great universities of the time. In 1666 she published the already mentioned *Observations upon Experimental Philosophy*. Other works were *Philosophical Fancies* (1653), *Philosophical and Physical Opinions* (1655), and later the *Ground of Natural Philosophy* (1668). These works were not unrelated, but formed part of a larger project. '[H]er chief energies', as her biographer Sara Heller Mendelson explains, 'were poured into an effort to "systematise" her scientific notions.'[32] Further, as Maria de Santis has shown, Margaret Cavendish's natural philosophy was a conscious critique of the experimental method prevailing at her time. Recognising basic failures of the method, especially concerning the larger methodological problem of transdiction, Cavendish challenges the 'very definition of objectivity' promoted by the Royal Society and its members, proving that the knowledge derived from experimentalism is as flawed as the ancient superstitions.[33] Margaret Cavendish thus not only wrote unconnected, singular scientific treatises, but also aimed at creating an overall scientific and philosophical methodology and, ultimately, epistemology.

In the seventeenth century the act of authorship was assumed to be unsuitable for women. As Elaine Hobby in her study of women's writing in the seventeenth century points out:

> [W]omen were not supposed to enter the public world in any form, and that prohibition extended to a ban on "making public" their words. They had to find ways of making their writing acceptable, both to themselves and to others. As a result, not only do their works discuss politics and love, household management and education, they also examine, repeatedly, the problem of being a woman writer in their society.[34]

Cavendish exceeded contemporary negotiations about female virtue and literary production by not only devoting her writing to specifically male subjects but also by overtly advertising her other works and thus 'making public' her own authorship. Further, she denounced the narrow domesticity of women in literature and practice, lamenting the fact that 'when any of our Sex doth Write, they Write some Devotions, or Romances, or Receits of Medicines, for Cookery or Confectioners, or Complemental Letters, or a Copy or two of Verses [...] which Express our Brief Wit in our Short Works [...].'[35] Instead of being a competent mistress of the household and giving birth to children, Cavendish experimented with language and genre and 'delivered' many texts.[36] Indeed, she likened her literary creation to children of her own, re-signifying 'the masculine metaphor of text-as-child.'[37] Therefore, by writing and publishing actively, Margaret Cavendish fashioned herself doubly as a hermaphrodite – as a monster who violated the rules of nature by an active participation in a predominantly male world, and as an individual who generally attracted attention with her singular appearance and attire. Fellow writers such as Mary Wroth and Aphra Behn were both vigorously condemned as monstrous creatures, as 'Hermophrodite in show, in deed a monster.'[38] There were, though, other women contributing directly or indirectly to the scientific discourse of the seventeenth century: Anne Finch (1661–1720) with her book *The Principles of the Most Ancient and Modern Philosophy* (1692), Aphra Behn, who translated *A Discovery of New Worlds* (1688), and the influential Katherine Ranelagh, sister of Robert Boyle, amongst others. As Londa Schiebinger has shown, apart from the above exceptions women worked in the background of scientific institutions and were seldom recognised for their achievements. By writing and even publishing scientific treatises Margaret Cavendish not only challenged the monopoly of male authorship in general but also its dominion of scientific knowledge and truth. Sandra Harding concludes:

> [w]hether science itself was to be considered masculine or feminine, there never was serious debate about the gender of nature or the gender of the scientist. From ancient to modern times, nature – the object of scientific study – has been conceived as unquestionably female. At the same time, it is abundantly clear that practitioners of science – scientists themselves – have overwhelmingly been men.[39]

By assuming authorship in the domain of science Cavendish subverts this binary opposition of male/science and female/nature, reclaiming a lost access to scientific knowledge, which precedes the New Science of the mid-seventeenth century. This disenfranchisement is represented in the iconography of science and nature. Whilst in works like Cesare Ripa's *Iconologia* (1618) or Galileo's *Il Saggiatore* (1623) science is represented by a female figure, science, especially in England after the establishment of the Royal Society, is represented by male figures of authority. Cavendish was very aware of this development:

> [T]hough the Muses, Graces and Sciences are all of the Female Gender, yet they were more esteemed in former Ages, than they are now; nay, could it be done handsomely, they would now turn them all from Females into Males: so great is grown the self-conceit of the Masculine, and the disregard of the Female Sex.[40]

Nothing represents this re-gendering of science better than the title of Francis Bacon's early and initially unpublished writing, *The Masculine Birth of Time* (published in 1603), which marks the end of centuries of unfruitful science and the pursuit of false knowledge and the birth of an active, virile and productive – hence male – science. In this unfinished essay, in the form of a monologue addressed by an older man in authority to a younger man, Bacon rejects a whole tradition of philosophy, claiming that the path to knowledge is blocked by idols and misconceptions and vanity.[41] This idolatry, which prevents the acquisition of true knowledge, is of course further explained in the later *The Advancement of Learning* (1605), where Bacon sees the light of knowledge obstructed by the 'Idols of the Tribe', the 'Idols of the Palace' (or 'Market-Place'), the 'Idols of the Cave' and the 'Idols of the Theatre'.[42] The human mind has to be cleansed of the 'false preconceptions' in order to make it receptive to the true knowledge and teaching. The birth of the masculine science is the death of the 'effeminate' science of Antiquity, and what is left of the traditional iconography is the domination of the female body of nature illuminated by the light of masculine science. Although the Royal Society was not a homogeneous group of scientists, professionals and philosophers with uniform methods of scientific enquiry, the official historiographical account by Abraham Cowley and Thomas Sprat regarded the Society as the true follower of Bacon. Their contemporary, Joseph Glanvill, proposed in his *Scepsis Scientifica* (1665) that Bacon's 'Salomon's House in the NEW ATLANTIS was a Prophetick Scheam of the Royal Society,' and repeated this comparison in his supplement to Bacon's *New Atlantis*.[43] Abraham Cowley introduces Thomas Sprat's *History of the Royal Society* (1667) with the verses:

> Philosophy, I say and call it, He,
> For whatsoe're the Painters Fancy be,
> It a Male Virtu seems to me.[44]

Margaret Cavendish enters this early scientific discourse with a number of scientific tracts and uses contemporary methodological disputes as a vehicle to vindicate her own concerns. These writings develop her own theories and arguments instead of being a mere translation of existing works or a compilation of scientific tracts and treatises solely for 'the use of Ladies'.[45] As a woman writer, a 'she-scientist', she already counters the gendering of writing, especially scientific writing, by assuming authorship and wide-ranging distribution of her writings. Further, she subverts the contemporary struggle between fact and fiction, between axioms and myths, between reason and fancy by fictionalising empirical facts and methodologies in her novel, *The Blazing World*. Cavendish not only created a 'transgendered' and 'transgeneric' text but she conceived a genuinely Baroque text which originated exclusively from, as she frequently stressed, her singular spontaneous imagination.

The Description of A New World Called The Blazing World is a unique mixture of travel tale, romance and scientific treatise. When Margaret Cavendish adds to the *Observations* the fantastic tale of *The Blazing World*, she not only intends to 'delight her reader with variety', but actively complements a work of reason with a work of imagination.[46] For her, the two faculties of reason and fancy are not oppositional, but spring from the same 'rational parts of the matter'.[47] In fact, both faculties are a necessary complement to each other. With this device, Margaret Cavendish not only creates the first science fiction text, but science fiction in its truest sense. While she uses her reason to present scientific theories in the

Observations, she fictionalises the scientific theories in *The Blazing World*. Whereas in the *Observations* she endeavours to objectively discuss contemporary scientific methods, *The Blazing World* serves to attack scientific notions in a much more open and satirical manner. I may only point out the numerous quarrels between the scientists in *The Blazing World* that are only resolved by the dissolution of the scientific societies. It is striking that in the *Observations*, Margaret Cavendish already stages the dispute amongst the scientists and philosophers of *The Blazing World* as a dispute amongst the different faculties in her mind:

> When I was setting forth this Book of *Experimental Observations*, a Dispute chanced to arise between the rational Parts of my Mind concerning some chief Points and Principles in Natural Philosophy; for some New Thoughts endeavouring to oppose and call in question the Truth of my former Conceptions, caused a war in my mind, which in time grew to that height, that they were hardly able to compose the differences between themselves, but were in a manner necessitated to refer them to the Arbitration of the impartial Reader, desiring the assistance of his judgment to reconcile their Controversies, and, if possible, to reduce them to a setled peace and agreement.[48]

Again, in the *Observations* Cavendish discusses the subject of 'Thawing or Dissolving of frozen bodies' and 'Whether cold doth Preserve Bodies from Corruption?', coming to the conclusion that 'such bodies as have been thorowly frozen, after being thawed, are most commonly spoiled.'[49] This musing on the preservation of bodies by freezing is echoed in *The Blazing World*, where, after the passage to the other pole, the heroine sees 'all the men dead, found small comfort in life; their bodies which were preserved all that while from putrefaction and stench, by the extremity of cold, began now to thaw, and corrupt [...].'[50] It is left to the creative imagination of the reader to believe that the lady survives 'by the light of her beauty, the heat of her youth, and protection of the gods [...].'[51]

The data and facts collected in the *Observations* are applied in the fiction of *The Blazing World*, creating a true hermaphroditical work. Not only does Cavendish imply that science has to be practicable and serve humanity, she also declares that, against the statutes of the Royal Society, fact and fiction are complementary, not mutually exclusive. In her view, to insist on prescribed axioms and rules is to omit possible other findings, as exemplified in the paradox of transdiction. She in fact rejects the 'logic of either-or' in science, cultural and gender politics as being reductive and simplistic.[52]

In addition to the heterogeneous association of the *Observations* and *The Blazing World*, the latter work itself consists of 'mixt forms': the 'romancical', the 'philosophical' and the 'fantastical' – genres which again were conceived as gendered in the seventeenth century. Whereas the philosophical form as the scientific essay was, as I have shown above, associated with the male reader and writer, the literary forms of the 'romanical' and 'fantastical' were associated with the female reader and, paradoxically, writers.[53] Although Margaret Cavendish borrowed a popular literary genre, the romance, as a mode of writing in *The*

Blazing World, she again adapted it to her purposes. She was highly critical of this genre, which only prepared women readers to 'fall in love with the feign'd Heroes and Carpet-Knights, with whom, their Thoughts secretly commit Adultery, and in their Conversation and manner, or forms or phrases of Speech, they imitate the Romance-Ladies.'[54] Indeed, Cavendish's romances are not about falling in love with 'feign'd heroes', but are a pursuit for individuality and subjectivity, as Cavendish's earlier tale of 1656, *Assaulted and Pursued Chastity*, proves.[55]

This tale of 'virtue in distress' narrates the heroine's quest for independence and individuality while escaping the persistent advances of a Prince. Her voyage of self-discovery and self-empowerment culminates in the heroine's intervention as a commander of the Queen's army in the Land of Amity. In the end, the heroine gives in and marries the Prince – the generic conventions of romance are fulfilled but clash strangely with rest of the text. Again, in *The Blazing World* the reader encounters a virgin in distress. It begins with the abduction of a young lady by a merchant who takes her onto his ship. Sailing to the Northern hemisphere of this world, a storm surprises them and blows them to another world. Only the young lady survives, who drifts helplessly through the New World until she encounters strange inhabitants. The animal-men rescue the lady and bring her to the capital where the Emperor instantly chooses to make the lady the Empress of the New World. In order to learn and reform, the Empress discourses with native scientists and philosophers on every subject which seems of importance to her. When the Empress desires a companion, she finds her alter-ego, Margaret, Duchess of Newcastle, from her former world. The women are true soul mates and platonic lovers, communicate literally as free spirits, move through countries and bodies together. They not only reform Civil War-ridden England, but also the kingdom of the New World to their own design. Whilst the tale *Assaulted and Pursued Chastity* has its paradoxical finale in marriage and the subsequent silencing of the heroine, the marriage in *The Blazing World* leads to the acquisition of political and economic power by the heroine. By modifying the romance genre beyond recognition, Cavendish confronts the traditional plot lines which confirm and re-enforce binary gender roles. Also, as a romance writer, she appropriates the genre to present alternatives for women's lives.

A third element of *The Blazing World* is, according to Cavendish, the 'fantastical', thus relating the book to the general faculty of imagination, synonymous in its early modern use with fancy. More specifically, and not strictly disconnected from the romance element, *The Blazing World* subscribes to and reworks the genre of the imaginary voyage in the same way as she alters the traditional plot line of the romance. The contribution of women to the genre of imaginary voyages in the seventeenth century is rare. As Nancy Armstrong and Earla A. Wilputte have suggested, travel tales like the much later *The Life and Strange Surprising Adventures of Robinson Crusoe, of York, Mariner* (1719), were recommended to women readers because of their obvious didactic messages. However, 'when they are written by women – and it is a genre which attracted few women authors perhaps because, the Edgeworths aside, it was as immodest to travel in the mind as in the body – they are quests to discover feminine individuality and discourse.'[56] The above short summary of the plot of *The Blazing World* has shown that the flight of the heroine, which turns quickly into a imaginary travel narrative, in fact allows her to reverse her fate as an impotent, disenfranchised woman and to become an Amazonian Empress. Further, with her retreat into the imaginary, Margaret Cavendish defies the discursive conflict between 'naive empiricism' and 'extreme scepticism' negotiated in the contemporary travel literature.[57]

With the establishment of the Royal Society and the pursuit of knowledge acquired through empirical experiments, Old Science was condemned as nothing but romance and fiction.[58] But the belief in an empirical approach was not unchallenged. Sceptics like Margaret Cavendish and later Newton implicitly and explicitly criticised the 'new telescopical faith' and pointed out the relativity of sensual knowledge.[59] This negotiation between romance and true history, between Old Science and Empiricism was specifically apparent in the travel literature of the time. The Royal Society issued guidelines for writing travel journals and accounts, not only trying to persuade the traveller to keep exact geographical, historical and anthropological notes but also to keep up an objective approach and style in writing. As Michael Nerlich and Amy Diane Boesky have shown, the original 'romance plot of travel, conquest, and return' told and retold by explorers and travellers in the early modern period was authorised and valorised by this new scientific discourse.[60] Consequently, as Michael McKeon suggests, imaginary travels and voyages 'printed during the Restoration and early eighteenth century are likely to deal with the question of historical truth in a manner peculiar to an age for which that question has become momentous. The contemporary editors of texts originally composed in an earlier era, for example, are apologetic in the current mode even about works that have been conventionally understood to be allegorical or fabulous.'[61] Margaret Cavendish goes beyond the mere apology or authorisation for her fantastic travel tale to claim that 'although I have neither power, time nor occasion to conquer the world as Alexander and Caesar did; yet rather than not to be mistress of one, since Fortune and the Fates would give me none, I have made a world of my own: for which no body, I hope, will blame me, since it is in every one's power to do the like.'[62] This return to her own imaginary resources allows Margaret Cavendish to transgress the rules of the Royal Society when dealing with travel literature and the faculties of imagination and fancy. With this retreat to fancy and the celebration of the self, Margaret Cavendish leaves the ambiguity of the genres negotiating their space within romance, true history and anti-romance and simply surpasses current accounts, imaginary voyages and contemporary utopian writings.

This multiplicity of genres and literary modes is echoed again in Margaret Cavendish's poetics. The Royal Society not only decreed the most adequate methodology for scientific investigation but also prescribed, as we have already seen in the context of travel accounts, the recording of the process of scientific inquiry and experiments. According to Thomas Sprat, false rhetoric would result in the propagation of false philosophy. Thus, one of the aims of the Society was to find a new form of scientific writing. 'Now the best means, that can be devis'd to bring that about,' writes Sprat, 'is to settle a fixt, and Impartial Court of Eloquence; according to whose censure, all Books, or Authors should either stand or fall.'[63] This 'Court of Eloquence' should have been an English version of the *Académie Française*, not only to cleanse the scientific language from the 'imagination of poets', but to create a male language appropriate to transmit philosophical and scientific knowledge.[64] In his biographical introduction to *The Works of Mr Abraham Cowley*, Sprat distinguishes between a male and female style when he claims that 'there is a kind of variety of Sexes in Poetry, as well as in mankind: that as the peculiar excellence of the Feminine kind, is smoothnesse and beauty; so strength is the chief praise of the Masculine.'[65] Cavendish again does not conform but searches for a 'natural' poetic style and imagery whilst criticising at the same time contemporary notions of poetry and literary expression. But in subjects even less suitable for the female pen Cavendish is most critical about style and language. In the advertisement 'To The Reader' of the *Observations* she complains:

> The truth is, if any one intends to write Philosophy, either in English, or any other language, he ought to consider the propriety of the language, as much as the Subject he writes of; or else to what purpose would it be to write? If you do write Philosophy in English, and use all the hardest words and expressions which none but Scholars are able to understand, you had better to write it in Latine; but if you will write for those that do not understand Latin, Your reason will tell you, that you must explain those hard words, and English them in the easiest manner you can; What are words but marks of things? And what are Philosophical Terms, but to express the Conceptions of ones mind in that Science? And truly I do not think that there is any Language so poor, which cannot do that [...].[66]

Cavendish experiments freely with language in her own writing, trying to develop a 'natural' language model, which moves away from classical rhetoric and prescribed language models. Critics of her dramatic oeuvre have called her plays 'confused', 'undramatic' and 'intolerable' because of Cavendish's unusual choice of imagery, symbolism, rhetoric and finally her erratic structuring.[67] This criticism has also been applied to the rest of her works. Despite the disclaimers Cavendish placed in the Prefaces of most of her volumes, acknowledging the coarse language and imperfect structure of all of her writing, she ultimately believes that her singular 'artlessness' and ignorance is in fact liberating and ultimately more creative. Margaret Cavendish thus arrives at using metaphors, analogies, similes and prolixities imaginatively and creatively – rhetorical figures which the new science excluded from scientific pursuits, but which make knowledge and language accessible to a larger readership:

> Since I desire to be perspicuous in delivering my opinions, and to remove all those scruples which seem to obstruct the sense thereof, I have chosen rather to be guilty of prolixity and repetition, than to be obscure by too much brevity.[68]

Deborah Taylor Bazeley and Verena Oleijniczak have shown that Cavendish uses rhetorical figures like allegory, metaphor, copia and simile to express her deep scepticism of cultural gender conventions that are exclusive and limiting:

> Many of Cavendish's conceits explode the conventional binarisms, e.g., animate–inanimate, organic–inorganic, human–animal, mind–matter, fiction–existence, by which we compartmentalise and understand the world. She similizes the human brain to a beehive, a barrel of wine, and a garden.[69]

This literary suspension of traditional binarisms brings us back to our theoretical point of departure. The narrative structure of *The Blazing World*, as well as its poetic rhetoric, uses elements of associative writing, of non-linear, elliptical and enigmatic narratives – an interplay between metaphors, metonyms and symbols. Indeed, Cavendish displays a Baroque usage of rhetoric and structure where 'basic images' such as allegory and metaphor 'tend to break their frames, form a continuous fresco, and join broader cycles [...]':

> The object [of the rhetorical figure] itself overflows its frame in order to enter into a cycle or a series, and now the concept is what is found increasingly compressed, interiorised, wrapped in an instance that can ultimately be called 'personal'.[70]

Whilst Cavendish does not advocate a specifically feminine rhetoric, she vindicates a writing strategy that creates these 'personal' texts. According to Cavendish, these texts should be imaginative and spontaneous, open and non-exclusive in structure and language.

I have shown that the original *Observations upon Experimental Philosophy. To which is added, The Description of a New World Called The Blazing World* is a complex work, exhibiting an intricate generic mixture of a scientific treatise and a fictional work and, as originally planned, a play. The individual parts of the larger work themselves are multifarious works which play with contemporary genre conventions. The *Observations* and *The Blazing World* explore specifically the constraints of gender on genre and surpass these constraints by resorting to the realms of multiplicity and heterogeneity. Although the superficial structure of the larger work, and *The Blazing World* itself, displays a triangular design, the text consists of a multiplicity of genres, a multiplicity of viewpoints, and uses rhetorical figures that confront conventional binarisms. This 'defiance of discourse' deconstructs political and social constraints in a very modern way, especially the cultural construction of gender.[71] As such, Cavendish displays the deterritorialisation of the Baroque, which revises and reinvents notions of unity and harmony by allowing the singular and the individual to be the essence of being.

Notes

[1] Virginia Woolf, *A Room of One's Own* (London: The Hogarth Press, 1929, repr. London: Granada, 1985), p. 60.

[2] Woolf, *A Room of One's Own*, pp. 59–60.

[3] Whilst a reading of Cavendish's work in the context of French *écriture féminine* is enlightening and helpful, I suggest that Deleuze's notion of the Baroque truly helps to uncover Cavendish's ungendered mode of singularities and of perspectivism. It must be mentioned though that Hélène Cixous's clearly utopian notion of 'bisexuality' comes perhaps the closest to Cavendish's poetic project. Cixous's conception of *écriture féminine* is based, on the one hand, on her understanding of the pre-oedipal imaginary and, on the other, on an essentialist concept of femininity. Elements of her associative and heterogeneous writing practice as a specifically non-essentialising category can already be found in Cavendish's oeuvre. In fact, it would be possible to read Cavendish's poetics of hermaphroditism in the seventeenth century as the precursor of writing as *différance* in the twentieth century. See Hélène Cixous, 'The Laugh of the Medusa', trans. Keith Cohen and Paula Cohen, in Elaine Marks and Isabelle de Courtivron (eds.) *New French Feminism: An Anthology* (New York: Schocken Books, 1981), pp. 245–264. For an interesting discussion on *écriture féminine* see Susan Sellers, *Language and Sexual Difference: Feminist Writing in France* (Basingstoke: Macmillan, 1991); Ingeborg Weber (ed.) *Weiblichkeit und weibliches Schreiben* (Darmstadt: Wissenschaftliche Buchgesellschaft, 1994); and Toril Moi, *Sexual–Textual Politics: Feminist Literary Theory* (London and New York: Routledge, 1988).

[4] See Gilles Deleuze, *The Fold: Leibniz and the Baroque*, trans. Tom Conley (London: The Athlone Press, 1993). I thank Rita Casale for an enlightening discussion on this.

[5] Gilles Deleuze and Félix Guattari, *Qu'est-ce-que la philosophie?* (Paris: Éditions de Minuit, 1991), cit. 'Translator's Foreword' in *The Fold*, pp. ix–xx, p. xvii.

[6] I borrowed the term 'heterocosmos' from Amy Diane Boesky who defines it as 'the poetics of world making' in Cavendish's work. Amy Diane Boesky, 'The Rhetoric of Reform: English Utopian Narrative, 1516–1667', (unpublished doctoral thesis, Harvard University, 1989), p. 145. See also Amy Diane Boesky, *Founding Fictions: Utopias in Early Modern England* (Athens: University of Georgia Press, 1996). For a different reading, see John Rogers, *The Matter of Revolution: Science, Poetry and Politics in the Age of Milton* (Ithaca: Cornell University Press, 1998), Chapter 6.

[7] Deleuze, *The Fold*, p. 3.

[8] Deleuze, *The Fold*, p. 120.

[9] Deleuze, *The Fold*, p. 30.

[10] Deleuze, *The Fold*, p. 126.

[11] Deleuze, *The Fold*, p. 134.

[12] Deleuze, *The Fold*, p. 31.

[13] For the iconography of the hermaphrodite in art and sculpture, see Andrea Raehs, *Zur Ikonographie des Hermaphroditen: Begriff und Problem von Hermaphroditismus und Androgynie in der Kunst* (Frankfurt: Peter Lang, 1987).

[14] See Ruth Gilbert, '"Probleme of Sexes": Representing the Renaissance Hermaphrodite' (unpublished doctoral thesis, University of Southampton, 1996), Chapter 1.

[15] See Raehs, *Ikonographie*, Chapter 10, and John Read, *Prelude to Chemistry: An Outline of Alchemy, its Literature and Relationships* (London: G. Bells & Sons, 1936, repr.

Cambridge, Mass. and London: MIT Press, 1966), p. 208.

[16] Gilbert, 'Renaissance Hermaphrodite', p. 20.

[17] See Emma Donoghue, *Passions between Women: British Lesbian Culture 1668–1801* (London: Scarlet Press, 1993).

[18] 'Introduction', in Jean R. Brink, Maryanne C. Horowitz and Allison P. Coudert (eds.) *Playing with Gender: A Renaissance Pursuit* (Urbana: University of Illinois Press, 1991), p. xx; Deborah Taylor Bazeley, 'An early challenge to the precepts and practice of modern science: The fusion of fact, fiction, and feminism in the works of Margaret Cavendish, Duchess of Newcastle, 1623–1673' (unpublished doctoral thesis, University of California, San Diego, 1990); and Gilbert, 'Renaissance Hermaphrodite'.

[19] Brink et al, *Playing with Gender*, p. xi.

[20] Bazeley, 'An early challenge', p. 31.

[21] Gilbert Herdt (ed.) *Third Sex, Third Gender: Beyond Sexual Dimorphism in Culture and History*, (New York: Zone Books, 1994).

[22] *Physical Opinions* (1655), p. 60. Earla W. Wilputte has argued that the *Observations*, as well as *The Blazing World* itself, displays a binary structure which has its foundation in Plato's concept of philosophical and spiritual elements in mankind. I, on the other hand, suggest that *The Blazing World* discloses a three-fold structure and that in fact three generic variations on the theme were originally planned. I therefore support Deborah Taylor Bazeley's argument that the triangular discourse is the basis of these works. Bazeley though herself ignored the dramatic fragment in *Plays Never Before Printed.* See Earla W. Wilputte, 'Margaret Cavendish's Imaginary Voyage to The Blazing World: Mapping a Feminine Discourse', in Donald W. Nicol (ed.) *Transatlantic Crossings: Eighteenth-Century Explorations* (St.Johns: Memorial University of Newfoundland, 1995), pp. 109–111, and Bazeley, 'An early challenge', Chapter 3.

[23] See also an enlightening discussion of this point, in Marina Leslie, 'Gender, Genre and the Utopian Body in Margaret Cavendish's Blazing World', *Utopian Studies,* 7 (1996), 6–24.

[24] *Observations* (1666), 'To the Reader', sig. f recto.

[25] *Orations* (1662), p. 229. See also *Worlds Olio* (1655), p. 215: 'But Women now adaies affecting a Masculincy, as despising their own sex, practise the behaviour of Men, not the spirits of Men; nor their Heroick Behaviour, but their Wilde, Loose, Rude, Rough or foolish affected Behaviour; they practise the Masculine Confidency or Boldness, and forget the Effeminate Modesty; the Masculine Vice, and forget the Effeminate Virtues; as to talke Impudently, to Swagger, to Swear, to Game, to Drink, to Revell, to make Factions, but they practice not Silence, Sobriety, Reservedness, Abstinency, Patience, or the like; they practice the Masculine Cruelty, quitting their tender and gentle Natures, their sweet and pleasing Dispositions; But these Actions and Humours are so far from preferring our Sex to a higher Degree, that they do debase and make us worse than other Creatures be.'

[26] *Sociable Letters* (1664), pp. 245–248.

[27] Deleuze, *The Fold*, pp. 61, 133.

[28] Margaret Cavendish, 'A Piece of Play', in *Plays* (1668), p. 4.

[29] *Plays* (1668), pp. 6–7.

[30] *Plays* (1668), p. 1.

[31] Bazeley, 'An early challenge', Appendix A; Wolfgang van de Daele, 'The Social

Construction of Science: Institutionalisation and Definition of Positive Science in the Latter Half of the Seventeenth Century', in Everett Mendelsohn, Peter Weingart and Richard Whitley (eds.), *The Social Production of Scientific Knowledge* (Dordrecht: Reidel, 1977), pp. 27–54 and Londa Schiebinger, *The Mind has no Sex? Women in the Origins of Modern Science* (Cambridge, Mass.: Harvard University Press, 1989).

[32] Mendelson says: 'As she explained her method, she deduced effects by analogy. She inferred the internal motions of animals or other phenomena by their external motions, or by their forms, figures, or shapes. She had long since abandoned the simple materialistic atomism of her earliest works for a system of hierarchical spiritual and material forces. These, she named "rational matter", "sensitive matter", and "inanimate matter". All three together made up the "infinite matter of nature", but each higher form was a purified quintessence of the others.' See Sara Heller Mendelson, *The Mental World of Stuart Women: Three Studies* (Brighton: Harvester, 1987), pp. 42–43.

[33] Maria de Santis, 'Projecting a New Science: Restoration and Eighteenth-Century Scientific Method' (unpublished doctoral thesis, Columbia University, 1992), Chapter 2. According to de Santis, 'transdiction' is the justified integration of speculative knowledge into a strictly empirical and inductive methodology to analyse non-observable phenomena. A striking example is the research into atoms.

[34] Elaine Hobby, *Virtue of Necessity: English Women's Writing 1649–88* (London, Virago Press, 1988), p. 1.

[35] *Sociable Letters* (1664), p. 226.

[36] See Kathleen Jones, *A Glorious Fame: The Life of Margaret Cavendish, Duchess of Newcastle, 1623–1673* (London: Bloomsbury, 1988).

[37] Gilbert, 'Renaissance Hermaphrodite', p. 181. On the gendering of textual bodies see Martina Mittag, 'Soma, Sema, Sexus: Territorialisierung der Körper im frühneuzeitlichen Diskurs', in Heide Wunder (ed.) *Geschlechterperspektiven: Forschungen zur Frühen Neuzeit* (Königstein: Ulrike Helmer Verlag, 1998), pp. 395–407.

[38] Lord Edward Denny, 'To Pamphilia from the father-in-law of Seralius', quoted from Josephine A. Roberts, 'An Unpublished Literary Quarrel Concerning the Suppression of Mary Wroth's "Urania" (1621)', *Notes and Queries*, 222 (1977), 532–535 (p. 533).

[39] Sandra Harding, 'Women look at science', *Women: A Cultural Review*, 1 (1990), 99–105 (p. 101).

[40] *Observations* (1666), p. 350.

[41] Benjamin Farrington, 'Temporis Partus Masculus: An Untranslated Writing of Francis Bacon', *Centaurus*, 1 (1951), 193–205.

[42] Francis Bacon, *The Advancement of Learning*, ed. by G.W. Kitchin (London: J. M. Dent & Sons Ltd., 1973).

[43] Thomas Sprat, *History of the Royal Society*, ed. by Jackson J. Cope and Harold Whitmore Jones (London: Routledge & Kegan Paul, 1958), p. xii. Joseph Glanvill, *Essays on Several Important Subjects in Philosophy and Religion* (London: John Baker, 1676), pp. 1–2.

[44] Abraham Cowley, 'To the Royal Society', stanza 1, ll. 5-7, in Sprat, *History*, sig. B recto.

[45] In 1739 Elizabeth Carter translated Francesco Algarotti's *Il Newtonianismo per le dame* (Naples, 1737) as *Sir Isaac Newton's Philosophy Explained for the Use of Ladies*, 2

vols (London: E. Cave, 1739). As de Santis has shown, the Restoration and the early eighteenth century saw the development not only of general educational literature but also of popular scientific works for women. In opposition to Cavendish's writing and contemporary male treatises, these tracts for women did teach fundamental scientific knowledge as ultimate truths without discussing and analysing the methodology behind them.

[46] *Writings* (1994), p. 124.

[47] *Observations* (1666), p. 132.

[48] 'An Argumental Discourse Concerning some principal subjects in Natural Philosophy, necessary for the better understanding, not only of this, but all other philosophical works, hitherto written by the authoress', in *Observations*, sig. h recto–verso.

[49] *Observations* (1666), p. 131.

[50] *Writings* (1994), p. 126.

[51] *Writings* (1994), p. 126.

[52] Bazeley, 'An early challenge', p. 122.

[53] The Interregnum and the Restoration clearly upheld a paradoxical notion about women's writing. On the one hand, the act of writing and most certainly the desire to publish was seen as unfeminine and immodest; on the other hand the women who actually wrote and even published were not immediately condemned but were judged according to male literary, but even more according to certain moral standards. As Janet Todd argues in her book, *The Sign of Angellica: Women, Writing and Fiction, 1660–1800* (London: Virago, 1989), p. 41: 'two poles of women's writing were speedily formed: the modest and the immodest. The first was personified in the professional and flamboyant stray Behn as "Astrea" [...] with her bawdy plays glorifying rakes and free livers and her poems on male impotence or female passion. The second was typified by the refined, retiring poet and playwright of heroic tragedy, Katherine Philips or "Orinda", isolated in Wales but at the centre of a network of platonic friendship "as innocent as our Design".'

[54] Todd, *Sign of Angellica*, pp. 39–40.

[55] *Natures Pictures* (1656), pp. 220-272.

[56] Wilputte, 'Imaginary Voyage', p. 109, and Nancy Armstrong, *Desire and Domestic Fiction* (Oxford: Oxford University Press, 1987), pp. 3–27.

[57] See Michael McKeon, *Origins of the English Novel 1600–1740* (Baltimore and London: Johns Hopkins University Press, 1987).

[58] Sprat, *History*, p. 4.

[59] McKeon, *Origins*, p. 72.

[60] Michael Nerlich, *The Ideology of Adventure. Studies in modern Consciousness, 1100–1750*, trans. by Ruth Cowley, 2 vols, Theory and History of Literature, 42–3 (Minneapolis: University of Minnesota Press, 1987); Boesky, 'Rhetoric of Reform', pp. 80–81.

[61] McKeon, *Origins*, p. 105.

[62] *Writings* (1994), p. 124.

[63] Sprat, *History*, p. 43.

[64] Sprat, *History*, p. 416.

[65] Thomas Sprat, 'An Account of the Life and Writings of Mr. Abraham Cowley Written to Mr. M. Clifford', in *The Works of Mr Abraham Cowley. Consisting of Those which were formerly Printed: And Those which he Design'd for the Press, Now Published out of the*

Author's Original Copies (London: Printed by J. M. for Henry Herringman, 1668).

[66] *Observations* (1666), sig. d1 verso–e recto.

[67] Cf. Woolf, *A Room of One's Own*, pp. 59–60 and Douglas Grant's *Margaret the First*. Scholars still are researching evidence for any performances of the plays by Cavendish. Current stagings of plays have proven that they are indeed performable. *The Convent of Pleasure*, published in 1668, was staged in 1995 at the University College of Ripon and York St. John in York. *The Female Wits*, written in the late 1650s or early 1660s, was directed by George Pensotti in 199 at the Canal Café Theatre, Little Venice, London (see infra, pp. 103–5).

[68] *Observations* (1666), pp. 185–186.

[69] Bazeley, 'An early challenge', p. 137; Verena Olejniczak, 'Unendliche Welten. Margaret Cavendishs imaginative Konstruktion der Wirklichkeit zwischen Skepsis und Platonismus', *Mitteilungen des Zentrums zur Erforschung der frühen Neuzeit*, 1 (1994), 222–259. Book II, Part I of *The Worlds Olio* is a particularly good example for this explosive writing practice of Cavendish.

[70] Deleuze, *The Fold*, p. 125.

[71] Lennard J. Davis, *Factual Fictions: The Origins of the English Novel*, (New York: Columbia University Press, 1983), p. 12.

5

Autobiography, Parody and the *Sociable Letters* of Margaret Cavendish*

James Fitzmaurice

The autobiographical sketch 'A True Relation' added by Margaret Cavendish to the end of her collection of tales in verse and prose, *Nature's Pictures* (1656), is on the surface a homey piece of writing. It would appear that Cavendish wanted to use the addendum to reinforce the picture of harmonious family life that she had conjured up with the frontispiece at the beginning of that volume. The frontispiece, as explained in one prefatory poem, presents a warm and loving woman who reads her stories aloud for the entertainment of her husband and stepchildren. The fire burns brightly and the family is content. Nevertheless, a closer look at 'A True Relation' reveals there were the same rivalries, tensions and irritations in the Cavendish family that obtain in ordinary life. She was, for example, a little uneasy about the relationship between money and status where she and her husband were concerned. Her husband, then a marquis, had considerable status. Many in the court of Henrietta Maria – at least at the time of the wedding – felt that Margaret's family, the Lucases, was not sufficiently noble to make such a match desirable for him. Margaret, on the other hand, had been raised in an environment where money was abundant and is not afraid to say so in 'A True Relation'. *Sociable Letters* (1664) is not an autobiography, but it also contains a large amount of autobiographical detail – detail that is always obliquely presented and sometimes veiled under the guise of anagrams. *Sociable Letters* often deals with even more personal and intimate problems than does 'A True Relation'; problems such as its author's medical condition and the difficulties that arise when married men are attracted to women other than their wives. William, the Marquis, had such a history with women, and while the couple got along very well, that history always seemed to be lurking in the back of Margaret's mind.

Margaret and William both enjoyed parody as a literary form, and the parody that they composed frequently has biographical or autobiographical import. Sometimes this parody is harsh and satirical. On other occasions, it is gentle and even loving. In his elegy on Jonson, 'To Ben: Jonson's Ghost' (about 1637), William parodies his master in a way that is loving:

* The author wishes to thank the staff of the rare book and manuscript rooms at the Huntington Library, Cambridge University Library, and the University of Nottingham Library for various sorts of help including the checking of references.

> I would write of Thee, Ben; not to approue
> My witt or Learneing; but my Iudgement, Love.
> But when I think or this, or that, to chuse;
> Each part of Thee, is too big for my Muse.
> Should I compare Thee to Romes dust, that's dead?
> Their witt, to Thine's as heauy as thy lead.[1]

William pays homage to Jonson by offering a parody of Jonson's compact style. He also judiciously parodies Jonsonian judiciousness, for he refuses to claim for himself either Jonson's wit or learning. Nevertheless the passage is a little disconcerting in its inclusion of the metaphor of size and weight. If Jonson possessed *gravitas*, he was also a large and heavy man. It is of course true that personal references were fair game for Jonson. He joked on the topic of his own 'mountain belly' in 'My Picture Left in Scotland', and he may have teased the diminutive William on the subject of short stature in the Welbeck and Bolsover entertainments.[2] Disconcerting as this poem might be for readers today, it is nevertheless clear that William felt close enough to Jonson to be able to have a laugh with the man even after Jonson had died.[3]

Another parody in which William probably had a hand was pointedly satiric in character. Margaret writes in *Sociable Letters* about attending a meeting of 'Holy Sisters and Holy Brothers', a meeting which is clearly fictional. She offers what she says is a quoted passage, but what amounts to a parody of Calvinist theology as propounded by lay preachers:

> A Holy Brother stood up and Preached thus:
> Dearly beloved Brethren and Sisters, We are gathered together in the Lord with Purity of Spirit to Preach his Word amongst us, We are the Chosen and Elect Children of the Lord who have Glorified Spirits and Sanctified Souls, we have the Spirit of God in us, which Inspires us to Pray and to Preach, as also to Call upon his Name and to Remember him of his Promise to Unite and Gather us together into his New Jerusalem, separating us from Reprobates, that we may not be Defiled with their Presence.[4]

The satire continues to hammer home the point that Puritan lay preachers were self-righteously convinced of their own holiness and of the fallen nature of everyone else. A second passage also offered as a quote is equally satiric, but it is a little complicated as regards authorship. Cavendish tells us that Mr. N.N., who was at the prayer meeting, decided to adopt the dress and the speaking style of the brethren – apparently for fun. N.N. took off his 'peruick, and put on a nightcap, wherein he appeared so like a Holy Brother, as they took him for one of their sect.'[5] Ironically, his particular Calvinist line drives the faithful away, for he says that nobody really knows who is among the elect and who is not. The audience is not flattered and not pleased. The problem of authorship arises when we realise that Mr. N.N. elsewhere in *Sociable Letters* is clearly William, Marquis of Newcastle.[6] Since William often did contribute brief pieces to Margaret's books, the parody spoken by Mr. N.N. easily could belong to the husband rather than the wife.

Uncertainties of this sort abound in *Sociable Letters* and often were part of a set of puzzles involving anagrams and intended for the entertainment of the reader.[7]

Quite a few of these anagrams obliquely develop a worry that pestered Margaret: William once had a weakness for female companionship, and he might perhaps return to his old ways. Before he met her, William was known for enjoying 'softer pleasures', to use the words of Edward Hyde, Earl of Clarendon.[8] In the *Life* of William, Margaret makes reference to this reputation, apparently treating it as a bit of trivia. She writes, 'I know him not addicted to any manner of Vice, except that he has been a great lover and admirer of the Female Sex', and then she goes on to another subject.[9] In 'A True Relation', she trivialises a similar sort of interest in women on the part of her brothers. The brothers avoid the more serious male failings of hawking and hunting and are generally admirable, 'unless to love a mistress were a crime.'[10] Nevertheless, her continued discussion of the brothers' interest in women gives the apparently small failing more seriousness. She says that she only knows about her brothers' behaviour by way of rumour and that rumour is usually a matter of lies, or at the best exaggeration. If what is being said is lies, then maybe the subject is significant and loving a mistress can be a crime.

Margaret Cavendish never really makes up her mind about just how trivial or important it is when men get involved with women who are not their wives. Nor is she always uniform in her condemnation of the women these men find attractive. In *Sociable Letters* she devotes an entire letter to Aspasia, a courtesan who eventually married the Athenian Prince, Pericles. Margaret believes Aspasia to be thoroughly unclean but at the same time credits her as a fine rhetorician. Margaret does not say so, but it is clear that William found women with some of these same rhetorical powers as Aspasia attractive – in particular his cousin's widow, Christiana Cavendish, Countess of Devonshire. Margaret's opening statement about Aspasia is largely a disinterested assessment of a historical figure, an assessment based on Margaret's recent reading of Plutarch's *Lives* – which she jokingly calls 'Lies':

> It was my chance to read the Life of Pericles the Athenian, in which Story he is Commended for his Gravity, Government, and Wisdom; this Pericles I did much Admire all the time I read of him, until I did read where it was mentioned of his marrying Aspasia, a famous Courtesan, and then I did not think him so Wise a man as I did before, in that he would not rule his Passion better, but to marry a Whore; neither doth Gravity and Wantonness suit well together, for to my imagination a Grave Cuckold doth appear most Ridiculous.[11]

When Margaret says that he 'would not rule his Passion better', she is in accord with the sort of analysis of Pericles that would have been made a few years before in Renaissance England. When she mentions in passing that Aspasia is a 'whore', she is harsh in the manner of Restoration writers like the Earl of Rochester. Further, her word choice is not quite accurate, since a whore and a courtesan were by no means the same. Aphra Behn's courtesan, Angellica Bianca from *The Rover* may be called a 'whore', but only by stupid men like Ned Blunt. It seems likely that Margaret Cavendish uses the word 'whore' because she finds the mistresses of

Restoration England irritating and a potential source of competition for the attentions of her husband. What makes the situation interesting is that she gives Aspasia her due:

> But it seem'd that she had an Attractive Power, especially on such as they call Wise men, as Statesmen, Philosophers, and Governours, and all this Power lay in her Tongue, which was a Bawd for the other end; nay, so well (it is said) she could Speak, that not only such men as forementioned did come to hear her, and to learn to speak Eloquently by her, but many also brought their Wives to hear her.[12]

Margaret might have given her readers a more lengthy lesson on the dangers of passion to 'Wise men, as Statesmen, Philosophers, and Governours', but instead she trims her sails and credits Aspasia as a woman of powerful words. She does not make this concession without a witty insult, also reminiscent of the Earl of Rochester, but she does give credit where it is due.[13]

Christiana, Countess of Devonshire, was no Aspasia, but she did share some of Aspasia's skill with words. Christiana was also a flirt. In the following letter she probably responds to flirtation initiated by William, all of this interaction taking place some years before he met his future second wife, the then Margaret Lucas. If William did initiate the flirtation then the letter serves to offer further evidence of his history as a 'lady's man':

> My lord I hop it is for your secret sins and not your declarde sickness that you undergoe soe great a penance since you cane so easily submit to a volantary martyrdome I wish I could translate my faults to haue them comprehended within <your> sufferings. soe littell compasione haue I of your compfartings. yet I am not soe destitute of pitty to deny you to a better aduise then I believe you tak to your self.[14]

Christiana goes on to give him medical counsel in this letter, but in another she both flirts and holds out the possibility of William's being present for a visit of the Queen and Prince Rupert to the Devonshires' home, Chatsworth:

> My Lord I did not know you hade soe ill a neighbor [presumably herself], I beseech you hasten to a remoue, I wish this place weer worthy to recieue you, or If you think any part of it fitt to serue you your lot shall commande it absolutely. I hard the last night. The queen intends me the honour to come hither, the prince elector has threatende me a surpriis a good while, the queen hiering of it. Told him she would mak him her guest hier, when, I am not certyne this day I meane to goe to inquire if your lo pleas to mak your self of the number to attend the queen you may be assured of a weelcome, in last I rest your seruant
>
> CDEVONSHIRE[15]

Flirtation, it would seem, was blended by both William and Christiana with court politics. William was ambitious to become governor to the young prince Charles, later Charles II, so a royal visit to the neighboring estate of Chatsworth would have provided a fine opportunity to work on this goal.

Margaret was well aware that sex might have a strong connection to the application of political power – both mild forms of sexual attraction as evidenced in flirtation and more serious manifestations as in the liaisons of lawyers and judges. She complains in *Sociable Letters* that men who are 'honest', or who would like to return to being virtuous, have little likelihood of fair treatment before the law when they compete with courtesans – that is to say, mistresses:

> But I believe Mr. P.C. will not easily clear himself from her, for Courtesans are often assisted by the Powerful, insomuch as in any Law-sute or petitioning Request, they shall be heard, and their Sute granted, although against all Law or Right; Such Power and Favour hath Concupiscence, as to corrupt Magistrates, bribe Judges, fee Lawyers, flatter Courtiers, and the truth is, intice, allure, and perswade most of Mankind.[16]

Justice can be perverted by mistresses who have strong political connections, and, even more frightening to 'honest' women, such women are very competitive on the marriage market. The letter continues:

> Courtesans are so Prevalent and Fortunate, as they do not onely get themselves Husbands, when Beauty and Lovers begin to leave them, but marry more Richly and Honourably for Dignities, than Honest, Chaste Widows, or Pure and Innocent Virgins, which is apt to make Honest and Chast Women to doubt, their Honesty and Chastity is not blest with such good Fortune as Dishonesty is.[17]

As with Aspasia, an enormous strength for courtesans sometimes resides in their ability to use language, and marriages can be undermined by articulate but less than virtuous women:

> [Men] love the Company and Conversation of Wanton and Free Women, insomuch that a Courtesan shall have a greater and stronger Power to Cause and Perswade Men to do Actions not onely to the Ruin of their Estates and Families, but to the Ruin of their Honours and Reputation, nay, to make them Unnatural, Extravagant or Base, than an Honest Chast Wife hath to Perswade her Husband to keep his Estate, Honour, or Honesty.[18]

The best defence against this particular threat, then, would appear to derive from language emanating from wit and intelligence on the part of the wife. Margaret, however, knows that wives who are brilliant conversationalists are by no means safe from women who are pretty but who cannot say an intelligent word. She parodies her own emphasis on the dangers of wit among courtesans in yet another letter:

> Sir W.C.'s Wife you know hath a Conversable and Ingenious Wit, yet not being very handsom, her Husband hath got him a Mistress, who is very beautiful and handsom, but yet she is a Fool; a Friend of his ask'd him why he chose a Fool for his Mistress? he said, he did not Court her for her Wit, but for her Beauty; for, said he, now I have a Mistress for Delight, and a Wife for Conversation.[19]

Strangely, the wife is not at all angered by this arrangement and is happy to observe that her wit will outlast the mistress's beauty. The wife goes on to claim to be thoroughly spiritual and completely above such mundane matters as physical attraction:

> For Wit is Spiritual and not Corporeal, it lives with the Mind, and not with the Body, being not subject to the gross Senses, for though Wit, said she, may be known by Words and Actions, yet those are but the Pictures of Wit's Works, not Wit it self, for that cannot be Drawn, it is beyond all Draughts; and so much Difference, said she, is between my Husband's Mistress and his Wife, as a Picture and an invisible Spirit, which Spirit can both Help and Hurt, Delight and Terrifie, Damn and Glorifie.[20]

The wife of W.C. is just a little too spiritual to be believed, and her protestations offer something of a parody of the spirituality of the wife of another W.C., William Cavendish. Should the reader have any question about the desirability of the marriage of the wife of W.C., the letter ends with just a touch of sarcasm:

> But, Madam, this is to let you know the [wife's] Wit, Discretion, and Temper, which is more than most of our Sex hath; and so leaving her to her Wit, and her Husband to Reformation, and his Mistress's Beauty to Time, I rest,
> Madam,
> Your most faithful Friend and Servant.[21]

The wife of W.C. is left to the dubious consolation of her ethereal wit and to the probably wan hope that her unfaithful husband will someday reform. Although Margaret Cavendish had her own ethereal side, she was not one to ignore the dangers of pretty women for her own W.C.

Where unfaithful husbands are concerned, perhaps the most sarcastic parody in *Sociable Letters* is to be found in the story of the newly wed Lady M.L. The initials of this young bride correspond to those of Margaret Cavendish before marriage when she was Margaret Lucas, and the tale of Lady M.L. shifts and twists what actually happened to Margaret Lucas when she was being courted by William, Marquis of Newcastle. Lady M.L's future husband never showed any signs of loving her; William wrote Margaret Lucas a book-length manuscript full of love poems.[22] Lady M.L.'s husband had to be talked into the marriage by friends; William married against the advice of nearly everyone. Lady M.L.'s husband was rich; William's estates were in the control of the Parliament. On the other hand, Lady M.L.'s husband is like William in significant ways, or at least like the picture of William elsewhere painted by Margaret. He is handsome, 'Dignified with Title', 'Valiant, Generous, and Wise.'[23]

Satire in the letter becomes apparent with the parody of the tale of the patient Griselda. Lady M.L.'s husband, like Chaucer's Walter, decides to test his wife's loyalty and endurance. The husband of Lady M.L. does not make any show of abusing her children however, for she – like Margaret Cavendish – has none; rather he takes a mistress and the patient Lady M.L. becomes a 'slave' to this woman. No amount of punishment seems to bother the insanely stoical Lady M.L., however. The ethereal wife of Sir W.C. would seem to be closer to ordinary reality:

> He [Lady M.L.'s husband] desired by this means to keep me [Lady M.L.] from Jealousie, and to learn me Patience; neither did I think my self Unhappy, that he Tortured me, nay Threatned Death to me, to Force me to Serve his Concubines, because I took more Comfort in that my Resolution was so Strong, as neither Pain, nor Fear of Death could Alter it, and Gloried more in my Sufferings, than Grieved for my Pains.[24]

As it turns out, the most crucial test for the saintly Lady M.L. comes when the husband threatens to divorce her. She believes that 'to be Divorced, is to Live in Disgrace and Scorn, which is Worse than any Pain, or Death.' Thus she is greatly relieved, even happy, to learn two letters later that the threat of divorce is not real, her 'Countenance [becoming] as Joyful, as formerly it was Sad.' The mistress, however, remains in place and 'Love makes [Lady M.L.] Wink at her Husband's Faults [...], which every Good Wife ought to do.' Sarcasm oozes from this second letter, and it is clear from other parts of *Sociable Letters*, and from stories in *Nature's Pictures*, that Margaret Cavendish felt unfaithful husbands deserved to be punished with unfaithful wives.[25] For their own part, overly patient wives merit biting satire rather than admiration.[26]

It is, of course, a supreme irony that the Lady M.L. of these two letters carries the initials of Margaret Lucas. Lady M.L. resembles William's first wife far more than she does his second. According to Geoffrey Trease, William spent a good deal of time trying to seduce the countess of Rutland a near neighbour in Derbyshire, while married to the first wife, Elizabeth.[27] Trease also believes that he penned verses to one of the servant girls:

> With love's hopes long my phansy thou hast fed;
> Now, since my wife is safely brought to bed,
> Thou art my Gossip, honour me to stand [...].
> Think not, though I grow old, I am no other
> But a dull handycraft Mechanique Lover:
> What though my youth's declin'd; I am afraid
> You'll think me a Patriarch with my handmaid.[28]

While Trease's evidence is piecemeal, it does appear that William had a good deal of interest in women other than his wife and that the sickly Elizabeth did nothing to oppose her husband.

Letters from an otherwise unknown Elizabeth Darcye to William show how an intended mistress might need to be as patient as a wife. These letters, written while William was married to his first wife, give evidence of a woman who had no interest in taking a lover but who also felt herself to be in no position to condemn the advances of a powerful aristocrat:

> My Lord
> giue me leave I besech your Lordsp to think yr judgment cannot but be much better then to place any contintise happyness in confrance with my unworthy selfe, for yr Lo:shp Ienorge is quicke & I am so inaprensive that it must needs be a purgatory to yr Lo:shp to frame yr discorse to my capacitye.[29]

William is not put off by Elizabeth Darcye's professed lack of intellectual ability and persists in his advances in what appears to be a second letter following the first. Elizabeth Darcye is again both patient and evasive:

> My Lord
> I acount it a uery great honour that you are pleased to retaine me in your thoughts which is nowe ways worthy of the Lest aspecte from your Lordshp + therefore I admire your Lo:shp transcendinge expressions in your Lordshp desire to see me, that doth not desarue soe hie a favure my Lo: I will study noe complements to returne to your Lo:shp againe but I am realy my Lord your most ingaged and faithfull humble Saruant.[30]

While in the first letter quoted here Elizabeth Darcye tries to escape the amorous embraces of the then Earl of Newcastle by pleading diminished intellectual capacity, in this letter she tries to beg off by explaining that she is not socially worthy to be the object of his attention. He is over and over again a 'lordship' and she a something else. A third letter, which seems to follow the first two in date of composition, shows the continued patience of the writer, but is just a little more pointed. Someone found her reading what is probably a love-letter from William and the experience caused her 'disquiet' thoughts as well general ill health. In any event, she does not expect to be able to visit William as long as her family remains under threat of 'the smalle Pockes & purples', which have killed neighbouring children.[31]

The Lady M.L. turns up in two more letters from *Sociable Letters* and is neither patient nor long suffering in either one of them. In the first letter, difficulties regarding a husband's fidelity are mixed with the topic of the lady's health. The Lady M.L. suffers from melancholia, a condition that Margaret Cavendish acknowledges elsewhere as a problem in her own life. Margaret's variety of melancholia, however, causes genuine physical impairment, while the Lady M.L. is simply guilty of malingering. The Lady M.L. is consequently in danger of losing her husband to one of the women servants:

> But if [Lady M.L.'s] Melancholy proceed from want of Variety of Company, I pitty both her Husband and Attendants, for most commonly a Peevish Frowardness doth attend that Melancholy, they will Quarrel with every Thing, and not be Pleased with Any, take Exceptions at every Word, complain of being Sick, but know not where their Pains are, even as Weary of Themselves, which makes their Husbands many times Weary of Them, and to Divert the Grief of their Wives Troubles, they Solace with their Wives Maids, who are more Pleasant Company, being not troubled with the Splene, as not having a Husband.[32]

What then is the connection between Lady M.L. and the woman who was once called Margaret Lucas? There is no single answer, and it would appear that Margaret Cavendish presents her reader with a puzzle. One solution that the reader might find would be to see in Lady M.L. a gentle parody of the public image that Margaret created for herself as a serious woman who sought seclusion in order to be able to write books. Too much time away from the husband might be dangerous even for such a committed writer. Since Margaret Cavendish goes on to say that melancholia is a disease of the wealthy and undisciplined, another solution readers might have tried out was that Margaret used the Lady M.L. to laugh at those among her detractors who felt that she, Margaret Cavendish, lacked focus and intellect. Mary Evelyn, for instance, wrote that Margaret was, 'rambling as her books, aiming at science, difficulties, high notions, terminating commonly in nonsense.'[33] Margaret would get the laugh by writing a parody of the sort of criticism expressed by Mary Evelyn. This game would have been dangerous, but Margaret was not timorous where her public image was concerned.

If the readers of *Sociable Letters* found the story of the 'froward' Lady M.L. entertaining as a puzzle, then another Lady M.L. in another letter was likely to amuse them even more. In this letter, Margaret answers a specific piece of criticism offered by a specific detractor. It was widely reported that Bishop John Wilkins, author of *The Discovery of a World in the Moone*, had suggested that Margaret built castles in the air.[34] In Letter 113, the Lady M.L. parrots Wilkins's suggestion and Margaret Cavendish, as semifictional letter writer, responds:

> The Lady M.L. spoke of me, saying, I liv'd a Dull, Unprofitable, Unhappy Life, Imploying my time onely in Building Castles in the Air. Indeed, if I were of her Ladiships Humour, I should be Unhappy, but as I am, I would not change the Course of my Life with her Ladiship, might I have the years of Methusalem to boot; and as for the Minds Architecture, as Castles in the Air, or Airy Castles, which are Poetical Conceptions, and Solitary Contemplations, which produce Poems, Songs, Playes, Masks, Elegies, Epigrams, Anagrams, and the like, they will be more lasting than Castles of Wood, Brick, or Stone, and their Architecture, if well Designed and Built, will be more Famous, and their Fame spread farther than those of Stone, viz. to the View and Prospect of divers Nations, if Translated into divers Languages.[35]

The semifictional Margaret Cavendish goes on to attack the Lady M.L. in language that contains phrases that might have been used by Mary Evelyn:

> So leaving [the Lady M.L.] to her Little Wit, and Many Words, to her Gossiping-Life and her Light Heels, I rest,
> Madam,
> Your faithful Friend and Servant.[36]

The Lady M.L., like Bishop Wilkins, is what might be called a proto-Philistine. Further, she has little intellect, talks too much, and, in being light-heeled, is of dubious morals. It is not even necessary to figure out the puzzle to be entertained by this picture. When one considers the connection via initials between the Lady M.L. and Margaret Lucas, the letter becomes quite daring as well as entertaining.

In Letter 8, Margaret Cavendish presents an intimate autobiographical look at the particular sort of melancholia to which she was subject. The letter is generally clinical in tone, though it does contain small comic passages:

> You were pleas'd to invite me unto a Ball, to divert my Melancholy Thoughts, but they are not capable of your Charity, for they are in too deep a Melancholy to be diverted; like as bodies that are starved, and almost dying for hunger, so weak as they cannot feed, at least that want strength to nourish or digest, having not life enough to re-kindle the vital fire, which want of food hath neer put out.[37]

Her husband and her physician both blamed her sedentary life for her melancholia.[38] She did not, they said, get the sort of exercise that she needed. She did not agree, and in this particular letter she uses metaphors of food and digestion to point at what she believed to be a major source of her illness, diet. At one point in *Sociable Letters*, for instance, she says that she had to be bled because she made the mistake of eating fruit. She is by no means merely a food faddist or a hypochondriac and is able to have a little fun at her own expense:

> In truth, my leaden Sprits have soder'd up my Joynts so stiff that they will not move so agilly, as is requir'd in Dancing; I am fitter to sit upon a Grave, than to tread measures on a Carpet.[39]

There is just a bit of self-parody here – self-parody that looks forward to the so-called graveyard school of poets. The letter also contains a puzzle for its readers, though a puzzle that is not based on anagrams.

> My Mind is benighted in Sorrow, insomuch as I have not one lighted thought, they are all put out with the memory of my Loss. Thus, Madam, Memory hath made an Oblivion; but though it hath buried for the present the worldly Joys of my Life, yet it hath not buried my grateful Thanks for your Favours, for which I am,
> Madam,
> Your most humble S.[40]

What is the 'Sorrow', and what the 'Loss'? Her husband had lost a great deal to the ravages of the English Civil Wars – rents not collected, houses fallen into disrepair, and woodlands stripped of trees. 'Sorrow' is an even more mysterious word, for Margaret never depicts William as sorrowful. Rather he bears up under adversity with uniform, if not entirely believable, good nature. It is, of course, Margaret who feels sorrow in this letter, but the mystery of the source of the sadness remains.

If references to loss and sorrow offer serious problems of autobiographical interpretation in Letter 113, the solution to the puzzle of 'who is the Lady T.M.?' in Letter 15 is much more light-hearted and entertaining. Simply stated, her initials are the last and first letters of the name Margaret. Lady T.M.'s suitor's identity is even more transparent, for Lord N.W. carries the reversed initials of William Newcastle. The letter is built around a complicated joke, in which Margaret, the semi-fictional letter writer, berates Lord N.W. for praising Lady T.M., that is 'another woman'. Margaret has this sort of fun with two fictional manifestations of herself and a fictional version of William at the end of *The Blazing World* (1668). There William enjoys platonic pleasures offered to him by the souls of Margaret Newcastle and her alter ego, the Empress of the Blazing World.

In Letter 15, there is gently satiric self-parody, for the Lord N.W. praises Lady T.M. in terms that Margaret always associated with herself and the praise is a little cloying:

> [Lord N.W. says] Nature had Crown'd [Lady T.M.'s] Soul with a Celestial Crown, made of Poetical Flame [...], her Celestial Crown was set with Understanding, Judgement and Wit, also with clear Distinguishings, oriental Similizings [...]. She had a powerful Perswasion and the tongue of Eloquence [...], and Fame's house was her Magnificent Palace.[41]

Margaret Cavendish frequently wrote that she hoped her poetry would bring her fame. She published two editions of *Orations*, ample testimony to her belief that she 'had a powerful Perswasion and the tongue of Eloquence.' Finally, she was proud of her 'similizings'. Just as the reader becomes thoroughly weary of the Lord N.W.'s praise for this woman who so resembles Margaret Cavendish, N.W. finishes and Margaret Cavendish, the semifictional letter writer, offers a sceptical response:

> I could not chuse but smile to hear such Poetical commentations of a Woman, doubting none of our Sex was worthy of such high, and far-fetch'd praises; he ask'd me why I smil'd? I told him, I smil'd to observe how the Passion of Love had bribed his Tongue.[42]

The Lord N.W. persists in his praise for Lady T.M. and Margaret Cavendish, again as semifictional letter writer, serves up the reader with her punch line:

> I [Cavendish as letter writer] pray'd him to give me leave, or to pardon me, if I told him, that his Speech shew'd, or express'd him a Temporal and Imperial Courtier, as to praise one Lady to another, and to give so many Praises to an absent Lady, as to leave no Praises for the present Lady: He pray'd me to pardon him that Errour, and that hereafter he would alwayes Praise the Lady he was present with.[43]

The joke continues as Margaret Cavendish, the semifictional letter writer, admits that the praise awarded to 'another woman' had almost caused her to be turned to 'Vinegar' or dissolved into 'Vitriol' by envy. She archly says that she avoided these 'spotted Vices' only narrowly by being, in essence, perfect. The letter abounds with such ironies.

What did William think of the autobiographical content of *Sociable Letters*? He wrote commendatory verses for the volume, but those verses say little about autobiography or anagrams. On the other hand, William probably knew something about Margaret's worries about his one-time abiding interest in the opposite sex, and it may well be that he teases her on this account in commendatory verses printed with the first edition of *Nature's Pictures*:

Gallants and Ladies, what do ye lack? pray buy
Tales a la mode, new Fashion'd here do lye:
So do romancies, your grave studies, too,
Academies of Love, teaching to woo
And to be woo'd, corrupts more Virgins then
Hot Satyrs turn'd to Amorous Courtly Men:
But these are innocent; then be not nice,
Will you not buy, because they teach not Vice?
Nature will teach you that; then do not look
To do't by Art and Learning by the Book;
A Vestal Nun may reade this, and avow it,
And a Carthusian Confessor allow it.[44]

The speaker of these verses at first says that 'Academies of Love' found in *Nature's Pictures* will undo more virgins 'then / Hot Satyrs turn'd to Amorous Courtly Men'. That is, Margaret's book will have the same effect on virtuous women that William himself at one time had. William, it appears, teases Margaret on the subject of her worries about his past.

The speaker then changes course, saying that *Nature's Pictures* is so innocent that it might be read by a 'Vestal Nun' or a 'Carthusian Confessor'. The exaggerated compliment merely continues William's teasing. Had Margaret's worries been based on a serious threat to her marriage, it is unlikely that William would have engaged in such playfulness. Thus William, like Margaret, includes autobiographical reference in what he writes and leaves it to the reader to figure out what is happening and to be entertained.

Notes

[1] Quoted from Francis Needham (ed.) 'A Collection of Poems by Several Hands', *Welbeck Miscellany, 2* (Bungay: Richard Clay and Sons, 1934), p. 43. The poem is also found in E. H. Craig (ed.) *Ben Jonson: The Critical Heritage* (London: Routledge, 1990), p. 181 and in *Ben Jonson* edited by C. H. Herford and Percy and Evelyn Simpson, 11 vols (Oxford: Clarendon Press, 1925–1963), XI, p. 489.

[2] According to Nick Rowe, Jonson claimed a high degree of 'playfulness [...], familiarity and license' in his dealings with William. See Nick Rowe, '"My Best Patron": William Cavendish and Jonson's Caroline Dramas', *The Seventeenth Century*, 9 (1994), 197-212 (p. 205).

[3] Thomas Greene writes of a 'dialogue of affectionate malice' that sometimes exists between parodist and subject. Perhaps there is a very small portion of malice in William's elegy. See Thomas M. Greene, *The Light in Troy: Imitation and Discovery in Renaissance Poetry* (New Haven: Yale University Press, 1982), p. 46.

[4] *Sociable Letters* (1664), Letter 76, p. 88.

[5] *Sociable Letters* (1664), Letter 76, p. 88.

[6] See *Sociable Letters* (1664), Letter 196, p. 45 which deals with William's financial problems and the ingratitude of 'C.R.', who is no doubt Charles II.

[7] A marginal note in the Emmanuel College, Cambridge, copy of *Sociable Letters* shows that at least one reader went so far as to try to solve a part of the puzzle. 'N.W.' in Letter 33 is identified as William Newcastle.

[8] Cit. *Margaret the First*, p. 61.

[9] *Life* (1667), p. 149; *Margaret The First*, p. 75.

[10] *Life* (1667), p. 159.

[11] *Sociable Letters* (1664), Letter 30, pp. 42–3.

[12] *Sociable Letters* (1664), Letter 30, p. 43.

[13] Cf. 'A Heroick head is liker to be balanced with an humble taile', in *The Letters of John Wilmot, Earl of Rochester*, ed. by Jeremy Treglown (Oxford: Blackwell, 1980), p. 75.

[14] Christina Cavendish, Duchess of Devonshire to William Cavendish, Earl of Newcastle, University of Nottingham, MS Pw 1 56, fol. 1 recto.

[15] Christina Cavendish, Duchess of Devonshire to William Cavendish, Earl of Newcastle, University of Nottingham, MS Pw 1 58, fol. 1 recto.

[16] *Sociable Letters* (1664), Letter 36, p. 49.

[17] *Sociable Letters* (1664), Letter 36, p. 49.

[18] *Sociable Letters* (1664), Letter 36, p. 49.

[19] *Sociable Letters* (1664), Letter 35, p. 47.

[20] *Sociable Letters* (1664), Letter 35, p. 48.

[21] *Sociable Letters* (1664), Letter 35, p. 48.

[22] The manuscript was published by Douglas Grant as, *The Phanseys of William Cavendish, Marquis of Newcastle, Addressed to Margaret Lucas* (London: Nonesuch, 1956).

[23] *Sociable Letters* (1664), Letter 153, p. 164.

[24] *Sociable Letters* (1664), Letter 153, pp. 164–5.

25 *Sociable Letters* (1664), Letter 36, p. 49: 'But leaving such men to their own Heads, and their Wives to their Neighbours Beds, I rest, Madam, Your faithful Friend and Servant'. A wife likewise cuckolds an unfaithful husband in 'The Matrimonial Agreement', in *Natures Pictures* (1656), p. 121.

26 In *The Worlds Olio* (1655), Cavendish doubts that Penelope was patient and rather believes that she enjoyed teasing the suitors (see p. 133).

27 Geoffrey Trease, *Portrait of a Cavalier: William Cavendish, First Duke of Newcastle* (London: Macmillan, 1979), p. 57.

28 Trease, *Portrait*, pp. 56–67.

29 Elizabeth Darcye to William Cavendish, Earl of Newcastle, University of Nottingham, MS Pw 1 106, fol. 1 recto.

30 Elizabeth Darcye to William Cavendish, Earl of Newcastle, University of Nottingham, MS Pw 1 107, fol. 1 recto.

31 Elizabeth Darcye to William Cavendish, Earl of Newcastle, 14 June 1636, British Library, Add. MS 70499, Cavendish Papers 1604-1659, fol. 204 recto:

> Right Ho^{ble}. The last time I had <the> Honour to here from your lo: I was so unexpectedly surprised with companye which did much disquiet my thoughts, & made <me> both then and euer since indisposed to health, which is one reason that ere now I haue not giuen your Honour [...] an acounte that I haue not parsonably waited upon y^{r} lo: and noble lady, but the ci<e>hfe [*sic*] lett is the smalle Pockes & purples are so seased upon many children in Astone & three died of them the last weeke that it makes me extreamly afread ether to come or send to afamlaye I so eceedingly honoure as your lo:, therfore I beseech your lo:^{p} and your lady a corrddinge to your acustemed goodness sensure faourably [*sic*] of me still lett me be esteemed of as one that is
>
> your
> Lo:^{shp} most faithfull
> and most humble
> Saruant
> Eliza: Darcye.
>
> Astone the 14 of Iune 1636

32 *Sociable Letters* (1664), Letter 34, p. 47.

33 John Evelyn, *Diary and Correspondence of John Evelyn*, ed. by William Bray, 4 vols (London: Henry Colburn, 1857), IV, pp. 8–9.

34 *Margaret the First*, p. 203. Grant doubts that Wilkins has the 'face' to make such a remark to a 'woman of Margaret's rank'.

35 *Sociable Letters* (1664), Letter 113, p. 121.

36 *Sociable Letters* (1664), Letter 113, p. 122.

37 *Sociable Letters* (1664), Letter 8, pp. 17–18.

38 *Margaret the First*, p. 105.

39 *Sociable Letters* (1664), Letter 8, p. 18.

40 *Sociable Letters* (1664), Letter 8, p. 18.

[41] *Sociable Letters* (1664), Letter 15, p. 24.

[42] *Sociable Letters* (1664), Letter 15, p. 24.

[43] *Sociable Letters* (1664), Letter 15, p. 25.

[44] *Natures Pictures* (1656), sig. b. These commendatory verses are not included in the second edition, *Natures Picture* (1671).

PART II

DRAMA

6

Writing for the Brain and Writing for the Boards: the Producibility of Margaret Cavendish's Dramatic Texts

Judith Peacock

There is no clear evidence of Margaret Cavendish's plays having had any influence on the dramatic writing of Aphra Behn. Contemporary scholars treat Margaret Cavendish as a separate, unique, eccentric and wholly original woman writer, ahead of her time, claiming no influence and not exerting an influence on the women writers that were to follow her. She did, however, turn her attention and her pen to one of the most social forms of literary culture. Drama not only offered her an opportunity to explore her own vacillating and often contradictory ideas about gender roles but her dramatic writing also demonstrates a theoretical exploration and an understanding of the constraints of the form, that mark these writings as less eccentric or formally independent than critics have conceded to date.

At the same time, Aphra Behn's position in the burgeoning Restoration theatre environment, and her rapid research, adaptation and production of plays for demanding professional companies, makes it seem highly unlikely that she would not have encountered Cavendish's work.[1] What is clear is that if either of the companies monopolising the theatrical entertainment business of the time knew of Cavendish's work, neither of them attempted a production of a Cavendish play. A consideration of the differences between the plays of Cavendish and Behn gives an indication as to why Cavendish's plays did not make it to the boards. Differing approaches to representation of gender and women's position in their social and literary contexts, has major implications for the producibility of their respective dramas. Aphra Behn's plays were producible because her gender politics, while subversive, did not threaten accepted mores concerning marriage and gender roles. Cavendish's utopian separatist scenarios, on the other hand, would have been deeply disturbing to a society just emerging from a crisis concerning social position and changing sites of power.[2] Current scholarship has tended to focus on claiming her dramas as feminist tracts,[3] or has concentrated on notions of the performability of gender. Cavendish's theatrical viability, that is, whether her plays would or could function as theatre is seldom addressed. Contemporary scholars have rarely progressed beyond reviewing the critics who have since the 1660s dismissed Cavendish's dramas as undramatic. From Virginia Woolf's assessment of her writing as 'higgledy-piggledy'[4] to Douglas Grant's dismissal of her plays as 'utterly undramatic'[5] the general consensus is still that 'Behn was the first woman to write theatrically.'[6] I contend, however, that it is precisely because they were not produced that they are viewed as dramatically stolid and unproducible.

Much has been made of the unwieldy structure of Cavendish's plays or their long discursive passages, but even a brief analysis of production practices of the 1670s will show that such features were not insurmountable obstacles to production. A consideration of a prompt book of a play by James Shirley that was revived successfully after the Restoration shows that standard contemporary treatment tailored plays to conform to prevailing theatrical trends and the limitations of both the playhouse and the audience of the day. Likewise, production of Cavendish's plays would have influenced the form in which they survived, and our understanding of Cavendish as a dramatist would be very different.

Margaret Cavendish's two volumes of plays, *Playes* (1662) and *Plays, Never before Printed* (1668) are generally assessed in terms of their significance to Cavendish's oeuvre as a whole, and seldom considered in relation to the dramatic tradition in which they can be seen to be a significant bridge between the drama produced before the theatres were officially closed in 1642 and their formal re-opening at the restoration of Charles II in 1660.

In spite of Cavendish's protestations about her intentions for her plays they constitute a major contribution to the dramatic endeavour of the Interregnum. Susan Wiseman, among others, has shown that the period between 1642 and 1660 was not a dramatic or theatrical wasteland, but in fact a time of essential transition for dramatic form and theatrical practice.[7] The most obvious survivor of the closure of the public theatres was the private performance; those performed for invited guests, without payment, in private or domestic space, and written and performed by members of the household. Set in this context Margaret Cavendish's plays become an important link between the writing and traditions of the 1630s and 1640s, and Restoration Theatre as we understand it today.

Margaret Cavendish was born in 1623 and was nineteen when the theatres were formally closed. Her youth and social status may have limited her access to the public theatres prior to the closure, although she does claim that her family made regular trips to London and visited the theatre during those visits.[8] Her most extensive dramatic experience during her youth may well have been the country house masque, but once she became Lady in Waiting to Queen Henrietta Maria, at Oxford in 1643, she would have became part of a very active theatrical coterie.[9] Charles maintained a small company of players in Paris and The Hague until 1646. It is recorded in *The Kingdom's Weekly Intelligencer* of 23 February 1647 that William Cavendish actually wrote for these players before they were disbanded.[10] Margaret Cavendish's experience of professional theatre on the Continent, with its female players, also had a significant impact on her thinking about drama.[11]

We know that copies of Cavendish's *Orations* were presented to John Edgerton, Earl of Bridgewater (the Duke's son-in-law) and the volume of *Playes* (1662) in the Widener Collection at Harvard may also have belonged to him.[12] It seems likely that as well as being circulated in literary circles these volumes could well have come into the hands of Killigrew and Davenant, the two theatre company licensees.

It is tempting to believe that since William Cavendish had five plays staged by the Duke's company between 1661 and 1674, his wife's plays could have been made available to that theatre management. The fact that Pepys was under the impression that Margaret Cavendish, rather than William, had written *The Humorous Lovers*, which he saw in March and April 1667,[13] seems to suggest that either her plays were in circulation in London, or that there had been gossip about the possibility or probability of the Duke's Men staging one of her plays.

A careful comparison of some of Margaret Cavendish's plays with those of Aphra Behn is useful in so far that it can show why one woman's plays enjoyed production in the public theatres and the other's did not. Cavendish's *Plays, Never Before Printed* was published in 1668, coinciding with Etheredge's success, *She Would if she Could*, now considered the first 'Restoration' comedy, which was only two years before Aphra Behn's first commercial success *The Forc'd Marriage* in 1670. It is possible that Behn did not encounter Margaret Cavendish's plays, but it seems highly unlikely, given that once Behn started writing for the theatre she appears to have scoured already published plays for her source material, gleaning from earlier successes and foreign playtexts. *The Luckey Chance* and *The Rover* were drawn from James Shirley's *The Lady of Pleasure* (1635) and Killigrew's *Tomaso* (1664) respectively, and she drew heavily on Molière.[14] In some ways Cavendish's experience of the theatre and the writing of plays was far superior to Behn's. She had experience of the English public theatres before moving to Court, first hand experience of the private theatricals of Henrietta Maria's Court, and the experience of French and Flemish Theatre, with its professional female performers. In marrying William Cavendish she married an experienced writer for the theatre who had also collaborated with a number of the esteemed playwrights of the 1630s and 1640s.[15] There is, however, no record of her plays being considered by the Dukes or the Kings Men, for production.

Aphra Behn was only 20 when the public theatres re-opened, but by the time she produced her first success ten years later, she had acquired a thorough grasp of what was wanted by the managements and how to produce it. In spite of hostility from other playwrights, Behn was part of an urban literary and theatrical milieu, while Cavendish was writing her plays in the 1650s, in exile and outside of that culture. One of her numerous epistles 'To the Readers' in *Playes* (1662) makes it clear that she was writing the plays in the 1662 volume during the official closure of the theatres:

> The reason I put out my Playes in print, before they are Acted, is, first, that I know not when they will be Acted, by reason they are in English, and England doth not permit, I will not say of Wit, yet not of Playes.[16]

If Behn had the stimulation of her environment and the harsh realities of maintaining herself to goad her, Cavendish had the support of a loyal husband. Both women chose to voice their opinions on a variety of subjects, like parental control and financially contracted marriages, and in a variety of literary forms. In their dramatic material, however, they both presented a female voice that had not been heard quite so publicly before. They also both had the courage to seek fame of the immortal kind, at the risk of courting fame of the disreputable kind. If their writing careers have points in common, there is also much that sets them apart. It is these differences in their practice that have an influence on the producibility of Margaret Cavendish's plays.

Both women wrote plays dealing with a woman's right to perform themselves in public, that is, their right to appropriate for themselves a voice and an active role within, or without, the structure of family or society. Cavendish and Behn both appropriated a role for themselves and for their heroines. Without a tradition or history of women's writing to draw on, both women drew on the only traditions they had available to them. While Cavendish drew on her experience of the performance traditions prior to 1660, Behn drew on those theatrical practices rapidly becoming established in the decade following 1660. Hence the major difference in their practice is in what would now be termed the area of 'professionalism'.[17] Writing during the time of the ban on public performance Cavendish was writing without a view to professional production. The Interregnum, as Susan Wiseman has pointed out, constituted a period of temporary equality between men and women writers when neither sex could write dramatic material with a view to professional production, as the theatres were closed.[18]

It was precisely professionalism, economic exchange and consumption that Cavendish despised. Nor did she appreciate the talents of professional performers and was vigorous in her criticism of 'mercenary Players' who did not benefit from the edifying effects of the drama:

> they only Act for the lucre of Gain, and not for the grace of Behaviour, the sweetness of Speech, nor the increasing of Wit, so as they only Act as Parrots speak, by wrote, and not as Learning gives to Education; for they making not a benefit of the wit, but only by the wit receive it; not neither into their consideration, understanding, nor delight, for they make it a work of labour, and not of delight, or pleasure, or honour; for they receive it into the memory, and no further than for to deliver it out [...] as soon as the Play is done, their wit and becoming graces are at an end, whereas the nobler sort, that Act not for mercenary Profit, but for Honour, and becoming, would not only strive to Act well upon the Stage, but to practise their actions when off from the Stage.[19]

Nor did she tailor her material for a consuming public:

> they will perchance say that my Playes are too serious, by reason that there is no ridiculous Jest in them, nor wanton Love, nor Impossibilities; also 'tis likely they will say that there are no plots, nor designs, nor subtil Contrivances, and the like; I answer, that the chief Plots of my Playes were to imploy my idle time, the designs to please and entertain my Readers, and the contrivance was to join edifying Profit and Delight together [...].[20]

Aristocratic hostility towards the professionalisation and democratisation of what Cavendish held to be the ideal of cultural education is clearly apparent here. *The Female Academy* depicts an institution that encourages the women's participation in oration, while in *The Convent of Pleasure* the encloistered women perform in theatrical entertainment. Far from being used in an educative capacity, as it might have been in an academy, acting and drama is depicted in *The Convent of Pleasure* as the preserve of the leisured and separate, in spite of the fact that 1660s London was very aware of the re-establishment of the professional theatre.

Defending herself from criticism Aphra Behn prefaces her 1678 play *Sir Patient Fancy* with a request that her audience should attribute 'all its faults to the Authours unhappiness, who is forced to write for Bread', a plea for consideration of the professional constraints of writing for 'the age'. She claims she is 'not ashamed to owne' her professional status, although she adds, 'this way of writing [...] even I despise as much below me.'[21] Economic necessity establishes her as a professional writer, bearing in mind that writing of any form was only beginning to be understood as a profession.[22] There were also the problems of what profession or professional could mean for an aristocrat as opposed to a member of the bourgeoisie, let alone what it might mean for woman as opposed to a man. The woman writer had already been labelled 'the new-fangled whore' and as such she was paid to display.[23] How much display was needed to survive and how it could be reconciled with remaining popular were real problems. Whatever accusations were levelled at the woman who chose to make her material available to the public, Behn had other issues to negotiate, most of them equally harsh. The economic realities of theatre as a business venture included trying to survive to a third night, competition with the rival playhouse, placating the cast, managing theatre finances, as well as problems with printers, patrons and booksellers. Cavendish was writing without economic pressures. Publication cost something, but something she could afford. Economic resources generated Cavendish's texts, while for Behn, her texts generated economic resources.

While she claims to have no interest in staging her plays, Cavendish gives long instructions for how her plays should be *read*. These, however, imply a reading aloud, and the instructions concern themselves with liveliness and sense:

> Indeed Comedies should be read a Mimick way, and the sound of their Voice must be according to the sense of the Scene; and as for Tragedies, or Tragick Scenes, they must not be read in a pueling whining Voice, but a sad serious Voice, as deploring or complaining [...] but when as a Play is well and skillfully read, the very sound of the Voice that enters through the Ears, doth present the Actions to the Eyes of the Fancy as lively as if it were really Acted [...].[24]

These could constitute instruction for reading aloud to oneself, as Elaine Hobby has suggested, 'a kind of closet drama, intended to be recited aloud by a reader in the privacy of her (or his) own home,' but this idea is not borne out by her prologues and epilogues addressing the 'spectator.'[25] In *The Apocriphal Ladies* her prologue even makes reference to the spectators 'eyes' and 'sight':

Noble Spectators, this play that you'l see,
Is taken out of Britains History [...]
But if it pleases not your Eyes or sight
She doth not care, since it pleas'd her to write [...].[26]

Cavendish's claim that the only stage for which she wrote was 'My brain the Stage'[27] is much undermined by the fact of publication and by her reference to how her plays should be made real in the reading. Not only does she demonstrate her awareness of the state of the public theatres in England, in her epistle 'To the Readers' but suggests a further practical reason why her plays might not be performed. She ends with her claim that she neither expects nor wishes them performed:

> [...] but the printing of my Playes spoils them for ever to be Acted; for what men are acquainted with, is despised, at lest neglected; for the newness of Playes, most commonly, takes the Spectators, more than the Wit, Scenes, or Plot, so that my Playes would seem lame or tired in action, and dull to hearing on the Stage, for which reason, I shall never desire they should be Acted; but if they delight or please the Readers, I shall have as much satisfaction as if I had the hands of applause from the Spectators.[28]

Cavendish's stage directions, although simple, set up a decidedly practical framework for her plays that is in direct opposition to her notion of her brain as her stage, and the 'theatre of the mind'. It is, in fact, much like the practical framework of the court masque. In the tableau in *The Convent of Pleasure* 'The *Scene* is opened, and there is presented a Rock as in the Sea, whereupon sits the Princess [...]; the rest of the Ladies sit somewhat lower, drest like Water Nymphs [...].'[29] Dawn Lewcock has shown that scenic effects were in use at court and that later:

> staging derived from the court masque stage devised by Inigo Jones for James I and Charles I. The masque stage had used sliding shutters, the *machina ductilis*, or the turning platform or spindle, the *machina versatilis*, to show spectacle and embellish effects [...] but the general public theatres had not had this facility before and few outside the Interregnum court circle would have seen it or had working experience of it.[30]

Cavendish is dramaturgically aware, describing the scene as 'opened', the princess sitting higher, the ladies 'somewhat lower' and so controlling spectacle and visual effect. It would appear too that she was able to adapt, or at least experiment with contemporary theatrical trends. *The Sociable Companions; or the Female Wits* features the witty couples sparring towards marriage so typical of the popular plays of the Restoration. This active engagement is in direct contrast to the almost anti-marriage separatism of *The Female Academy* and *The Convent of Pleasure*, and shows a pragmatic post-war view of marriage as a form of survival.

All three girls are well born but cannot rely on their cavalier brothers to provide for them. In collusion with the prevailing trends, where the rising gentry would cast about for women with titles and good connections, but no dowries, *The Sociable Companions, or The Female Wits*, shows the heroines landing professional husbands by craft and intelligence. The play ends with four marriages about to take place.[31]

Behn was, from 1670, along with Thomas Otway, a mainstay of The Dukes Company, managed between 1668 and 1673 by Lady Davenant, Sir Richard Davenant's widow.[32] Behn tailored much of her writing to the talents of the stars of the day, creating roles for Elizabeth Barry, Thomas Betterton, William Smith, Betty Currer, Mary Leigh and the comic talents of Cave Underhill and James Nokes. She had notoriously high standards concerning production of her work. Her epistle to the reader prefacing *The Dutch Lover* (performed in 1673) explains that the play:

> was hugely injur'd in the Acting, for 'twas done so imperfectly as never any was before [...] the Plot being busie [...] and so requiring a continual attention, which being interrupted by the intolerable negligence of some that acted in it, must needs much spoil the beauty on't. My Dutch Lover spoke little of what I intended for him, but supply'd it with a great deal of idle stuff, which I was wholly unacquainted with, till I had heard it first from him; so that Jack-Pudding ever us'd to do: which though I knew before, I gave him yet the part because I knew him so acceptable to most o' th' lighter Periwigs about the Town [...] I intended him a habit much more notably ridiculous, which if it can ever be important was so here [...] Lastly, my Epilogue was promis'd me by a Person who had surely made it good, if any, but he failing of his word, deputed one, who had made it as you see [...] The Prologue is by misfortune lost.[33]

In the 1690 dedication to *The Widow Ranter*, which was performed and failed months after her death in 1688, G. J. (probably George Jenkins) sympathised:

> The Play had not that Success which it deserv'd [...] The main fault ought to lye on those who had the management of it. Had our Authour been alive she would have Committed it to the Flames rather than suffer'd it to have been Acted with such Omissions as was made [...] and Lastly, many of the Parts being false Cast, and given to those whose Tallants and Genius's suited not our Authors Intention [...].[34]

Both the epistle and dedication indicate the realities of professional production; the lottery of casting and the risk of clumsy editing (as is made clear below) for example. Behn shows an awareness of the risks to her writing in passage from play to performance. Cavendish makes clear in one of her epistles 'To the Readers', that she understands editing to be important to the crafting of the texts and the actual writing process:

> I Have heard that such Poets that write Playes, seldome or never join or sow the several Scenes together; they are two several Professions, at least not usual for rare Poets to take that pains; like as great Taylors, the Master only cuts out and shapes, and his Journy-men and Apprentices join and sow them together; but I like as a poor Taylor was forced to do all my self, as to cut out, shape, join and sow each several Scene together, without any help or direction; wherefore I fear they are not so well done but that there will be many faults found; but howsoever, I did my best indeavour, and took great pains in the ordering and joining thereof, for which I hope my Learned Readers will pardon the errors therein, and excuse me the worker thereof.[35]

Cavendish probably based her metaphor on the collaborations between the Duke and other playwrights, but she shows no awareness of editing as it might pertain to production. She is however concerned for her plays' reception, fearing that they might be 'hissed off from the Stage'.[36] Her concern is indeed justified. Her depiction of alternative female environments, like the convent and the academy, in which women conduct their own lives, without interference from men or indeed society, would have been considered deeply disturbing by the audiences of the 1660s.

In *The Female Academy* women claim the right to speak and discourse on chosen topics, but to avoid the stigma that attaches to speaking in public the woman speak in a self-created privacy. The women have a voice, that can be heard through the grille or grate that separates them from the outside world. In a reversal of the traditional position, the women are heard but not seen. This disrupts traditional courtship patterns and is a source of social anxiety for both the male and female auditors outside the Academy. This display of intelligence without access also serves to eroticise the activity of debate. Their vocal power is being flaunted along with their independence, and men are reduced to frustrated supplicants:

> Those women that retire themselves from the Company of men, are very ungratefull; as, first to Nature, because she made them only for breed; next to men who are their Defenders, Protectors, their Nourishers, their Maintainers, their Instructers [...] wherefore it is a great ingratitude, nay a horid ingratitude in those women, that denye men their Company, Conversation, and Communication; wherefore men have not only Reason to take it ill, but to be angry with those women that shun or restrain their Company from them [...].[37]

Having exhibited their intelligence in a context that has not compromised their modesty or virtue, at the end of the play the women make themselves available for marriage, as potential intellectual partners. In *Loves Glory and Deaths Banquet*, Lady Sanspareille embraces the possibility of censure by expressing her ideas in a public, albeit a controlled scholarly environment, and again this incites her male auditors to adulation verging on desire:

honour this Virgin whose wit is supreme, whose judgement is Serene as is the Sky [...] her words so sweet, like to harmonious musick in the Aire, that charms our Senses and delights the Soul, and turns all passions in our hearts to love [....].[38]

Everything Margaret Cavendish wrote was intended for publication. Publishing, however, may be simply the business of seeing one's ideas in a printed, bound volume, but it is also to invite public examination. Here again we are reminded of the prologue to *The Apocriphal Ladies* and her references to 'eyes' and 'sight'. Although cloistering her characters and only allowing fractured erotic glimpses, Cavendish was, in creating these characters and in her own copious publication, one of the first of the generation of female writers who, to quote Ros Ballaster, 'wilfully made its sex visible.'[39]

If Cavendish's heroines are experimenting with ways of living outside of conventional familial structures, the dominant theme in Behn's dramas is that of a woman's position within the prevailing conventions of marriage and the family, and all her plays focus on oppressive familial relationships. For a play to have any kind of success in the theatre, attacks on the status quo needed to be extremely subtle or adding to an argument already under discussion.[40] In Behn's case I think she was doing both. In crafting sympathetic characters like the sisters Florinda and Hellena in first part of *The Rover, or, the Banish't Cavaliers* (1677) and Lady Fulbank and Leticia in *The Luckey Chance* (1687) and placing them within the confines of the arranged marriage or impending arranged marriage, she was adding to the debate about the right of children to make their own choice of marriage partner.[41] In Cavendish's *The Sociable Companions; or The Female Wits* Lady Prudence asks her father's permission to choose her own marriage partner. She not only chooses very wisely, choosing an older man who loves her to the point of rejecting her dowry, she also defends her choice at a public gathering:

> Concerning the Church and State, since they do allow of buying and selling young Maids to Men to be their Wives, they cannot condemn those Maids that make their bargain to their own advantage, and chuse rather to be bought then sold, and I confess I am one of the number of those; for I'le rather chuse an old Man that buys me with his Wealth, then a young one, whom I must purchase with my Wealth; who, after he has wasted my Estate, may sell me to Misery and Poverty. Wherefore, our Sex may well pray, From Young Mens ignorance and follies, from their pride, vanity and prodigality, their gaming, quareling, drinking and whoring, their pocky and diseased bodies, their Mortgages, Debts and Serjeants, their Whores and Bastards, and from all such sorts of Vices and Miseries that are frequent amongst Young Men, Good Lord deliver Us.[42]

Lady Prudence views her younger suitors as rapacious and dangerous whatever their birth or breeding. Behn's city comedies, on the other hand, depict the older men as lecherous, mercantile and misogynistic. They have definite rates of exchange for their women. In *The Luckey Chance* Sir Cautious Fulbank values his wife's chastity as being worth £300; Francisco in *The False Count* (1682) refuses to pay Julia's ransom;[43] and in *The Amorous Prince* (1671) Laura's father and brother are prepared to make her available as the Prince's mistress in return for political favour.[44] Behn's young heroes have little other than their sexual attractiveness to commend them. If Behn's characters are suggesting a rejection of marriage as practised, the plays present a complaint rather than a real criticism of marriage as an institution. Women's limited options and parental control are being addressed but a serious suggestion of alternative domestic arrangements is not negotiated. The stronger suggestion is that marriage is only an honourable institution, when the parties concerned are committed out of love for one another. Depictions of women devising environments that are not under male control as in Cavendish's *The Convent of Pleasure* and *The Female Academy*, offer living arrangements that render men superfluous. Cavendish even suggests that the convent is a means of relieving women of the burden of depending on men for their livelihood as well as resolving the dilemma of the woman who has no dowry with which to secure such a livelihood. These utopian scenarios suggest women taking care of their own future rather than fighting off the competition as Hellena does Angelica Bianca in *The Rover*.

Both Cavendish and Behn are writing about that fantasy space between two states of ownership, a fictitious period of autonomy between being owned by a father and being owned by a husband. In *The Rover* this period lasts only the duration of the carnival. The reality for most women was that of moving directly from one state of being owned to the other. Indeed in all the plays discussed the heroines have few choices apart from marriage. Cavendish, however, presents her readers with unnerving alternatives. While Hellena in *The Rover* is trying to escape the convent, Lady Happy in *The Convent of Pleasure* embraces the idea of withdrawal from the world and its social pressures. The courtesan Angelica Bianca in *The Rover* appears to represent a woman making her own choices, but she is still totally dependent on her paying customers to survive. The tenuous balance of her unmarried life is disrupted when she confuses financial barter with pledges of love. While Behn was depicting Angelica Bianca in a sympathetic light, the courtesan too, is a socially sanctioned role and does not threaten existing structures. Behn, herself a widow, enjoyed the only acceptable single state, that of widowhood. By engaging in professional activity, and entering into the discussion of sexual behaviour, she forfeited her right to respectable widowhood, no matter how discreet her private life. Her performance of a professional persona was to attract the label of 'punk-poetess' that was to serve as a warning for those women who might have hoped to follow in her footsteps.[45] Both Cavendish and Behn were forced to bear the brunt of resentment from both men and women, for moving from silence to discourse. Cavendish, married to a respected aristocrat, had no prospects to mar and Behn, not on the marriage market, had already discarded the commodity value of her honour. In embracing fame at the risk of infamy, both women speculated with changes in accepted female roles. In the very act of writing for publication or performance they followed where their heroines led.

If Cavendish's heroines use separation and withdrawal to realise their objectives, Behn's comedies, in common with the other more popular writers of the period, focus on active engagement between the sexes. The better known popular comedies of the Restoration period feature a sparring courtship; the heroines make a show of autonomy and freedom. They sparkle with wit and intelligence, all of which helps them to bring the rake into submission and tempt him into settling down. The happy ending is the marriage itself. Restoration heroines like Etheredge's Harriet in *The Man of Mode* (1676) and Congreve's Millamant in *The Way of the World* (1700) have not actually gained financial, intellectual or even physical independence. They enter negotiated marriages, with promises of greater fairness, but they are marriages nonetheless. Behn's women characters engage in witty exchanges with their suitors, not just displaying their intelligence, but using wit to challenge the men. Hellena in *The Rover*, for example, does not shy away from the business of finding and securing a lover or husband:

> nay I am resolv'd to provide my self this Carnival, if there be ere a handsome proper fellow of my humour above ground [...] have I not a World of Youth? a humour gay? a Beauty passable? a Vigour desirable? [...] and sense enough to know how all these ought to be employ'd to the best advantage; yes I do and will [...].[46]

At the same time, she is only prepared to deal with Willmore on her own terms. When he balks at marriage she is quick to point out the consequences of his 'we'l have no Vows but Love,' with 'what shall I get? A cradle full of noise and mischief, with a pack of repentance at my back?'[47] Behn is also concerned with the notion of honour as it pertains to love. In *The Town-Fopp* (1676) it is clearly deemed more honourable to honour earlier vows made during a prior betrothal:

Bell[mour]	[...] Besides, Sir, I have given my Heart and Faith, And any second Marriage is Adultery.
Lord [Plotwell]	Heart and Faith, I am glad 'tis no worse; if the Ceremony of the Church has not past, 'tis well enough.
Bell[mour]	All Sir, that Heaven, and Love requires, is past.[48]

Both *The Town-Fopp* and *The Luckey Chance* feature marriages that need to be 'undone' in favour of real love:

Dia[na]	[...] undo that knot, that ties us two.
Lord [Plotwell]	How! this Request from thee! who lov'd him once, and wish'd no good beyond possessing him.

Dia[na]	Heaven hast not, Sir, decreed us for each other, Something of Fate or Chance Has otherwise dispos'd those first Resolves.
Lord [Plotwell]	Too virtuous Maid , I know thou dost but feign, His wickedness has forc'd thee to this change.
Dia[na]	No, Sir, were he the only Man Of kind and good, I never wou'd be his. – And if you shou'd compel me, I shou'd live The infamous Reproach of my whole Sex.
Lord [Plotwell]	Well, and you Sir, that are the cause of this, What canst thou say to move me for thy Pardon?
Bell[mour]	[...] I only say *Celinda* is my Wife [...].
Lord [Plotwell]	There only wants the ceremony of the Law to undo What's between you and *Diana*, if she remain a Virgin.[49]

Behn depicts a society where individuals are at odds with established institutions. Her older characters attempt to take advantage of accepted marital practices, while the younger characters try to circumvent them. Rejecting the passive acceptance of parental choices, they choose to take an active role in selecting their marriage partners, and privilege love over duty.

In *The Rover* Behn's women are almost as physically active as the men. Hellena in Act I Scene 1 describes marriage as 'a worse Confinement than a religious Life' and she and Florinda escape their domestic confines, run around the town, don disguises and outwit their families. Behn at the same time does not deny the dangers inherent in such freedom, and in Act IV, Scene 3 Florinda is almost raped, as a result of her mobility. In spite of the underlying threat of danger (used to great dramatic effect by Behn) this is in contrast to the confinement and enclosure of most of Wycherly and Congreve's women. In Cavendish's *Bell in Campo*, Lady Victoria marches a female army off to war and gives instructions as to the bracing physical activity that should occupy their spare time, although this seems characteristic of only one character in her plays:

> Be it known, observed and practiced, that none unless visibly sick to be idle, but imployed in some Masculine action, as when not imployed against an Enemy, and that they are not imployed about the works, forts or trenches, but have spare time to imploy themselves, in throwing the Bar, Tripping, Wrastling, Running, Vaulting, Riding, and the like exercise.[50]

More generally, Cavendish's heroines achieve autonomy by withdrawal and separation. The convent in the *Convent of Pleasure* is a means to escape from male demands and enjoy the company of like-minded women. It is the women's choice, and it is not permanent. In Behn's *The Rover* it is the confinement of a convent, chosen by her brother, that Hellena is trying to escape. One of Behn's most memorable characters, Hellena moves out of the house to find herself a husband, and so wrest her life from control by the male members of her family. Behn's treatment of physical activity as a form of autonomy is also facilitated by her use of the breeches part in other plays like *The Town-Fopp.*[51]

Cavendish's female characters reveal and exhibit. She creates the intellectually fertile woman, highly desirable, and carefully displayed, or the celebrity-heroine whose army can make up for the inadequacies of their male counterparts, but whose post-war role is to be exhibited and adored in procession and then to negotiate domestic changes. It is the separation of women into independent all-women groups that creates a social anxiety that results in attention to the women's discourse. They thus emphasise the margin to which they have removed themselves, and it is the display of discourse that creates an exchange between viewer and viewed. Behn requested:

> the Priviledge for my Masculine Part the Poet in me [...] to tread in those successful Paths my Predecessors have so long thriv'd in, to take those Measures that both the Ancient and Modern Writers have set me, and by which they have pleas'd the World so well.[52]

In taking these 'measures', Behn pits her heroines against a patriarchal social order which acts out a form of liberal contract theory. The tyrannous parent or husband justifies her heroines' 'disobedience' to 'unjust commands'. To give up being acted for, women must act for themselves. Where the social order offers only containment and commodification the heroine has to enter the marketplace to perform the role of broker for herself. It was only in this carefully constructed performance that the Self, the Woman and the professional could be reconciled and protected. Behn's own experience of actively selling her resources in the theatrical marketplace is performed by her characters who must 'hang out their sign', to attract and negotiate a livelihood, or go out into the streets to avoid marital or religious confinement.[53]

If both Cavendish and Behn set significant precedents, they set them in these very different ways and by exploiting different structures. Cavendish exploited her position of marital security in both the sexual and financial arenas. She also spoke from the lofty position of aristocratic privilege within which she could discuss the idea of female agency and capacity. Behn exploited the mercantile realities of the London stage in the 1670s. She wrote stageable material that not only contributed to the escalating contemporary discussion of marriage taking place on the stage and in the pamphlet wars, she added to the discourse by using her professional visibility, her woman's perspective on the institution of marriage, delivered from the stage by yet another professional female, the actress.

The form or structure of Cavendish's plays may have been less problematic for a theatre management than her subject matter. Her representation of gender and women's ability to control their position in society by separation, withdrawal or controlled display may well have constituted a problem for any theatre manager who might have considered staging one of her plays in the 1660s and 1670s. As Susan Wiseman has shown, Cavendish's dramatic construction appears less eccentric than critical opinion has claimed, when compared to Thomas Killigrews's ten act drama, among others.[54] In any event, professional production of her plays would have significantly influenced that structure. Another major difference between Cavendish's plays and those of Behn, is the form in which they survived. Behn's plays were published after their performance and were revived after her death. Original play texts are much modified in performance and often tailored for the limitations of the lead players as well as the playhouse. *The Widow Ranter*, referred to earlier, suffered significant editing at the hands of the theatre management during its posthumous revival:

> For example, they thought fit to leave out a Whole Scene of the *Virginian Court of Judicature* [...] on which depended a great part of the Plot, and wherein were many unusuall and very Natural Jests which would at least have made some sort of People laugh: In another Part of the Play is Omitted the appearance of the Ghost of the *Indian King* [...].[55]

Cavendish's plays were never subjected to the rigours of professional editing. Just how rigorous this could be is made quite clear by surviving Restoration promptbooks.

James Shirley provides a good working model because at least sixteen of Shirley's plays were revived after 1660, and the innovations of the Restoration stage and the production values of the theatre had a significant effect on those revivals.[56] The eighteen year period during which the professional theatre was banned provided a gap in the traditions established during the early part of the century. While Davenant and Killigrew were men of the pre-Interregnum theatre, as were many of their surviving older actors, they were compelled to respond to the challenges of a younger, more novelty-hungry audience.

An analysis of the changes made to texts and the approaches to staging and interpretation can lead us to a tentative mapping out of a form of 'direction' that probably characterised a company's priorities when mounting a production. I have chosen to consider Shirley's plays in attempting to recognise a characteristic approach to production during the 1660s and 1670s because there are four known, marked, promptbooks available for study.[57] Close study of these promptbooks gives us some information about how Restoration innovations (moveable scenery, female performers and improved permanent theatres) and Restoration attitudes (explicit interest in sexual behaviour, changing attitude to marriage and the family) may have affected the staging and acting approaches and hence the overall approach to production. For the managements who chose to revive his plays Shirley may have represented a playwright with a proven track record, but their primary concern may well have been cost. It cost half as much to license a revival than to license a new play.[58]

The actual markings in the extant promptbooks of Shirley's plays differ according to the company that held the license. The prompter for the Duke's company used a different set of signs for marking entrances or scene changes, but these are fairly clear and are of backstage interest rather than dramatic significance.[59] The markings that influence the dramatic content of the plays are the cuts and textual changes. Comparing uncut passages with passages as they were performed for a Restoration audience it appears that dramatic priorities were clarity, action and plot. This would appear to be standard treatment of a text in order to render it producible, given the practical constraints of the professional theatre in the 1660s and 1670s.

The prompt-copy of Shirley's *The Maides Revenge* in the Harvard Theatre Collection, a 1639 First Quarto used by the King's Company, contains extensive (although badly cropped) manuscript prompt notes for performance probably at Lincolns Inn Fields in 1673–74.[60] I have indicated the passages cut from the text by square brackets and striking out the text. The largest passages are generally removed from the beginning and end of the play, those sections that appear to feature the least stage action. I offer sections from the first act of the play to show the extent of some of the editing that took place.

Act I, scene 1 starts with very uncertain cuts. Lines that are definitely scored through delete blood and kin references. The first substantial removal of text takes place after the entrance of the sisters' father, Gaspar de Vilarezo:

> *Vil*[*arezo*]*:* Give your observance then, I know their businesse,
> *Catalina* and *Berinthia* are the starrs
> Direct them hither, *Gaspars* house shall give
> Respect to all, [~~but they are two such Iewels,~~
> ~~I must dispose maturely, I should else~~
> ~~Returne ingratitude upon the heavens~~
> ~~For leaving me such pledges, nor am I,~~
> ~~Like other fathers carried with the streame~~
> ~~Of love toth youngest, as they were in birth~~
> ~~They had my tendernesse, *Catalina* then~~
> ~~Is eldest in my care, *Berinthia*~~
> ~~Her childs part too, both faire and vertuous;~~
> ~~But daughters are held losses to a family,~~
> ~~Sonnes onely to maintaine honour and stemme~~
> ~~Alive in their posterity, and now I think on't,~~]
> My sonne *Sebastiano* hath been slow
> In his returne from *Lisbone*, oh that boy

Renewes my age with hope, and hath returnd
My care in education, weight for weight,
with noble quality, [~~well belov'd by th' best~~
~~O' th Dons in *Spaine* and *Portugall*, whose loves~~
~~Do often stretch his absence to such length~~
~~As this hath beene~~]

Cou[nt de monte Nigro]:
[...] oh my *Dona*
Catalina! Well would I were so happy once to
Maintaine some honorable duell for thy sake, I shall
Nere be well, till I have kild some body; ~~fight, tis true~~
~~I have never yet flesh: my selfe in blood, no body~~
~~Would quarell with me, but I finde my spirit prompt~~
~~If occasion would but winke at me, why not? Wherefore has~~
~~Nature given me these brawny armes, this manly bulke,~~
~~And these Collossian supporters, nothing but to sling~~
~~The sledge, or pitch the bare, and play with~~
~~Axletrees;~~] if thou lovest me, do but command me
some worthy service; pox a dangers I weigh 'em no
More than fleabitings, would some body did hate that
Face, now I wish it with all my heart. [...]

Vila[rezo]: Sebastiano, thou hast largely recompenc'd
Thy tedious absence, you shall dishonour me,
Vnlesse you thinke your selfe as welcome here;
As at your *Eluas* Castle, [~~*Vilarezo*~~
~~Was once as you are Sprightly, and though I say it~~
~~Maintaind my fathers reputation,~~
~~And honour of our house with actions~~
~~Worthy our name and family, but now,~~
~~Time hath let fall cold snow upon my haires,~~
~~Ploughed on my browes the furrowes of his anger,~~
~~Disfurnished me of active blood, and wrapt me~~
~~Halfe in my seare cloth, yet I have minde~~
~~That bids me honour vertue, where I see it~~
~~Bud forth and spring so hopefully~~.]
Anto[nio]: You speake all noblenesse, [~~and encourage me~~
~~To spend the greenenesse of my rising yeares~~
~~So to thadvantage, that at last I may~~
~~Be old like you.~~]
Vila[rezo]: Daughters speake his welcome, *Catalina*.
Cata[lina]: Sir you are most welcome.
Count [*de monte Nigro*]: Howes that? she sayes he is most welcome, he were

Not best love her, [~~she never made me such a reverence~~
~~For all the kisses I have bestowed upon her since~~
~~I first opened my affection,~~] I do not like this
Fellow, I must fain to use doctor *Sharkins* cunnning.[61]

It is easy to see from this vigorous editing that unwieldy texts presented no problem to a management intending to stage a particular play. It is worth remembering that Shirley was not present to protect his text in any way, and Aphra Behn's complaints about the management's treatment of *The Dutch Lover* had to be made at the time of publication. It is possible that a theatre management might have considered it impolitic, given Cavendish's social status, to give her plays a similar draconian editing.

Lynda R. Payne suggests that 'with extensive editing and rearranging of scenes, three [of Cavendish's plays] – *Love's Adventures*, *Bell in Campo* and *The Convent of Pleasure* – may contain the dramatic elements and liveliness necessary to succeed on stage.'[62] I would draw her attention to the first professional staging of *The Sociable Companions; or The Female Wits*, which took place at the Canal Café Theatre in London in January 1995. It ran for 4 weeks to capacity houses and broke the theatre's box office record. Paula Webb reviewing the production for *Time Out* (January 25–February 1 1995) claimed 'its theatrical merit is no less than that of Cavendish's male contemporaries.'

Gweno Williams in referring to her student performance of some of the scenes from *The Convent of Pleasure* makes much of her decision not to cut or edit any of Cavendish's text. 'There was an agreed commitment to keep the text intact in performance, without any cuts.'[63] Even Cavendish herself removed scenes from her plays when they seemed too long. One example is *The Presence* where 29 scenes 'were design'd to be put into the *Presence*; but by reason I found they would make that Play too long, I thought it requisite to Print them by themselves.'[64] A play, whether for public or private performance is not a sacrosanct literary text. It is a working document that forms the basis of the resulting performance, and is ultimately defined by the performance. This is the reason most plays are published after performance. Unsuccessful plays were very often not published at all.

Williams's commitment to preserving Cavendish's printed text inviolate undermines the complementary nature of production and performance. Without the performance the play remains a text, its dramaturgical potential unexplored. What is characteristic of producing a public performance is that play is modified for the stage. It was so in Shakespeare's time and is still the case today. It is intrinsic to the very nature of public and professional performance that the play becomes tailored to the requirements of the theatre. Williams' experiment also only covered Act 2, scene iv to Act 4, scene iv which might well prove sections of a play performable, but does nothing to prove the play producible. Assessing the producibility of a play requires a consideration of the entire play. Some scenes are more strongly crafted than others, weaker scenes need the overall structure of the play to support them, and a management needs a whole play to offer an audience. One would never assess the producibility of a Behn or Shirley play based on a number of performed scenes.

Margaret Cavendish's *The Sociable Companions; or the Female Wits* succeeded on the London stage because it was treated like any other reasonably well-crafted play text. It was treated as Aphra Behn's *The Rover* was treated by the Royal Shakespeare Company in 1986, and as any other piece of drama written to be performed whether in the 1660s or the early twenty-first century.[65] Texts are proved performable when performed and producible when produced. Promptbooks prove that a dramatic text becomes a play when it is handed over to players. To treat Cavendish's plays as a sacred text that cannot be tampered with is to deny her work the ability to prove its dramaturgical potential. What the plays need is a professional approach that has the courage to make considered and creative editorial decisions. *The Sociable Companions; or The Female Wits* needed surprisingly little editing. Some scenes were moved to facilitate exits and costume changes, as plays have always had to be adapted to the practicalities of the playhouse. Interestingly enough, when a rehearsed reading was staged at the Theatre Museum (Covent Garden, 1993) the stage was vast and the play was untouched. The reading (which was witnessed by Williams) did communicate as a museum piece. With scenes following as written, and entrances and exits not facilitating pace and motivation, the play lacked momentum. Once committed to a specific professional venue and handed over to professional director, with a history of working with Shakespearean comedy, the play sprang to life. Very few directors or producers would consider it essential or even advisable to stage *Hamlet* in its entirety, whether from a 'good' or 'bad' text.

It seems clear that Margaret Cavendish's relationship with the professional theatre managements of the 1660s would have been facilitated by her social position as well as her connections through the Duke. Evidence of Restoration production values, as can be seen by the treatment of texts revived during the first two decades of the Restoration, shows that Cavendish's texts would have been handled in much the same way as Shirley's or Behn's by the management prepared to attempt a performance of any of her plays. These factors strongly suggest that subject matter was the real obstacle to a staging of her texts. For a twenty-first-century audience her subject matter is no obstacle. An interested director might even consider her discussion of gender relations topical. The 1995 production of *The Female Wits* proved that at least one play by Margaret Cavendish is not just producible, but indeed 'good box-office'. We can judge Margaret Cavendish's dramas by the product on stage. Cavendish may have considered her brain the stage, but when a demanding London theatre critic declared Cavendish's play as good as those written by her male contemporaries, it was because she saw evidence of that on the boards.

Notes

[1] Gerard Langbaine, in *An Account of the English Dramatick Poets. Or, Some Observations and Remarks On the Lives and Writings, of all those that have Publish'd either Comedies, Tragedies, Tragi-Comedies, Pastorals, Masques, Interludes, Farces, or Opera's in the English Tongue* (Oxford, 1691), includes Margaret Cavendish, alongside William, listing all her published plays in detail, attaching the titles of her other published works at the end (see pp. 390–394). Langbaine also notes that one of her plays *The Comical Hash* had 'not been in any Catalogue before.' (p. 392), suggesting that all the others have been listed in other catalogues, not necessarily his own. While this particular catalogue was published three years after Behn's death in 1688, the plays were quite clearly in circulation during the period in which Behn was producing plays for The Duke's Company.

[2] On the Civil War and its effect on Cavendish's dramatic writing see Susan Wiseman, 'Gender and Status in Dramatic Discourse: Margaret Cavendish, Duchess of Newcastle' in *Women, Writing, History*, pp. 159–77.

[3] See, for example, Nancy Cotton, *Women Playwrights in England c.1363–1750* (New Jersey: Associated University Press, 1980), p. 42.

[4] Virginia Woolf, *A Room of One's Own*, (London: Hogarth Press, 1929), p. 59.

[5] *Margaret the First*, p. 161.

[6] Cotton, *Women Playwrights*, p. 60.

[7] See Susan Wiseman, *Drama and Politics in the English Civil War* (Cambridge: Cambridge University Press, 1998), 'Introduction: how the drama disappeared', pp. 1–16.

[8] Sophie Tomlinson, '"My Brain the Stage": Margaret Cavendish and the Fantasy of Female Performance' in *Women, Texts and Histories*, pp. 134–36 (p. 138).

[9] On Margaret Cavendish and the literary milieu of Henrietta Maria's court see Anna Battigelli, *Margaret Cavendish and the Exiles of the Mind* (Lexington: University Press of Kentucky, 1998), pp. 11–38.

[10] *Kingdom's Weekly Intelligencer sent abroad to prevent mis-information*, Number 198, Tuesday February 23–Tuesday March 1646, p. 438.

[11] Tomlinson, 'My Brain the Stage', pp. 134–5.

[12] The copy of Cavendish's *Orations* (1662) owned by the Earl of Bridgewater is Harvard University Library, Houghton *f EC65 N4322 662o (A). It is bound in calf with the Bridgewater crest stamped in blind on both covers. See the letter of thanks from John Bridgewater to Margaret Cavendish dated 30 December 1662, in *Letters and Poems* (1676), pp. 77–8. The Harvard University Library copy of *Playes* (1662) is Harry Elkins Widener Collection, HEW 7.10.18 F.

[13] Samuel Pepys, *Diary*, 30 March 1667, April, 1667, cit. Helen McAfee (ed.), *Pepys on the Restoration Stage*, (Newhaven: Yale University Press, 1919), pp. 171–72.

[14] For a near-contemporary view of Behn's borrowings see Langbaine, *An Account of the English Dramatick Poets*, pp. 17–18.

[15] Nancy Cotton contradicts herself in *Women Playwrights in England c.1363–1750* when she persists in referring to William Cavendish as an 'amateur playwright' as opposed to 'professional' playwrights like Shirley, Dryden and Shadwell who 'turned the Duke's sketches into professional plays which were then performed in the London theatres.' (see p. 48). By her own admission 'By the Restoration persons of the highest social rank in England were writing for the public stage.' p. 40.

[16] 'To the Readers', *Playes* (1662), unsigned page between sig. A3 and sig. A4 (sig. χ verso).

[17] Cavendish and Behn can be seen as examples of the steady progress from patronage towards professionalism. Richard Helgerson in *Self-Crowned Laureates. Spenser, Jonson, Milton and the Literary System*, (Berkeley and London: University of California Press, 1983) describes the changing attitudes towards literary production. Cavendish's literary ambitions are characteristic of what Helgerson calls the 'laureate' tradition. Behn, on the other hand, was forced to argue with booksellers to extract just payment for verses, and was reputed to have produced a play within six days in the hopes of another successful benefit in the theatre. See Warrren Chernaik, *Sexual Freedom in Restoration Literature*, (Cambridge: Cambridge University Press, 1995), p. 161.

[18] Wiseman, *Drama and Politics in the Civil War*, p. 92.

[19] *Playes* (1662), 'To the Readers', unsigned page between sig. A4 and A5 (sig. 2χ recto).

[20] *Playes* (1662), 'To the Readers', unsigned page between sig. A5 and sig. A6 (sig. 3χ recto).

[21] Aphra Behn, 'To the Reader', *Sir Patient Fancy: A Comedy As it is Acted at the Duke's Theatre.* (London, 1678), sig. A verso.

[22] John W. Saunders's whistlestop treatment of the Interregnum and Restoration in *The Profession of English Letters* (London: Routledge, 1964) makes no mention of any women dramatists during this period.

[23] Catherine Gallagher, 'Who was That Masked Woman? The Prostitute and the Playwright in the Comedies of Aphra Behn', in Janet Todd (ed.) *Aphra Behn, New Casebooks* (Basingstoke: Macmillan Press, 1999), pp. 12–31 (p. 13). See also Derek Hughes, 'The Masked Woman Revealed; or, the prostitute and the playwright in Aphra Behn criticism', *Womens Writing*, 7:2 (2000), 149–164.

[24] *Playes* (1662), untitled note, sig. A6 verso.

[25] Elaine Hobby, *Virtue of Necessity; English Women's Writing 1646–1688* (London: Virago, 1988), pp. 110–111.

[26] 'Prologue' preceding *A Comedy of the Apocriphal Ladies* in *Playes* (1662), p. 635.

[27] 'The Dedication', *Playes* (1662), sig. A2 recto.

[28] 'To the Readers', *Playes* (1662), unsigned page between sig. A3 and A4 (sig. χ verso).

[29] *The Convent of Pleasure*, IV.1, p. 41 in *Plays* (1668).

[30] Dawn Lewcock, 'More for Seeing than for Hearing: Behn and the use of Theatre' in Janet Todd (ed.) *Aphra Behn Studies* (Cambridge: Cambridge University Press, 1996), pp. 66–83 (p. 66).

[31] *The Sociable Companions; or The Female Wits* is the first play in the 1668 volume, published with *The Presence, Scenes, The Bridals, The Convent of Pleasure* and *A Piece of a Play*. However, it could be argued that this play was the last written, in that it shows a progression in subject matter and formal construction.

[32] Leslie Hotson, *The Commonwealth and Restoration Stage* (Cambridge Mass.: Harvard University Press, 1928), p. 227.

[33] Aphra Behn, *The Dutch Lover, a Comedy acted at the Dukes Theatre* (London, 1673), 'An Epistle to the Reader', sig. a verso.

[34] G. J.'s dedication 'To the much Honoured Madam Welldon', in Aphra Behn, *The*

Widow Ranter or, The History of Bacon in Virginia. A Tragi-Comedy, Acted by their Majesties Servants (London, 1690), sig. A2 recto–verso.

[35] 'To the Readers', *Playes* (1662), unsigned page between sig. A5 and A6 (sig. 3χ verso).

[36] 'The Epistle Dedicatory', *Playes* (1662), sig. A3 recto.

[37] Cavendish, *The Female Academy*, III.14 in *Playes* (1662), pp. 664–5.

[38] Cavendish, *Youths Glory, and Deaths Banquet*, III.9 in *Playes* (1662), p. 140.

[39] Ros Ballaster, 'Seizing the means of seduction: Fiction and feminine identity in Aphra Behn and Delarivier Manley' in *Women, Writing, History*, pp. 93–108 (p. 95).

[40] *The Whole Duty of Man laid down in a plain way for the meanest reader* was published in 1658 and ran into many editions, and stated that if a parent 'will enjoin a child, upon mere motives of advantage, to marry, where there is no foundation of love, nor prospect of content; it is hardly to be thought, that such instances are to be complied with.' Cit. Alan Macfarlane, *Marriage and Love in England: Modes of Reproduction 1300–1840* (Oxford: Basil Blackwell, 1986), p. 129.

[41] See Susan Staves, *Players' Sceptres. Fictions of Authority in the Restoration.* (Lincoln and London: University of Nebraska Press, 1979), pp. 114-118, and Robert D. Hume, *The Rakish Stage. Studies in English Drama 1660-1800*, (Carbondale and Edwardsville: Southern Illinois University Press, 1983), p. 177. See also Lawrence Stone, *Road to Divorce, England 1530-1987* (Oxford: Oxford University Press, 1990), pp. 149-150 on the increase in private separation deeds.

[42] *The Sociable Companions; or The Female Wits*, p. 95, in *Plays* (1668).

[43] Aphra Behn, *The False Count, or, A New Way to play an Old Game. As it is Acted at the Dukes Theatre.* (London, 1682), IV.2, p. 45

[44] Aphra Behn, *The Amorous Prince, or the Curious Husband. A Comedy, As it is Acted at his Royal Highness, the Duke of York's Theatre* (London, 1671), III.1, pp. 35–8.

[45] Gallagher, 'The Prostitute and the Playwright', p.16.

[46] Aphra Behn, *The Rover, or, the Banish't Cavaliers. As it is Acted at His Royal Highness the Duke's Theatre* (London, 1677), I.1, p. 2.

[47] Aphra Behn, *The Rover*, V.1, p. 80.

[48] Aphra Behn, *The Town-Fopp: or Sir Timothy Tawdrey. A Comedy* (London, 1677), II.3, p. 22.

[49] Behn, *The Town-Fopp*, V.2, p. 64.

[50] Cavendish, *The First part of Bell in Campo*, III.11 in *Playes* (1662), p. 592.

[51] See 'Transvestite Heroines and the Plays in Which They Appear' in Jacqueline Pearson, *The Prostituted Muse: Images of Women & Women Dramatists, 1642–1737* (New York and London: Harvester–Wheatsheaf, 1988), pp. 100–118. Interestingly Cavendish's *The Convent of Pleasure* is one of the few plays to use a transvestite role for an actor, as opposed to the breeches part for an actress. In III.1 the Prince infiltrates the convent dressed as a princess, and then requests Lady Happy's permission to masquerade as a man. In *The Sociable Companions, or The Female Wits* Harry Sencible is dispatched disguised as a chambermaid in an attempt to marry Dick Traveller to an old woman of great fortune. These are both clearly transvestite *roles* as opposed to Cavendish's earlier experience of men playing women's parts before the formal closure of the theatres in 1642.

[52] Aphra Behn, *The Luckey Chance, or An Alderman's Bargain. A Comedy. As it is Acted by their Majesty's Servants. Wriiten by Mrs. A. Behn* (London, 1687), 'Preface', sig

[A5] recto.

[53] Janet Todd, *The Sign of Angelica: Women, Writing and Fiction 1660–1800* (London: Virago, 1989), pp. 1–10.

[54] Wiseman, *Drama and Politics*, p. 92.

[55] G. J.'s dedication 'To the much Honoured Madam Welldon', Behn, *The Widow Ranter*, sig. A2 recto.

[56] William B. Van Lennep (ed.) *The London Stage 1660-1800, Part 1, 1660-1700* (Carbondale: Southern Illinois University Press, 1965), lists nineteen plays, attributed to James Shirley, performed between 1660 and 1700. (see pp. cclxxiv-cclxxv).

[57] These can all be found in Edward A. Langhans, *Restoration Promptbooks*, (Carbondale and Edwardsville: Southern Illinois University Press, 1981).

[58] 'Articles of Agreement between Herbert and Killigrew', 4 June 1662, document 139 in Judith Milhous and Robert D. Hume (eds.) *A Register of English Theatre Documents 1660–1737*, 2 Vols (Carbondale: Southern Illinois University Press, 1991), I, 34.

[59] For detailed information on prompt copies see Langhans, *Restoration Promptbooks*, and idem, *Eighteenth Century British and Irish Promptbooks. A Descriptive Bibliography* (Connecticut: Greenwood Press, 1987).

[60] James Shirley, *The Maides Revenge. A Tragedy. As it hath beene acted with good Applause at the private house in Dury Lane, by her Majesties servants* (London, 1639), Harvard Theatre Collection. See facsimile reproduction 13, Langhans, *Restoration Promptbooks*, pp. 197–231. On the probable dates of performance see Langhans, *Restoration Promptbooks*, pp. 35–7.

[61] Shirley, *The Maides Revenge*, I.1, sig. B2 recto–B4 verso, Langhans, *Restoration Promptbooks*, pp. 200–203.

[62] Linda R. Payne 'Dramatic dreamscape; Womens Dreams and Utopian Vision in the works of Margaret Cavendish, Duchess of Newcastle' in Mary Anne Schofield and Cecelia Macheski (eds.) *Curtain Calls. British and American Women in the Theatre 1660–1820* (Athens: Ohio University Press, 1991), pp. 18–33.

[63] Gweno Williams, '"Why may not a Lady write a good play?" : Plays by Early Modern women reassessed as performance texts' in S. P. Cerasano and Marion Wynne-Davies (eds.), *Readings in Renaissance Women's Drama Criticism, history and performance 1594–1998* (London: Routledge, 1998), pp. 95–107 (p. 100).

[64] Cavendish, *Scenes*, p. 93 in *Plays* (1668).

[65] On the Royal Shakespeare Company's adaptation of Behn's play, performed in the Swan Theatre, Stratford Upon Avon in 1986 see John Barton, 'Director's Note' in Simon Trussler (ed.) *An adaptation of The Rover (The Banished Cavaliers) by Aphra Behn. A programme/text with commentary by Simon Trussler* (London: Methuen, by arrangement with the Royal Shakespeare Company, 1986), p. 5.

7

'Making a Spectacle': Margaret Cavendish and The Staging of the Self

Rebecca D'Monté

In Mary Russo's work on women and carnival theory, she asks, 'in what sense can women really produce or make spectacles out of themselves'?[1] This is a particularly suggestive question when used to consider the life and work of Margaret Cavendish, Duchess of Newcastle. At a time when women writers were supposed to present themselves as modest and unassertive, Cavendish deliberately presented herself as ambitious for fame and glory. She was a prolific dramatist whose plays were collected into two volumes, published in 1662 and 1668, although these probably remained unperformed during her lifetime. Intriguingly, any play produced from the first volume would have made her the first female dramatist on the English professional stage, preceding Katherine Philips's adaptation *Pompey* by a year, Frances Boothby's *Marcelia* by seven years, and Aphra Behn's first play *The Forc'd Marriage* by eight years.[2] Regardless of whether these were performed or closet plays, however, these plays evince an almost obsessive concern with female spectacle and display, whilst the staging of Cavendish's own body also created a theatrical context in which her plays could be read.

The idea of staging the self or recreating oneself through performance was one that was endemic to seventeenth-century culture, a period when bodies 'made a display of themselves.'[3] Charles I, for instance, fell in love with the future queen of England when he saw her appearing in a masque at the French court (he himself was 'in disguise on his way to woo the Infanta of Spain'), whilst Henrietta-Maria's entry into England popularised the masque, which relied on spectacle, particularly of the female body.[4] The idea of display reached its inevitable apogee in the newly opened Restoration playhouses, which took on the function of licensed areas of voyeuristic pleasure. Guido Ruggiero has noted that from the beginning of the seventeenth century, buildings were being built not just to be seen, but to 'stage' those inside.[5] These included the playhouses where audiences could display themselves as much as the actors on the stage. Certainly, the introduction of actresses to England in 1660 brought with it an automatic exploitation and fetishisation of their bodies, particularly the shoulders, breasts and legs, whilst female dramatists – especially Aphra Behn – found ways to capitalise on the professed links between 'Poetess' and 'Punk'. Moreover, the audience displayed themselves as much as the actors on the stage, with Charles II, amongst others of the élite, using the playhouse as a place to exhibit his mistresses.[6]

Cavendish's plays show an awareness of this sexualised atmosphere surrounding notions of acting and display. Whilst commenting on the dangers implicit in the power of 'looking' – surveillance, control, suspicion – she also explores the ambiguous qualities of performance to enhance both her role as a woman writer and that of her female characters.[7] These women can be seen to *deliberately* present themselves as a form of theatrical spectacle as they indulge in a seductive striptease, publicly unveiling, revealing, and displaying their bodies: at the grate in *The Religious*, *The Convent of Pleasure* and *The Female Academy*, before a largely male audience in *Youths Glory and Death's Banquet*, *The Publick Wooing* and *Natures Three Daughters*, in the army camp in *Love's Adventures*, *Bell in Campo* and *The Lady Contemplation*.[8] Initially, many women seem to stage themselves as platonic love objects. Lady Ambition in *Wits Cabal* wishes 'that Nature had made me such a Beauty, as might have drawn the Eyes of the whole World as a Loadstone to gaze at it.'[9] In the first part of *The Lady Contemplation* (1662) the eponymous heroine's fantasies revolve around her feminine charms. She imagines going to meet her husband-to-be along 'streets strewed with dead Lovers, which had lived only on hopes, so long as I lived amongst them.'[10] Although she assumes a masculine role by rousing the troops, this is couched in conventional 'courtly love' terms where a woman's persuasive powers are seen to lie with her beauty.

More complexly, as we have seen in *The Several Wits*, Caprisia is consistently told that she has to temper her sharp and dangerous tongue. This she initially refuses to do, stating that she is only carrying on the tradition started by 'Grandmother Eve in Paradise'.[11] However, like Kate in *The Taming of the Shrew* (1594), when Caprisia finally falls in love with a man who is prepared to overlook her faults, her language changes from that of a shrew to that of a dutiful woman; indeed, as aforementioned, she practices how to behave, how to become an 'ideal' woman. Whether she apportions blame for her 'froward' ways to fortune, nature or education, the results are the same; she is in danger of silencing the only weapon she has against unwelcome advances: her witty tongue. Yet, by couching this compliancy in platonic love terms, Caprisia transfers her potency to more accepted places for a woman – 'eyes', 'smiles' – whilst also 'feminising' her sharp tongue:

> My smiles shall be as Baits, my eyes as Angels, where every look shall be a hook to catch a heart; I'l teach my tongue such art, to plant words on each heart, as they shall take deep root, from whence pure love shall spring.[12]

Thus, whilst Caprisia professes herself to be 'neither dishonest, unchaste, base or unworthy', she can make-believe that she can continue to control men through the love she inspires, drawing a sense of power from the only asset she has been left, her sexuality.[13]

In displaying themselves as potential objects of desire to an audience of male admirers, these women can be seen to take up positions similar to those adopted by the ladies at the Caroline court who employ the seductive language and visual appeal of platonic love. The role of the lady-in-waiting was to heighten the glamour of the queen by presenting herself as desirable and seductive, behaviour at odds with conventional views of modest womanhood; indeed Ann Rosalind Jones has described her as providing a 'generalised erotic function directly opposed to the silent fidelity demanded of the private woman.'[14] The exhibitionist and provocative nature of such a role would have been further intensified when considered alongside the feminocentric court's favoured masques, and Henrietta Maria's popularisation of the cult of platonic love, which fused petrarchan idealisation of Elizabeth I with French romance and pastoral drama. Central is the vision of woman as paradox: she is passive but cruel, virtuous but seductive, witty but aloof. Above all, her beauty inspires devotion. Like the Court ladies, her 'role is essentially one of "setting herselfe at gaze", playing *prima donna* to an audience of spectator servants whom she keeps at a distance through her artful language and wit'.[15] Yet, when Patricia Parker connects the popularity of Petrarchism with the reign of Elizabeth I, describing it as 'a politicised lyric structure inscribed within the complex sexual politics of the exceptional rule of a woman in an otherwise overwhelmingly patriarchal culture,' she astutely shows how the power of the woman is dissipated through replacing the world of politics with the world of courtly love.[16] Playing mistress to her male courtier–lover, she is the dominant partner but her control of the situation is nominal.

Nevertheless, whilst working within these literary and social conventions, Cavendish reverses beliefs concerning the platonic lady's fabricated potency, suggesting something far more subversive in the process. Unlike the platonic love poets who often portray women as passive recipients of male (sexual) desire, Cavendish's female characters frequently control their own discovery and display to explore the ambiguous qualities of theatrical performance. Although realising a conventional 'feminine' power through ensnaring men with their beauty, they also achieve a transgressive 'masculine' power through their control over language and learning, and their manipulation of the 'gaze'. Two of Cavendish's female orators, Lady Sanspareille in *Youths Glory* and Madamoiselle Grand Esprit in *Natures Three Daughters*, stage themselves before a largely male audience, with the theatrical trope particularly invoked in the case of Sanspareille who stands on 'a place raised and railed with guilt rayles.'[17] Whilst Lady Mother Love tells her daughter to display herself amongst potential suitors, and 'shoot such sharp darts through your eyes, as may wound the hardest and obduratest hearts,' Sanspareille disdainfully rejects this yielding form of power, replying 'Amorous affections, madam, and wanton glances are strangers to my eyes and heart.'[18] She does not want the 'vulgar fame' which is attached to those women who inspire others through their beauty and exists only in the here and now, but seeks for something more elevated and enduring: 'when fame is in'thron'd, all Ages gazes at it; and *being thus Supremly plac'd up high; like as an Idol gets Idolatry*: Thus singularity as well as merit, advances fame.'[19] Sanspareille can here be seen to stage herself in exactly the same way that a woman would if she were at court, but for an entirely different purpose. She deliberately draws attention to her gender by presenting her body *solus* in front of an increasingly appreciative audience. The female orator's choice of costume also accentuates this concept of 'staging' as she dresses first 'in black; fit for the gravity of the company,' and then 'in white Satin, like as a bride.'[20] For the first lecture, she 'enters upon the mounted place [...]. The Company upon her entrance seems to be struck with amaze of her beauty.' The fact that she is displaying herself as a seductress as well as a rhetorician is underscored by the philosopher's comment that they have all been invited 'to feast our eyes, not our eares.'[21] After the lecture, 'the Audience holds up their hands in admiration.'[22] Thus Sanspareille deftly lures her audience into acknowledging her intellectual gifts through the more conventional channels of appreciating her beauty and chastity first.

In *The Female Academy*, Cavendish moves from the staging of one female orator to the staging of a group. The female academy, like the convent of pleasure, is made up of unmarried women, with both plays specifically presenting retreat as a theatrical performance. In particular, the learned ladies of the academy *emphasise* their withdrawal: they enter the all-female enclave 'to speak wittily and rationally, and to behave themselves handsomly, and to live virtuously.'[23] To accentuate this display of their virtue, Cavendish provides a precise layout of the inside and outside of the academy, which segregates space according to gender, and which allows the female orators to be seen and heard through 'a large open Grate'. Susan Wiseman perceptively comments that whilst 'the listening men are allowed to watch the women orate upon the public stage [...] they are marginal, silenced onlookers to the discourses':

> A situation is set up similar to the one depicted in the frontispiece to Cavendish's *Poems and Fancies*, in which the figure of the author sits looking at the viewer, who is separated from the female figure by a railing in the foreground of the picture [...] the play presents the male gaze as controlled by and subjected to the female object of the gaze, rather than vice versa.[24]

The spectator/reader watches the men watching the women orators through a grate in the wall. The gaze is therefore doubly controlled – by Cavendish and by her female characters who retain ocular freedom (when their orations are not in progress there is nothing to look at), and freedom of speech (they choose what is being said, and therefore heard, by the men). At the end of the play, it is discovered that the learned ladies have not retired from society at all. The Matron points out the Gentlemen's understandable mistake: 'these Ladies have not vowed Virginity, or are they incloystred; for an Academy is not a Cloyster, but a School, wherein are taught how to be good Wives when they are married.'[25] With this description, Cavendish seems to be foreshadowing the work of Bathsua Makin who set up her school in order to educate women to be good companions for their husbands. Nevertheless, Cavendish's whole play would seem to militate against such a reading, as it is taken up with presenting female learning purely for scholarly intent rather than for the getting of a husband. Moreover, through staging their bodies at the grate, the Ladies have allowed men to 'gaze on their Beauties, and praise their sweet Graces', whilst more unconventionally providing themselves with an opportunity to display their intellectual skills.[26]

The correlations between display of the (feminine) body and display of the (masculine) intellect are further directed and regulated by Cavendish's literary technique which incorporates such figures of rhetoric as *copia*, *hyperbole*, and *emblazoning*. The lengthy speeches of many female characters, sometimes running into several pages, deliberately stop the dramatic flow of the play and call attention to the figure of the woman speaker standing apart. Rather than being considered as a somewhat unsophisticated method for introducing philosophical and moral arguments into the drama, this flagrant showcasing of eloquent loquaciousness bears directly on Cavendish's views about education, and as such figures unorthodox views on female learning and rationality. Moreover, a correlation can be made between these discursive orations and Cavendish's own psychological need for *all* of her words to be uttered, as instanced by her play, *The Presence* (1668), where twenty-nine of the scenes are removed because they make the play too long, but are then resurrected at the end with an explanatory note.[27] Further links between Cavendish's staging of her female characters and her own self-proclamatory style are illustrated by Nancy Vickers's comments on the verb 'to blazon' which, in the seventeenth century, conflated the French *blasonner* definition of heraldic ornamentation with the English 'to blaze': 'to proclaim as with a trumpet, to publish [...], and, by extension, to defame or celebrate.'[28] In her reading of Vickers's argument, Patricia Parker usefully reminds us at this point of the *Oxford English Dictionary* definition of 'display': '"to unfold or spread out, to describe at large in representation or narrative, and to exhibit ostentatiously to the view". It involves simultaneously an act of unfolding, offering to the eye, and the more static sense of something to be gazed upon and seen.'[29] In many ways, this linking of narrative technique and control of the 'gaze' anticipates Laura Mulvey's seminal work on the cinema:

> Going far beyond highlighting a woman's to-be-looked-at-ness, cinema builds the way she is to be looked at into the spectacle itself. Playing on the tension between film as controlling the dimension of time (editing, narrative) and film as controlling the dimension of space (changes in distance, editing), cinematic codes create a gaze, a world, and an object, thereby producing an illusion cut to the measure of desire.[30]

Cavendish's seemingly disjointed movement between scenes thus takes on the function of the modern-day cinematic dissolve and, more importantly for the purposes of display, has the effect of focusing attention on the female figure, either singly or in a group, whose predicament – often connected to male oppression – mirrors one another.[31] Beyond this, in using the blazon, which was a chief tool of petrarchan poets, Cavendish assumes control of the way in which the female body is represented; this becomes even more interesting when it is applied to figures like the Amazon rather than the more customary platonic lady. In re-appropriating and redirecting the 'male gaze', then, Cavendish expressly comments on issues of control and authority.

Judith Butler exposes the ease with which the balance of power can be shifted if desire is defined from a female rather than male perspective:

> For that masculine subject of desire, trouble becomes a scandal with the sudden intrusion, the unanticipated agency, of a female 'object' who inexplicably returns the glance, reverses the gaze, and contends the place and authority of the masculine position. The radical dependency of the masculine subject on the female 'Other' suddenly exposes his autonomy as illusory.[32]

This notion of the female Other is apparent in both Cavendish's short stories and plays, where 'the woman as stranger effortlessly and instantaneously seduces all who encounter her, and is able to profit by the recognition of her own status as fetish.'[33] So, the heroine of Cavendish's short story, *The Contract*, is always seen 'masked, muffled, and scarfed.'[34] She bears a striking similarity to Lady Sanspareille, both in the way that she dresses (she appears first in black, like a widow, and then in white satin, like a bride), and in the way that she stages herself (when she takes her place amongst the audience for a masque, 'it was as if a curtain was drawn from before her, and she apeared like a glorious light; whereat all were struck with such amaze.')[35] As Kate Lilley points out, 'these narratives centre on the strangeness of woman, both inherent and circumstantial, and her ability to solicit and shape "the gaze of wonder".'[36] Unlike more customary representations of the courtly mistress, or indeed the martial lady, whose femininity becomes 'the objectified and also eroticised and sexualised construct of women,' Cavendish thus presents such women obliquely, capitalising on the position of Woman as Other.[37]

This is particularly noticeable in two works with striking similarities, the fantastical *Description of a New World Called the Blazing World* (1668), and one of Cavendish's most polemical plays, *Bell in Campo* (1662). In the former, the female newcomer is reborn as Empress and focus is specifically drawn to her newly emblazoned appearance:

> on her head she wore a cap of pearl, and a half-moon of diamonds just before it; on the top of her crown came spreading over a broad carbuncle, cut in the form of the sun; her coat was of pearl, mixed with blue diamonds, and fringed with red ones; her buskins and sandals were of green diamonds: in her left hand she held a buckler, to signify the defence of her dominions; which buckler was made of that sort of diamond as had several different colours, and being cut and made in the form of an arch, showed like a rainbow; in her right hand she carried a spear made of a white diamond, cut like the tail of a blazing star, which signified that she was ready to assault those that proved their enemies.[38]

This description bears a resemblance to iconographic representations of a real-life female leader, Elizabeth I, particularly in the famous 'Rainbow' portrait by Marcus Gheeraerts the Younger (c. 1600).[39] This detailed listing of material trappings intensifies the Empress's power; moreover, as Lilley notes, 'It functions iconographically to ratify a seduction which has already occurred within the narrative – the seduction of the Blazing World by the young lady – and which is now extended to the reader.'[40]

Initially, in *Bell in Campo*, Lady Victoria rejects her feminine body and men's opinion that women 'are only fit to breed and bring forth Children.' She counsels her 'Heroickesses' to view their bodies in a non-sexual way, to train themselves for active service rather than passive domesticity, by 'Throwing the Bar, Tripping, Wrastling [*sic*], Running, Vaulting, Riding, and the like exercise.'[41] Nevertheless, her victories on the battlefield are also seen in sexual terms. Victoria's husband, the Lord General, says 'tis fit to these women above all others we should yield ourselves Prisoners, not only in love but in Arms' and sends a letter to be publicly read which declares that 'we are not only taken Captives by your Beauties, but that we acknowledge we are bound as your Slaves by your Valours.'[42] Like the Empress of *The Blazing World*, Cavendish provides us with a detailed inventory of Lady Victoria's clothing and accoutrements. Again, similar to the Empress, the description of Victoria also possibly alludes to another actual female ruler. In this case, the Amazon's entrance, rapturously received by crowds of people in the centre of the town, carries resonances of Henrietta Maria's reception in Oxford in 1643, but extends this into a conclusive triumphal *gestus*.[43] It starts with the entry of 'many Prisoners which march two and two, then enter many that carry the Conquered Spoils, then enters the Lady Victoria.'[44] Here it is the woman herself who displays the treasures *on* her body, not only to enhance her own beauty, but also to signify her far-reaching authority. Cavendish deliberately intertwines symbolic descriptions of power, majesty and femininity: Victoria's revealingly short coat as well as her (phallic) crystal bolt, her curled and loosely flowing hair as well as her laurel garland. Martin Butler has suggested that 'the feminine attractiveness of these women was for each a measure of their political authority,' with the 'romantic motifs' of platonic love operating 'as devices to explore certain aspects of the relationship between ruler and people (the subject's public 'love').'[45] Again, Victoria stages herself not just in front of a public fictional audience but a private actual reader as well, with Susan Wiseman noting that:

> Where the courtly lady is constructed by the text, she perhaps becomes available to the reader in the position of the courtier. Her erotic function may be grounded in insistence on her chastity, like that of a *femme forte*, but the heroine's assumption of masculine roles and prerogatives constitutes a representation of a society radically transformed in terms of gender relations.[46]

It is interesting to note therefore that in the description of Lady Victoria, Cavendish brings together in one woman the figure of the courtly lady, the

Amazon, and the writer, thus conflating literary, mythical and actual constructions of womanhood. Victoria is not only seen as a platonic love object but as the creator and narrator of her own self, an idea made clear by her use of birth imagery:

> worthy heroickesses, at this time Fortune desires to be the Midwife, and if the Gods and Goddesses did not intend to favour our proceedings with a false deliverance, they would not have offered us so fair and fit an opportunity to be the Mothers of glorious Actions, and everlasting Fame.[47]

The triumphal display of a woman who has succeeded both in the feminine domain of love and the masculine spheres of war and literature is counterpoised by an antithetical act of seduction, this time where attempts are made to negate, deny or absent the female body. Here Cavendish makes use of the *mise en scène* to contrast the death of Madam Jantil and the triumphant successes of Lady Victoria. Where the passionate wife-turned-Amazon uses images of childbirth and labour to convey a sense of activity, opportunity and creativity, by contrast the sexually redundant widow is totally bound up in the world of death. She lies on the ground, trying literally to bury herself in the earth as she proclaims her own elegy, 'Death is generous and sets us free,/Breaks off our Chains, and gives us liberty'.[48]

Curiously, whilst Jantil ostensibly attempts to dis-place her body, she also engages in an act of display by providing a full description of her new surroundings:

> my Chamber and the Bed therein to be hung with white, to signify the Purity of Chastity [...]; my Closet to be hung with black, to signify the darkness of Death, wherein all things are forgotten and buried in Oblivion.[49]

This provides a visual framework by which to read a later scene in the second part of the play. Here a Tomb is described as being 'thrust upon the Stage'. Madam Jantil appears 'attired in a rich Cloth of gold girt loosly about her, and a Mantle of Crimson Velvet lined with powdered Ermins over that.' Her hair is 'all unbound hung loose upon her Shoulders and Back, upon her Head a rich Crown of Jewels, as also Pendant Jewels in her Ears, and on her Wrists costly Bracelets.'[50] She then proceeds to strip herself of these worldly vanities on stage, taking off her clothes and jewels, and dressing in a plain white garment and a black veil, this latter garment being a direct reference to a previous incident in which Lady Victoria had incited her troops to 'take courage, cast off your black Veil of Sorrow, and take up the Firematch of Rage.'[51] Francis Barker's brilliant commentary on the displaced body – the 'tremulous private body' – is particularly pertinent here:

> as the flesh is de-realised, representation, which becomes at last representational, is separated from it and puts in train a mode of signification for which, to borrow a

word from Derrida, the body has become supplementary. Neither wholly present, nor wholly absent, the body is confined, ignored, exscribed from the discourse, and yet remains at the edge of visibility, troubling the space from which it has been banished.[52]

In rejecting the objects that, Cavendish suggests, symbolise both femininity and power, Madam Jantil is in denial against a sense of self. She is so totally subsumed into her husband's identity that when he dies, she has to die as well, almost as a form of Indian suttee. Inverting Victoria's public act of triumph, Jantil performs a private act of defeat. Here again the female protagonist is once more observed by the reader, an instance perhaps of what Catherine Clément has called 'an attack of spectacle [...] a celebration of their guilt used as a weapon, a story of seduction.'[53] More darkly, this seduction conjures up the taboo image of necrophilia, a metaphor already hinted at in *Youths Glory*.[54] Here Lady Innocence appears alone 'drest in white, and her hair bound up in Several coloured Ribbons.' Preparing to commit suicide, she crowns herself 'Queen of Innocence', strewing flowers as she speaks. In this most voyeuristic of plays, where the women are under constant surveillance or conversely deliberately display themselves, the stage directions tell us that as Lady Innocence stabs herself, 'Lord de L'amour comes and peeps through the Curtain; or Hanging, and speaks to himself, whilst she is a dying.'[55] As she is silenced through death, her lover finds his voice to profess her innocence and his repentance. The woman educates through her actions but they are the actions of death. In both *Youths Glory* and *Bell in Campo*, Cavendish juxtaposes scenes to deliberate effect, troubling the boundaries between male and female spheres of activity. Where Lady Victoria seduces the spectator through her assumption of a feminised martial role or Lady Sanspareille with her usurpation of the learned role, conversely Madam Jantil and Lady Innocence display themselves as victims of a reduced female existence. Peter Daly confirms that 'the corpse is an emblem that instructs', and in deliberately staging their own deaths, these women in turn become a sacrificial symbol of the society from which they are attempting to disassociate themselves through removal of their corporeal bodies.[56]

In displaying the displacement of their bodies, then, Madam Jantil and Lady Innocence stand as *exempla* of the possible fate of women like Lady Victoria and Lady Sanspareille, and the passivity with which they lived their lives is contrasted with both the single-minded way in which they approach their deaths and the vibrancy of the lives of their counterparts. Yet Cavendish does not allow us to draw simple parallels, particularly in the case of Lady Sanspareille. Escaping from the fate of a court lady who displays her seductive charms only in order to catch a husband, Sanspareille's pursuit of the intellectual life is presented in commendatory terms by her creator as she is seen to successfully broach masculine territory whilst remaining unequivocally virtuous. It is unsurprising, then, that her untimely and unexplained demise has puzzled several critics. Jacqueline Pearson has conjectured that it expresses the 'irresolvable conflict between [her] womanhood and the public role,' a sense, perhaps, that boundaries continue to exist for all those women who wish to create a new identity for themselves.[57] Linda Payne, too, asks, 'Was it just too inconceivable that this remarkable woman could continue to bloom in a public role, particularly when further estranged from her sex by her vow of celibacy?'[58] It is my contention, however, that by considering this character not just as a female orator but *specifically* as a virgin, and one who deliberately puts her virginity on display, we can perhaps contemplate a more affirmative option.

Generally, in Cavendish's plays, a women chooses to remain a maid so as to apply herself to her studies or because she has seen examples of bad marriages. Here, however, there is a sense here that Cavendish is drawing attention to the very state of virginity itself, particularly as it is viewed in patriarchal society. If, in the seventeenth century, a woman's virtue was often seen as a way for men to gain power and status over other men, Cavendish represents the figure of the virgin as one who is not meek and passive but, rather, assertive and active. In addition, by withdrawing their bodies from society, Cavendish seems to suggest that women can add value to what has not been possessed. Freud's observation that by denying something – in this case female sexuality – one draws attention to it, is borne out by Margaret Higgonet's comments on female destructiveness: 'The focus on chastity, of course, involves that precisely which distinguishes wōman as woman, and does so in terms of possession by man, fetishistically.'[59] Sanspareille deliberately stages herself as both a stranger (a female orator) and as a fetish (chaste/sexual object of desire). After whipping her audience up into a frenzy of anticipation, she enters in her bridal costume, 'her Father and the audience, which are all Lovers; these stand gazing upon her', and goes on to state that 'since I cannot be every mans wife, I will dye every mans Maid.' The stage directions directly invoke the cruelty of the platonic mistress who spurns her lovers' addresses: 'All her Audience, her Lovers, goeth out silently, some lifting up their eyes, others their hands, some striking their hands on their breasts, and the like.'[60]

However, here she presents herself as something far more than the constructed woman of platonic love poetry. Rather, she is a real (virginal) woman who is deliberately withdrawing her body from public view, and who achieves sanctification in doing so. The possibility of sexual fulfilment – visual or aural – will no longer exist. She eschews earthly marriage, instead achieving apotheosis as she goes to a more fitting nuptial alliance in Heaven – the 'Death's Banquet' of the title.[61] Her funeral hearse, with a 'silver Crowne [...] placed in the midst' is 'born by six Virgins all in white, other Virgins goe before the Herse, and Strew Flowers, white Lillies and white Roses'.[62] A contemporary view that 'There is a law in heaven, that the heavenly Bride may at one time have but one Husband' is echoed both in *Youths Glory* and one of Cavendish's orations on Virginity:

> a Virgin's Soul it is, Cloth'd with white Innocency, and so fitter for their Company, as also for the Robe of Glory, which the Gods will give me. As for my Body,

though it be Young, yet it is only fit for Death, as being Due to him, for that was made of Earth.[63]

The enigmatic title of the play seems to recall a part of the Bible concerned with the resurrection of the dead:

> If the dead are not raised, 'Let us eat and drink, for tomorrow we die.' Do not be deceived [...]. What you sow does not come to life unless it dies [...]. What is sown is perishable, what is raised is imperishable. It is sown in dishonour, it is raised in glory. It is sown in weakness, it is raised in power. It is sown a physical body, it is raised a spiritual body.[64]

Through rejecting the corporeal in favour of the spiritual, Lady Sanspareille thus ensures that her virtuousness and the lessons that she has preached will always be remembered. Moreover, she permanently safeguards her chastity whilst ensuring that this will be forever associated with her wisdom, and in doing so, receives validation from both heaven and earth.

As I have shown, Margaret Cavendish's plays deliberately make a spectacle of the female body, whether by displaying the body as a platonic love object or, more complexly, by displacing the body within the narrative, thereby problematising the relationship between seduction and spectacle. In providing a variety of different perspectives on the idea of the staging of the female body, Cavendish also comments on what she sees as the special relationship between women and the theatre. One of the themes proposed in *The Female Academy* is that of theatre, for which women are particularly suited because of their capacity to stage themselves, 'for we delight more in Scenes than in Battels.'[65] Again, in *Youths Glory*, Lady Sanspareille's mother accuses her of being 'transformed from what you should be, from a sober, young maid, to a Stage-player, as to act Parts, speak Speeches, rehearse Verses, sing Sonets, and the like.' Sanspareille's rejoinder is that 'Theators were not only Schools to learn or practise in, but publick patterns to take example from' and that 'Thrones are but glorious Theaters, where Kings and Princes, and their Courtiers acts their parts.'[66]

Margaret Cavendish was certainly conversant with the theatrical world. We know that her husband was patron to a number of dramatists and wrote plays for public performance with the considerable help of professional writers, including Dryden and Shadwell. The Newcastle family, including the Duke's daughters, Jane Cavendish and Elizabeth Brackley, wrote and acted in plays at Bolsover Castle and, although Cavendish was not involved in these activities, she would have had knowledge of them, as well as Jonson's elaborate spectacles held at Newcastle's residences in honour of Charles I. Moreover, her role as maid of honour to Henrietta Maria afforded her opportunities to see the Queen and her attendants take part in a number of court entertaiments, as well as visit public playhouses. There is also evidence that, when exiled in Antwerp, she became enamoured of a troupe of female actresses who were performing nearby.[67] The metaphor of acting, therefore – of displaying the self in public – was one that Cavendish found particularly suggestive and which she gradually introduced into her life and her works. Several critics have already noted the former. Kate Lilley describes Cavendish as an 'exemplary instance of woman as spectacle,' whilst Kathleen Jones says that 'her public persona was a theatrical mask she created to hide behind.'[68] Here, as Susan Wiseman has pointed out, 'it is the Duchess herself who is displayed and observed.'[69]

This is made clearer when examining Cavendish's *deliberate* manipulation of her own self-image. As Margaret Lucas, daughter of a family ravaged by the Civil War, she presents herself in her autobiography as painfully shy and awkward. Yet, moved by a spirit of adventure, a romantic fancy, or more possibly a pragmatic need to seek protection against her family's political enemies, she chose to follow Henrietta Maria's court which went into exile soon after. Here she became known as Mistress Bashful, even after assuming a higher status in life by marrying the Marquis of Newcastle.[70]

Originally rejecting the theatrical qualities implicit in the role of court lady, Cavendish nonetheless becomes far more forthright in the presentation of a public self after her prestigious marriage in 1646, and it is important to note that *both* the Newcastles stage themselves in order to affirm their status, an aristocratic necessity during this time of political instability.[71] After the publication of Margaret Cavendish's first work in 1653, she seems to embrace the 'idea of acting as a means of becoming or self-realisation,' and of 'performance as a metaphor of possibility.'[72] Pertinently, Sophie Tomlinson notes that:

> performance means crossing the boundary between inside and outside, animating the self in front of the gaze of others. This fantasy depends on self-projection, not self-withdrawal; even though the self is part of the audience.[73]

As 'Mad Madge', a role created by others and dependent on the exhibition of herself for the benefit of an audience, Cavendish deliberately exploits her position as Other.[74] In doing so, she demands a response and is able to create a specifically theatrical environment for the production (writing) and reception (reading) of her work.[75] Her very public visits to places like the Royal Society, the playhouse and the Court, are described by contemporaries in terms of performances given before crowds of eager and inquisitive onlookers. The visual impression so carefully cultivated by Cavendish mesmerises Mary Evelyn, who acknowledges (if somewhat ironically) the seductive appeal of the Duchess's performance: 'my part was not yet to speak, but to admire.'[76]

As her costume, gestures, and demeanour were considered excessive, inappropriate, and even deranged, so her writings were viewed in the same way. Dorothy Osborne's comment that Cavendish's book of poems is considered 'ten times more extravagant than her dress' shows, as Lilley has said, 'the atextual way in which Cavendish's work – and indeed life – has tended to be read as a vehicle for or by-product of personality.'[77] Pepys, too, conflates the text and the body when he comments on Cavendish's appearance at the theatre for a performance of Newcastle's *The Humorous Lovers* (1677). His mistaken assumption that the play is by Cavendish alters the way that he views her behaviour as he records how 'she at the end made her respect to the players from her box and did give them thanks.'

The situation is made even more ironic by the fact that the play was mainly written by Shadwell. Again, a letter from Charles North to his father in 1667 comments on this event and describes the Duchess as 'all ye pageant now discoursed on: Her brests all laid out to view in a play house with scarlett trimd nipples.'[78] Cavendish has become the ultimate spectacle of female availability, publicly displayed for male consumption. Her theatrical appearance in a theatre playhouse becomes a performance in itself, the staging of another self far removed from the 'dull, fearful, and bashful' creature she describes in her autobiography. This act of self-creation is both excessive and transgressive as it flagrantly violates set boundaries between text/body, fiction/reality, public/private. Indeed, it becomes the spectacle of the 'grotesque [...] body of becoming, process, and change.'[79]

Returning to Mary Russo's original question, then, how is it possible for women to make spectacles themselves and of themselves if they are constrained by society's prescriptions concerning female behaviour and 'estranged [...] from their own bodies as signs in culture'?[80] In reply, I would suggest that Margaret Cavendish not only produces spectacles out of transgressed boundaries but specifically *because* they provide her with a way of transgressing those boundaries. Her unconventional calls for fame (in the plays and other works), the frequent displays made of herself and her female characters, and the dramatic interplay between the chaste woman and her seductive staging, show us the unique ways in which Cavendish tried to reappropriate her own body. Writing becomes the most powerful expression of individuality, something denied to women by men. In this way, Cavendish can perhaps be seen to begin to struggle with Hélène Cixous's maxim that 'Woman must write herself: must write about women and bring women to writing, from which they have been driven away as violently as from their bodies.'[81] Through conflating the woman and the image, the writing and the body, Cavendish transforms female margins of text into spaces of potential power. This transference of sexuality into textuality, as Teresa de Lauretis has observed, allows a female writer to recreate herself both in her own time and through time, thus providing both herself and her reader/audience with a spectacle of yet other selves waiting to be discovered:

> The struggle with language to re-write the body beyond its precoded, conventional representations is not and cannot be a reappropriation of the female body as it is, domesticated, maternal, oedipally or preoedipally en-gendered, but is a struggle to transcend both gender and 'sex' and recreate the body other-wise: to see it perhaps as monstrous, or grotesque, or mortal or violent, and certainly also sexual, but with a material and sensual specificity that will resist phallic idealisation and render it accessible to women in another sociosexual economy.[82]

Notes

[1] Mary Russo, 'Female Grotesques: Carnival and Theory', in Teresa de Lauretis (ed.) *Feminist Studies, Critical Studies* (Bloomington: Indiana University Press, 1986), pp. 213–29 (p. 217).

[2] For a full discussion concerning the likelihood of contemporary performance of Cavendish's plays see Judith Peacock's essay in this collection.

[3] Michel Foucault, *The History of Sexuality*, 2 vols (London: Allen Lane, 1979), I, p. 3.

[4] Juliet Dusinberre, *Shakespeare and the Nature of Women* (Basingstoke: Macmillan, 1975), p. 268. For further examples on the use of court spectacle, see Paula R. Backscheider's *Spectacular Politics: Theatrical Power and Mass Culture in Early Modern England* (London: Johns Hopkins University Press, 1993). Barry O'Connor has also persuasively argued that Restoration portraits depicted royal and aristocratic subjects as if they were actors upon a stage. See Barry O'Connor, 'Late Seventeenth-Century Royal Portraiture and Restoration Staging', *Theatre Notebook*, 49 (1995), 152–64. Terry Castle's comment that the eighteenth-century masquerade 'had its undeniably provocative visual elements: one took one's pleasure, above all, in seeing and being seen', also seems relevant here when placed alongside seventeenth-century views of the female writer, the emergence of the actress, and Caroline court culture. See Terry Castle, *Masquerade and Civilization: The Carnivalesque in Eighteenth-Century English Culture and Fiction* (London: Methuen, 1986), p. 38.

[5] See Guido Ruggiero 'Marriage, Love, Sex, and Renaissance Civil Morality', in James Grantham Turner (ed.) *Sexuality and Gender in Early Modern Europe: Institutions, Texts, Images* (Cambridge: Cambridge University Press, 1993), pp. 10–30.

[6] The idea that what happened in the audience was as much of an entertainment as that which occurred onstage is illustrated at several points in Pepys's diary. For example, on 20 April 1661 Pepys disparages the onstage production, but notes his pleasure about 'so many great beauties' in the audience, including 'Mrs Palmer, with whom the King doth discover a great deal of Familiarity'. On 23 July of the same year, Pepys notes that 'I sat before Mrs Palmer, the King's mistress, and filled my eyes with her, which much pleased me.' See Robert Latham and William Matthews (eds.) *The Diary of Samuel Pepys*, 11 vols. (London: Bell and Hyman, 1970), II, pp. 80, 139.

[7] For further details on Cavendish's dramatic engagement with the darker side of surveillance with its sexual connotations of scopophilia and voyeurism or authoritarian undertones of discipline and punishment, see my thesis, 'Re-Presenting the Female Body in Seventeenth-Century Drama: The Plays of Margaret Cavendish, Duchess of Newcastle, and Aphra Behn (unpublished doctoral thesis, University of London, 2000).

[8] All these plays appear in Cavendish's first volume of plays in 1662, with the exception of *The Convent of Pleasure* which appears in the 1668 volume.

[9] Margaret Cavendish, *The First Part of the Play Called Wits Cabal*, in *Playes* (1662), pp. 247–80 (II.12, p. 260).

[10] Margaret Cavendish, *The First Part of the Lady Contemplation*, in *Playes*, pp. 181–211 (I.1, p. 183).

[11] Margaret Cavendish, *The Comedy Named The Several Wits. The Wise Wit, The Wild Wit, The Cholerick Wit, The Humble Wit*, in *Playes* (1662), pp. 78–119 (II.9, p. 85).

[12] *The Several Wits*, IV.37, *Playes* (1662), p. 114.

[13] *The Several Wits*, IV.33, *Playes* (1662), p. 111.

[14] Ann Rosalind Jones, 'Nets and Bridles: Early Modern Conduct Books and Sixteenth-Century Women's Lyrics', in Nancy Armstrong and Leonard Tennenhouse (eds.) *The Ideology of Conduct: Essays on Literature and the History of Sexuality*, (London: Methuen, 1987), pp. 39–72 (p. 44).

[15] Sophie Tomlinson, '"My Brain the Stage" : Margaret Cavendish and the Fantasy of Female Performance', in *Women, Texts and Histories*, pp. 134–63 (p. 138).

[16] Patricia Parker, *Literary Fat Ladies: Rhetoric, Gender, Property* (London: Methuen, 1987), p. 61.

[17] Margaret Cavendish, *Youths Glory and Deaths Banquet. The First Part*, in *Playes* (1662), pp. 121–52 (III.9, p. 135). This is in direct contrast to the reality afforded Anna Maria van Schurman, often described as the century's foremost learned lady, who was 'granted the rare privilege of attending lectures at the University of Utrecht, though she had to stand behind a curtain.' See Merry Wiesner, *Women and Gender in Early Modern Europe* (Cambridge: Cambridge University Press, 1993), p. 135.

[18] *Youths Glory*, I.3, *Playes* (1662), p. 127.

[19] *Youths Glory*, II.5, *Playes* (1662), p. 130.

[20] *Youths Glory*, III.9, *Playes* (1662), p. 136; Margaret Cavendish, *The Second Part of Youths Glory and Deaths Banquet*, in *Playes*, pp. 153–80 (II.5, p. 158).

[21] *Youths Glory*, III.9, *Playes* (1662), p. 136.

[22] *Youths Glory*, III.9, *Playes* (1662), p. 139.

[23] Margaret Cavendish, *The Female Academy*, in *Playes* (1662), pp. 652–79 (I.1, p. 653).

[24] Susan Wiseman, 'Gender and Status in Dramatic Discourse: Margaret Cavendish, Duchess of Newcastle', in *Women, Writing, History*, pp. 159–77 (p. 165).

[25] *The Female Academy*, V.29, *Playes* (1662), p. 679.

[26] *The Female Academy*, III.14, *Playes* (1662), p. 665.

[27] Cavendish's verbose prefaces and epistles to the Reader have also been commented upon by several critics including Jacqueline Pearson in '"Women May Discourse ... as Well as Men": Speaking and Silent Women in the Plays of Margaret Cavendish, Duchess of Newcastle', *Tulsa Studies in Women's Literature*, 4 (1985), 33–45, and Sylvia Brown's 'Margaret Cavendish: Strategies Rhetorical and Philosophical Against the Charge of Wantonness, Or her Excuses for Writing So Much', in *Critical Matrix: Princeton Working Papers in Women's Studies*, 6 (1991), 20–45.

[28] Nancy J. Vickers, 'This Heraldry in Lucrece' Face', in Susan Rubin Suleiman (ed.) *The Female Body in Western Culture: Contemporary Perspectives* (Cambridge, Mass.: Harvard University Press, 1986), pp. 209–22 (p. 213).

[29] Parker, *Literary Fat Ladies*, p. 127.

[30] Laura Mulvey, *Visual and Other Pleasures* (Basingstoke: Macmillan, 1989), p. 25. Theories on the construction of the gaze have since been challenged, but Mulvey's comments are still pertinent. See also E. Ann Kaplan's 'Is the Gaze Male?', in Ann Snitow, Christine Stansell and Sharon Thompson (eds.) *Powers of Desire: The Politics of Sexuality* (London: Virago, 1984), pp. 321–38.

[31] Linda R. Payne has also made a similar connection. See 'Dramatic Dreamscape: Women's Dreams and Utopian Vision in the Works of Margaret Cavendish, Duchess of

Newcastle', in Mary Anne Schofield and Cecilia Macheski (eds.) *Curtain Calls: British and American Women and the Theater 1660–1820*, (Athens: Ohio University Press, 1991), pp. 18–33 (p. 30).

[32] Judith Butler, *Gender Trouble: Feminism and the Subversion of Identity* (London: Routledge, 1990), p. vii.

[33] See Kate Lilley, 'Introduction' in *Writings* (1994), pp. ix–xxxiv (p. xvii).

[34] Margaret Cavendish, *The Contract*, in *Writings* (1994), pp. 18–33 (p. 30).

[35] *The Contract*, in *Writings* (1994), p. 14.

[36] *Writings* (1994), 'Introduction', p. xvii.

[37] Marianne Hester, *Lewd Women and Wicked Witches: A Study of the Dynamics of Male Domination* (London: Routledge, 1992), p. 74.

[38] Margaret Cavendish, *The Description of a New World called the Blazing World*, in *Writings* (1994), pp. 119–225 (p. 133).

[39] This has also been noted by Claire Jowitt, 'Imperial Dreams? Margaret Cavendish and the Cult of Elizabeth', *Women's Writing*, 4 (1997), 383–99 (pp. 391–92).

[40] *Writings* (1994), 'Introduction', p.xxvi.

[41] Margaret Cavendish, *The First Part of Bell in Campo*, in *Playes* (1662), pp. 578–600 (p. 592).

[42] Margaret Cavendish, *The Second Part of Bell in Campo*, in *Playes* (1662), pp. 607–33 (II.5, p. 612; III.8, p. 616).

[43] See *Glorious Fame*, p. 22.

[44] *The Second Part of Bell in Campo*, V.20, *Playes* (1662), p. 623 [misprinted as p. 625].

[45] Martin Butler, *Theatre and Crisis 1632–1642* (Cambridge: Cambridge University Press, 1984), p. 29.

[46] Wiseman, 'Gender and Status', p. 169.

[47] *The Second Part of Bell in Campo*, I.3, *Playes* (1662), p. 609.

[48] *Bell in Campo*, IV.21, *Playes* (1662), p. 602.

[49] *Bell in Campo*, IV.21, *Playes* (1662), p. 600.

[50] *The Second Part of Bell in Campo*, II.7, *Playes* (1662), p. 613.

[51] *Bell in Campo*, IV.17, *Playes* (1662), p. 596.

[52] Francis Barker, *The Tremulous Private Body: Essays on Subjection* (London: Methuen, 1984), p. 63.

[53] Catherine Clément, 'The Guilty One', in Hélène Cixous and Catherine Clément, *The Newly Born Woman*, trans. Betsy Wing (Manchester: Manchester University Press, 1986), pp. 1–59 (p.10).

[54] I am reminded here too of the fate of Cavendish's dead mother during the ransacking of the family graves. See *Glorious Fame*, p. 70

[55] *The Second Part of Youths Glory*, IV.19, *Playes* (1662), pp. 173–74.

[56] Peter M. Daly, *Literature in the Light of the Emblem: Structural Parallels between the Emblem and Literature in the Sixteenth and Seventeenth Centuries* (Toronto: University of Toronto Press, 1979), p. 147.

[57] Pearson, 'Silent Women', p. 41.

[58] Payne, 'Dramatic Dreamscape', p. 29.

[59] Margaret Higgonet, 'Speaking Silences: Women's Suicide', in Suleiman, *Female Body*, pp. 68–83 (p. 74).

[60] *The Second Part of Youths Glory*, II.5, *Playes* (1662), pp. 158, 161.

[61] Stanley Stewart notes that 'the theme of virginity, so much a part of monastic lore, was a favoured motif in the legends of the saints' lives. Even the *Book of Margery Kempe* treats sexual abstinence as almost coincidental with virtue', Stanley Stewart, *The Enclosed Garden: The Tradition and the Image in Seventeenth-Century Poetry* (London: University of Wisconsin Press, 1966), p. 32.

[62] *Youths Glory*, V.22, *Playes* (1662), p. 177.

[63] Francis Rous, *The Mysticall Marriage; or, Experimentall Discoveries of the Heavenly Marriage Between a Soule and her Saviour* (London: Printed by W. I. and T. P. for I. Emery, 1635), p. 17. Margaret Cavendish, 'A Young Virgin's Dying Speech', in *Orations* (1662), p. 139.

[64] I Corinthians 15.33, 36, 42–44.

[65] *The Female Academy*, IV.12, *Playes* (1662), p. 670.

[66] *Youths Glory*, I.3, *Playes* (1662), pp. 126–27.

[67] See Tomlinson, 'Female Performance', pp. 134–36.

[68] *Writings* (1994), 'Introduction', p. ix; *Glorious Fame*, pp. 1–2. Even contemporaries like Mary Evelyn and Samuel Pepys made reference to this aspect of Cavendish's theatrical self, with Pepys saying, 'The whole story of this Lady is a romance, and all she doth is romantic', *Diary*, VIII, p. 163.

[69] Wiseman, 'Gender and Status', p. 160.

[70] Cavendish goes on to fictionalise this side of her own character in the creation of two figures called Lady Bashfull, who appear in the plays, *Loves Adventures* and *The Presence*. As these plays were published in both *Playes* (1662) and *Plays* (1668), it would suggest that the figure of the bashful female character held significance for Cavendish. Interestingly, although Cavendish repeatedly asserted her own subservience and shyness in her autobiography, this is done in rather a self-conscious manner as she presents herself as she feels she *ought* to, the conventionally modest wife and daughter.

[71] For example, whilst in exile the impecunious Duke purchased a new coach in which his wife could take public excursions, described by the Duchess as 'a tour where all the chief of the town go to see and be seen', *True Relation* (1814), p. 28. Again, although strapped for cash, they rented not just any house in Antwerp, but one that belonged to its most famous citizen, the artist Rubens. See Hero Chalmers, 'Dismantling the Myth of "Mad Madge": The cultural context of Margaret Cavendish's authorial self-presentation', *Womens Writing*, 4 (1997), 323–39 (p. 327).

[72] Tomlinson, 'Female Performance', p. 137.

[73] Tomlinson, 'Female Performance', p. 150.

[74] Frequent references by contemporaries to her 'eccentric' behaviour include Pepys's comment that she was 'a mad, conceited, ridiculous woman', *Diary*, IX, p. 123, and Dorothy Osborne's observation that she was 'a little distracted' and that there were 'many soberer People in Bedlam', *Letters to Sir William Temple*, ed. by Kenneth Parker (Harmondsworth: Penguin, 1987), pp. 75, 79. Even Charles Lamb, one of her champions, saw her as rather fantastical and singular.

[75] Again, David Robinson's research reminds us that the Newcastles were very canny in their understanding of what would now be termed 'media hype'. For example, Newcastle's play, *The Humorous Lovers* was put on in London just after Cavendish's publication of her

husband's biography, and timed to coincide with one of their few visits to London. See David Robinson, 'What's a Nice Muse Like You Doing in a Text Like This? or: (Pro) Lesbian Readings of Margaret Cavendish's Works' (unpublished conference paper, Margaret Cavendish Conference, University of East Anglia, 1996).

[76] Cit. Tomlinson, 'Female Performance', p. 159. Cavendish specifically refers to her intention of creating an original and visual spectacle when she states in *True Relation* (1814): 'I took great delight in attiring, fine dressing and fashion, especially such fashions as I did invent my self, not taking that pleasure in such fashions as was invented by others', p. 31. She then reattributes such mannerisms to her fictional characters, such as the Lady in her short story, *The Contract*.

[77] *Writings* (1994), 'Introduction', p. xiii.

[78] Cit. Tomlinson, 'Female Performance', p. 159.

[79] Russo, 'Female Grotesques', p. 219.

[80] Russo, Female Grotesques', p. 217.

[81] Hélène Cixous, 'The Laugh of the Medusa', trans. by Keith Cohen and Paula Cohen, in Elaine Marks and Isabelle de Courtivron (eds.) *New French Feminisms: An Anthology* (New York: Schocken Books, 1981), pp. 245–64 (p. 245).

[82] Teresa de Lauretis, 'Sexual Indifference and Lesbian Representation', in Sue-Ellen Case (ed.) *Performing Feminism: Feminist Critical Theory and Theatre* (London: Johns Hopkins University Press, 1990), pp. 17–39 (p. 29).

8

'The Closet Opened': A Reconstruction of 'Private' Space in the Writings of Margaret Cavendish*

Julie Sanders

The closet is frequently used as a metonym for 'private space' in literature of the early modern period, and yet, in a manner comparable to Margaret Cavendish herself when she declared via the character of Lady Happy in *The Convent of Pleasure*: 'My Cloister shall not be a Cloister of restraint, but a place of freedom [...],'[1] I intend in this essay to challenge traditional concepts of privacy and the closet in the seventeenth century, most obviously by challenging the category of closet-drama, but also by challenging the role or function of the closet space within the 'real' early modern household and within fictional texts.

One obvious critical model in this is provided by the work of Margaret Ezell. In her seminal article on the work of the Cavendish sisters, Ezell questions the application of the term 'closet' to their literary productions: 'These pieces were not "closet" poems in the sense that they were hidden and anonymous,' she says, going on to refute the highly gendered usage of the term: 'When Donne writes for a limited readership in a specific environment, it is referred to as "coterie" writing: when a woman of the period does so, it becomes "closet" writing, a negative and diminishing adjective [...].'[2] Mary Ellen Lamb has explained what she sees as the essentially feminine understanding of the closet or cabinet: 'the cabinet image seems evocatively feminine, as a representation of a dark, secret, interior space where "meaning" grows until it forces itself out into the world.'[3] The womb connection is inescapable here, as is the sense of an interior and sexualised female space, but so too is the sense of the vulnerability of this feminised space to masculine penetration, construction and redefinition. Ezell's work establishes, in contradistinction to the isolated, withdrawn and inherently unstable 'closet' image, a notion of controlled, or family, readerships for the texts she is discussing, relevant to the Sidney family as much as to the Cavendishes. Here though, I want to expand on ways in which these challenges to our understanding of closet-space can in turn shed light on our critical understanding of Margaret Cavendish's work and life.

Increasingly, the private theatricals of early modern households are being seen to have been very public and political in their purpose, often working in opposition

* I am indebted to all the participants of the Margaret Cavendish conference at the University of Oxford in June 1997 for their comments on a shorter version of this essay.

to court theatricals of a similar or related form; this must perforce lead to a re-evaluation of the female contribution to these events. Cavendish's plays, we are frequently informed, were not written to be performed, but were written as 'private' drama, and yet they frequently employ tropes of performance and of public speaking. The women's theatre of *The Convent of Pleasure*, the oratory of plays such as *The Female Academy* and *The Bridals* are just a few examples, and it is this conscious redefinition, or destabilisation, of concepts of the private and the public that I intend to explore here.

In the first part of Lady Mary Wroth's prose romance, the *Urania* (1621), the writing and reading of the text's female protagonist, Pamphilia, is spatially and linguistically associated with the cabinet or closet:

> She went to her bed again, taking a little cabinet with her wherein she had many papers and, setting a light by her began to read them. But few of them pleasing her, she took pen and paper, and being excellent in writing, writ these verses following [...].[4]

A cabinet or closet could refer to a particular small room within a house, usually a location of literary or epistolary endeavour, and in seventeenth-century literature these were often associated with female members of the household who could find private creative potential within them, impossible elsewhere: a room of their own, as it were. The cabinet in the quotation here, though, is a portable desk, suggesting that the independent social and intellectual space that Pamphilia is able to find through the acts of reading and writing is not confined to a single private space with clearly determined parameters, but instead travels with her. Helen Wilcox, in an important investigation of the hiddenness, or otherwise, of feminine space, has stressed the 'public' significance of travel for seventeenth-century women.[5] The supposed 'private' space of the writing cabinet or closet is here blurring the edges of sites of more overt 'public' enactments and representations, and transforming our perception of the character of Pamphilia as it does so.

Already, then, we are becoming aware of the semantic slippage of terms such as 'closet' or 'cabinet' within seventeenth-century texts. Cabinets can be portable writing desks or small writing rooms in themselves; closets can be small private spaces or larger family rooms (possibly containing the potential for theatrical performance in the instance of closet-drama). They can even be shared spaces containing books and materials of readership. Lady Anne Clifford and her husband, the Earl of Dorset, clearly shared the 'library' that was held within his 'private' closet at Knole. This is clear from accounts of her use of that space in her diaries. Whilst on certain occasions she describes being read to within her own closet (a further implication of the complicated operation of the term 'private' in application to these spaces – often these spaces were intimately shared, by male and female aristocrats alike, with personal servants, always therefore containing the risk of events there being made 'public' on some later occasion).[6] On one specific occasion Clifford writes, 'The 26th I spent the evening in working and going down to my lord's closet, where I sat and read much in the Turkish history and Chaucer.'[7] Margaret Cavendish's employment of the closet-space in her own writings also suggests an interaction between men and women within or around these locales, indicating the household closet's potential operation as a site of shared space, an interpretation recently resisted by Lisa Jardine in her account of closets, in *Reading Shakespeare Historically*.

Although Jardine claims, justifiably, with reference to Middleton and Rowley's play, *The Changeling* and the use of Alsemero's closet in the plotline, that:

> The man of property's 'closet' was the physical place of his greatest privacy. His closet was adjacent to his sleeping quarters, and contained his books, his correspondence and his most private possessions. It was generally locked, inaccessible to anyone but himself and his most intimate personal servants. The woman of the household might have her own closet or 'cabinet', which might contain her personal effects and toiletries, but she would not have access to her husband's.[8]

The extracts from the Clifford diaries alone cast doubt on the certainty of this statement in application to related 'real-life' locations. Cavendish's own play, *The Matrimoniall Trouble*, features a dialogue between a husband and wife occurring at the very site of the masculine closet or study. Although admittedly Sir William Lovewell in that text describes his wife, Lady Hypochondria, as a 'stranger here', his manner towards her is far from unwelcoming.[9] This may say something more general to us about the operations of elite household space, for it is undoubtedly that sector of society's understanding of social space that is my overriding concern here, as well as the social dynamics of the Cavendish household *per se*. Patricia Fumerton has suggested that 'privacy' was an unattainable or at least an eternally receding state of being for aristocrats, male and female alike, at this time.[10]

The social historian Mark Girouard has emphasised that in the formal English country house from the Caroline period onwards the withdrawing chambers that had developed in architectural design in the late Middle Ages and Tudor periods became more prominent as sites of reception and public display: 'More often, drawing chambers became more accessible, less like private sitting rooms and more like general reception rooms.'[11] Bedrooms too became more public, not least in royal residences: 'The king's serious business was carried on in his closet, sometimes called his cabinet.'[12] The political significance of these spaces in the seventeenth century should not, then, be underestimated. The making public of the contents of closets became a popular activity in the Civil War and Interregnum years, with the publication of letters of both King Charles I and his Queen, Henrietta Maria, under the respective titles of *The King's Cabinet Opened* and *The Queen's Closet Discovered*.[13] Linguistically, those politicised associations have present day vestiges in the 'private' space for our own governmental 'Cabinet' and its public significance in terms of the policy dictates decided there for the country at large. That these seventeenth-century closets or cabinets were sites for communication, talking shops of sorts, is something I want to argue for as crucial in Cavendish's personal and literary perceptions of these spaces, as is their proximity to the space of the bedchamber and therefore to erotic, sexual potential.

It has frequently been argued that the retreat, architecturally and socially, from the medieval Great Hall constituted a retreat into an increasingly defined private sphere: Philippe Ariès and Georges Duby's recent multi-volumed history of private life is no exception to this.[14] I would prefer, though, to think in terms of a shift of power centres. After all, servants also retreated from these central spaces, often operating in rooms directly juxtaposed to the master's or mistress's closet; the management of the house was not withdrawing but relocating itself. That closets were not central topographically is not to say that they were marginal in social or political terms.

The gendered history of closet spaces also demands reinvestigation. The implication of Jardine's comments is that whilst the male closet held literary and sometimes political significance, equivalent female spaces were of more lowly status. Again, there would appear to be firm evidence to the contrary in this period seventeenth century, not least the Duchess of Portsmouth's (Charles II's mistress) use of her space of *levée*, the bedchamber, for the purposes of political negotiation with supporters and representatives of court factions in the late seventeenth century,[15] and indeed earlier in the century with Queen Anna of Denmark's exploitation of her private space. Anna made sure court appointments to her chambers became politically significant in her rejection of those women favoured by James, and in a letter of February 1604, Edward Somerset made observation of the 'female common welthe' of Anna's locked privy chamber: 'mayny tymes the dores ar lokt; but the plotting and malice amongst them is sutche, that I think envy hathe tyed an invisibl snake about most of their necks, to sting on another to deathe.'[16] The male construction of these spaces, the mapping on to them of masculine anxiety or fantasy, should not be underestimated in our reading of contemporary accounts of them.

Louise de Kerouaille (the Duchess of Portsmouth) must surely have sought regal precedent for her activities from the comportment of another significant Frenchwoman at the Stuart court, Charles I's wife, Queen Henrietta Maria, and her highly political employment of closet spaces, and indeed 'closet drama' (as it has come to be known, the term is a retrospective nineteenth-century one) at the pre-Civil War Caroline court.[17] It is no mere coincidence that the critical emphasis of late has been on the impact on Margaret Cavendish's later thinking about, and representation of, female space and community of her time as a lady in waiting to Henrietta Maria.[18]

Closets and cabinets are sites, then, of theatre, actual and political, but also of literary productivity. In Part Two of Mary Wroth's *Urania*, Pamphilia and Amphilanthus become erotically involved with one another within the loaded space of her closet, perhaps significantly through his act of reading her romantic compositions. The enclosed female space here is penetrated not only by public male figures such as Amphilanthus, but by public concepts such as authorship and identity. There are a number of fictional female authors in the *Urania*, of whom Pamphilia is merely the foremost, and they all store their poetry within their cabinets. Cabinets and closets therefore resonate with the sense of authorly creativity and identity, and of the public circulation of texts, for all that they seem on the surface to contain and constrain them.

I want to argue here that private female closets and analogous spaces are significant to Cavendish's dramatic works and to her own public self-construction. The picture that adorns her edition of *The World's Olio,* for example, depicts her writing in her closet (figure. 1.2), and she frequently mentions her residence in this space of contemplation in her autobiographical texts.[19] These constitute a very public manipulation of images of privacy by the publicity-conscious Cavendish, and gesture towards the paradoxical entity that was 'private space' in this period. I want to use as facilitating texts two of Cavendish's plays, *The Convent of Pleasure* and *Lady Contemplation*, in order to discuss the theatricalised and eroticised usage of such spaces in her 'closet-drama', and to ruminate on the possible significance of 'private' space in her own life.

The performative nature of private space in Cavendish's work can of course be most readily located in Lady Happy's self-sufficient female commune in *The Convent of Pleasure*. The persistent reiteration throughout the early scenes of Lady Happy's plan to 'incloister' herself in all female community leaves us in little doubt that Cavendish means here to represent some form of female withdrawal from the public world, not least of heterosexual relations:

MEDIATOR:	But surely you will not incloister your self, as you say.
LADY HAPPY:	Why, what is there in the public World that should me to live in it?[20]

The choice of terminology is worth some reflection. In *A True Relation*, Cavendish describes her mother's widowed life as one of incloistering: 'She made her house her cloister, enclosing herself, as it were, therein; for she seldom went abroad, unless to church.'[21] In this account, only the horrors of war force her mother out of this space into a world of homelessness, something I will argue for later as significant in Cavendish's own life experience. In *A True Relation*, Cavendish suggests that her own life mirrored her mother's in its preference for solitude and retreat as opposed to public mirth, and the character of Lady Contemplation makes comparable statements in the course of that eponymous play.[22] But I want to argue for these self-images as self-conscious constructions, and to suggest that Lady Happy's incloistering is in fact an inversion of Elizabeth Lucas's: one fashioned for mirth and for freedom rather than restraint. Happy will not, as Sir Fancy Poet says of Lady Contemplation, 'smother [her] thoughts, and stifle [her] conception in the close Closet of Study,' but will be empowered by the space for thought the convent affords her.[23] Though in her autobiography Cavendish might claim never to have 'taken delight in closets or cabinets,' they were precisely cabinets 'of toys' – her closets will not be compensatory places of play, but rather areas of genuine self-staging.[24]

In *The Convent of Pleasure*, Lady Happy resists Mediator's interpretation of a life of seclusion as necessarily one of privation: 'retiredness bars the life from nothing else but Men.'[25] This is a sensually and materially indulgent community, and of course in truth her women spend much of their time in performance. Not only do we have the centrally positioned Act III 'play-within-a-play' (evidence I think of Cavendish's sense of dramatic structure and of Jonsonian and Shakespearean influences: her genuine understanding of theatrical form is often underestimated in the critical anxiety to stress the impossibility of her plays ever being staged in her own life) about the perils of the female condition in society, staged to the problematic gaze of the newly arrived 'convert', the Princess of masculine habit, but also no fewer than two quasi-masques, which themselves pay homage, through their pastoral and maritime settings, to Jonsonian and Caroline experiments in that form.

I have written elsewhere of the influence of the Caroline dramatist James Shirley's own play about female closet-drama, *The Bird in a Cage* (1633) on Cavendish's engagement in *The Convent of Pleasure* with the trope of female play-acting in a closeted space of withdrawal from mainstream society.[26] In comparison to the rather more ambivalent stances of Shirley's public theatre play (which would therefore, of course, have been performed by male actors), the emphasis in Cavendish's play text, as Hero Chalmers has stressed, is on pleasure, on the recreational enjoyment to be had by these birds in a cage (and Madam Mediator herself uses that concept to describe the female votaries of Nature: 'I doubt all my sweet young Birds are undone'):[27]

> LADY HAPPY: I intend to incloister my self from the World to enjoy pleasure, and not to bury my self from it; but to incloister my self from the incumbred cares and vexations, troubles and perturbance of the World.[28]

Yet it would be erroneous to ignore Cavendish's retention of Shirley's flirtation throughout the dramatic structure of his play with the concept of male heterosexual penetration of this closeted space (most obviously figured by the Jupiter–Danäe storyline of the play, performed in their phallic tower of incarceration by Princess Eugenia and her waiting women – again a theatricalised troupe analogous to Henrietta Maria and her female court players – and further figured in Rolliardo's gained access inside the carefully managed stage property of the birdcage, which is carried into the female space of performance). In this play, that is to say *The Convent of Pleasure*, we have Monsieur Takepleasure and the others devising various hapless schemes to penetrate the convent walls where not even a grate for oral communication with the outside world has been allowed – it is intriguing to say the least that Cavendish resists the option favoured by many other texts about withdrawal of retaining a chink of outside light from a keyhole or a window to facilitate both the voyeuristic male gaze and therefore eventual penetration.[29] The account within Wroth's *Urania* of a servant's entrapment of the devious Queen of Romania elicits a remarkably dense series of paragraphs which engage with this paradoxical concept of the private room of the closet and the public 'performance' of privacy and withdrawal into it:

> He plotted to undo her, and watched the opportunity, which he obtained by his diligent prying – that bringing him to discover going into her cabinet with this stranger, pretending there to show him some jewels. They were no sooner within the room (she having but put the door a little to, not close), but her enraged enemy came, and finding means of discerning what was to be seen, lost it not but stood still looking in. She (whose thoughts carried her to higher points than care) took no heed of that which most concerned her, for there he saw her will all passionate ardency seek and sue for the stranger's love, yet he, unmovable, was no further wrought than if he had seen a delicate play-boy act a loving woman's part and, knowing him a boy, liked only his action.[30]

As this extract makes manifest, the private closet-space is automatically sexualised by the entrance of another person into this intimate region: the overt puns Wroth makes on jewels here emphasise this transformation. This is also represented by the author in overtly theatricalised terms, and therefore provides an important precedent for Cavendish's engagement with the theatrical potential of the closet–arena or area.

The Jupiter–Danäe story as employed in Shirley's *The Bird in a Cage* is also revealing here: Jupiter pierces Danäe's tower confines in the form of a shower of gold travelling through the keyhole (a trope which was translated in turn by more prosaic seventeenth-century writers, from Jonson through to Shirley, as a very literal bribing of the guards). Cavendish, as I have mentioned, excludes any crack in the convent's structure that would facilitate masculine invasion of this kind, and yet I do question how hermetically sealed her female convent community truly is. Madam Mediator is the very socially active go-between, who manages to keep the choices of the intensely private Lady Happy very public. Even more importantly perhaps, we do have a Rolliardo-esque penetration of the female troupe by the disguised 'Princess', who actually watches and eventually participates in the convent theatricals and therefore in the dramatic and erotic economy of this closet space.[31]

In seventeenth-century prose fiction by women, closet spaces take on highly paradoxical significations. Retreat into such spaces, into supposed 'privacy', is often overtly performative, made 'public' in numerous episodes in Wroth's aforementioned *Urania* and Madame de Lafayette's *Princess de Cleves*. Both these texts exhibit a fondness for penetration tropes and motifs, and both are *romans à clef* – only surface fictions that constantly invite the reader to find real-life parallels and equivalent spaces with which to invade and redefine the story. Cavendish's own fondness for employing the material of genuine experience in her play texts and in her other generic experimentations needs no reiteration here, but does add further texture to my argument for the centrality of visible private spaces in her writings.

This tendency may not have been unique to Cavendish. The historian Anne Laurence has indicated the special relevance of this for the female 'performance' of devotion. 'Private' prayers in 'private' closets must be overheard in order for godliness to be fully registered, and this fact, for Laurence, contributes to what she describes as the 'ambiguous privacy' of the closet.[32] Matthew 6.6 may have counselled: 'But thou, when thou prayest, enter into thy closet, and when thou hast shut the door, pray to thy Father which is in secret,' but servants might be placed to overhear (and again we have this important theatrical and literary manoeuvre figuring in the quotidian practices of the early modern household), or friends might be informed of the act.[33] Once more, then, we have the conscious blurring of socially defined thresholds – of limens between public and private, but also between ranks, the sexes, and social groups. On a related theme, Alan Stewart has written of Lady Margaret Hoby's personal diary:

> [...] the (private) closet is placed in contrast to her (public) bedchamber, where she is often accompanied by the gentlewomen, acting as a sign to distinguish public praying – that is praying in company – from private, solitary praying which takes place in her closet. For example, on Thursday, 13 September 1599 she concludes her day: 'Then I wrought tel almost : 6 :, and praied with Mr. Rhodes [her chaplain], and privatly in my Closett' [...] When Lady Margaret goes in to her closet, she does not merely withdraw to privacy, but rather she enacts that withdrawal publicly, and records it textually, indicating a space of secrecy outside the knowledge of the household [...] The closet is thus constructed as a place of utter privacy, of total withdrawal from the public sphere of the household – but it simultaneously functions as a very *public* gesture of withdrawal, a very public sign of privacy [...].[34]

When the Queen of Romania in Wroth's *Urania* leaves the door to her cabinet slightly ajar, she seems to be to be inviting the servant to overhear her 'performance', and Wroth (a performer herself in the very public spectacles of the court masques for Queen Anna as well as an author of closet-drama) describes the ensuing 'scene' in deliberately theatrical terminology. Cavendish's own interest in the masque form and its potential for female self-stagings and empowerment is made manifest in Acts IV and V of *The Convent of Pleasure* and elsewhere in her literary canon. It seems significant that when Lady Happy speaks in the guise of the Sea Nymph in the watery masque of Act IV, it is to assert her power, and that she articulates that power in terms of access to the sea's cabinets and closets:

> My Cabinets are Oyster-Shells,
> In which I keep my Orient-Pearls
> To open them I use the Tide,
> As Keys to Locks, which opens wide,
>
> No Prince on Earth hath more resort,
> Nor keeps more Servants in his Court.[35]

The masque, let alone the female commissioned masques of Queen Anna and Queen Henrietta Maria, would have been a remembered form; there was of course a need for the private and constrained to substitute for the public and performed at the time when Cavendish was writing. The Interregnum's problematic relationship with dramatic forms (and yet constant engagement with them, albeit in displaced contexts) may consequently invest her closet drama with a very strong sense of needing to be staged to the world in alternative forms to prohibited straight drama.[36] At a time when public theatre in England was under ban we have to assume that the nature of 'private' drama may have been decisively altered or redefined. In some respects as the only possibility or recourse for dramatic performance, so-called 'closet-drama' may have been rendered more 'public' in its self-understanding and its composition than the label allows. Indeed, this may even have been the case prior to the Interregnum for women who were, after all, forbidden access to the public stages of England prior to 1660, and yet who found all kinds of access to performance culture in the early Stuart period, as studies of Mary Wroth, Arbella Stuart, Queen Anna and others have indicated.[37] The gendered, supposedly non-performative site of the closet, and the related form of closet-drama, needs serious re-interrogation in this light, and performance history needs to rethink the performative vacuum it has implied existed between 1642 and 1660.

An often quoted phrase of Margaret Cavendish's is from the *Sociable Letters*: 'my Fancy set up a stage in my Brain [...] and the Incorporeal Thoughts were the Several Actors,'[38] and as Jane Milling has argued there are related arguments to be made about the extent to which Cavendish did use these intensely private sites of experience[39] (the closet and, more importantly, even her own mind – 'her closet theatre of the mind', as Sophie Tomlinson terms it)[40] to stage herself to the world. The 'private space of the thinking subject', the space of the mind, was also of fascination to her (indicated in her interest in the work of Hobbes and Descartes), and in turn destabilises any easy understanding of 'privacy' as it operates in her work.

In a recent article, Ronald Huebert has suggested that there are four different understandings of 'privacy' in operation in the early modern period, a period in which, he argues, 'privacy was emerging as a category of experience in its own right':[41] private as being that which is not public, a lack, an absence or lack of status therefore, privation or deprivation (a meaning which, as we have seen, Cavendish – through the medium of Lady Happy – resists, suggesting that she saw the 'private' as a potentially empowering locale, perhaps because of that intrinsic association with status); ownership or property (again linked to power and social standing); secrecy (as in private and confidential – although as we have seen private spaces often operate in Renaissance drama or prose as sites of overhearing, surreptitious audiences, and discovery; secrets are intended to be known);[42] and finally interiority. Huebert cites one of Stephen Gosson's numerous late-sixteenth century arguments against theatre in *Plays Confuted in Five Actions* (1582) in which he advises introspection as a way of resisting theatrical blandishments:

'Enter every one into your selves, and whensoever you heare that playe againe, or any man els in private conference commend Playes, consider not, so much what is spoken to colour them as what may be spoken to confounde them.'[43] The thought of theatre is seen to get into the imagination and from thence to corrupt it. I would suggest that this interiority functions almost in reverse in Cavendish: the thoughts of theatre, the possibilities of the public and performed enter the private space of her mind, her 'brain the stage', and empower it from within. On the contentious subject of just how theatrical Cavendish's drama really is, it is worth remembering that Renaissance playgoers persistently described 'hearing' rather than 'seeing' plays: in a society where the ear was attuned to the imaginative potential of the words, why should the theatrical experience of a read closet-drama be at all diminished by comparison with mainstream public theatre? Perhaps in this way Cavendish found a means of very public speech. The closet becomes in this reading a theatre of immense public significance and potential, and I would suggest that Cavendish exploited the space in this way throughout her own life, literally and figuratively speaking.

There are then, it will be clear, important socio-historical and literary significances, as well as intellectual arguments, that accrue around the household and imaginative spaces of closets or cabinets. As the instances from Cavendish's work and from Wroth's *Urania* evidence, closets have been largely over-determined as 'private' spaces. 'Privacy' *per se* as a governing concept during the Renaissance is now under scrutiny and accordingly 'privacy' as an attainable or even desirable state of being for early modern men and women must be queried. If we are to fully comprehend the functions and symbolic significances of closet-space(s), it is paramount that we challenge pre-determined assumptions about the particular meanings and cognisance of 'public' and 'private' within the period with which we are dealing.

The 'private room' was, paradoxically, often the heart of the early modern house, if not architecturally, then certainly within the context of the individual's experience of it. Early modern houses were constructed to be read, they were 'emblematic statements', and 'private' rooms were necessarily part of that reading process – thus rendering them public intellectual property. Contemporary, 'real-life' examples such as the painted oratory or closet of Lady Drury at Christchurch Mansion in Ipswich, which is extant, or the private apartments of William Cavendish at Little Castle, Bolsover could be offered as indicators of how material space mapped the mental and imaginative space of its occupants.[44]

Margaret Cavendish's closet was a subject of contemporary discussion and speculation, and the inherently 'theatrical' public aspect of designated private space, already hinted at, is thus confirmed.[45] Whilst William Cavendish's painted private apartments articulate a series of retreats into fantasy and nostalgic constructions of a paradisiacal harmonious pagan and Christian past, it is to be remembered that retreat and nostalgia were political tropes and motifs in the decades leading up to the English Civil wars and beyond.[46] Cavendish's is a performed retreat that has distinctly public and political motives and signification. The nostalgia for Caroline feminocentric theatre and culture that Margaret Cavendish's drama evinces can be read as a very public expression of political sympathies, as well as an expression of her own sense of a lost privacy. Cavendish was part of a community of exiles, uprooted, without their own spaces into which to retreat, and her creation of these compensatory empowered arenas in her drama and her prose should perhaps be considered in this light.[47]

Such exploitation and reconfiguration of the 'private' closet space raises important questions for many seventeenth-century women's literary performances. There has been a strong and valid critical interest in recent decades in retrieving non-canonical women's writings from the early modern period, and this has led to an emphasis being placed upon so-called 'private' texts – usually diaries or comparable autobiographical writings ('private' here usually operating as a synonym for 'unpublished', which again is problematic). The *Her Own Life* collection has been influential in establishing a genuine academic space for these texts, but their incorporation into the canon has carried with it its own distorting effects. Women writers in the seventeenth century have become identified, perhaps over-identified, as predominantly private and domestic authors ('domestic' may be another misleading term; on a number of occasions here I have had recourse to mention the very 'public' nature of the aristocratic household). Women's works have consequently been assigned to categories or genres that would seem to fit or confirm this label. Yet, as Helen Wilcox has suggested, this cannot by definition constitute the whole story:

> Autobiographical writing appears to be introverted, and these texts the most inward-looking of the genre; however, the act of inscribing a self involves the creation of a new self, a publicly accessible one, available in the shared language in spite of an absent or limited audience [...] Autobiographical writing may thus breach the divide between private and public, and in its very essence mirror the women's lives, poised at the borderline between hiddenness and expressiveness.[48]

Lady Anne Clifford may bemoan her loneliness at Knole (she describes herself as 'like an owl in the desert' while her husband, the earl of Dorset, is depicted gallivanting off to social gatherings such as the races), and the private genre of diary writing may constitute an effort on her part to stave off this overwhelming privacy, and yet the pages of her diary also indicate a life constantly overheard or overseen, where observing servants are omnipresent, and where her very placement in a closet room would be a fact known to several people.[49] The paradoxes persist and our understanding of genre in relation to the closet-space may also require detailed reinvestigation as a result.

Finally, there is the very public circulation of printed and manuscript texts of so-called 'closet-dramas'. If the prose style of female fiction writers such as Mary Wroth or Margaret Cavendish, with their highly individuated syntax styles, consciously resisted containment within patriarchal expectations, then the drive exhibited by both these women to publish – to make their texts public and therefore to be read – also constitutes a challenge to that restrictive 'private' space of the closet, or at least a reconstitution of it. The question of public and private spaces forms a crucial part of a number of current debates within early modern scholarship. In order to fully explore the complexities of those terms it is necessary that we include subtle redefinitions of the physical, textual and imaginative space of the closet within the discourse of that debate so that they become indeed spaces for freedom and not cloisters of restraint.

Notes

[1] Margaret Cavendish, *The Convent of Pleasure*, ed. by Jennifer Rowsell (Oxford: Seventeenth Century Press, 1995), I.2, p. 11. All subsequent references to the *Convent of Pleasure* are to this edition.

[2] Margaret J. M. Ezell, '"To Be Your Daughter in Your Pen": The Social Functions of Literature in the Writings of Lady Elizabeth Brackley and Lady Jane Cavendish', *Huntington Library Quarterly*, 51 (1988), 281–296 (p. 284).

[3] Mary Ellen Lamb, *Gender and Authorship in the Sidney Circle* (Madison: University of Wisconsin Press, 1990), p. 190.

[4] Lady Mary Wroth, *Urania*, in Paul Salzman (ed.), *An Anthology of Seventeenth-Century Fiction* (Oxford: Oxford University Press, 1991), p. 76.

[5] Helen Wilcox, 'Private Writing and Public Functions: Autobiographical Texts by Renaissance Englishwoman', in S. P. Cerasano and Marion Wynne-Davies (eds.), *Gloriana's Face: Women, Public and Private in the English Renaissance* (London: Harvester Wheatsheaf, 1992), pp. 47–62 (p. 54).

[6] See extracts in Elspeth Graham, Hilary Hinds, Elaine Hobby, and Helen Wilcox (eds.), *Her Own Life: Autobiographical Writings by Seventeenth-century Englishwomen* (London and New York: Routledge, 1989). See, for example, p. 44.

[7] Anne Clifford, *The Diaries of Lady Anne Clifford*, ed. by D. J. H. Clifford (Stroud: Alan Sutton, 1990), p. 248. Alan Stewart in 'The Early Modern Closet Discovered', in *Representations*, 50 (1995), 76–100, suggests the different experience of closet space on the part of Anne and her husband, highlighting that whilst he reads in his, she is read to in hers. This account however neglects those occasions on which she enters his space to read, an intriguing act of self-insertion and retrieval along the lines Stewart explores elsewhere in his essay.

[8] Lisa Jardine, *Reading Shakespeare Historically* (London: Routledge, 1996), especially pp. 126–127 and 150–151.

[9] *The Matrimonial Trouble*, II.5, *Playes* (1662), p. 461.

[10] Patricia Fumerton, *Cultural Aesthetics: Renaissance Literature and the Practice of Social Ornament* (Chicago and London: University of Chicago Press, 1991), esp. Ch.3: 'Secret Arts: Elizabethan Miniatures and Sonnets', pp. 67–110.

[11] Mark Girouard, *Life in the English Country House: A Social and Architectural History* (Harmondsworth: Penguin, 1980), p. 130.

[12] Girouard, *English Country House*, p. 135.

[13] See Annabel Patterson, *Censorship and Interpretation: The Conditions of Writing and Reading in Early Modern England* (Madison: University of Wisconsin Press, 1984), p. 209.

[14] Philippe Ariès and George Duby (eds.) *A History of Private Life*, trans. Arthur Goldhammer, 3 vols (Cambridge, Mass. and London: Harvard University Press, 1987–1989): see in particular III, *The Passions of the Renaissance*, especially pp. 228–229.

[15] See Girouard, *English Country House*, p. 150 and R. Malcolm Smuts (ed.), *The Stuart Court and Europe: essays in politics and political culture* (Cambridge: Cambridge University Press, 1996).

[16] Cit. Barbara Lewalski, *Writing Women in Jacobean England* (Cambridge, Mass.: Harvard University Press, 1993), p. 23. See also Leeds Barroll, 'The Court of the First Stuart Queen', in Linda Levy Peck (ed.) *The Mental World of the Jacobean Court* (Cambridge: Cambridge University Press, 1991), pp. 148–168.

[17] My thanks to Alexandra Bennett for discussions on this topic.

[18] I am of course indebted here to the work of Sophie Tomlinson and Hero Chalmers. See Sophie Tomlinson, 'She That Plays the King: Henrietta Maria and the Threat of the Actress in Caroline Culture', in Gordon McMullan and Jonathan Hope (eds.), *The Politics of Tragicomedy: Shakespeare and After* (London: Routledge, 1992), pp. 189–207, and Hero Chalmers, 'The Politics of Feminine Retreat in Margaret Cavendish's *The Female Academy* and *The Convent of Pleasure*', *Women's Writing*, 6 (1999), 81–94. I am deeply grateful to Hero for allowing me to read this article in draft form and for her invaluable discussions of this material.

[19] See extracts from Cavendish, 'A True Relation', in Graham et al, *Her Own Life*, pp. 89–100.

[20] *The Convent of Pleasure*, I.2, p. 9.

[21] Graham et al, *Her Own Life*, p. 91.

[22] *The Second Part of the Lady Contemplation*, I.6, *Playes* (1662), p. 217.

[23] *The Second Part of the Lady Contemplation*, IV.19, *Playes* (1662), p. 230.

[24] Graham et al, *Her Own Life*, p. 96.

[25] *The Convent of Pleasure*, I.2, p. 9.

[26] See my '"A Woman Write a Play!": Jonsonian Strategies in the drama of Margaret Cavendish, or Did the Duchess Feel the Anxiety of Influence', in S. P. Cerasano and Marion Wynne-Davies (eds.), *Readings in Renaissance Drama by Women* (London: Routledge 1998), pp. 293–305.

[27] *The Convent of Pleasure*, V.2, p. 35.

[28] *The Convent of Pleasure*, I.2, p. 11. See Chalmers, 'Politics of Female Retreat'.

[29] See Domna C. Stanton, 'Recuperating Women and the Man behind the Screen', in James Grantham Turner (ed.), *Sexuality and Gender in Early Modern Europe: Institutions, Texts, Images* (Cambridge: Cambridge University Press, 1993), pp. 247–265.

[30] Wroth, *Urania*, p. 89.

[31] Sophie Tomlinson has argued for the significant operation of 'erotic spectacle' in Cavendish's writing. See Sophie Tomlinson, '"My Brain the Stage": Margaret Cavendish and the Fantasy of Female Performance', in *Women, Texts, and Histories*, pp. 134–63. See also Susan Wiseman, 'Gender and Status in Dramatic Discourse: Margaret Cavendish, Duchess of Newcastle', in *Women, Writing, History*, pp. 159–177.

[32] Ann Laurence, *Women in England, 1500–1700: A Social History* (London: Weidenfeld and Nicolson, 1994). I am also indebted to her unpublished symposium paper, 'The Ambiguous Privacy of the Closet: How Private Was Women's Space in the Early Modern Period?', Wormleighton, Warwickshire 1995.

[33] Ariès and Duby stress the rather curious blend of communal and personal piety that makes up the Christian faith at this time. See *History of Private Life*, p. 69.

[34] Stewart, 'Early Modern Closet', p. 81. Extracts from Hoby's diary are reproduced in Suzanne Trill, Kate Chedgzoy, and Melanie Osborne (eds.), *'Lay By Your Needles, Ladies Take the Pen': Writing Women in England, 1500–1700* (London: Arnold, 1997).

[35] *The Convent of Pleasure*, IV.1, p. 32.

[36] Susan Wiseman's research on Interregnum drama has had a profound influence on my thinking. See her *Drama and Politics in the English Civil War* (Cambridge: Cambridge University Press, 1998). See also Dale B. J. Randall, *Winter Fruit: English Drama, 1642–1660* (Lexington: University Press of Kentucky, 1995).

[37] See, for example, Lewalski, *Writing Women in Jacobean England, passim*. I am also indebted to the ongoing research of Clare McManus on the subject of elite female performance.

[38] *Sociable Letters* (1664), p. 408.

[39] Jane Milling, 'Lady Contemplation's Philosophical Fancies: The Closet Drama of Margaret Cavendish', unpublished symposium paper, Wormleighton, Warwickshire, 1995.

[40] Tomlinson, 'My Brain the Stage', p. 155.

[41] Ronald Huebert, 'Privacy: The Early Social History of a Word', *The Sewanee Review*, 105 (1997), 21–38 (p. 29). My thanks to Ronald Huebert for sending me an advance copy of this article and for his exchanges on this subject.

[42] See Helen Hackett, '"Yet Tell Me Some Such Fiction": Lady Mary Wroth's *Urania* and the "Femininity" of Romance', in *Women, Texts,and Histories*, pp. 39–68.

[43] Stephen Gosson, *Plays Confuted*, cit. Huebert, 'Privacy', pp. 33–34.

[44] I am indebted here to Peter Davidson for ideas and thinking on this issue.

[45] John Evelyn records visits to the Newcastle residences in his diaries and letters. See *The Diary of John Evelyn*, ed. by E. S. De Beer (Oxford: Clarendon Press, 1955). Richard Flecknoe mentions her closet in a poem included in the obscure *Collection of Letters and Poems, Written by Several Persons of Honour and Learning, Upon Divers Important Subjects to the late Duke and Duchess of Newcastle* (London, 1678). I thank James Fitzmaurice and Marie-Louise Coolahan respectively for these references.

[46] On the decoration of the Bolsover apartments see Timothy J. Raylor, '"Pleasure Reconciled to Virtue": William Cavendish, Ben Jonson, and the Decorative Scheme of Bolsover Castle', *Renaissance Quarterly*, 52 (1999), 402–39.

[47] See Chalmers, 'The Politics of Female Retreat'.

[48] Wilcox, 'Private Writing and Public Functions', p. 60.

[49] Graham et al, *Her Own Life*, p. 42.

PART III

POETRY

9

Imagining the Mind: Cavendish's Hobbesian Allegories

Jay Stevenson

This paper discusses imagining the mind as a central literary strategy throughout Cavendish's works. I point out that she has frequent recourse to this strategy in her poems, plays, prose fiction and philosophy, and suggest that this strategy helps legitimate her writing in physiological as well as rhetorical terms, as a process of playful mental and social ordering. I also suggest that her readers are ambiguously implicated in this playfulness, invited to accede to the ordering power of Cavendish's own mind, or to laugh at the extravagance of that imagined and imagining power.

Elsewhere I have argued that Cavendish's self-reflexive and self-contradictory philosophical writings reflect her mechanist–vitalist conception of the mind, or soul.[1] In this paper, I want to extend my previous discussion by looking at excerpts from some of Cavendish's literary writings – poems, tales and plays – that figure and enact the mind. These representations of mind in Cavendish help justify thinking, speaking and writing as sufficiently ordered or in need of self-ordering. At the same time, they continually police themselves against mental and social disorder resulting from the threats of enthusiasm and atheism.

In representing the mind, Cavendish raises questions about knowing. Two emergent early modern epistemological strategies, rationalism and empiricism, constitute important new approaches to the problem of knowing. Each provides a way of testing secular and religious knowledge and authority and offers the hope of an orderly resolution to religious and political dispute. These two approaches, however, were not fully reconciled to one another. In fact, they can be seen as results of an analytical split imposed on a less rigorous vitalist world-view in which meaning, agency, mind and substance are seen both to reside in all things and to transcend them. Empiricism and rationalism, in contrast, impose a division between matter and mind, each emphasising one over the other as the basis of knowledge. Put simply, the difference between rationalism and empiricism is that the former pursues knowledge independently of sensed experience while the latter aims to rely primarily on the evidence of the senses. In other words, empiricism begins with matter whereas rationalism begins with mind. The two orientations coexist in a state of unresolved dialectical tension throughout the seventeenth century.[2]

One expression of this tension was widespread invective against the twin epistemological menaces of enthusiasm and atheism. It makes sense to regard enthusiasm as a species of rationalism gone wrong. The mind, left wholly to its own devices, fills itself with factitious ideas of religious devotion or philosophical truth. Such spurious thinking was perceived as perniciously liable to set itself up as authoritative and thence to spread to whole communities. Enthusiasm was exposed and denounced in treatises that regard the enthusiastic mind and its fabrications empirically, stripping them of their metaphysical pretensions by objectifying them as mere physiological manifestations. Thus, enthusiasm was seen as a kind of medical condition.[3]

There is a pronounced enthusiastic strain in Cavendish. She frequently allows her imagination to get carried away with itself. Moreover, her enthusiasm is shared by a number of the female protagonists of her plays and narratives who are not only enthusiastic themselves, but indoctrinate others in enthusiasm with elaborately crafted speeches. Thus Cavendish parodies enthusiasm, even while suggesting it is a source of her own discursive abilities.

Atheism, conversely, was attributed to an excessive or misguided kind of empirical impulse. When the mind, preoccupied with tangible things, stubbornly insists on disregarding its own immaterial essence, it ignores its connection with God and loses its ability to apprehend and acquiesce to divinity. Atheism was denounced in treatises urging that the new empirical science be implemented with cautious humility and pious reflection.[4] Much of Cavendish's work smacks of atheism in that it suggests the mind has no direct spiritual connection to God, but is wholly physical and left to its own devices.

Enthusiasm and atheism are psychological and political manifestations of the opposed epistemological positions of rationalism and empiricism. Both menaces are symptomatic of disorder in the mind and in the commonwealth. Seventeenth-century treatises view these problems as related, indeed as over-reactions to one another. Each problem may breed its opposite. Cavendish, in her many representations of mind, engages both problems simultaneously, suggesting the mind is both detached from any informing source of absolute truth and prone to embrace ideals of its own devising. Thus, atheist and enthusiast tendencies complicate one another in Cavendish. She counters her enthusiasm by suggesting her mind is its own world, and its beliefs and ideas are physiological accidents. In turn, she disguises her atheism by asserting religious and other ideals of virtue as among those that promote order in her mind.

On one hand, the mind in Cavendish is so completely subject to empirical scrutiny that each thought is a concrete, physical symptom of itself. At the same time, mind is so completely prior to experience that nothing reliably exists except as thought. Indeed, Cavendish's writings about the mind suggest that *everything* is thought and that all thought is the tangible figment of its own imagination.

This astonishing relativist writing creates a space for itself by celebrating the provisional mental and social order it reflects. In so doing, it continually suggests that psychological and social order must be imagined. Imagination, then, is a force that imposes order. Indeed, Cavendish's own imagination, together with the writings that enact it, is necessary for her own mental and social well-being. Her representations of mind exercise and order her own thoughts while they appeal to her readers for approval and acceptance.

The force of Cavendish's imagination, however, is ambiguously directed toward her readers, particularly in plays and narratives centred around her magnificently virtuous heroines, most notably the play, *Youth's Glory, Death's Banquet* and the romance, *The Description of a New World Called the Blazing World*. These works, in relating the rise to fame of their magnificent heroines, dramatise the social power of factitious ideals of virtue, which the protagonists supposedly embody. In representing factitious virtues, Cavendish invites the factitious respect of her readers.

The force of Cavendish's imagination, in other words, is deployed against her readers even while it is dramatised and implicitly exposed within the text. Cavendish, like her heroines, is an enthusiast who wants to spread her enthusiasm to her readers just as her imaginary counterparts want to persuade their auditors of their transcendent virtue. At the same time, she, like them, is slyly sceptical of the very virtues she seems to espouse and invites her sceptical readers to laugh at the credulity depicted in her narratives.

Cavendish repeatedly uses the idea of her own mind to frame her writings. The 1662 volume of her plays is prefaced by a poem identifying them as dramas enacted on the stage of her brain:

> [...] all the time my Playes a making were,
> My brain the Stage, my thoughts were acting there.[5]

This 'theatre of the mind' trope is presented partly as a consolation for Cavendish's belief that her plays would never be acted on stage. Not only did she suspect they were too unorthodox to be successfully performed, but they were apparently written during the Interregnum before the reopening of the public theatres. There is a sense, then, in which Cavendish is only pretending to be a playwright. This very pretence, however, becomes for Cavendish an integral aspect of dramatic representation. In imagining itself as a stage, her brain produces plays. Emphasising their imaginary origin in her brain, Cavendish deftly acknowledges the many senses in which her plays might be thought not to be real plays: not only will they not be performed, but they were written by a woman – someone, in other words, whose literary credentials are suspect. At the same time, however, her brain authorises her plays as, in fact, performable, indeed as actually performed in her mind. As dramatisations of the very thought they represent, her plays have an undeniable empirical reality.

Like her drama, many of her narratives are framed as mental figurations. A prefatory poem to her book of tales, *Nature's Pictures Done With Fancy's Pencil to the Life*, says that the subsequent tales are told and heard by 'Figures' of Cavendish's absent friends, raised like phantoms 'in the Circle of my Brain.' These mental friends gather around a fire, which 'was of Fancy, which I made / Within the Glandule of a Chimney laid.'[6] The glandule is a portion of the brain thought to be the seat of understanding. Thus her stories as well as plays are framed as allegories representing and enacting a process of self-consolation: here the imaginary friends are comforting substitutes for absent real ones, and they tell tales intended to disperse the cold and tedium of winter.

Of course, it is hardly surprising that the tales are mental manifestations; traditionally, the tale is an especially fanciful narrative form. Here, however, specifying the scene of storytelling as mental reifies the consumption of the tales as well as their production. Cavendish's mind imagines not only the tales, but also an audience for them. Her mind comprises a fictive, discursive community. Cavendish presents not only her drama and narrative, but also her philosophy as the self-reflexive activity of her mind. Again, her mind imagines not only her philosophy, but also an appropriate social setting:

> I was very Studious in my own Thoughts and Contemplations, when I writ it for all that time my Brain was like an University, Senate, or Council Chamber, wherein all my Conceptions, Imaginations, Observations, Wit, and Judgement did meet to Dispute, Argue, Contrive, and Judge for Sense, Reason, and Truth.[7]

In presenting her philosophy as the result of a community of mental impulses, Cavendish qualifies any rational pretensions she may be thought to have in writing philosophy. Cavendish's 'Thoughts' have minds of their own. Her mind is embattled, and the knowledge it produces is the result of a political process rather than simply the reflection of an ideal or empirical truth. As we shall see, Cavendish's sense of knowledge as socially contingent is woven into the plots of many of her plays and narratives in which female orators, philosophers and rulers deploy rhetorical and political force to establish their authority. In these prefatory allegories, Cavendish is drawing attention to the fact that she is imagining herself as a playwright, a storyteller and a philosopher. This strategy of self-representation obviously qualifies any absolute status she might seek for her work, suggesting her ideas are *just* ideas, with no necessary authority or grounding in extra-mental reality. We are invited not to regard her writings about the mind as authorised by a rational self, except insofar as the mind's authority – and its order – is produced by that mind. Cavendish, in effect, imagines her own discursive power. Although her discursive authority is imagined, however, it is literally self-realising. In generating representations of itself, her mind provides irrefutable testimony of its own discursivity. Manifestly, her brain thinks and her thoughts can be written down. *Cogito ergo scribo*.

Such a thoroughly empirical and self-sufficient attitude towards discourse suggests an atheistic bent to her thinking. If Cavendish's thoughts are simply self-creating, she would seem entirely lacking in any spiritual connection with God according to the criteria of her theist contemporaries.[8] Not surprisingly, then, a number of Cavendish's representations of mind address religious questions, dramatising the psychological implications of belief in God. For example, some allegorical narratives about the mind in *Nature's Pictures* suggest that religious ideals are mental constructs conducive to psychic order. In 'An Expression of the Doubts and Curiosity of Man's Mind', for example, a man's 'thoughts' go off to learn what happens to the soul after death. When Reason, their guide, tells them the answer cannot be known, the thoughts get angry and abandon her. After inquiring of academicians, courtiers, soldiers and alchemists, and receiving different answers from each, the thoughts get back together with Reason who introduces them to Faith. The story concludes with an alliance formed among the 'thoughts', Reason and Faith.[9] Seemingly, this happy ending figures a triumph of rationalism. Empirical inquiry fails to yield the sought-for knowledge of the afterlife, which may only be intimated with the help of Reason. Reason, however, fails to transcend the empirical frame of the allegory. The abstractions, Truth, Faith and Reason, because they are psychologised as mental states, are significant chiefly as such. The conflicts these allegories present are resolved through the harmonious ordering of the mind. The suggestion of a transcendent truth which, as the tales insist, cannot be known, is important chiefly insofar as it conduces to mental order. These tales depict divine order *qua* mental order, locating abstract value in the mind *per se*, rather than in an unknowable afterlife. In representing mental order as teleologically paramount, the allegory secularises transcendent religious and personal virtue as psychological well-being, reversing the more common allegorical presentation of mental integrity as a means to a social or religious end.

In obvious contrast, *Pilgrim's Progress* suggests mental integrity is not an end in itself, but a means to a higher religious end. Could Christian's acceptance into heaven function as a metaphor for a mental state? Could Bunyan's allegory be interpreted as a fable about psychological well-being? The narrative is certainly slippery and especially marked by the ambiguity characteristic of allegory in general. The events it represents are ambivalently psychological events, simulacra of actual events, and 'dark' shadowings of a transcendent truth that cannot be perfectly known. Christian's salvation, however, is not simply analogous to his psychological state, but contingent on it. He must master his inner fears *in order* to cross through the River of Death to the Celestial City. Failure to maintain faith would not result simply in mental anguish but damnation. Narrative closure is achieved not simply with the reaffirmation of faith, but with Christian's arrival and acceptance by God and the Saints.[10]

Thus, Bunyan's allegory is largely blind to the self-reflexive sense in which Christian's uncertainty, together with sectarian politics, requisition transcendence. Bunyan does not emphasise the possibility that the effect of transcendence his allegory seeks to produce may stem from a self-fulfilling psychic and political desire. He presents transcendent atonement as a solution for the problem of mental struggle without suggesting that such atonement may be merely imaginary, taking place as an effect of mental resolution. Cavendish's religious allegories, on the other hand, repeatedly associate transcendent atonement with reflexive self-ordering. In Cavendish, moreover, mental order is fictive, depending upon the mind's acceptance of ideas toward which the narrative exhibits scepticism. There is a disjunction between the narrated and the narrating mind, which have opposed attitudes toward transcendent ideals. The narrated mind 'believes' these ideas and thus attains resolution. The narrating mind promotes these ideals merely as a means of bringing about resolution.

The importance of mental order is evident in Cavendish's political allegories as well as her religious ones. Like her religious allegories, her political allegories make contradictory use of ordering ideals. In these, the purpose of achieving mental order is not necessarily to resolve the social problems they seem to be concerned with. Instead, social order is achieved allegorically as a way of resolving mental problems. In 'Fancy's Monarchy in the Land of Poetry', for example, mental faculties are allegorised as state officials and the five senses are military commanders patrolling the borders.[11] Good government makes for a good mental state, rather than vice versa. Here order is achieved through, and figured as, the discipline of writing poetry. While the ideals advanced in the mind's poetry are persuasive enough to regulate the mind, they are not asserted for their own sake by the writing mind of Cavendish, but are shown to serve the purpose of achieving mental order.

Similarly, in 'Of the Indispositions of the Mind', a sick mind seeks help from divines and moral philosophers who disagree about the nature of the mind's disease and about the appropriate cure.[12] The wrangling of these doctors and theologians exacerbates the mind's indisposition to the point of refiguring it. The mind's disease may be purged only after it purges the physicians, the first step in a self-healing process. The mind then goes on to cure itself with 'Herbs of Grace, Fruit of Justice, Spice of Prudence, Bread of Fortitude' and other aliments, suggesting that social and religious virtues are chiefly important as a means of achieving mental well-being. This mental order is provisional and *a posteriori*, rather than absolute.

Clear evidence that mental order in Cavendish is not absolute is to be found in allegories that depict the mind in an embattled condition without resolving the conflict. One such depiction is presented in the poem, 'The Prey of Thoughts', which presents thoughts and feelings as animals in a kind of Hobbesian state of nature, preying on, and hiding from, one another:

If Thoughts be the Mindes Creatures, as some say,
Like other Creatures they on each do Prey.[13]

'Ambitious Thoughts' represented as hawks, prey on 'Hopes' represented as partridges. 'Suspicious Thoughts' are hounds that pursue a 'Timorous Doubt' in the shape of a hare. The poem depicts internal conflict and suggests that there is no absolute king of the mind's jungle, but that all thoughts are similarly motivated by the exigencies of survival.

The allegory suggests the mind is a kind of ecosystem that establishes a precarious balance through inner conflict. Even virtues, Hope, Gratitude, Patience and Love are predators and/or prey:

Grateful Thoughts do feed on Thoughts of Thanks,
And are industrious, as prudent Ants.
But Thoughts of Love do live on several Meat,
Of Feares, of Hopes, and of Suspition eat.[14]

Far from being transcendently redemptive, Gratitude and Love are two of many kinds of feeders. Although they are associated with the qualities of prudence, industry and hope, they are also implicated in a moral and psychic economy of survival characterised equally by fear and suspicion. Indeed, they are derogated by their association with penury – they are insect-like and dependent. Here, then, the mind Cavendish represents lacks an ideal external ordering principle. Instead, ideals are in competition with the rest of the 'thoughts'.

Cavendish's work includes a variety of allegorical figurations of the mind that suggest mental order is contingent and subject to the interplay of independent, and sometimes conflicting, mental impulses. Such allegories are included in her philosophical writings that represent the mind as made up of 'atoms' in various states of order and disorder. Her writing thus describes and enacts conflict and order, at times demonstrating her rational and rhetorical powers to impose order and at other times enacting her own mental fragmentation.

The self-consuming, self-ordering mind represented in Cavendish's work can be found elsewhere as satire on atheism and enthusiasm. Swift, for example, provides this allegorical allusion to Hobbes in his two-pronged satire, 'The Mechanical

Operation of the Spirit':

> It is the opinion of choice virtuosi, that the brain is only a crowd of little animals, but with teeth and claws extremely sharp, and, therefore, cling together in the contexture we behold, like the picture of Hobbes's *Leviathan*.[15]

Swift characterises the mind by alluding to the famous drawing of Hobbes's allegory for the commonwealth, the 'artificial man', in which numerous individual men come together to provide its shape and substance. Swift's idea that the 'animals' in the mind are attached to one another by their teeth may glance at Hobbes's understanding of human nature as being somewhat predatory. Hobbes's understanding of human nature as motivated by self-interest, together with his materialist view of the psyche, contributed to his notoriety as an atheist.

Swift's image parodies Hobbesian mechanistic psychology in representing the mind as self-conflicted and fragmentary.[16] Indeed, in various places throughout 'Mechanical Operation', Swift actually demonstrates some of the problems he has with the mechanistic philosophy of mind by writing from the subject position of the sort of mind Hobbes seems to theorise: a mind that is not subject to the control of a transcendent reason, but internally divided by conflicting physical impulses.

Swift's satire fails, perhaps deliberately, to appreciate the importance of inductive method as a stabilising feature in Hobbesian psychology. For Hobbes, the testing of sense impressions against one another leads to reliable knowledge and guards against enthusiastic delusion. Swift, however, represents the mechanist mind as fragmented and vitalistic.

Swift was not the first writer to satirise mechanistic psychology as fraught with the very sort of mental conflict it attempts to explain. As early as 1645 the Aristotelian, Alexander Ross refuted Kenelm Digby's vitalist modification of Cartesian mechanism. Digby believed that concrete ideas are atoms given off by the things they represent and sucked by the eyes and ears into the mind where they are stored as memory. Ross has some fun with Digby's theory by saying:

> if the atoms of two armies fighting should rush into your brain by the eye, they will make a greater motion then Minerva did in Jupiter's braine: you would call for a Vulcan to cleave your head, and let out those armed men, who would cause greater struggling in your head, then the twins did in Rebecca's womb.[17]

Like Swift, Ross suggests that mechanist psychology theorises a mind unable to control either itself or the independent, self-moving, physical entities that comprise thought.

Similarly, the Cambridge Platonist, Ralph Cudworth portrays mechanist psychology as ridiculous, saying that according to the mechanist view of mind:

> every Atom of Matter must needs be a distinct Percipient, Animal, and Intelligent Person by itself [...]. Every Man would be a heap of Innumerable Animals and Percipients.[18]

Cudworth argues that if mere matter put in motion can think, as Hobbes seems to suggest, then each unit of matter, or atom, is its own authority. Human subjectivity would be infinitesimally fragmented, not unlike a brain swarming with tiny soldiers or predatory animals.

Such a subjectivity is Godless. Thus, people without God are people who do not think clearly. Dryden suggests as much in *The Hind and The Panther* where he evokes mechanist psychology to characterise equatorial pagans as having physical souls unanimated by Godly spirit. They are 'a slimy-born and sun-begotten tribe', who:

If they think at all, 'tis sure no high'r
Than matter, put in motion, may aspire.
Souls that can scarce ferment their mass of clay;
So drossy, so divisible are They [...].[19]

Thus the subjectivity theorised by mechanist psychology could be thought rationally inferior to a dualist psyche, whose spiritual aspect helps assure its clarity and integrity. Left to its own devices, without the ordering spiritual influence of God, the empirical brain wallows in the living mud it is made of. Such is the mind Cavendish theorises throughout her work, even ascribing to herself this mind's fragmented, reflexive perspective. Cavendish, however, does not merely accept the stigma of irrationality, but attempts to legitimate the material imagination. She does this by celebrating enthusiasm as psychologically salutary.

While her mental allegories about religion in the mind suggest that religious experience is physiological rather than divine, they do not discredit sectarian religious practice, as many of her contemporaries did, so much as characterise the imagination as quasi-religious – as capable of deep, though physical, sensibilities that can help order the mind. Moreover, these allegories do not ridicule certain minds for being especially prone to delusory physical influences, but instead suggest that all thought is physically generated.

Cavendish suggests, for example, that religious ideals have a material, psychological significance in the poem, 'A Prospect of a Church in the Mind'. This begins:

Standing at Imagination's Window high,
I saw a prospect in the Mind to lye.[20]

Here the imagination is figured as a window of a church, a window that is also self-reflexively imagined. Cavendish seems to be on the outside of her mind looking in, yet she has to enter her imagination to produce this effect. The imagination, then, gives itself shape here as it looks through itself at itself.

Here she sees 'An Isle of Thoughts so long [...] / Fill'd full of Fancies Light.'[21] A pun on 'light' suggests an ambivalence towards religious inspiration. The fancies are light, or insignificant, but at the same time they produce the light of inspiration. The poem goes on to suggest further associations of religion with the unreliability of the mind. While the thoughts are worshipping, 'All sorts of Opinions in Pulpits seemed to Preach, / False Doctrine for Truth might many teach.'[22] These lines suggest the poem is a satire on spurious religious authority and that the 'thoughts' are being led astray.

If it were simply the case, however, that the poem is satirical, we might expect to find the imaginary status of the church presented in a critical manner, implicating it in this false doctrine. To the contrary, the poem exhibits a tone of sincere reverence that attaches, not to God or to faith, but to the imagination and its power to generate concrete images for feelings and other mental abstractions:

> Pillars of Judgments thick stood in a row,
> And in this Isle Motion walked to and fro.
> Feare, Love, Humility kneel'd down to pray,
> Desires beg'd of all that pass'd that way.
> Poore doubts did seem, as if they quaking stood,
> Yet were they lapt in Mantles of Hope good.[23]

Judgements here are without doctrinal content, but are structurally necessary to the church of the mind. They are important, not because of what they say, but because of the function they serve. Their structural, as opposed to doctrinal, significance further suggests Cavendish's secular conception of religion.

Similarly, 'Motion', who acts as an usher in the church, suggests Cavendish's secular attitude, since 'motion' is one of the fundamental principles, along with matter, of the new mechanist philosophy and psychology espoused by Hobbes and others (see the passage from Dryden, above). Obviously, however, the poem is not detached and rational about its depiction of the church of the mind, but deals sympathetically with the feelings, Fear, Love, Humility, Hope and the rest, that implicitly account for religious belief. Indeed, the 'poore doubts', 'lapt in mantles of Hope' suggest the material, as opposed to spiritual, benefits of religious consolation.

Clearly, Cavendish's mental church lacks the divine and institutional authorisation afforded the mind in Herbert's 'The Windows'. Here the mind is unreliable, 'brittle, crazy glass', until transfigured by God, who inscribes the window of the mind with its Christian destiny.[24] Herbert's poem, addressing God, makes it clear that the preacher's mind – and the church – have a transcendent source of authority. This transcendence is disseminated from God to his priests and thence to the congregation who, with the priest's help, discover it in themselves. Whereas Herbert depicts the internalisation of Holy writ and the institutional structure of a stable Anglican hierarchy as divinely authorised and inscribed in the mind, Cavendish depicts religion as imagined and imaginary.

Cavendish's allegories of the mind imply that the ideas of order and of transcendence they entertain are provisional, physically gratifying and are produced by the mind itself. This production often seems coterminous with the act of writing mental allegory. As we shall see, imagined order is self-reflexively enacted in many of Cavendish's plays and narratives as well. While working within assumptions regarding the unreliability of the enthusiastic mind, Cavendish suggests that all minds are similarly unreliable, and that unreliable thought does not preclude mental order, or even social order. Indeed, a number of Cavendish's plays and narratives resolve in a social order predicated on enthusiasm. Much as ideals of virtue and authority in her figurations of mind are represented ironically as promoting mental order, the ideal virtues ascribed to the female protagonists of Cavendish's plays and narratives serve to promote an imagined social order.

Few readers of Cavendish's plays and narratives have understood the female protagonists as the intentionally comic figures I take them to be, although many have found them unintentionally ridiculous.[25] The reason, I think, is that Cavendish's humour is not contained within the text, but extends to characterise the relationship between Cavendish and her readers. Cavendish is self-consciously an enthusiastic philosopher who would like to infect her readers with her humorous enthusiasm. Her writing, then, is part of the brash performance her work enacts and describes, and Cavendish wears the mask of her protagonists.

Cavendish, then, is complicitous with her protagonists in their comic, yet heroic, attempts to win fame as orators and philosophers. She helps them by refraining from acknowledging the meta-fiction of female magnificence for the cynical power play that it partly is. Their speeches assert and disguise a relativist and materialist philosophy that belies the idealist virtues their auditors ascribe to them. In representing audiences who flock to see them and who are rapt by their transcendent brilliance, Cavendish imagines the sort of fame she herself desires, predicated on virtuous ideals to which she does not herself subscribe.

The play, *Youths Glory, Deaths Banquet*, for example, is an extravagant, exaggerated, self-conscious solicitation of approval. The protagonist, Lady Sanspareille, is both transcendently virtuous and calculatingly, ambitiously in pursuit of fame. Philosophers to whom she lectures agree to:

> honour this Virgin whose wit is supreme, whose judgment is Serene as the Sky, whose life is a Law unto herselfe and us, virtue her handmaid, and her words so sweet, like to a harmonious musick in the Aire, that charms our Senses and delights the Soul, and turns all passions in our hearts to love, teaches the aged, and instructs the youth, no Sophister, but Mistress still of truth.[26]

Cavendish invites her readers to endorse this view, but half-jokingly, since the lecture that elicits this response, though indeed brilliant, sets forth an elaborate justification of 'selfe love' bolstered by a relativist and imaginative material philosophy. Her auditors, then, love her because she so brilliantly manages to love herself.

In staging this play in her mind, Cavendish imagines that she, like Lady Sanspareille, will have an approving audience for her discourse. To garner approval for her protagonist, Cavendish goes so far as to write her wryly comic play disingenuously as a tragedy. The tragic death of Lady Sanspareille serves rhetorically to emphasise the virtues ascribed to her, providing the bereaved auditors of the play with the opportunity to dilate further on her transcendent magnificence. Her death also compounds the burden of judgement placed on the play's readers, who must decide whether the parody of idealism is still amusing in light of it. Her death, moreover, provides an occasion for materialist joking. As one of her friends remarks in response to the universal lament that she died so young: 'She cannot be kept longer because she was not unbowelled.'[27] She is, and has always been, all body after all.

If we take seriously the self-reflexive introductory frame to the volume of plays in which *Youth's Glory, Death's Banquet* appears and read the play as enacted on the stage of Cavendish's brain, the adulation Lady Sanspareille receives makes sense as a figuration of the mental drama of Cavendish's thoughts rallying around the idea of the female philosopher. In other words, we can, and should, read the character's magnificence as imaginary, a self-pleasing fiction with which Cavendish orders her mind and teases her readers.

The drama of the success of the female orator, then, is played out in Cavendish's plays and narratives by her female protagonists while it is played out self-reflexively in Cavendish's mind by her own thoughts. This is the case in *The Blazing World*, Cavendish's best-known work, in which the resplendent virtue of the protagonist, the Empress, results from imaginative creation and ordering. This creation and ordering involves both the Empress's creation of speeches and spectacles that order her subjects and Cavendish's creation of the narrative that orders her mind and the 'world' of the text.

The magnificent heroine appears absolutely brilliant to her subjects and to the Emperor, who make her their ruler upon first hearing her speak. The Blazing World with all its inhabitants, however, is explicitly the imaginary creation of the Duchess of Newcastle, herself a character in the romance. The romance self-reflexively narrates its own invention. Its writing is part of its plot, and both writing and plot address themselves to the imagined and self-realising success of female discourse. The two women, Cavendish and her protagonist, are in league in bringing this success about. Indeed, they consult with one another, not only about subjugating worlds, but also creating them:

> At last, when the Duchess saw that no patterns would do her any good in the framing of her world; she resolved to make a world of her own invention, and this world was composed of sensitive and rational self-moving matter; for as the sensitive did move and act both to the perceptions and consistency of the body, so this degree of matter at the same point of time (for though the degrees are mixed, yet the several parts may move several ways at one time) did move to the creation of the imaginary world; which world after it was made, appeared so curious and full of variety, so well ordered and wisely governed, that it cannot possibly be expressed by words, nor the delight and pleasure which the Duchess took in making this world of her own.[28]

This world is created out of the self-moving matter of the Duchess's imagination; it materialises itself in her brain. Its order and government, together with the pleasure it affords, are features of this imagining. The romance's self-imagining reifies not only mental order, but at least potentially social order as well. Just as the Empress's discourse and staged self-display subjects the inhabitants of the Blazing World to her rule, the self-display of the text of *The Blazing World* is intended to subjugate Cavendish's readers:

> If any should like this world I have made, and be willing to be my subjects, they may imagine themselves such, and they are such, I mean, in their minds, fancies or imaginations; but if they cannot endure to be subjects, they may create worlds of their own, and govern themselves as they please.[29]

This cagey relativist remark offers a choice among imagined realities and orders. The alternative to Cavendish's solipsistic empire is some other self-produced power. She suggests, then, that power and order are always self-produced and imaginary.

Interest in Cavendish has increased in recent years, and she has elicited deeply mixed responses in regard both to her abilities as a writer and to the politics of her self-representations. Clearly, her apparent lack of rational control and her failure to represent female virtue convincingly are part of her elliptical strategy of self-display and not, as has often been thought, evidence of her lack of training as a writer. It seems clear as well that she cultivates and, I think, deserves, a complex and approving response, involving amusement and admiration.

Notes

[1] Jay Stevenson, 'The Mechanist–Vitalist Soul of Margaret Cavendish,' *Studies in English Literature 1500–1900*, 36 (1996), 527–543. For valuable discussions of reflexivity and self-contradiction in Cavendish see Sandra Sherman, 'Trembling Texts: Margaret Cavendish and the Dialectic of Authorship', *English Literary Renaissance*, 24 (1994), 184–210, and Catherine Gallagher, 'Embracing the Absolute: The Politics of the Female Subject in Seventeenth-Century England', *Genders*, 1 (1988) 24–39.

[2] I am indebted to Michael McKeon for the insight that Cavendish's figurations of mind may be understood as engagements with this dialectic.

[3] See Henry More, *Enthusiasmus Triumphatus, or a brief discourse of the nature, causes, kinds and cure of enthusiasm* (London, 1662), reprinted with an introduction by Michael V. Da Porte by The Augustan Reprint Society, 118 (Los Angeles: William Andrews Clark Memorial Library, 1966); and Meric Casaubon, *A Treatise Concerning Enthusiasm as it is an effect of nature but is mistaken by many for either divine inspiration or diabolical possession* (London: Roger Daniel, 1655), reprinted with an introduction by Paul J. Korshin (Gainesville, Florida: Scholar's Facsimile and Reprints, 1970). Korshin cites scholarship on the reaction to enthusiasm on p. xxiv, including Philip Harth, *Swift and Anglican Rationalism: The Religious Background of A Tale of a Tub* (Chicago: University of Chicago Press, 1961), pp. 72–5; Aharon Lichtenstein, *Henry More: The rational theology of a Cambridge Platonist* (Cambridge, Mass.: Harvard University Press, 1962); and Stanley Grean, *Shaftesbury's Philosophy of Religion and Ethics: A Study in Enthusiasm* (Athens: Ohio University Press, 1967).

[4] More is one of a number of philosophers who takes this view (More, *Enthusiasmus*, pp. 1–2). Hobbes in particular underwent attack for religio–philosophical reasons. See Samuel I. Mintz, *The Hunting of the Leviathan: Seventeenth-Century Reactions to the Materialism and Moral Philosophy of Thomas Hobbes* (Cambridge: Cambridge University Press, 1962); and, pp. 293–298.

[5] *Playes* (1662), sig. A2 recto.

[6] *Natures Picture* (1671), 'The Preface', sig. c verso.

[7] *Physical Opinions* (1663), 'Epistle to the Reader', sig. b3 verso.

[8] With the exception of Hobbes, most new philosophers, including the 'empiricists,' ascribed a spiritual aspect to the mind, or soul, that assured its ability to discern truth. See Walter Charleton, *The Immortality of the human soul, demonstrated by the light of nature in two dialogues* (London: William Wilson, 1657); Henry More, *The immortality of the soul so farre forth as is demonstrable from the knowledge of nature and the light of reason* (London: J. Flesher, 1659); Joseph Glanvill, *Philosophia Pia, or, a discourse of the religious temper and tendencies of the experimental philosophy which is expressed by the Royal Society* (London: J. Macock, 1671); and Robert Boyle, *The Christian Virtuoso, shewing that by being addicted to experimental philosophy a man is rather assisted than indisposed to be a good christian,* (London: Edward Jones, 1690).

[9] *Natures Picture* (1671), pp. 107–113.

[10] John Bunyan, *Pilgrim's Progress*, ed. Roger Sharrock (London: Penguin Books, 1987).

[11] *Natures Picture* (1671), pp. 227–231.

[12] *Natures Picture* (1671), pp. 234–246.

[13] 'The Prey to Thoughts', (ll. 1–2), *Poems and Fancies* (1653), p. 150.

[14] 'The Prey to Thoughts', (ll. 29–32), *Poems and Fancies* (1653), p. 150.

[15] Jonathan Swift, *A Tale of a Tub with Other Early Works*, ed. Herbert Davis (Oxford: Blackwell, 1965), p. 181.

[16] On Hobbes's psychology, see J. W. N. Watkins, *Hobbes' System of Ideas: A Study in the Political Significance of Philosophical Theories* (London: Hutchinson University Library, 1965), esp. pp. 4–8 and 50–54. On mechanistic psychology in general see John Yolton, *Thinking Matter: Materialism in Eighteenth-century Britain* (Minneapolis: University of Minnesota Press, 1983); Carolyn Merchant, *The Death of Nature: Women, Ecology, and the Scientific Revolution* (San Francisco: Harper and Row, 1980); and Lester King, *The Philosophy of Medicine: The early Eighteenth Century* (Cambridge, Mass.: Harvard University Press, 1978).

[17] Alexander Ross, *The Philosophical Touchstone: or Observations upon Kenelm Digby's Discourses of the nature of Bodies and of the reasonable Soule* (London: James Ross, 1645), p. 48.

[18] Ralph Cudworth, *The True Intellectual System of the Universe* (London: Richard Royston, 1678), p. 72, cit. Yolton, *Thinking Matter*, p. 7.

[19] John Dryden, *The Hind and the Panther*, I, ll. 311, 316–19, *The Poems and Fables of John Dryden*, ed. James Kingsley (Oxford: Oxford University Press, 1970), p. 363.

[20] 'A Prospect of a Church in the Mind', (ll. 1-2), *Poems and Fancies* (1653), p. 143.

[21] 'A Prospect of a Church in the Mind', (ll. 9–10), *Poems and Fancies* (1653), p. 143.

[22] 'A Prospect of a Church in the Mind', (ll. 19–20), *Poems and Fancies* (1653), p. 143.

[23] 'A Prospect of a Church in the Mind', (ll. 11–16) *Poems and Fancies* (1653), p. 143.

[24] *The English Poems of George Herbert*, ed. C. A. Patrides (London: J. M. Dent and Sons, Everyman's Library, 1974), pp. 84–5.

[25] Among those who have, in passing, derogated Cavendish's narrative and dramatic ability are Marjorie Nicolson, *Voyages to the Moon* (New York: MacMillan, 1948), p. 224; and Rose Zimbardo, *A Mirror To Nature: Transformations in Drama and Aesthetics 1660–1732* (Kentucky: University of Kentucky Press, 1986), p. 58.

[26] *Playes* (1662), p. 140.

[27] *Playes* (1662), p. 165.

[28] *Writings* (1994), p. 189.

[29] *Writings* (1994), pp. 224–225.

10

Margaret Cavendish's *Poems and Fancies* and Thomas Harriot's Treatise on Infinity

B. J. Sokol

Careful reassessment is needed of the self-proclamations of absolute originality that recur in the works of Margaret Cavendish, Duchess of Newcastle. These claims are justified in some senses, yet have misled many critics who have dismissed Cavendish's supposedly wholly untutored forays into the realms of scientific and mathematical thought as worthless or misguided.

As opposed to ignorance, an awareness of advanced and highly technical theoretical work of her period will be shown to underlie some of the uncustomary subject matter of Cavendish's *Poems and Fancies* (1653).[1] Such a demonstration will not deny the uniqueness or originality of Cavendish's 1653 folio, a first step in a remarkable publishing career. This volume is not only palpably unorthodox in content, style and presentation, but was also a new departure in being, and consciously being, very nearly the first collection of poems in English by a woman ever to be published.

If we amend 'in English by a woman' to 'by a woman in England', Cavendish's book does indeed mark a publishing first. But as Sandra Sherman points out, Anne Bradstreet's slightly earlier collection, *The Tenth Muse Lately Sprung Up in America*, was 'published – ostensibly without [Bradstreet's] consent – in London, 1650.'[2] We should note that Bradstreet's ostensible disavowal corresponded with a norm – traditionally even male authors (especially those of high social standing) 'ostensibly' claimed to have not authorised the publication of their work, or to have been unwillingly forced into publication. Not least remarkable about Cavendish's singular literary self-presentation was that she did no such thing, but the reverse. In defiance of customary constraints of gender, and also of long-standing conventions of authorial false modesty, her numerous prefaces and many other self revelations in her more than a dozen folios repeatedly and openly assert her personal ambition for recognition, praise, fame and – if possible – literary or intellectual immortality.[3]

As has been often remarked, Cavendish was also frequently candid about fears that her bid for fame through writing might be harmed by weaknesses she could not overcome, including a very deficient education. Yet sometimes she also defiantly claimed that a lack of outside influence, or even of all learning and retention, might be beneficial to her imagination.[4] Taking literally her frankness about her own fancifulness, frivolity and ignorance, a number of scholars have taken Cavendish too much at her own word.[5] For Cavendish may have been far from truly candid, and on the contrary may have hoped that some readers would detect behind her false–naive pretence her actual acquaintance with very new and challenging ideas. Just like Robert Frost, another autodidact poet fascinated by advanced science, she may have feigned naivete in contexts where she in fact wanted to be contradicted by the truly knowing.[6] In fact Cavendish's self-professions of having had no external influences, such as 'any English Booke to Instruct me',[7] may have been a ploy attempting to attract the notice of the truly knowing to allusions in her work to subtle and arcane, yet highly important elements of the most advanced theoretical thinking of her time.

Many of Cavendish's critics negatively assess her scientific thinking against what they wrongly think to be the true model for seventeenth-century science, a supposedly 'prevailing Baconian paradigm' of pure empiricism.[8] Bizarrely, some even take the genuine science of the period to have been only technological, a pragmatic discipline with wholly 'utilitarian aims'.[9] Several others misapply, as if the issue were somehow humorous, Robert Kargon's comment that Cavendish's scientific views embarrassed renowned contemporary atomists.[10] Kargon's historical account makes it clear however that the cause of this embarrassment was not solely because Cavendish's views were extreme or silly. The real reason was not wry, but religio-political: Cavendish's tendency to radical materialism in her atomism suggested 'a tenderness toward atheism which was dangerous for one so closely tied to the suspect atomic philosophy.'[11]

With some honourable exceptions,[12] most twentieth-century critics have excused, dismissed or condemned Cavendish's theorising intellect. But, oddly, many who have so judged her have seemingly overlooked the huge importance of the fact that not experimentation alone, but rather experiments or observations led and interpreted by mathematical theories, underlie all the momentous advances of seventeenth-century European science. The imaginative insights of, for instance, Kepler, Descartes or Newton contributed at least as much as any new emphasis on experimentalism. If this truth was not well understood by many of the gentlemanly 'virtuosi' of the early Royal Society, there is no excuse for ignoring it now.[13] So, although it has been cited to her supposed discredit, there is in fact justice and wisdom in Cavendish's observation 'that Experimental and Mechanical Philosophy cannot be above the Speculative part, by reason most Experiments have their rise from the Speculative.'[14]

We will find in particular in Cavendish's poems allusions to aspects of the most advanced, and indeed eventually the most fruitful, mathematical topics of her age. These allusions show her both informed about and intuitively attracted to the abstruse studies that lead to the development of the infinitesimal calculus. As we know from hindsight, this development forged the way to the most fruitful physical theories of that or almost any age. But, very interestingly, recent investigators argue persuasively that interest in the pre-calculus was driven, as far as motivation was concerned, at least as much by meta-mathematical issues, such as heuristics or logical foundations,[15] as by practical considerations of enabling computation or measurement.

It may be useful to summarise briefly a brilliant recent discussion by Paolo Mancosu of one such motivation. Mathematical thinkers of the earlier seventeenth century were troubled about the apagogical or 'indirect' methods of proof by *reductio* often found in classical mathematics. Although these 'indirect' methods were widely believed to establish adequately the validity of propositions that were already put into question, these methods were criticised because they were in no way indicative of how these propositions might be arrived at or even surmised.[16] Because known apagogical methods of proof offered no help in finding out propositions, but could only verify them, they did not supply mathematicians with what Wallis called an 'Art of Invention'.[17] In fact, Archimedes and Theon had possessed some infinitistic geometrical methods giving practical help with heuristic problems, but the existence of these methods was unknown and had to be reinvented in the seventeenth century. While doing this, seventeenth-century mathematicians re-exploring such techniques added newly a concern with their validity – that is, they sought to refine and extend infinitistic heuristic methods into 'direct' or ostensive modes of proof.[18] So they had a greater intellectual goal than to seek a useful Art of Invention, and indeed eventually they did replace some classical apagogical proofs with methods simultaneously discovering and ostensively verifying geometrical truths.

Andrew Marvell, whose work Margaret Cavendish may have seen in manuscript,[19] wrote poetry subtly dealing with problems and paradoxes of 'indirect' proofs, and he probably thereby alluded to the closely allied scientific method of verification by *reductio ad impossible* championed by Descartes.[20] Cavendish shows no sign of matching Marvell's great subtlety in the comprehension of logical issues, but as we have seen she did realise that speculative hypotheses are often a vital prerequisite for experimentation. Her insight is in exact accord with Descartes's understanding of how 'indirect' logical methods should motivate and direct the design of experiments in order to test speculative hypotheses.[21]

Atomism, and the use of speculative theory to direct the design of experiments, are of course well-known aspects of the new science; the puzzling of early seventeenth-century mathematics about infinity and infinitesimals is less so. Before 1653 the mathematical materials of what was to be the pre-calculus were in an embryonic state. Margaret Cavendish appears to have had her knowledge of them from an acquaintance with 'De Infinitis', a group of little-known and abstruse manuscript studies by the English mathematician Thomas Harriot (1560–1621).[22] In these studies Harriot not only anticipated the thinking that led to the development of the infinitesimal calculus, but touched also on conundrums of infinity resolved only recently, or still partly in question.

Recent scholars have revised earlier opinions that the extreme usefulness of the infinitesimal calculus as a computational technique led both its inventors and its pre-inventors to overlook severe logical deficiencies in their understanding of its basis.[23] The claim of the newer historians is just the opposite – they hold that following Cavalieri's publication in 1635 of his innovative pre-calculus method of 'indivisibles', seventeenth-century mathematicians were deeply concerned to resolve its foundational weaknesses.[24]

Harriot's studies. 'De Infinitis', composed at a time probably well in advance of his death in 1621, address the same paradoxes of the infinite and infinitesimal that concerned the later seventeenth century.[25] Although they have indeed remained obscure until now, there is good evidence that Margaret Cavendish could have encountered Harriot's pioneering studies of infinity. A selection of Harriot's voluminous mathematical manuscripts were transcribed by her savant brother-in-law Sir Charles Cavendish (1591–1662), to whom *Poems and Fancies* is dedicated. Sir Charles was a pivotal figure in contemporary intellectual life,[26] and he was Margaret Cavendish's close companion, especially when she was stranded in England and writing her first book.[27] He was also, to some degree, her scientific mentor.

The facts concerning Charles Cavendish's transcriptions of Harriot need some amplification. A substantial number of folio sheets scattered through Harriot's now disordered manuscripts are headed 'De Infinitis'. Many of these bear varied sub-headings, and there are several associated studies among Harriot's other scientific papers. A great part of this work on infinity is carefully copied out in British Library, Harleian MS 6002 by the same hand that collects a variety of scientific and philosophical material in Harleian MSS 6001, 6002 and 6083. Despite some confusions, this hand and the collection were correctly attributed in 1949 by Jean Jacquot to Sir Charles Cavendish.[28]

Sir Charles Cavendish's copies of Harriot's papers on infinity appear in two groups. Both end with a well-justified comment on the difficulty of deciphering Harriot's writing.[29] The first group, comprising Harleian MS 6002 fols. 2 recto–6 recto, concludes with Cavendish's modest remark, 'From Mr Hariots loose papers, some of which I could not well reade so there may be some what amiss, which if there be are to be imputed to me & not to him.'[30] The second group comprises Harleian MS 6002, fols. 6 verso–10 recto. In it Cavendish transcribes completely Harriot's manuscripts, British Library, Add. MS 6782, fols. 362 recto–371 recto. This section is followed by Cavendish's remark: 'From Mr Harriots other papers as difficult in some places to be read as the former.'[31] Yet, where close scrutiny and/or mathematical contexts allow precise comparisons, Cavendish's transcriptions of Harriot appear to be exact.[32]

The papers in the first group of Cavendish's transcriptions of Harriot's 'De Infinitis' are concerned with 'continuous' proportions and the sums of resulting infinite series,[33] with infinite sets of geometrical points producing a parabola,[34] and with questions of infinity arising in regard to motion, time and space.[35] In this and in the second group of Harriot's 'De Infinitis' papers there is close consideration of numerical convergence, of geometrical tangents, and of continuous motion. Thus these papers show interest in all the ingredients, if not the substantive contents, of the future differential calculus.

Harriot also showed interest in general questions of numerical convergence or divergence, which eventually became the underpinning of the theory of the calculus. Certainly Harriot treated the sums, differences and limits of convergent or divergent infinite series in a wide variety of contexts. Divergent series feature in his calculations of compound interest,[36] and in his extensive work on the exponential growth of human populations.[37] The one published work of Harriot's lifetime, his famous 'briefe and true report' of his investigations in North America, also addressed in a practical context the mathematics of limits; here an applied political arithmetic was aimed at questions of sustainable food production, and consequent possible coexistence of populations.[38]

Although, as is usual for him, Harriot provided no clear motivating narrative for the complex calculations in his mathematical manuscripts 'De Infinitis', Sir Charles Cavendish transcribed, among the first group of these papers, some general reflections:

> of contradictions that spring from diverse suppositions [about infinity] it can not trulie be sayed that the one parte or the other is false. for they are true consequences from their suppositions & in that respect are both true. but that which followeth is that one of these suppositions is necessarilie false from whence one of the pointes of the contradiction was inferred. as in the reason of Achilles and other reasons of Zenoes.[39]

So paradoxes of infinity were of special interest to Harriot, who hoped to reduce false suppositions to absurdities.

A repeated mention is made at the end of the first group of Harriot's papers 'De Infinitis' of a particular paradox attributed to Zeno, and forward reference is made to a solution: 'The method used in an other paper of Achilles.'[40] This 'other paper' containing a method or solution is included in the second group of Harriot's papers 'De Infinitis' as arranged by Cavendish, and it is followed there by a discussion of some further paradoxes of infinity. The start of this subsection of 'De Infinitis', headed 'Ratio Achilles', is an incomplete discourse in which Harriot recalls that Aristotle's *Physics* VI, 9 reported Zeno's paradox concerning a race between Achilles and a tortoise only to illustrate a point about motion, but offers that the problem may have more interest regarding questions of infinity than Aristotle noted.[41] Zeno's famous Achilles paradox argues that if the world's fastest runner were to allow a tortoise a moderate head start in their race, then the tortoise must win no matter how far they run. For by the time Achilles reaches the place where the tortoise began the race the tortoise will have run some distance onward to a second point beyond his own starting place. But by the time Achilles will have reached that second point the tortoise will have moved forward from there to a third point, and be still ahead of Achilles. The same argument could be repeated over and over again forever, so the tortoise would always retain a lead over Achilles, who could never overtake the tortoise.

The flaw in this argument was well understood by Harriot. 'De Infinitis' often instances how infinitely extended 'continuous progressions' with a ratio of less than one have a finite sum. Thus the ever-decreasing intervals of time required for Achilles to reach the tortoise's 'last' position, although infinite in number, sum up to a finite amount of time – at that time Achilles will overtake the tortoise.

In another example of the same principle, 'De Infinitis' shows how an infinite succession of rectangular shapes, each exactly half as large in area as the former, have in total a composite area equalling exactly double the area of the first shape. Harriot illustrates this example with a diagram showing the first of an infinite series of rectangles each having equal bases but with declining heights, and he places these figures adjacent to one another.[42] He thus demonstrates how to create an overall shape having infinite length and ever decreasing height which covers a finite area.[43]

Harriot offers an algebraic method of finding just when and where Achilles will overtake the tortoise (see illustration. 10.2).[44] To this solution Harriot appends 'to find that point geometrically is set downe in my other papers de infinitis.' This geometrical solution is found in Harriot's manuscript British Library, Add. MS 6785, fol. 437; just as Newton later was to offer geometrical demonstrations alternative to algebraic ones, Harriot supplements his algebra with a more 'classical' solution by geometrical construction.

Although he showed where Achilles must overtake the tortoise, Harriot was too acute to abandon the troubling questions posed by notions of infinity. Thus, immediately following his algebraic solution of Zeno's problem of Achilles, Harriot adds a series of further passages, the first beginning: 'Nowe I will propound some difficulties to be considered of.' (see illustrations. 10.1 and 10.2)[45] The first passage discusses paradoxes concerning the 'peripherie' and 'superficie' of a circle, assuming both are 'compounded ex atomis.' The main paradox here considered is an apparently necessary yet also seemingly impossible density of points located at the center of any circle. A second, related passage discusses 'another difficultie [that] ariseth from the square, if a line be compounded ex atomis the diametrall line will be found to be equall to the side.' Both these paradoxes, arising from Harriot's hypothesis that any line or area contains infinitely many points, involve problems of counting and matching infinite quantities not understood until recently.[46]

Harriot's following claim to have a method 'whereby will be found the means for the solution of all' is not sustained. Only the later integral calculus was to provide a general method for determining the 'superficie' of areas bounded by smooth curves. Logical difficulties underlying this calculus, arising from apparent paradoxes in the summation of infinite infinitesimal 'atoms', were resolved only in the nineteenth century. The first part of Harriot's supposed 'solution of all', involving a dialectic of 'discretum' versus 'continuum' in 'essence' 'ratio' and 'quidditie' is of little value.[47] However, what he lays down next, in seeming conclusion at the end of his papers 'De Infinitis', is true if incomplete:

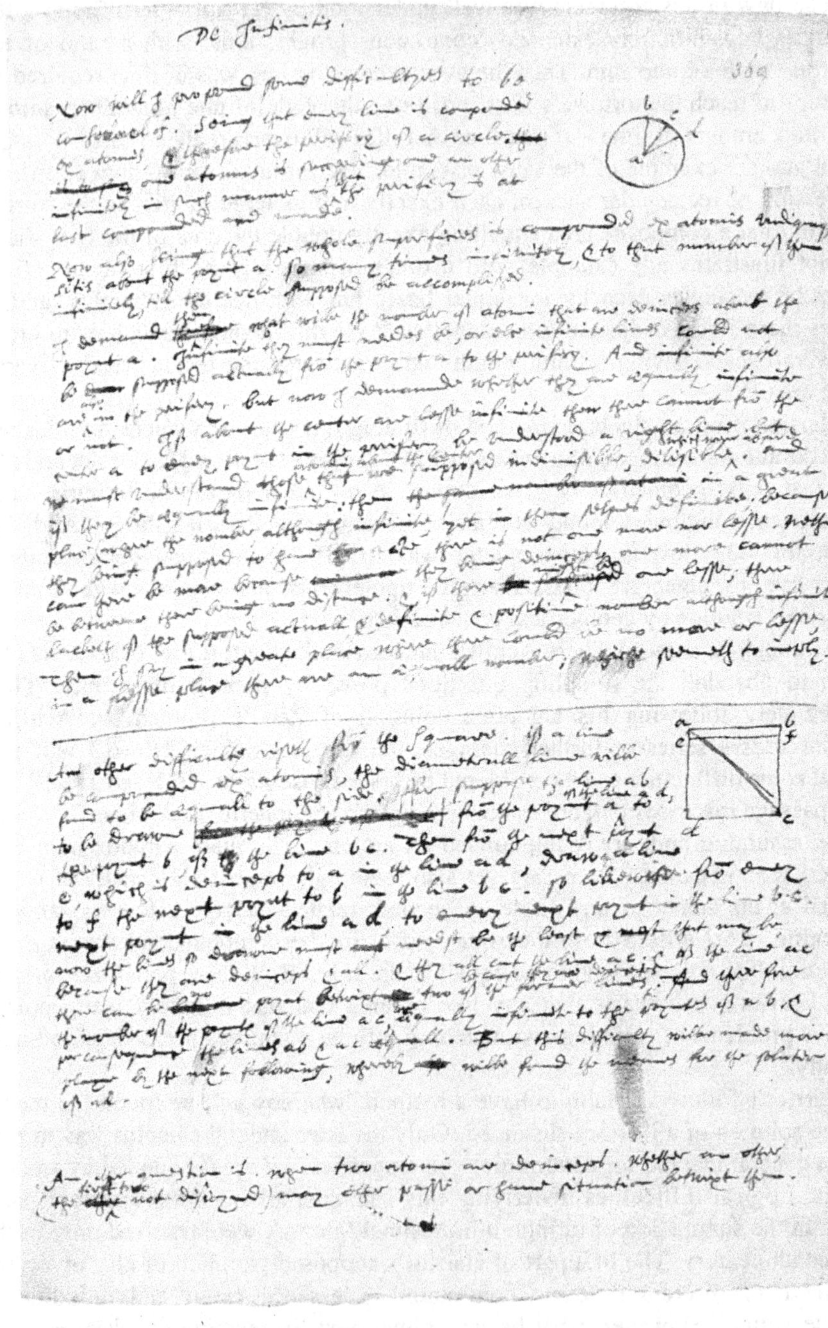

Illustration 10.1: Thomas Harriot, 'De infinitis', by permission of The British Library, Additional MS 6782, fol. 369 recto

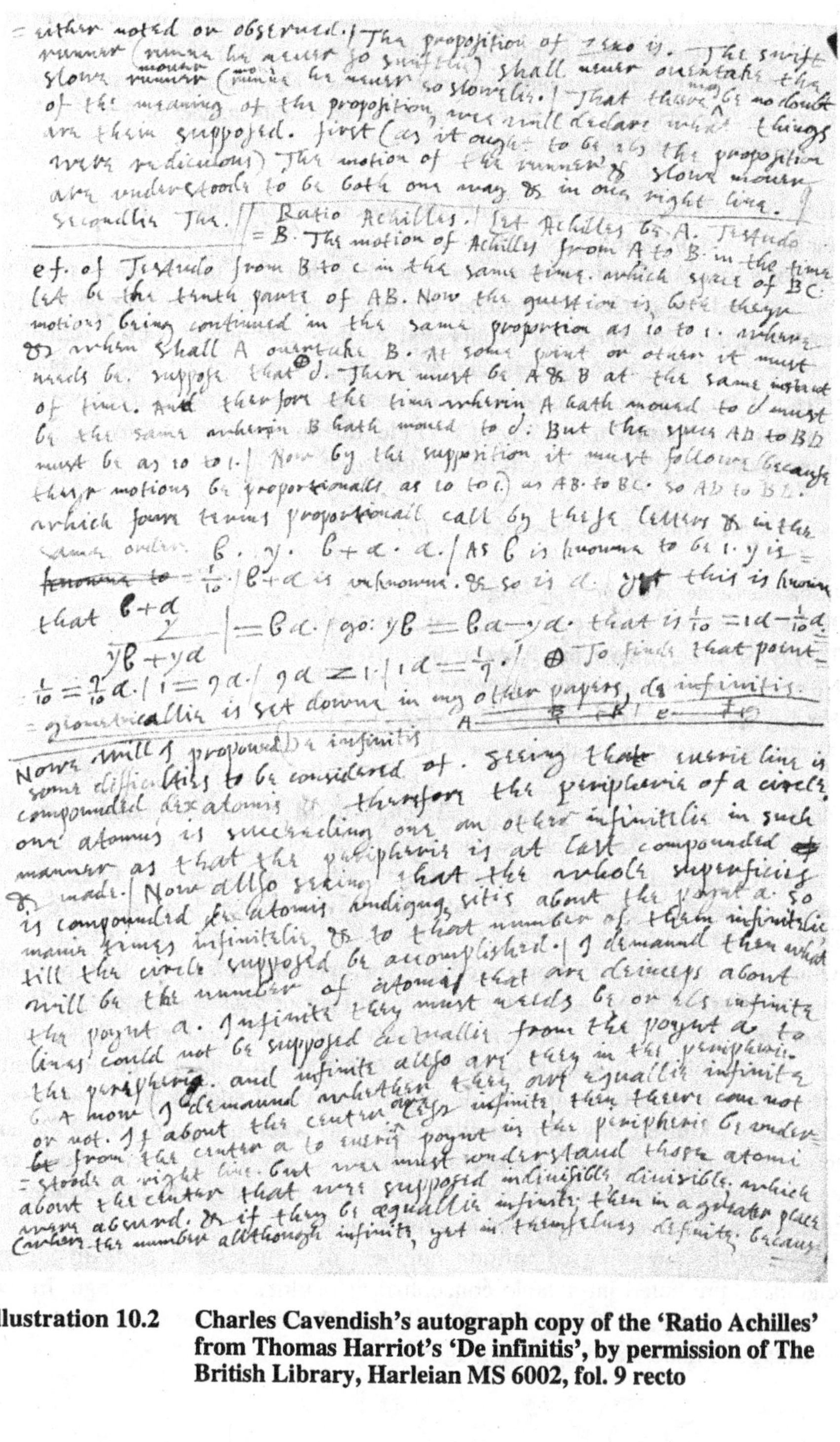

Illustration 10.2 **Charles Cavendish's autograph copy of the 'Ratio Achilles' from Thomas Harriot's 'De infinitis', by permission of The British Library, Harleian MS 6002, fol. 9 recto**

> That there may be two magnitudes given, of which the one shall be infinite in respect of the other & yet in respect of two other magnitudes they shall be finite [...] That a finite line may have an infinite number of parts if all the parts be in continuall proportion. Their number must be compounded of an infinite number of finite parts and an infinite number of infinite parts.[48]

Here the final use of the term 'infinite' means infinitesimal, a notion Harriot approached but did not fully conceive.

Harriot's true but restricted final understanding that if 'a line be understood to be compounded of poyntes, the number of them is infinite,'[49] left him with difficulties concerning measures of infinity and of the 'continuum' which remained unexplained until very recent times, and are still partly unresolved. Such subtleties are reflected in a short poem of Margaret Cavendish. The concept of this appears to have been drawn directly from Harriot's 'circle' dilemma, introduced by his 'Nowe I will propound some difficulties to be considered of':

> In the Center Atomes never Separate.
>
> Just at the Center is a point that's small,
> Those Atomes that are there are wedg'd in all;
> They lye so close, firme in one Body binde,
> No other Forme, or Motion can unwinde:
> For they are wreath'd so hard about that point,
> As they become a Circle without joynt.[50]

Here an asterisk at the poem's end refers to Margaret Cavendish's cryptic marginal comment: 'As it were without partition, but it is but one.' The very language of this recalls Harriot's conundrum: 'wee must understand those atomii about the center that were supposed indivisible divisible, which were absurd' (see illustrations. 10.1 and 10.2).[51]

Other allusions to refractory problems in pure mathematics, also possibly relating to Charles Cavendish's transcriptions of Harriot's papers, appear in *Poems and Fancies*. Two of these concern the unsolved classical problems of 'squaring the circle' and of 'doubling the cube'. Harriot's concern with geometrical atoms indicates the direction taken in later-developed analytical approaches to such problems. Harriot himself moved in similar directions when he reconsidered ancient methods of determining areas by decomposition of polygons into triangles,[52] and when he showed an understanding, as we have seen, that sums of infinite numbers of geometrical areas might converge to a finite quantity.

However the summing of infinite numbers of infinitesimal parts in all but special cases presented intractable conceptual difficulties to Harriot's age. In two linked poems Margaret Cavendish described problems presented by the inconclusive stage of understanding of that age:[53]

The Circle of the Brain cannot be Squar'd

A Circle Round divided in foure Parts,
Hath been a Study amongst Men of Arts;
Ere since Archimedes, or Euclid's time,
Hath every Brain been stretch'd upon a Line.
And every Thought hath been a Figure set,
Doubts Cyphers are, Hopes as Triangulars meet.
There is Division, and Substraction made,
And Lines drawne out, and Points exactly layd.
But yet None can demonstrate it plaine,
Of Circles round, a just Foure Square remaine.
Thus while the Braine is round, no Square will be,
While Thoughts are in Divisions, no Figures will agree.

Another to the same Purpose

And thus upon the same account,
Doubling the Cube must mount;
And the Triangular must be cut so small,
Till into Equall Atomes it must fall.
For such is Mans Curiosity, and mind,
To seek for that, which hardest is to find.[54]

Cavendish's borrowing here, although in service of a moral allegory of human psychology, suggests that she did not at all overlook existing scientific 'method or authority' out of self-will, nor that she was wholly 'unable to develop a systematic understanding of the work of others.'[55]

Indeed, through her choice to make applications in poetry of mathematical concepts which were pondered and described by her advanced thinking brother-in law – concepts all the more subtle for being unresolved – Cavendish showed that she appreciated the huge importance of abstruse mathematical theoretical thinking to modern science. She certainly recognised this importance far better than did a modern commentator who faults her for a supposedly foolish 'disregard for the methods and utilitarian aims' of scientific inquiry.[56]

Only four years before *Poems and Fancies* appeared, the first Latin translation of Descartes' *Géométrie* notified the world at large of an epochal marriage between the questions of ancient mathematics and the techniques of modern analysis powered by algebra.[57] That this marriage was destined to solve all the ancient problems of geometry, and to beget moreover unimaginable mathematical riches in new theoretical and heuristic forms, could not have been fully foreseen by Cavendish or any of her contemporaries. But some intuition seems to have been abroad that great events were starting, and in that hopeful excitement Cavendish and others extended their imaginations to revive, revise, or wholly innovate older ideas on questions about infinity, energy, motion and matter. What has been established here is the existence in the literary imagery of *Poems and Fancies* of references to some of the subtle and abstruse problems that motivated the deep researches of contemporary mathematicians, and that these references were probably inspired by the infinitistic speculations of Thomas Harriot. Further investigations may well reveal other aspects of Cavendish's writings showing both an actual acquaintance with, and possibly some prescient grasp of, the just-forming mathematical theoretical foundations of modern science.

Notes

[1] The pagination of *Poems and Fancies* (1653) is inconsistent and partly repetitive, but in all the following citations there are no ambiguities.

[2] Sandra Sherman, 'Trembling Texts: Margaret Cavendish and the Dialectic of Authorship', *English Literary Renaissance*, 24 (1994), 184–210, (p. 192n).

[3] See Jean Gagen's lucid and informative 'Honor and Fame in the Works of the Duchess of Newcastle', *Studies in Philology*, 56 (1959), 519–538, and the more highly theorised study of Sherman.

[4] See Sylvia Bowerbank, 'The Spider's Delight: Margaret Cavendish and the "Female" Imagination', *English Literary Renaissance*, 14 (1984), 392–408, especially pp. 396–7. Cavendish's defiance is discussed also in Sherman, 'Trembling Texts', pp. 191–194, which begins, 'In virtually all of her works Cavendish's ostensible strategy is that of the female with no access to literary/scientific discourse.' The qualifier 'ostensible' suggests to me the possibility not only of the contradictions discussed by Sherman, but also of purposeful rhetorical posturing, as will be described.

[5] Although sympathetic to the Duchess, Charles Firth believed her admission that she 'prides herself that her views are all her own, and all new,' making it inevitable that 'as might be expected from these confessions, the ponderous tomes on science and philosophy which the Duchess published are entirely valueless.' See *Life* (1906), p. xxviii, Myra Reynolds, *The Learned Lady in England 1650–1760* (Boston: Houghton Mifflin Co., 1920), p. 49, similarly concludes, 'the inaccuracy and amazing self-confidence of [Cavendish's scientific] studies render them worse than futile.' Down through the twentieth century the litany continues that Cavendish's meagre knowledge spoiled her chances in science. In addition to critics listed in note 12 below, who excuse her supposed faults by her exclusion from learning, Sara H. Mendelson, *The Mental Life of Stuart Women: Three Studies* (Brighton: Harvester Press, 1987), pp. 37–38, concedes that 'In her magpie-like way Margaret had picked up some scientific and mathematical ideas,' but judges that 'scientific topics of the early 1650s can be discerned clearly in Margaret's work, albeit grotesquely transformed.' (p. 28).

[6] The game that Frost played with scientists and intellectuals by shamming the role of an 'ignorant farmer' while alluding to abstruse and advanced ideas is discussed in B. J. Sokol, 'Poet in the Atomic Age: Robert Frost's "That Millikan Mote" Expanded', *Annals of Science*, 53 (1996), 399–412.

[7] *Poems and Fancies* (1653), sig. A6 recto. For unusual, and I believe well-warranted, mistrust of such self-assertions see Stephen Clucas, 'The Atomism of the Cavendish Circle: A Reappraisal', *The Seventeenth Century*, 9 (1994), 247–273 (pp. 261 and 272n).

[8] The phrase is from Bowerbank, 'Spider's Delight', p. 398. Its odd premise is repeated in various forms in many twentieth-century discussions of Cavendish. Firth contrasts Cavendish with 'the Royal Society and all those to whom the progress of physical science in England during the later half of the Seventeenth Century was due [who] were eagerly pursuing the experimental method.' (*Life* (1906), p. xxix). Reynolds contrasts Cavendish's supposed dogmatism, although not unique in 'the first half of the seventeenth century,' with the 'experimental method [which] was having its triumph.' (*Learned Lady*, p. 49) Gerald Dennis Meyer, *The Scientific Lady in England, 1650–1760* (Berkeley: University of California Press, 1955), p. 2, laments that Cavendish was 'certainly more active in her intellect than in her researches, a motivation that would have been thwarted or arrested had she been a follower of the empirical school of Bacon,' and blames this on 'Cartesian rationalism, the principles of which warped permanently her scientific outlook.' (p. 3) Echoes of this opinion, placing Descartes below Bacon as a scientist or methodologist of science, continue down to Mendelson, p. 37, which laments that 'the concept of science as an experimental discipline was not fully established until late in the seventeenth century', thus making space for Cavendish's grotesque propensity to theories.

[9] Samuel I. Mintz, 'The Duchess of Newcastle's Visit to the Royal Society', *Journal of English and Germanic Philology*, 51 (1952), 168–176 (p. 176).

[10] As in Bowerbank, 'Spider's Delight', pp. 398–399, which goes on to detail Cavendish's 'intuitive, if erratic, exposition and defense of Nature's ways.' Lisa T. Sarasohn, 'Science Turned Upside Down: Feminism and the Natural Philosophy of Margaret Cavendish', *Huntington Library Quarterly*, 47 (1984), 289–307, similarly applies Kargon's comment (p. 290), but later does explain that Cavendish's atomism was shocking because it lacked 'theological qualifiers' (p. 291). Sherman, 'Trembling Texts', (p. 200n), does not cite Kargon, but paraphrases that Cavendish's physical theories 'were so eccentric as to embarrass even committed atomists.'

[11] Robert Hugh Kargon, *Atomism in England from Harriot to Newton* (Oxford: Clarendon Press, 1966), p. 75. Clucas, 'Atomism', pp. 261–2, corrects Kargon's attribution of a single form of atomism to Cavendish, showing how her ideas evolved and transformed in her books following *Poems and Fancies*.

[12] A persuasive and detailed case is made for better understanding of the seriousness of the 'neo-atomism' of Margaret Cavendish and others in Clucas, 'Atomism', especially pp. 259–64. A just, if less specific, assessment of Cavendish's abilities appears in Marjorie Hope Nicolson, *Pepys' Diary and the New Science* (Charlottesville: University Press of Virginia, 1965); this discusses Cavendish pp. 103–114, concluding, 'Exhibitionist though she was, she had real intellectual interests and abilities.' Hilda L. Smith, *Reason's Disciples: Seventeenth Century English Feminists* (Urbana: University of Illinois Press, 1982) treats Cavendish (pp. 75–95), and judges: 'What she obviously missed [...] was the community of scholars to which only men had access, where her ideas would have been brought to others' attention and been argued, tested, and perhaps sharpened.' (p. 73) This position admitting qualified approval does not really coincide with finding excuses for Cavendish's supposedly bad science, as in: Bowerbank, 'Spider's Delight', especially p. 402; Sarasohn, 'Science Turned Upside Down', especially pp. 290–293; or Sherman,'Trembling Texts', especially pp. 189–90.

[13] See Walter E. Houghton Jr., 'The English Virtuoso in the Seventeenth Century', *Journal of the History of Ideas*, 3 (1942) 51–73 and 190–219.

[14] Quoted disparagingly from Cavendish's *Observations upon Experimental Philosophy* in Meyer, *Scientific Lady*, p. 4. Bowerbank, 'Spider's Delight', p. 400, similarly finds the elevation of speculative philosophy in this book whimsically 'curious'. What lies behind this is Cavendish's scepticism about microscopic and telescopic observations. Now that we know far more about 'systematic error' and other misleading artefacts of experimental design, a similar point made by Robert Frost in 'A Wish to Comply' has been seen in its seriousness in Sokol (see note 6). Even Cavendish's atomic intelligences, or fairies, are not necessarily so bizarre now as formerly, in the light of the quantum mechanical mystery of the collective 'decision' streams of particles appear to make when they begin to act in concert, as if they were waves, when encountering a diffraction apparatus. And indeed, far less anachronistically, Clucas, 'Atomism', pp. 261–262, locates the 'synthesis of materialism and vitalism' in her atomism in the contexts of serious and important contemporary thinking.

[15] See Paolo Mancosu, *Philosophy of Mathematics and Mathematical Practice in the Seventeenth Century*, (Oxford: Oxford University Press, 1996) and Antoni Malet, 'Barrow, Wallis, and the Remaking of Seventeenth Century Indivisibles', *Centaurus*, 39 (1997), 67–92.

[16] See Mancosu, *Philosophy of Mathematics*, pp. 24–28 and 59–64. Mancosu, *Philosophy of Mathematics*, pp. 105–117 treats the fascinating history from Kant's time to 1996 of the question of the necessity or otherwise of apagogical proofs.

[17] Mancosu, *Philosophy of Mathematics*, p. 63.

[18] Mancosu, *Philosophy of Mathematics*, p. 35.

[19] *Glorious Fame*, p. 81. A link between the Cavendish circle and Marvell was possibly through John Pell.

[20] See B. J. Sokol, 'Logic and Illogic in Marvell's "To His Coy Mistress"', *English Studies*, 71 (1990), 244–252.

[21] See René Descartes, *Discours de la Méthode*, ed. by Etienne Gilson (Paris: Vrin, 1987), p. 65.

[22] The *De Infinitis* writings are briefly treated in Kargon, pp. 24–6. I am doubtful of the conclusions drawn there that Harriot's interest was centred uniquely on 'a physical theory of nature' and so his infinitism concerned mainly a study of physical indivisibles. John Henry, 'Thomas Harriot and Atomism: A Reappraisal', *The History of Science*, 20 (1982), 255–96, questions Kargon's supposition that Harriot was unquestioningly an atomist, but identifies only classical mathematical paradoxes, and not the newer ones of Harriot's own time, behind the difficulties of his infinitistic thought. Henry stoutly dismisses the influence of Giordano Bruno on Harriot's *De Infinitis*, while Hilary Gatti, *The Renaissance Drama of Knowledge: Giordano Bruno in England*, (London: Routledge, 1989), pp. 57–65, asserts it.

[23] This earlier position, and the background of pre-calculus, are well presented in Morris Kline, *Mathematical Thought from Ancient to Modern Times* (New York: Oxford University Press, 1971), pp. 344–356.

[24] On Cavalieri's own anxiety over the logical problems of his method and his vain hopes to obtain Galileo's approval of his solution, see Mancosu, *Philosophy of Mathematics*, p. 50. On others' efforts to reform theoretically Cavalieri's method, see Malet, 'Seventeenth Century Indivisibles', especially p. 69.

[25] However Cavalieri first developed infinitary techniques in the 1620s, and Kepler published a primitive version of them in 1615. See Mancosu, *Philosophy of Mathematics*, pp. 38–39.

[26] See Jean Jacquot, 'Sir Charles Cavendish and his Learned Friends', *Annals of Science*, 8 (1952), 175–191.

[27] See Lisa T. Sarasohn, 'Science Turned Upside Down: Feminism and the Natural Philosophy of Margaret Cavendish', *Huntington Library Quarterly*, 47 (1984), 289–307, (p. 290); *Margaret the First*, pp. 90–91; and *Glorious Fame*, p. 94.

[28] According to the British Library Harleian Catalogue, Harleian MSS 6001, 6002 and 6083 are 'said to be made by Dr Pell from the papers of T. Harriot'. Contrary to this, British Library, Harleian MS 6083, fol. 147 recto, in illustrating a number of mathematical symbols, labels them 'Mr pells markes'. R. C. H. Tanner, 'Thomas Harriot as Mathematician', *Physis*, 9 (1967), 243–292 (p. 279), questions Jean Jacquot's attribution of these manuscripts to Charles Cavendish. She refers to Jacquot's 'Sir Charles Cavendish and his Learned Friends', *Annals of Science*, 8 (1952), 175–191, which seemingly only casually attributes Harleian MSS 6083 and 6002 (pp. 176n, 182, 183n) to Cavendish. However this was justified, since Jean Jacquot, 'Un Amateur de Science, Ami de Hobbes et de Descartes, Sir Charles Cavendish', *Thales*, 6 (1949–1950), 81–88, (p. 81), establishes by means of a handwriting comparison with Cavendish's letters to John Pell, that the great part of these Harleian manuscripts are Cavendish's autograph transcriptions of Harriot's work and other material.

[29] Sir Charles Cavendish's handwriting is often much clearer than Harriot's, but sometimes Harriot's writing illuminates his. Harriot's beautiful geometrical constructions are much more elegantly drafted than Cavendish's copies.

[30] British Library, Harleian MS 6002, fol. 6 recto.

[31] Harleian MS 6002, fol. 10 recto.

[32] There is an exact match between Harleian MS 6002, fol. 1 recto and Harriot's crucial 'summary' folio in British Library, Add. MS 6782, fol. 31 recto, fully analysed in B. J. Sokol, 'Thomas Harriot – Sir Walter Ralegh's Tutor – on Population', *Annals of Science*, 31 (1974), 205–12.

[33] British Library, Add. MS 6785, fols. 190 verso–191 recto and Harleian MS 6002, fol. 2 recto.

[34] Add. MS 6785, fol. 190 recto and Harleian MS 6002, fol. 3 recto.

[35] Harleian MS 6002, fol. 4 recto.

[36] Add. MS 6782, fols. 67–72.

[37] Add. MS 6782 and British Library, Add. MS 6788, *sparsim*. See Sokol, 'Population'. On Harriot's ability to employ exponential series see Jon V. Pepper, 'Harriot's Calculation of the Meridional Parts as Logarithmic Tangents', *Archive for History of Exact Sciences*, 4 (1968), 359–413 (pp. 376–7).

[38] See B. J. Sokol, 'The Problem of Assessing Thomas Harriot's "A briefe and true report" of his Discoveries in North America', *Annals of Science*, 51 (1994), 1–16 (p. 13).

[39] Harleian MS 6002, fol. 5 recto.

[40] Harleian MS 6002, fol. 6 recto. Like Harriot, Charles Cavendish was evidently fascinated by Zeno's famous paradoxes of motion; in addition to transcribing Harriot's work on the Achilles paradox Cavendish transcribed a 'Solution à L'Argument de Zenon' which he ascribed to 'Monsieur de Cartes', Harleian MS 6002, fols. 55 verso–56 recto.

[41] Add. MS 6782, fol. 367, Harleian MS 6002, fols. 8 verso–9 recto.

[42] Add. MS 6785, fol. 190 verso, Harleian MS 6002, fol. 2 recto.

[43] This construction is nearly equivalent to Torricelli's famous construction of a solid with a finite volume and yet with infinite linear dimension, published in 1643; see Mancosu, *Philosophy of Mathematics*, pp. 129–149 on the distinguished, widespread and avid philo-

sophical discussion of Torricelli's construction during the third quarter of the seventeenth century.

[44] Add. MS 6782, fol. 368 recto, Harleian MS 6002, fol. 9 recto.

[45] Add. MS 6782, fol. 369 recto, Harleian MS 6002, fols. 9 recto–9 verso.

[46] On the history of such paradoxes see Mancosu, *Philosophy of Mathematics*, pp. 118–129.

[47] Add. MS 6782, fol. 370 recto, Harleian MS 6002, fol. 9 verso.

[48] Add. MS 6782, fol. 371 recto, Harleian MS 6002, fol. 10 recto.

[49] Add. MS 6782, fol. 371 recto., Harleian MS 6002, fol. 10 recto.

[50] *Poems and Fancies* (1653), p. 30.

[51] Add. MS 6782, fol. 369 recto, Harleian MS 6002, fol. 9 recto.

[52] Add. MS 6785, fol. 119.

[53] At the conference 'Science and Literature in the Seventeenth Century', held at the University of Aberystwyth in 1997, Roberto Bertuol noted mathematical imagery in verses conflated from these two Cavendish poems, but discussed them from a very different perspective than here. Other poems in *Poems and Fancies*, such as 'The Squaring of the Circle' (p. 48), 'A Circle Squar'd in Prose' (pp. 48–49) and 'The Tra[n]section' (p. 50), use evident geometrical imagery. Less evidently but more interestingly geometrical is the image in 'Of many Worlds in this World' (p. 44), which begins, 'Just like unto a Nest of Boxes round, / Degrees of sizes within each Boxe are found.' Although Sherman ('Trembling Texts', p. 190) finds this image 'exactly corresponds to the regress of thoughts bounding a universe in the poet's mind,' an additional or perhaps alternative correspondence may be found with the new method of using laminar or planar indivisibles to determine geometrical volumes. If a drawing of nested shells were to be discovered in the context of efforts to replace the classical infinitistic method of exhaustion, the regress described in this poem to worlds 'thinner and lesse, and lesse still by degree' clearly would refer to insensible mathematical infinitesimals, rather than 'the contingency of [Cavendish's] own absolute selfhood.' (Sherman, 'Trembling Texts', p. 191). See also 'The Temple of Fame' in *Poems and Fancies*, sig. Bb1 (page numbered out of sequence as 146), ll. 9–10: 'just like the Cube, / Which to double hard is in dispute.' Here Cavendish states that she knows of mathematical controversies.

[54] *Poems and Fancies* (1653), pp. 47–48.

[55] Sarasohn, 'Science Turned Upside Down', pp. 302 and 294.

[56] Mintz, 'Visit to the Royal Society', p. 176; this concludes an argument that Cavendish ignored the 'utilitarian aims' distinguishing real science from mere entertainments for the Royal Society's virtuosi.

[57] The first publication of Descartes' geometry in French was in an appendix to *Discours de la Méthode*. See René Descartes, *Discours de la méthode pour bien conduire sa raison et chercher la verité dans les sciences. Plus la dioptrique, les meteores et la géometrie, qui sont des essais de cette méthode* (Leyden, 1637). On her own admission Cavendish lacked the languages and mathematics to make her fully able to understand this breakthrough, or the earlier struggles with indivisibles of Harriot, Kepler Cavalieri and others. But as Clucas points out 'she had a flourishing intellectual discourse with both her husband and his brother Charles' (Clucas, 'Atomism', p. 272n), and through these could easily have encountered new ideas.

11

A Well-Spun Yarn: Margaret Cavendish, and Homer's Penelope*

Emma L. E. Rees

A sixteenth-century Dutch broadsheet depicts in a series of woodcuts the preposterous consequences for a society where cultural norms have been inverted; where the world has been turned upside down.[1] It is a world where monarchs go by foot, and children beat their parents; where the sighted are led by the blind, and fish nest in the high branches of trees. Margaret Cavendish's own familiarity with this inversion trope is apparent in her poem, '*The* Ruine *of the* Island':

> To *Parents Children* unnat'rally grow,
> And *former Friend-ship* now's turn'd cruell *Foe.*
> For *Innocency* no *Protection* had,
> *Religious Men* were thought to be *stark mad.*[2]

Amongst the broadsheet's tableaux of the unthinkable is a scene inscribed 'Het wyf trect na de krych', or, 'The woman marches to war'.[3] A woman is standing, laden with weapons. She faces her seated husband, from between whose legs rises a distaff. Her stance is active, even aggressive; his is passive and domesticated, as he has been emasculated by the symbol of culturally inscribed femininity, the distaff. That this scenario is to be read as inherently grotesque and unnatural is made apparent by its presence in a world where ships go by land, and oxen drive their masters.

By the sixteenth century, the association of needlecraft with a passive femininity was thus deeply ingrained into the popular consciousness. The interconnection had connotations for women's sexuality. This metonymic relationship had been irrevocably forged by the far earlier exemplar of the famously chaste Penelope. Through an adroit manipulation of domestic images connected with varieties of needlework, Cavendish negotiates her position as a writing woman, and central to these passages, and arguably to much of her overall project is this motif of the virtuous Homeric Penelope. A reading of Cavendish's evocations of Penelope, and, to a lesser degree, of another classical exemplar, Ariadne, divulges how the author

* I should like to thank Stephen Clucas for organising the Cavendish Colloquium at Birkbeck College in December 1993, which gave me the opportunity first to present some of the ideas central to this paper. My thanks too to Richard E. Wilson for providing translations from the Dutch.

skilfully and pragmatically redefined notions of gender and femininity so that her act of publication should seem acceptable, even socially desirable, rather than monstrous and transgressive.

The cultural elision of needlework with a passive, virtuous femininity, which finds its ideal in Penelope, is etymologically reinforced.[4] Cavendish effects and exploits the possibilities of an established discursive shift which, in the broadest terms, may be characterised as a move from needle to pen. As late as the nineteenth century, the word 'work' used in the context of women's lives, refers almost invariably to 'needlework'. Further, that potent symbol, the 'distaff', being a staff onto which flax or wool was wound, by extension also came to refer to the female sex.[5] The Latin verb *texere* means 'to weave', and from this derive both 'textile' and 'text', and it is here that Cavendish identifies and seizes upon an opportunity to execute a literary transition from the occupation of needlework, or the creation of textiles, to the occupation of writing, that is, the creation of a text. It is predominantly in her subversive use of the figure of Penelope that she makes this shift appear natural and justifiable.[6] A brief examination of the edition of *The Odyssey* available to Cavendish, George Chapman's translation of 1614–15, may suggest how she formed this individual, and ultimately eminently serviceable, interpretation of the figure of Penelope.[7]

Throughout *The Odyssey*, Homer repeatedly associates masculinity with activity and exploration; femininity with a domestic seclusion focused on the needle or the loom. The success of the Phæacian civilisation encountered by Ulysses, for example, is attributable to its rigid organisation, whereby certain activities are gendered according to typically Homeric codes, so that the Phæacian men surpass 'All other countrimen in Art to build/ A swift-saild ship,' and the women 'For worke of webs past other women were.'[8]

In the second book of *The Odyssey*, one of Penelope's wooers, Antinous, denies that the unruliness of her uninvited suitors is their own fault, instead blaming her, and calling her 'first in craft', an ambiguous epithet pertaining both to her needlecraft and her cunning.[9] He reports how Penelope pleaded that she must finish weaving Laertes's shroud before choosing a new husband, and tells of her attendant three-year-long deceit in unravelling each night that day's weaving. Even the duped Antinous cannot fully conceal his admiration for Penelope's ingenuity. No other woman, he states, compares '(For solide braine) with wise Penelope.'[10] Her actions for three years appeared as those of a dutiful daughter-in-law, and the consequence of her subterfuge was that by not completing the shroud, she was actually preserving her chastity. Her deceit, then, operated not as a transgressive force, but rather one which reaffirmed cultural expectations of a woman's sexuality. That Chapman's Penelope possesses a strength which resides in her intellect rather than in her body is repeatedly emphasised, perhaps most clearly in Book IV. The suitors, once more led by Antinous, determine to set sail from Ithaca in pursuit of Telemachus, who has gone in search of his father, Ulysses. Their departure is detailed in a dispassionate, technical way, symptomatic of Homeric delimitations of masculine activity and decisiveness:

All hasted, reacht the ship, lancht, raisd the mast,
Put sailes in, and with leather loopes made fast
The oares, Sailes hoisted.[11]

This account is intercalary, appearing between two passages which centre on Penelope. In the first, she shrieks and offers up a prayer to Pallas to protect Telemachus, and the second describes her retreat to her chamber and refusal to eat or drink because her 'strong thoughts wrought so on her blamelesse sonne.'[12] Penelope's heightened emotions, her bodily debility, and her confinement, stand in stark contrast to the very physical, out-of-doors activity of Antinous and his men.

In 1651, Cavendish returned to England to appear before the Committee for Compounding at Goldsmith's Hall, in order to plead for revenue.[13] It was during this period apart from her husband, who remained in exile in Antwerp, that she began to write, her first volumes, *Poems and Fancies*, and *Philosophical Fancies*, appearing some two years later. Cavendish's first ever published words come in the form of a dedicatory epistle to her brother-in-law, Charles Cavendish. His 'Bounty *hath been the* Distaffe' for the threads of *Poems and Fancies*, a project which, through a sustained conceit, the author characterises as akin to a spinster's respectable, domestic endeavours.[14] Dressed in Charles's patronal mantle, Cavendish may go about the production of her own 'Garment *of* Memory,' the manufacture of which is represented as being implicitly similar to the '*more proper*' feminine activity of 'Spinning *with the* Fingers,' carefully differentiated from, and yet importantly comparable with '*studying or writing* Poetry, *which is the* Spinning *with the* braine: *but* I,' she continues:

> *having no skill in the* Art *of the* first (*and if* I *had,* I *had no hopes of gaining so much as to make me a Garment to keep me from the* cold) *made me delight in the* latter; *since all* braines *work naturally, and incessantly, in some kinde or other*; *which made me endeavour to Spin a* Garment *of* Memory, *to lapp up my* Name, *that it might grow to after* Ages: I *cannot say the* Web *is* strong, fine, *or* evenly Spun, *for it is a* Course peice; *yet* I *had rather my* Name *should go* meanly clad, *then* dye *with* cold.[15]

Cavendish's writing is seen as the natural, almost inevitable, consequence, of having an active imagination which might turn to less proper thoughts and activities if not occupied. Her rhetoric has transformed writing into a respectable pursuit for a woman, and the implication is that it operates with the same force, and to the same ends, as weaving did for Penelope.

This is an idea reinforced by Cavendish's epistle 'To Poets', wherein the author explicitly adopts Homer's figure, and rewrites her once more to function in defence of her writing. Again, writing is represented as a domestic activity like needlecraft, similarly helping a woman avoid the dangers of 'Idle Time', and all the potential sexual improprieties which that implies.[16] Cavendish compares herself with 'Chast Penelope' in the epistle, embracing a domestic discourse, whilst simultaneously characterising herself as unable to perform domestic activities.[17] In her negotiation of self as writer, she juxtaposes appearance and actuality, undermining the apparent passivity and complicity entailed by domestic images, and applying them instead to her writing.

Cavendish expresses apparently conventional anxieties about her first incursion into print, and attempts to stave off adverse criticism, or the parody of 'Poets Satyrs, *and their* Faiery Wits.'[18] The discourse she employs in her defence is expressly domestic. '*I hope you will spare me,*' she writes, '*for the* harth *is swept cleane, and a* Bason *of* water *with a* cleane Towell *set by, and the* Ashes *rake'd up.*'[19] Within, and precisely because of the existence of, this spruce homely setting, the author's desire is that her 'harmlesse Bookes rest' may be undisturbed. Significantly, the discursive realm into which the author would be forced by unfavourable comments about her publication, is masculine. Cavendish constructs her articulateness as being restricted to domestic discourses, so, in an imagined courtroom scenario, she would be rendered inarticulate and defenceless: '*I have,*' she complains, '*no* Eloquent Orator *to plead for me, as to perswade a* Severe Judge.'[20] Desirous of appearing non-threatening, the woman writer's assurance is that, should she transgress cultural delimitations of the feminine, she would be impotent.

However, Cavendish's self-identification, later in the same epistle, with Penelope, arguably attenuates this eloquent self-abasement. '*Tis true,*' she writes:

> *my* Verses *came not out of* Jupiters Head, *therefore they cannot prove a* Pallas: *yet they are like* Chast Penelope's Work, *for I wrote them in my* Husbands absence, *to delude* Melancholy Thoughts, *and avoid* Idle Time.[21]

Cavendish's construction of Penelope is neither as conventional nor as anodyne as it may, upon a first reading, appear. The explicit point of comparison being established between the two women is that each maintained her chastity whilst apart from her husband, her main means of doing so being writing, in Cavendish's case, weaving in Penelope's. By ostensibly aligning her writing with Penelope's weaving, Cavendish is assuring her audience that her sexual chastity will not be threatened by her publication of her work. However, Penelope, as this quotation suggests, and as Antinous inferred, is not an entirely unproblematic exemplar of female passivity and chastity. Underlying Cavendish's construction of her is a trace of pragmatic deceit implicit in her use of the ambiguous words 'Work', and '*delude*', and the evocation of Pallas, the goddess who was responsible for Ulysses's disguise upon his return to Ithaca. Penelope, then, functions not simply as a paragon of passive female domesticity, but as a motif of ingenuity and initiative, since, in her deception, she had outwardly attempted to protect her honour by weaving the shroud, and this ingenuity meant that by not finishing it she was preserving her chastity for longer. Like Penelope, Cavendish recognises the potential of the loom as a metaphor for self-expression and self-preservation, and the singularity of a woman with the imagination and artistic ability to exploit it.

The potency of the rich motif of Penelope endured in Cavendish's imagination after the Restoration, and is in evidence in her 1664 work, *CCXI Sociable Letters*. In Letter 150, in the same way that Penelope said she had to finish the shroud so that other women would refrain from criticising her, so the letter writer's sudden and extraordinary desire for creative domestic employment is sparked by neighbours gossiping that she does not give her maids enough to do. Like her classical predecessor, the letter writer turns initially to needlecraft, specifically spinning, but is dissuaded by her housekeeper, whose rhetorical function is to voice an intentional narratorial exposure of the cultural supposition that needlework is an inherently gendered activity. 'Nature hath made you a Spinster in Poetry,' she says, 'yet Education hath not made you a Spinster in Huswifry, and you will Spoil more Flax, than Get Cloth by your Spinning, as being an Art that requires Practice to Learn it.'[22] Needlework is here constructed as being a craft which is not naturally part of every woman's psyche, but which has to be taught. The letter writer represents herself as being surprised by her housekeeper's assertion, characterising herself with complicity, as to some extent sharing the patriarchal notion that she should be skilled at spinning:

> I thought Spinning had been Easie, as not requiring much Skill to Draw, and Twist a Thread, nay, so Easie I thought it was, as I did imagine I should have Spun so Small, and Even a Thread, as to make Pure Fine Linnen Cloth, also, that my Maids and I should make so much, as I should not have needed to Buy any, either for Houshold Linnen, or Shifts.[23]

The housekeeper goes on to articulate good reasons for rejecting each of the letter writer's proposed domestic schemes – silk-flower making is uneconomical, as is the making of jams and preserves, which, in addition, 'Breed Obstructions, and Rot the Teeth.'[24] Further, she tries to persuade the writer that her maids would be better occupied improving their minds by reading, and that 'any other Course of Life would be as Unpleasing, and Unnatural to you, as Writing is Delightful to you.' Modesty appears to prevail at this point as the writer wishes she had as much skill in writing as she has time in which to write, declaring: 'my Time and Paper is Unprofitably Wasted in Writing, as my Time and Flax would be in Spinning,' but the overall rhetorical sophistication of the letter operates as a concrete contradiction of this abstract avowal. Writing is convincingly portrayed as being her only option: '[I] was Forced to Return to my Writing-Work again, not knowing what else to do.'[25]

As the letter progresses, the writer's evocation of the Homeric Penelope functions in support of her self-characterisation as a spinster of, rather than with, yarns. The 'Idle Time' trope of *Poems and Fancies* is again invoked, as the writer claims that her virtue actually exceeds Penelope's legendary chastity, since her writing engrosses all of her senses. '[H]ad *Penelope*'s Ears been so Barr'd,' she writes:

> her Lovers Petitions, Sutes, and Pleadings, would have been kept without doors, like a Company of Beggars, they might have Knock'd, but not Entred, nor any of the Mind's Family would have ask'd them what they Desired; neither would the Tongue, the Mind's Almner, have given them one word of Answer, and then it was likely her Amorous Lovers would have gone away, and not stay'd to Feed upon her Cost and Charge, as they did.[26]

Had Penelope been a writer, she would have been even more virtuous. Cavendish, fully aware of Penelope's possession of both wile and virtue, has again taken Homer's figure and cunningly rewritten it, so that feminine virtue is not, as traditionally expected, tied up in the domestic activity of needlework, but, rather, in writing. Cavendish negotiates the reductively dichotomous, antithetical relationship of the 'masculine' pen and the 'conventional' needle, by writing about needlework, and explaining her relationship to it. This skilful compromise bridges the gap between textile and text, functioning as a brilliant and persuasive argument in her defence of herself as writer.

It cannot be ignored, however, that Homer's Penelope was ultimately exposed and brought some way back under patriarchal control, the paradigm of female initiative being, in the end, frustrated by men. It is partly on account of her son's protection that Penelope is at last reunited with her husband. Cavendish, too, had to employ numerous strategies to prevent herself being subsumed into conventional domestic roles, and to protect her identity as a writer, and her soliciting of Charles Cavendish's patronage in *Poems and Fancies* may be read as the inchoate expression of such strategies which so forcibly found expression in the later work.

Like Penelope, Ariadne used thread from the loom in an ingenious fashion, and her representation in Cavendish's work furthers the writer's imaginative exploitation of an association between tools of needlework, and female initiative and, ultimately, betrayal. In Letter 15, the Lady T. M. is reported as being rapturously described by Lord N. W. thus:

> She was a Lady fit to be the Empress of the whole world, for though Fortune had not given her a Temporal Imperial Crown [...], yet she was Crown'd at her Birth the Empress of her Sex; [...] her Celestial Crown was set with Understanding, Judgement and Wit, also with clear Distinguishings, oriental Similizings, and sparkling Fancies, a Crown more glorious than *Ariadne*'s Crown of Stars.[27]

The intellectual attributes of the Lady T. M. are praised above more traditional accomplishments and trappings of beauty and power, but, as was the case with the emblem of Penelope, the invoking of Ariadne is not altogether unproblematical. Theseus escaped from the minotaur's labyrinth with the help of Ariadne and her ball of thread, but subsequently abandoned her on Naxos, where she was found and wed by Dionysus, who crowned her with seven stars which became a constellation after her death.[28] As for the lady T. M., only the narrator's own spotless character prevents her becoming 'turn'd [...] all into Vinegar, or dissolv'd [...] into Vitriol' with envy.[29]

For both Penelope, then, the purpose of whose plot was to control her own body and sexuality, and Ariadne, who implicitly offered herself to Theseus when she handed him the ball of thread, the act of removal of that yarn from the sanctioned, domestic loom, connoted an act of enterprise rewarded by betrayal. Exposed to the suitors by her maids, the Homeric Penelope's intellectual scam is brought to an end, and her autonomy is further circumscribed by her husband's return to rule. The deserted Ariadne and the exposed Penelope both function paradigmatically within Cavendish's project of presenting herself as a writer.

In *Natures Pictures*, another of Cavendish's exilic works of the 1650s, however, the protagonist's defence of her chastity in 'Assaulted and Pursued Chastity' entails a more permanent self-determination, a fact which is legitimised by the author's construction of her heroine as not only part-Penelope, but, significantly, part-Ulysses too. The drive of *The Odyssey* is towards Ulysses's return to Ithaca in the thirteenth book, but narrative resolution cannot come about until he is recognised by Penelope in the twenty-third. Disguised by Pallas, Ulysses's self-revelation is protracted further by his deliberate misinformation.[30] Whilst Penelope's slowness in recognising him as her husband is attributable to this, it could also be read as a response to the implications for her of his return home. For Penelope, the homecoming necessitates a relinquishment of the power and self-rule she has enjoyed during his absence.[31] The loom she returns to is once again the site of a specifically feminine activity, its instrumental role in her discursively cunning preservation of her chastity having paid off, but also having come to an end. By contrast, Cavendish's tale, ostensibly about a woman as victim of assault and pursuit, becomes a text about a woman with agency who preserves her chastity through her own initiative. The female protagonist is at once Penelope, in her fierce preservation of her chastity, and, simultaneously, Ulysses, in her own eventual homecoming and concomitant assertion of rule. Cavendish's failure to stage a traditional homecoming for her heroine signifies her reluctance to have her subsumed back into an orthodox domestic setting where her considerable powers would have to be given up. By not returning to her native land of the Kingdom of Riches, the heroine, Travellia, does not have to yield the Ulysses part of herself and become all Penelope. Cavendish instead stages a bold compromise, settling her heroine in a new position. She writes:

> Then there was a declaration read to the army of the agreement of peace: and when it was read that the Prince should be Viceroy in the Kingdom of Amity, all the soldiers, as if they had been one voice, cried out, Travellia shall be Viceregency; which was granted to pacify them. Whereupon there were great acclamations of joy.
>
> But the Prince told his mistress, she should also govern him.
> She answered, that he should govern her, and she would govern the kingdom.[32]

The brazenness here of Travellia's answer is significant, and the set of circumstances she has been instrumental in bringing about point to her as the only natural choice of ruler. This is a romantic attachment underpinned by Travellia's awareness that her husband's government of her is purely nominal, since she possesses the real power, which resides in the support she enjoys from the populace and militia.[33] In effect, her statement that 'he should govern her' signifies less an assumption of a position of submission than a kindly, and ultimately insignificant, concession. As did Penelope, so Travellia employs her intellectual resources in order to preserve her chastity, but significantly unlike Penelope, marriage does not mean powerlessness, as Travellia resists coming home to the loom.

The Dutch woodcuts with which this paper began spun a fantastical tale of illogicality and transgression. In order to tell her own stories, and to deflect precisely such charges of monstrosity, Cavendish spins a complex web of self-representation and justification.[34] Having similarly shunned the distaff, she is in one sense analogous to the aggressive warrior woman of the broadsheet, armed, however, not with masculine weapons of war, but with the desire to spin stories. It is a desire which she first realises in *Poems and Fancies*, due to her inventive appropriation of the symbol of Penelope in order to eschew public impugnment of her reputation. It was essential for Margaret Cavendish's self-construction and presentation that she appear to surpass the paradigmatic Penelope, that is, that she does not relinquish her autonomy over her publications in a way analogous to Penelope's relinquishment of Ithaca to Ulysses upon his return home. Such self-identification was forcibly emphasised by Cavendish in the prefatory material of her first book, the 1653 *Poems and Fancies*, and, some three years later, in her imaginative refiguring of the epic topos of the homecoming in her 'Assaulted and Pursued Chastity'. Its confident and witty exposition was to find its fullest expression after the Restoration, in *CCXI Sociable Letters*. The prefatory material of *Poems and Fancies* may be read, then, as Cavendish's early, and somewhat tentative, exploration of the figure of the Homeric Penelope as a symbol replete with significance for the woman writer, whose very chastity could be called into doubt by the audacious and necessarily self-promoting act of publication.[35]

Notes

[1] Such broadsheets were common throughout Renaissance Europe. Their enduring significance and popularity are discussed by David Kunzle, 'World Upside Down: The Iconography of a European Broadsheet Type', in Barbara Babcock (ed.) *The Reversible World. Symbolic Inversion in Art and Society* (Ithaca: Cornell University Press, 1978), pp. 39–94. The particular woodcut to which I refer, published in Amsterdam by Ewout Muller, is reproduced in Babcock, pp. 46–7.

[2] *Poems and Fancies* (1653), p. 120.

[3] The original Dutch inscription makes no mention of the man's similarly reversed occupation, focusing instead solely on the woman's incongruous employment. Recent

interpreters have, however, seen it as necessary to provide a gloss which emphasises the man's role in the tableau. See, for example, 'wife goes to war and husband spins', Kunzle, 'World Upside Down', p. 45.

[4] By 'needlework', I intend to suggest the gamut of activities which involve threads, from spinning to weaving, knotting to embroidery. The emphasis is perhaps rather more on the 'work' than the 'needle'.

[5] Hence, in genealogical terms, the 'distaff side' is the female branch of a family.

[6] Needlework and female ingenuity are often paired in Greek myths, such as that of mute Philomela, who tells in a tapestry the story of her rape. For further etymology see Linda Woodbridge, 'Patchwork: Piecing the Early Modern Mind in England's First Century of Print Culture', *English Literary Renaissance*, 23 (1993), 5–45 (pp. 34–37); for needlework as 'inculcated not innate', see Rozsika Parker, *The Subversive Stitch: Embroidery and the Making of the Feminine* (London: The Women's Press, 1984), p. 104; for the etymology of 'text', see J. Hillis Miller, *Ariadne's Thread: Story Lines* (New Haven: Yale University Press, 1992), p. 7; on the gendered significance of 'work' see Laurie Yager Lieb, '"The Works of Women are Symbolical": Needlework in the Eighteenth Century', *Eighteenth-Century Life*, 10 (1986), 28–44; for Penelope as a potentially subversive, but ultimately virtuous, paradigm, see Cecilia Macheski, 'Penelope's Daughters. Images of Needlework in Eighteenth-Century Literature', in Mary Anne Schofield and Cecilia Macheski (eds.), *Fetter'd or Free? British Women Novelists, 1670–1815* (Athens: Ohio University Press, 1986), pp. 85–100.

[7] Cavendish was not entirely complimentary about Chapman's translation, presumably the one to which she is referring in *The Worlds Olio* (1655), p. 12, when she writes that '*Homer* is not yet matched in our Language; for though the worke was indeavoured to be translated, yet it is not like him.' Given her inability to read Homer in the original, or any language other than English, this opinion could only have been adopted from those who could.

[8] George Chapman, *Chapman's Homer: The Iliad, The Odyssey and the Lesser Homerica*, ed. by Allardyce Nicoll, 2 vols (London: Routledge and Kegan Paul, 1957), II, *The Odyssey* (Book VII), pp. 121–22. The nineteenth-century expression 'a well-spun yarn' suggests a degree of hybridisation of Homerically gendered social roles, since it derives from the stories sailors told each other to pass the time whilst weaving yarn into rope at sea. See Eric Partridge (ed.) *The Penguin Dictionary of Historical Slang*, sixth edition, abridged by Jacqueline Simpson (Harmondsworth: Penguin, 1988), p. 1060.

[9] *Chapman's Homer: The Odyssey* (Book II), p. 31.

[10] *Chapman's Homer: The Odyssey* (Book II), p. 32. The second account of the same plot and its subsequent exposure is told later, following Ulysses' return. Here, however, Penelope speaks for herself, telling her own story of how she spun the suitors a yarn. *Chapman's Homer: The Odyssey* (Book XIX), p. 332.

[11] *Chapman's Homer: The Odyssey* (Book IV), p. 84.

[12] *Chapman's Homer: The Odyssey* (Book IV), p. 85.

[13] The best account of this and other formative events in Cavendish's life remains Douglas Grant, *Margaret the First: A Biography of Margaret Cavendish Duchess of Newcastle 1623–1673* (London: Rupert Hart-Davis, 1957).

[14] *Poems and Fancies* (1653), sig. A2 verso. The potency of the distaff as domestic emblem with repercussions for the female writer is apparent twice more in *Poems and*

Fancies. In '*The Elysium*', poets 'The *World* as *Flax* unto their *Distaffe* bring / This Distaffe spins fine canvas of conceit, / Wherein the *Sense* is woven even, and strait', and in '*Of the* Spider', the spider's '*Body* is the *Wheele* that goeth round. / A *Wall* her *Distaff*, where she sticks *Thread* on, / The *Fingers* are the *Feet* that pull it long.' (pp. 142; 151).

[15] *Poems and Fancies* (1653), sig. A2 recto–verso.

[16] 'To Poets', in *Poems and Fancies* (1653), p. 122. In *The Worlds Olio* (1655), Cavendish questions Penelope's chastity which, she avers, was flawed because she allowed the suitors too much licence: 'she was Chast, but she gave her self leave to be Courted, which is a degree to Unchastity.' With two published volumes to her name, Cavendish may, by this later date, criticise even established exemplars from a position of superiority, as expressed in her conclusion that 'there is nothing dearer to a Man than his Fame, so a Wife should have a care to keep it.' (p. 133).

[17] *Poems and Fancies* (1653), p. 122.

[18] *Poems and Fancies* (1653), p. 121. The 'Faiery Wits' are characterised as at once ethereal, and, in keeping with an overall Lucretian tenor to her volume, as minuscule, atomised structures which '*passe through every* small Crevise, *and* Cranie *of* Errours, *and* Mistakes.' (p. 121).

[19] *Poems and Fancies* (1653), p. 121. This discourse recalls that of early conduct books like William Gouge's *Of Domesticall Duties: Eight Treatises* (London: William Bladen, 1622). The Puritan emphases of such works would have alienated Cavendish even had their stress on the importance of female domestic accomplishments not done so. On Gouge's demonstration of 'the essential idealism of the Puritan position', see N. H. Keeble (ed.), *The Cultural Identity of Seventeenth-Century Woman. A Reader* (London: Routledge, 1994), p. 145.

[20] *Poems and Fancies* (1653), p. 121.

[21] *Poems and Fancies* (1653), p. 122. In Greek mythology, Pallas sprang fully grown and armed from her father, Jupiter's, head. By contrast, the poet's work is '*gathered too soon*' (p. 122). Cavendish's use of the word 'Work' here, in relation to Penelope, perhaps recalls Antinous's 'first in craft', *Chapman's Homer: The Odyssey* (Book II), p. 31.

[22] *Sociable Letters* (1664), pp. 311–12.

[23] *Sociable Letters* (1664), p. 312.

[24] *Sociable Letters* (1664), p. 313.

[25] *Sociable Letters* (1664), p. 314.

[26] *Sociable Letters* (1664), p. 315.

[27] *Sociable Letters* (1664), p. 24.

[28] The image of the labyrinth also occurs later, in Letter 184, where it represents the impossibility of self-knowledge: 'the Nature of Mankind is like an Endless Labyrinth, past finding out.' See *Sociable Letters* (1664), p. 383. Perhaps Ariadne's experiences in the labyrinth might inform our reading of the often repetitive and stylistically confusing writing of Margaret Cavendish's oeuvre as a whole, and the meanderings of Ariadne's thread might stand as an analogue to the non-linearity of Cavendish's project.

[29] *Sociable Letters* (1664), p. 26.

[30] In the nineteenth book, for example, Ulysses tells his wife that he is from Crete, and Euryclea's recognition of his scar marks another step towards reassimilation in the court.

[31] Elizabeth Gregory also comments on this possibility: 'In insisting up to the point of Odysseus' return that she need not remarry, Penelope has stood on the threshold of a

repudiation of patriarchy.' See Elizabeth Gregory, 'Unravelling Penelope: The Construction of the Faithful Wife in Homer's Heroines', *Helios*, 23 (1996), 3–20 (p. 16). In Chapman's Homer, the reunion of Penelope and Ulysses is characterised in nautical terms, and they cling to each other with as much joy as 'sad men at Sea [...], their ship quite lost [...], craule up to Land.' *Chapman's Homer: The Odyssey* (Book XXIII), p. 399.

[32] Margaret Cavendish, 'Assaulted and Pursued Chastity', in *Writings* (1994), pp. 45–118 (p. 116).

[33] The idea that, in order to be a successful ruler, an individual had to have the militia on his or her side may be traced back to Machiavelli, who wrote that 'princes control their own destiny when they command enough money or men to assemble an adequate army and make a stand against anyone who attacks them'. Niccolò Machiavelli, *The Prince*, translated and ed. by Robert M. Adams (London: Norton, 1992), p. 30. It was an idea which William Cavendish echoed in the 1650s in his *Advice* to Charles II: 'without an Army in your owne hands, you are but a king upon a Curtesey of others.' Thomas P. Slaughter, *Ideology and Politics on the Eve of the Restoration: Newcastle's Advice to Charles II* (Philadelphia: American Philosophical Society, 1984), p. 5.

[34] The centrality of the image of the web to Cavendish's imaginative processes is explored in Sylvia Bowerbank, 'The Spider's Delight: Margaret Cavendish and the "female" Imagination', *English Literary Renaissance*, 14 (1984), 392–408.

[35] Janet Todd discusses the relationship between social constructions of femininity and female authorship in the seventeenth and eighteenth centuries in *The Sign of Angellica: Women, Writing and Fiction, 1660–1800* (London: Virago, 1989).

PART IV

NATURAL PHILOSOPHY

12

Margaret Cavendish and Henry More

Sarah Hutton

> I was very much surpriz'd when your Servant saluted me from so Illustrious a personage; but when he produced those noble Volumes as intended Testimony of your Ladiships respect, the unexpectedness of so great an honour made me suspect the Messenger of a mistake, and that he presented me with what was meant fitter for the Colledge, or at least to some more worthy and considerable person than myself. But he persisting still in the same story, my doubts were swallowed up into admiration of your Ladyship's singular and unparalleled goodness; which seems to me a Corrival with that excellency of your Wit, and to seek an equal share of Glory in searching out Objects of such condescending Acts of Civility and Bounty in these obscure corners of Academical Retirement, as the other in piercing into the greatest difficulties and the most dark and abstruse Recesses of Philosophy.[1]

So wrote the Cambridge Platonist, Henry More to the Duchess of Newcastle, who had just sent him a gift of some 'noble volumes' of her works. His letter is full of the flourish of compliment, modesty about the recipient as overdone as the praise for the sender (the gift is described by More as 'fitter for the Colledge, or at least to some more worthy and considerable person than myself.') He rounds off his letter with a rhetorically crafted apology for his unpolished manner of writing (in his haste to thank her he had not 'as yet fitly polished and adorned my Stile.') That was as much of a reply that the Duchess ever obtained from More, who took refuge in the excuse of haste to give thanks to explain why he could not indulge in 'longer converse with your Ladyship's most Elegant and Ingenious Writings.' He did take sufficient cognisance of the contents of the volumes to note that they contained a critique of his own philosophy. In an undated letter probably written at about the same time, he told his philosophical friend and erstwhile pupil, Anne Conway:

> My Lady of Newcastle hath sent two more Folios of hers to furnish my study, the one of poems, the other which is far the bigger, of letters wherein I am concern'd, above 30 of those letters being intended for a confutation of sundry passages in my writings.[2]

He continues:

> She is affrayd some man should quitt his breeches and putt on a petticoat to answer her in that disguize, which you Ladiship need not. She expresses this jealousie in her

book, but I beleave she may be secure from any on giving her the trouble of a reply.[3]

The first volume mentioned by More in his letter to Lady Conway could have been Margaret Cavendish's *Poems and Fancies* of 1653. The second was her *Philosophical Letters* of 1664. His reference to 'two more Folios' implies that he was already in receipt of other works by Cavendish. But there is no record of how many, or of what their titles might have been. In the following year (1666), More was to figure in Cavendish's *Blazing World* as one of the 'more famous modern writers', who, along with Galileo, Gassendi, Descartes, Van Helmont and Hobbes, are described as 'fine ingenious writers, but yet so self-conceited that they would scorn to be scribes to a woman.'[4] The last three, Descartes, Van Helmont and Hobbes, also figure with More in Cavendish's *Philosophical Letters*. The Duchess is a trifle unfair to include More among those who would not 'be scribes to a woman': he may have scorned to be scribe to the Duchess of Newcastle, but he could be described as scribe to the Countess of Conway, for he was both tutor and friend of Anne Conway, and had written at least one book at her behest.[5] In order to explain Cavendish's inclusion of More alongside such illustrious names in the history of science and philosophy, it is necessary to place both him and Margaret Cavendish in their contemporary intellectual context. This is a necessary first step to understanding the nature and scope of the satire on science and philosophy that occupies so much space in *Blazing World*. One source of information about the learned figures on whom Margaret Cavendish draws her own philosophical views and her opinions of them is her own *Philosophical Letters*, which contains important clues about several figures whom she subjects to critique in *Blazing World*.

The Context of Margaret Cavendish's Thought

Margaret Cavendish wrote at a time of enormous intellectual ferment, when new systems of thought were being proposed to replace for the Aristotelian synthesis that had dominated and shaped the intellectual horizons of Europe since the Middle Ages. Among the emergent new philosophies of the seventeenth century, the philosophy of Hobbes and of Descartes were challengingly new, though neither had attained a position of dominance. Alongside these, new techniques of observation and experiment were being developed and applied to the examination of the natural world. Such methods are epitomised most famously in the programme of the Royal Society.[6] The fact that Cavendish yokes together philosophers like Hobbes and Descartes with the *virtuosi* of the Royal Society, is a reminder that the twentieth-century distinction between science and philosophy did not obtain in the seventeenth century. What we call science was at that time natural philosophy, and much of the work of the philosophers Hobbes and Descartes was in the realm of natural philosophy. It should of course be remembered that to the seventeenth century Descartes was not just the author of the *Discourse on Method*, but he was probably better known as the author of a system of natural philosophy, *Principia philosophiae* (1644), which could be described as a treatise of theoretical physics.

Likewise, Hobbes was not a political theorist *tout court*, but also wrote on the science of nature: the first part of his *Elements of Philosophy* (published as *De corpore* in 1655) sets out the basis of his natural philosophy. Moreover, although the seventeenth century is traditionally regarded as an age of new science and new thought, it was not exclusively modern in its orientation. Alchemy was both an acceptable and a creative aspect of medicine as well as practical natural philosophy. For this reason, Cavendish's engagement with Jan Baptista van Helmont in *Philosophical Letters* does not represent a regressive position.[7] Nor does it contradict her interest in those like Descartes and Hobbes, who have since come to be called moderns.[8]

Henry More

Henry More is just such an example of a figure whom it is difficult to classify as either an ancient or a modern.[9] There are prominent features of his thinking which link him with the vitalistic philosophies of the Renaissance, and other aspects which show he was very much abreast of new developments. Having first made his name as a philosophical poet, More had by the time Cavendish's *Philosophical Letters* appeared (1664) secured his reputation as a philosopher through the publication of a collected edition of his writings, *A Collection of Several Philosophical Writings* in 1662.[10] More has come to be labelled a Platonist, and the titles of his books sound indelibly theological, particularly his *Immortality of the Soul* and his *Antidote against Atheism*, the two texts which are scrutinised in Cavendish's *Philosophical Letters*. Nonetheless, his philosophy was very up to date. More was constantly engaged with the thinking of his own day, in particular the philosophies of Descartes and Hobbes and developments in newly-emerging observational science promoted by the Royal Society. More's enthusiasm for Descartes (an enthusiasm which wore off with time) was accompanied with an intense hostility towards the philosophy of Thomas Hobbes.[11] Hobbes's philosophy appeared to him and most of his contemporaries to be the quintessence of atheism on account of Hobbes's attempt to explain the operations of nature and man in entirely material terms. The attraction of Cartesianism for More was that it was a dualist philosophy, which pre-supposed the existence of soul (mind) as well as body. Descartes's mechanistic concept of matter denuded material substance of all properties except shape, size and position. According to Descartes, all natural phenomena could be explained in terms of matter in motion. The attraction of this for More and other Cambridge Platonists was that it offered an argument for the existence of immaterial beings (hence of God), for the operations of material bodies could not be explained in terms of the properties of matter, but could only be explained by the presence of spiritual forces. Similarly, the human body was thought to require a guiding soul.[12]

For this reason (among others), it would be wrong to describe More as a Cartesian. His is an independent philosophy with affinities with Cartesianism. A central point of difference is the centrality of the concept of spirit. For More, not only are human beings composed of body and soul or spirit, but spirit, like body, is spatially extended and all corporeal things require the intervention of spiritual agency to give them life and movement. To put it another way, the entire universe, for More, is ensouled. According to More, God himself is *res extensa*, infinitely extended throughout the universe. To explain the operations of the created world, More posited the existence of what he called a *principium hylarchicum* or 'Spirit of Nature', which, like the World-Soul of the ancient Platonists, was an immaterial force moving, ordering and animating all physical phenomena. It acted as the agent of God, or agent of providence, carrying out God's designs in the natural world. More calls it, 'the vicarious power of God [...] upon this great *automaton*, the world.'[13]

More's entire intellectual project was a demonstration of the existence of spirit. It is to this that his book *The Immortality of the Soul* (1659) is devoted. And the spirits whose existence he sought to prove include not just the human soul and Spirit of Nature, but angels and devils, and, of course, God. It was an essential part of his argument for the existence of God that spirits exist. If you can persuade people of the existence of minor spirits through their observable operations, it is a short step to persuading them of the existence of a perfect and infinite spirit, i.e. God. More's two books, *Antidote against Atheism* and *Immortality of the Soul* go to considerable lengths to catalogue the operations of spirit in a range of observable phenomena, from the movement of the tides and the sympathetic vibration of strings, to the appearance of ghosts and the evidence of witchcraft. As he himself summed it up: 'That Saying is no less true in Politicks, *No Bishop, no King*, than this in Metaphysicks, *No Spirit, no God*.'[14] The logic of this position extended also to belief in the existence of evil spirits. And part of More's project was the collection of data that proved the existence of witches, poltergeists and demons. Accordingly, his *Antidote against Atheism* is devoted to relating stories of ghosts and witches reported to him by reliable witnesses.[15] In 1681 he edited and published Joseph Glanvill's *Sadducismus triumphatus*, a work which amounts to a catalogue of such occurrences.

It is not surprising, therefore, that when in *Blazing World* the Empress decides to discourse about the nature of the soul she should invoke Henry More, Doctor of Souls. And given Margaret Cavendish's decidedly materialist concept of nature it was inevitable that she should disagree with More, which is exactly what she does in her *Philosophical Letters*. Here she devotes one of the four sections to Henry More, giving him significantly more space than Hobbes and Descartes, who are treated together in the first section. In his turn, More receives less attention that Jan Baptista van Helmont.[16]

Margaret Cavendish's critique of Henry More is based on two of the books I have mentioned: his *Immortality of the Soul* and his *Antidote against Atheism.* At first glance it is easy to make fun of the woman would-be philosopher. Her critique of More (and of Hobbes, Descartes and Van Helmont, for that matter) seems at first sight to be piece-meal, scoring points at random and even irrelevantly. There is no systematic exposure of More's premises, no analysis of his objectives, not even consistency about which book is being discussed. But it would be wrong to dismiss Cavendish as a butterfly mind on the basis of the style of argument she adopts in this book. It is true that she does not use the kind of systematic argument that is a feature of seventeenth-century academic debate. But this is not surprising. She did not, after all, have a formal school and university education. Lack of philosophical formality does not necessarily denote lack of philosophical insight. The non-systematic character of argument is a feature of other writings by women philosophers and may be attributed in large part to lack of formal training.[17] And in any case, Cavendish's choice of epistolary form itself implies a loosening of polemical style. Her technique may be aptly compared to that of a gadfly: as, for example, when she catches Henry More out for inconsistency because he says that he intends to refute atheists yet admits that everyone believes in God.[18]

Furthermore, appearances are deceptive in respect of Margaret Cavendish's polemical style. There is indeed an organising principle for the points she makes, but it is not dictated by the books she criticises; rather it derives from her own philosophical position. Behind Cavendish's comments on More is a consistent philosophical standpoint, the very antithesis of More's. For Cavendish holds that 'there is nothing Nature but what is material.'[19] To that extent her discussion in *Philosophical Letters* confirms what she states in other writings. Indeed, she refers her reader back to 'my Philosophy [...] where you will find that all the several Parts of Nature are Living and Knowing, and that there is no part that has not Life and Knowledge, being all composed of rational and sensitive matter, which is the life and soul of nature.'[20] It is therefore probably true to say that in *Philosophical Letters* we learn more about Margaret Cavendish than about Henry More.

In *Philosophical Letters* Cavendish is careful to state her belief in God and in the immortality of the soul, and even in angels and devils, because they are mentioned in the Bible. But she says that the divine soul is a subject for churchmen ('divines'), and she utterly repudiates any idea that the operations of nature are to be explained by the actions of spirit. Where for Henry More matter is inert, requiring the intervention of spiritual action to cause it to move, for Cavendish matter is self-moving. Where More attributes the power of thinking not to bodies but to souls, Cavendish insists that matter can think. Nature, according to her, is 'knowing'. It is only because matter (or some part of it) is rational that thought is possible. Cavendish ascribes to matter, 'Notions, Conceptions, Imaginations, Deliberations; and anything else that belongs to the mind.'[21]

In *Philosophical Letters* she denies that matter is uniform in character, proposing instead that it is variegated, or rather variable, according to the kind of movement made or changes in movement: 'it is impossible to affirm, that self-moving Matter is either all rare, or all dense, or all hard, or all soft; because by its self-moving power it can be either, or both, and so by the change and variety of motion, there may be soft and rare Points, and hard and sharp Points, hard and contracted Globes, and soft and rare Globes [...].'[22] Matter cannot be annihilated: death or change is just a re-arrangement of the constituent elements of a body. Different parts of nature may have different amounts of knowledge. Indeed, vegetables and minerals may know more about themselves than Man does.[23] She dismisses the very idea that there is such a thing as spiritual substance. Immaterial substances are 'so many Hobgoblins to fright Children withal.'[24] Indeed, in many ways she seems to have much in common with Hobbes.[25] To summarise Margaret Cavendish's position vis-à-vis Henry More: everything that More explains as the result of the actions of spirit, Cavendish explains as actions of (refined) matter.

Nature and the Spirit of the Universe

That Cavendish's philosophical position is very much the obverse of More's can be highlighted by comparing her concept of nature with his Spirit of Nature. As is well known, Cavendish conceived of Nature as encompassing the entire created world and all the operations of natural things. Nature is both the agency of order and function, and the aggregate of material bodies that fill the world. In *Blazing World*, she writes:

> I find that nature is but one infinite, self-moving body, which by the virtue of its self-motion is divided into infinite parts, which parts, being restless, undergo perpetual changes and transmutations by their infinite compositions and divisions [...] there is no more but one universal principle of nature, to wit, self-moving matter, which is the only cause of all natural effects.[26]

In *Philosophical Letters* she expatiates further, reminding her reader that Nature is the instrument, or rather servant, of God. That nature is gendered female is emphasised in this account:

> First, that nature is infinite, and the eternal servant of God: Next that she is corporeal, and partly self-moving, dividable and composable; that all and every particular creature, as also perception and variety in nature, is made by corporeal self-motion, which I name sensitive and rational matter, which is life and knowledge, sense and reason [...][27]

In the *Grounds of Natural Philosophy* she underlines the subordination of Nature to God, a hierarchical relationship that emphasises the distinctness of Nature from God:

> God is an eternal creator; Nature, his eternal creature. God is an eternal master; Nature, God's eternal servant. God is an infinite immaterial being; Nature, an infinite corporeal being. God is immovable and immutable; Nature, moving and mutable. God is eternal, invisible, and of an incompoundable being; Nature, eternal divisible and compoundable. God is eternally perfect; Nature eternally imperfect. God is eternally inalterable; Nature, eternally alterable. God is without error; Nature, full of irregularities. God knows exactly or perfectly nature; Nature doth not perfectly know God. God is infinitely and eternally worshipped; Nature is the eternal and infinite worshipper.[28]

More's Spirit or Nature, or *Principium hylarchicum*, is very definitely not the stuff of which corporeal things are composed. But it is an organising and controlling principle in the natural world. Cavendish knew the summary description he gives of it *Immortality of the Soul*:

> *The Spirit of Nature* therefore, according to that notion I have of it, *is, A substance incorporeal, but without Sense and Animadversion, pervading the whole Matter of the Universe, and exercising a Plastical power therein according to the sundry predispositions and occasions in the parts it works upon, raising such* Phaenomena *in the World, by directing the parts of the Matter and their Motion, as cannot be resolved into mere Mechanical powers.*[29]

Like Cavendish's 'Nature', More's Spirit of Nature is conceived as the agent or instrument of God in the operations of the corporeal world. More calls it variously, 'a mute copy of the eternal Word [...] appointed to doe all the best services that Matter is capable of,'[30] and 'the Vicarious power of God upon the Matter.'[31] But unlike Cavendish's 'Nature', More's Spirit of Nature is very definitely non-material; he calls it, '*a substance incorporeal that does interesse it self in the bringing about some more general* Phaenomena *in the World.*'[32] Moreover, unlike Nature in Cavendish's philosophy, More's Spirit of Nature is unconscious of the actions it performs: it is 'a Substance devoid of all sense and perception, *and therefore uncapable of premeditated contrivance.*'[33]

These differences notwithstanding, there are nonetheless some uncanny parallels between Cavendish's Nature and More's Spirit of Nature. If we ignore, for a moment, that the latter is purely spiritual and immaterial and the former entirely material, the two have much in common. Certainly as far as their function and operations are concerned. Both are principles of conservation and order. Both are used to account for the disposition and movement of bodies in nature. Cavendish uses the same metaphor for the role of Nature as More does for the Spirit of nature: that of a servant to God. Cavendish's view that 'nature's soul adores and worships God as well as man's soule [doth]'[34] suggests the same kind of special relationship with the divine that More imputes to his Spirit of Nature. One might think that she should have been able to find some common ground with More on the subject of the Spirit of Nature, but this is not the case. She refuses to construe Nature even as the soul of Nature. She denies that physical bodies that constitute nature need spiritual assistance in its activities: 'Nature is not a Babe or a Child, to need such a Spiritual Nurse to teach her to go or move.'[35] She ridicules the Spirit of Nature as the '*Quarter-master General of his Divine Providence.*'[36] With devastating common sense in respect of divine omnipotence, she rejects the need for such a spiritual intermediary as the Spirit of Nature as the means whereby God imparts motion to matter: 'God can surely just as well give power of motion to matter as to Incorporeal Substance.'[37] Furthermore, she argues, that to posit an intermediary spirit between God and Creation, as also to argue that material things need superadded spirit to make them move or be capable of thought, is to commit the same error as the pagans in setting up a bevy of gods and demi-gods.[38] As in the case of the other philosophers whom she confutes in *Philosophical Letters*, Cavendish's critique of Henry More was one way of asserting her own 'singularity'. By underscoring the *differences* between her philosophy and his, she insures herself from the charge of being derivative or plagiarising. This distancing is taken further in *Blazing World*, where she adds ridicule to her armoury.

A Description of a New World Called the Blazing World

Although he is named only once, Henry More's part in *Blazing World* is larger than is normally recognised by Cavendish's modern editors and critics.[39] First of all, his name is invoked in the course of a long discussion about the nature of spirits. And spirits, as is well known, were a topic on which Henry More was a noted expert. As we have seen, More's *The Immortality of the Soul* is entirely devoted to proving the existence of immaterial spirits. Of course, More was not the only writer on spirits in his day. But what links the discussion of spirits in *Blazing World* with him specifically is the Empress's interest in constructing a Cabbala. Having been dissuaded from being instructed about 'The Jews Cabala', she proposes to study a literal interpretation of scripture, then to construct 'a philosophical Cabala' and finally 'a moral Cabala'. This triple approach to understanding the mysteries of scripture – literal, philosophical and moral – refers directly to the 'cabala' of Henry More's own making, his *Conjectura Cabbalistica: or, a Conjectural Essay of Interpreting the Minde of Moses according to a threefold Cabbala, viz. Literal, Philosophical, Mystical, or, Divinely Moral*, published in London in 1653.[40] Cavendish does not discuss More's *Conjectura Cabbalistica* in *Philosophical Letters*, but it is the case that some of the points made in *Blazing World* relate specifically to the claims of this work. For example, in *Conjectura Cabbalistica*, More gives a lengthy exposition of Pythagorean number symbolism; in *Blazing World* this is repudiated:

> Then she [the Empress] enquired whether there was no mystery in numbers. 'No other mystery,' answered the spirits, 'but reckoning and counting, for numbers are only marks of remembrance'. 'But what do you think of the number of four,' said she, 'which the Cabalists make such ado withal, and of the number ten, when they say that ten is all and that all numbers are virtually comprehended in four?' 'We think,' answered they, 'that Cabalists have nothing else to do but to trouble their heads with such useless fancies, for naturally there is no such thing as prime or all in numbers, nor is there any other mystery in numbers but what man's fancy makes.'[41]

In his *Defence of the Philosophick Cabbala*, appended to *Conjectura Cabbalistica*, More had explained:

> And for further eviction, we may yet adde that as *all numbers* are contained in *Four*

> virtually, (by *all numbers* is meant *Ten*, for when we come to *Ten* we go back again) so the root and foundation of all the Corporeal Creation is laid in this *fourth* day's work [...] For, as *Philo* observes, *Pythagorean*-like, *Ten* [...] is made by the scattering of the parts of *Four*, thus, 1, 2, 3, 4. Put these together now and they are *Ten.*[42]

The majority of the replies by the spirits to the Empress's questions, however, match Cavendish's critique of More in *Philosophical Letters*. For example, in *Blazing World* the spirits repeatedly insist that motion is not caused by spirit that imparts motion to matter, but matter is the cause of motion.[43] In *Blazing World*, matter is described as not uniform but varied: 'some parts of matter were rare, some dense, some solid, some fluid etc.'[44] As we have already noted, in *Blazing World*, Cavendish defines Nature as:

> one infinite, self-moving, living and self-knowing body, consisting of the three degrees of inanimate, sensitive and rational matter so intermixed together that no part of nature, were it an atom, can be without any of these three degrees.[45]

In *Philosophical Letters*, she refers the reader to 'my Philosophy where you will find that all the several Parts of Nature are Living and Knowing, and that there is no part that has not Life and Knowledge, being all composed of rational and sensitive matter, which is the life and soul of Nature.'[46] In *Philosophical Letters*, Cavendish tells More, 'I have said before that nothing is perishable or subject to annihilation in nature, and so no death.'[47] In *Blazing World*, we are told that death is merely change of the motion or configuration of matter,[48] and that, 'there is no beginning in nature, no not of particulars, by reason nature is eternal and infinite, and her particulars are subject to infinite changes and transmutations by virtue of their own corporeal, figurative self-motions so that there's nothing new in nature, not properly a beginning of anything.'[49] In *Blazing World*, the term 'Spirit of Nature' is not used, but the Empress does invoke the concept when she 'asked further whether there was any plastic power in nature.'[50] The term 'plastic' in the sense of 'shaping' or 'formative' is used by More's fellow Cambridge Platonist, Ralph Cudworth to name his equivalent of the spirit of Nature, namely, Cudworth's more famous doctrine of 'Plastic Nature'.[51] In *Philosophical Letters*, Cavendish derides the confusion of and profusion of experts' opinions about the soul: while there are so many opinions on the doctrine of the soul that 'the multiplicity confounds my choice.'[52] Cavendish tells More that this bewildering array of opinions on soul is like 'an Hodg Podg, Bisk or Olio.'[53]

Most of the views expressed in *Blazing World* can be found in other writings by Cavendish besides *Philosophical Letters*. But some of the detail indicates that she has mustered her opinions as part of a critique of Henry More. In addition to the allusions to *Conjectura cabbalistica*, two further details in *Blazing World* suggest a link with Henry More, or at least with her treatment of More in *Philosophical Letters*. As we have already noted, in *Philosophical Letters*, Cavendish makes an explicit separation between Reason and Faith: 'I avoid as much as ever I can, not to mix Divinity with Natural Philosophy; for I consider that such a mixture would breed more confusion in the Church, then do any good to either,' adding that it is impossible to prove Divinity 'by Mathematical Demonstration.'[54] She also insists repeatedly that divine matters should be left to divines, that the divine soul is a subject for theologians, not natural philosophers, and that in any case our minds are incapable of forming a true idea of God or of divine spirits because our minds are finite and material. In *Blazing World*, the spirits condemn those 'many divine philosophers that make a galimaufrey both of reason and faith,'[55] and dismiss the 'doctrine of the Platonists' in respect of the 'divine light', the soul of man and the soul's 'vital operation on the body.'[56] These Platonists are examples of those 'ancient and modern philosophers' who 'endeavour to go beyond sense and reason, which makes them commit absurdities, for no corporeal creature can go beyond sense and reason; no, not we spirits, as long as we are in our corporeal vehicles.'[57] We have already noted that in *Philosophical Letters* Cavendish had goaded More for seeking to convert atheists yet admitting that there was no one who was not a theist (since everyone has an idea of God). Likewise, in *Blazing World* the Empress asks 'whether there were any atheists in the world. The spirits answered that there were not more atheists than what Cabalists make.'[58] This must surely be a reference to the great Cabalist, More, addressing his writings to supposed atheists.

There are many other examples that could be cited. As in *Philosophical Letters*, the purpose of the allusions to More in *Blazing World* is to refute his philosophy. It is with consummate irony that Cavendish has her Empress consult spirits, whose very existence as incorporeal beings is impossible according to her own philosophy. There is further irony in the fact that these spirits are themselves authorities against the great champion of spiritual substance, Henry More. These spirits tell the Empress that the source of motion is not spirit but matter – a position that contradicts More but upholds Cavendish's own view.[59] Furthermore, the spirits lend support to this view by putting forward one of More's own suppositions, namely that every spirit must have a corporeal vehicle. The fly-men tell the Empress that earthly spirits are 'embodied and material' while airy spirits 'were always clothed in some sort or other of material garments, which garments were their bodies, made for the most part, of air.'[60]

In this way Cavendish exposes the shortcomings of More's philosophy of spirit, indicating that even the champion of immaterialism is obliged to make concessions to materialism in order to make his system work. In respect of Platonist philosophy, the overall effect in *Blazing World* is very similar to Cavendish's treatment of Royal Society science. She turns Cambridge Platonism upside down in exactly the same way, subjecting the Platonist philosopher, Henry More, to the same discomfiture as she inflicts on the Royal Society experimenters.

Nonetheless, as the narrative unfolds Cavendish stays with the Platonists to the extent that she exploits the Platonic doctrine of the airy vehicle of the soul to make possible the peregrinations of the Empress's and Duchess's souls and their meeting together inside the head of the Duke of Newcastle. This curious 'Platonic seraglio' as it is called, is entirely pure, free of any sexual taint because, as we are told, 'no adultery could be committed amongst Platonic lovers.'[61] In *Philosophical Letters*, however, Cavendish reaches the opposite conclusion. Dismissing all talk of spirits as 'poetical fictions', she concludes:

> By this you may plainly see, *Madam*, that I am no Platonick; for this opinion is dangerous, especially for married Women, by the reason the conversation of the Souls may be a great temptation, and a means to bring Platonick Lovers to a neerer acquaintance, not allowable by the Laws of Marriage, although by the sympathy of souls.[62]

Cavendish's dismissal of spirits as 'poetical fictions' is a clue to narrative strategy in the final episode *Blazing World.* If, on her own materialist account of being, the existence of spirits is impossible, they can only 'exist' as imaginary beings – that is, as fictions. Just as Cavendish's Duchess can become Empress of a world in her own imagination, so she can also commune with the souls of the Empress and her husband inside the head of the latter by virtue of a psychological theory – the Platonist doctrine of souls – that is, in her view, purely fiction.[63] Communication between souls within the head of a third party (as happens in the last part of *Blazing World*) is only possible in fiction. This element of Platonism that sustains and shapes the last episode of the *Blazing World* is therefore the hallmark fiction. If that is so, the great Platonist, Henry More, is by implication, a philosopher of airy nothingness – not a philosopher at all, but the inventor of poetical fictions. Ironically perhaps, Cavendish takes his writing (at least one of his books) at his own valuation, namely as conjecture (his *Conjectura cabbalistica*, is subtitled *A Conjectural Essay*).[64] And it was, after all, as a poet that he started his publishing career.[65] Devastating though this reduction of 'the pious and learned Henry More' might be, it also offers another way for Cavendish to put herself on an equal footing with one of her more famous and more intellectually respectable male contemporaries. After all, as her husband asserts in his prefatory Epistle to her *Philosophical and Physical Opinions*, 'there is not any one thing in the whole Book, that is not absolutely spun out by her own studious phancy.'[66]

Notes

[1] Anne Conway, *The Conway Letters: The Correspondence of Anne, Viscountess Conway, Henry More, and their Friends, 1642–1684*, ed. by Marjorie Hope Nicolson, rev. by Sarah Hutton (Oxford: Clarendon, 1992), p. 241.

[2] *Conway Letters*, p. 237.

[3] *Conway Letters*, p. 237.

[4] Margaret Cavendish, *The Description of a New World Called the Blazing World*, in Paul Salzman (ed.), *An Anthology of Seventeenth-Century Fiction* (Oxford: Oxford University Press, 1991), p. 306. Cavendish's acquaintance with the philosophy of Descartes, Gassendi and Hobbes probably dates from her years of exile in Paris. The Cavendish family into which she married took an active part in the intellectual life of Paris. Through their patronage of Hobbes and acquaintance with members of the Mersenne circle, they were thoroughly conversant with the scientific and philosophical developments of their day. See Jean Jacquot, 'Sir Charles Cavendish and his Learned Friends', *Annals of Science*, 8 (1952), 13–27; Helen Hervey, 'Hobbes and Descartes in the Light of some Unpublished Letters of the Correspondence between Sir Charles Cavendish and Dr. John Pell', *Osiris*, 10 (1952), 67–90.

[5] For More's friendship with Anne Conway, see *Conway Letters*. According to his biographer, Richard Ward, More wrote *Conjectura cabbalistica* at her request. See Richard Ward, *The Life of Henry More, Parts 1 and 2*, ed. by Sarah Hutton et al., Archives internationales d'histoire des idées, 167 (Dordrecht and Boston: Kluwer Academic, 2000), p. 122.

[6] See especially Lisa Sarasohn, 'Science Turned Upside Down: Feminism and the Natural Philosophy of Margaret Cavendish', *Huntington Library Quarterly*, 47 (1984), 289–307 for the relevance of the new science of the Royal Society to Cavendish's thought. Also, Sarah Hutton, 'Anne Conway, Margaret Cavendish and Seventeenth-Century Scientific Thought', in Lynette Hunter and Sarah Hutton (eds.), *Women, Science and Medicine 1550–1700* (Stroud: Alan Sutton, 1997), pp. 218–234.

[7] On Van Helmont, see Walter Pagel, *Jan Baptista van Helmont, Reformer of Science and Medicine* (Cambridge: Cambridge University Press, 1982).

[8] I might also add at this point that the new philosophies of the seventeenth century were woman-friendly in two important respects. First of all they were free of the misogynistic baggage that encumbered the philosophical system which they replaced, namely Aristotelianism. Secondly, most (though not all) of the new philosophers wrote in the vernacular and not in Latin: a great advantage to women denied the Latin-based education reserved for their male contemporaries. For a measure of the built-in misogyny of Aristotelianism see Ian Maclean, *The Renaissance Notion of Woman* (Cambridge: Cambridge University Press, 1980).

[9] See Sarah Hutton (ed.) Henry More: *Tercentenary Studies* (Dordrecht: Kluwer, 1990); and A. Rupert Hall, *Henry More: Magic, Religion and Experiment* (Oxford: Blackwell, 1990).

[10] More's first published work was *Psychodia Platonica; or a platonicall song of the soul* (Cambridge, 1642), reprinted in *Philosophical Poems* in 1647.

[11] On More and Descartes, see Alan Gabbey, 'Philosophia cartesiana triumphata: Henry More (1646–1671)' in Thomas M. Lennon et al. (eds.), *Problems of Cartesianism* (Kingston and Montreal: Queen's McGill University Press, 1982), pp. 171-250. On Hobbes

and the Cambridge Platonists, see Samuel I. Mintz, *The Hunting of Leviathan: Seventeenth-Century Reactions to the Materialism of Thomas Hobbes* (Cambridge: Cambridge University Press, 1962).

[12] For an account of Cambridge Platonism see Sarah Hutton, 'Lord Herbert and the Cambridge Platonists', in *Routledge History of Philosophy*, 10 vols (London and New York: Routledge, 1993-1999), *V: British Philosophy in the Age of Enlightenment*, ed. Stuart Brown, (London and New York: Routledge, 1996), pp. 20–42. On More, see Alan Gabbey, 'Henry More and the Limits of Mechanism' in Hutton, *Tercentenary Studies*, pp. 19–35.

[13] More, *Immortality of the Soul*, p. 203 in *A Collection of Several Philosophical Writings* (London, 1662). The works in this volume are separately paginated, all subsequent citations refer, therefore, to the pagination within individual works.

[14] More, *Antidote against Atheism*, p. 142 in *A Collection*.

[15] In such cases where verification was problematic, the reliability or trustworthiness of the observers was, of course, paramount. One of the dependable witnesses who was asked to gather reports of witchcraft was Anne Conway. Her reports are included in Joseph Glanvill's *Sadducismus Triumphatus*. See *Conway Letters*, p. 214. On More's interest in demonology see Allison P. Coudert, 'Henry More and Witchcraft', in Hutton, *Tercentenary Studies*, pp. 115–136.

[16] This distribution of attention should not be taken to mean that Cavendish failed to recognise the importance of Hobbes and Descartes. Such an interpretation is unhistorical, failing to take account of the relative standing of these various figures in the seventeenth century. On the contrary, Cavendish's choice of thinkers was very much 'state of the art'.

[17] Damaris Cudworth, Lady Masham is another example of a woman whose philosophical writing is not formally structured according to the rules of dialectic. See Sarah Hutton, 'Damaris Cudworth, Lady Masham: Between Platonism and Enlightenment', *British Journal for the History of Philosophy*, 1:1 (1993), 29-54. By contrast, Anne Conway, who did receive philosophical training, writes in a more formal philosophical manner.

[18] *Philosophical Letters* (1664), p. 137.

[19] *Philosophical Letters* (1664), p. 149.

[20] *Philosophical Letters* (1664), pp. 143–144.

[21] *Philosophical Letters* (1664), p. 173.

[22] *Philosophical Letters* (1664), p. 171.

[23] *Philosophical Letters* (1664), p. 162.

[24] *Philosophical Letters* (1664), p. 187.

[25] For an assessment of the relationship between Cavendish's philosophy and that of Hobbes see Sarah Hutton, 'In Dialogue with Thomas Hobbes. Margaret Cavendish's Natural Philosophy', *Women's Writing*, 4 (1997), 421–32.

[26] *Blazing World*, ed. Salzman, p. 281.

[27] *Philosophical Letters* (1664), sig. b4.

[28] *Grounds* (1668), p. 241.

[29] *Immortality*, p. 193, in *A Collection*.

[30] 'Preface', p. xv, in *A Collection*.

[31] *Immortality*, p. 13, in *A Collection*.

[32] 'Preface', p. xv in *A Collection*.

[33] *Immortality*, p. 12, in *A Collection*.

[34] *Philosophical Letters* (1664), p. 138.

[35] *Philosophical Letters* (1664), p. 149.

[36] *Philosophical Letters* (1664), p. 215.

[37] *Philosophical Letters* (1664), p. 195.

[38] This criticism of More's Spirit of Nature anticipates one of Pierre Bayle's criticisms of More's colleague, Ralph Cudworth, whose concept of Plastic Nature is very similar to More's Spirit of Nature. See Rosalie Colie, *Light and Enlightenment: A Study of the Cambridge Platonists and Dutch Arminians* (Cambridge: Cambridge University Press, 1957).

[39] The editions by Paul Salzman (1991) and Kate Lilley (1992) contain only the most cursory of references to More.

[40] Also printed in *A Collection*.

[41] *Blazing World*, p. 297.

[42] *Conjectura Cabbalistica*, p. 82 in *A Collection*.

[43] *Blazing World*, pp. 294, 298, 300.

[44] *Blazing World*, p. 297.

[45] *Blazing World*, p. 301.

[46] *Blazing World*, pp. 143–144. Cf. *Philosophical Letters* (1664), pp. 145, 171 (quoted *supra*).

[47] *Philosophical Letters* (1664), p. 221.

[48] *Blazing World*, pp. 148–149.

[49] *Blazing World*, p. 279.

[50] *Blazing World*, p. 295.

[51] See note 38 above.

[52] *Philosophical Letters* (1664), p. 230.

[53] *Philosophical Letters* (1664), p. 210.

[54] *Philosophical Letters* (1664), pp. 210–211.

[55] *Blazing World*, p. 293.

[56] *Blazing World*, p. 298.

[57] *Blazing World*, p. 299. Cavendish is referring here to the Platonic doctrine of the vehicle of the soul, much discussed by More, and according to which souls need a material container or vehicle. See, for example More, 'Immortality', II, ch.14; cf. *Blazing World*, p. 291.

[58] *Blazing World*, p. 299.

[59] *Blazing World*, p. 294.

[60] *Blazing World*, p. 291.

[61] *Blazing World*, p. 319.

[62] *Philosophical Letters* (1664), p. 219.

[63] '[W]hy should you desire to be Empress of a material world, and be troubled with the cares that attend government, whenas by creating a world within yourself, you may enjoy all, both in whole and in parts, without control or opposition, and may make what world you please and alter it when you please and enjoy as much pleasure and delight as a world can afford you', *Blazing World*, p. 311.

[64] He describes his Cabbalistic scheme to Lady Conway as 'births of my own braine', *Conway Letters*, p. 83.

[65] See note 10 above.

[66] Margaret Cavendish, *Physical Opinions* (1655), sig. A2.

13

Variation, Irregularity and Probabilism: Margaret Cavendish and Natural Philosophy as Rhetoric*

Stephen Clucas

Probably the most formidable obstacle to Margaret Cavendish's inclusion within the canons of philosophical and literary scholarship has been the perception of her work as incoherent, formless and disorganised. Even critics sympathetic to her 'free fancy and subjective expression' such as Sylvia Bowerbank, have regretted that she was not 'a more disciplined writer,' seeing her 'endlessly varied and fecundating' discourse as 'a cautionary tale for those of us who would suggest that craftsmanship and order are masculine, and artlessness and chaos are feminine.'[1] I would argue, however, that when viewed in relation to some of the aesthetic and natural philosophical contexts of the 1650s and 1660s, Cavendish's work seems less idiosyncratic and eccentric and, if not normative, then at least canonically comprehensible. Viewed in terms of the demands and imperatives of late twentieth-century canons – even recuperative, feminist canons like Bowerbanks's – much of Cavendish's work seems difficult to locate, if not downright perverse. Generically, stylistically and formally Cavendish's works in various literary and non-literary modes seem complex and even contradictory. This paper focuses on Cavendish's natural philosophical writings, which because of their apparent contradictoriness or unmethodical design have posed particular difficulties for intellectual historians. When her writings are placed within appropriate contexts, however, such as the discourses of conceited wit, and the essayistic probabilism of mid-seventeenth-century natural philosophical discourse, they become, I would argue, more comprehensible if not completely resolved.

In her 1983 study *Probability and Certainty in Seventeenth Century England*, Barbara Shapiro noted that the 'focus on the empirical and the probable, rather than the certain and the demonstrative' in mid-seventeenth century natural philosophical inquiry 'resulted in a philosophical style that strove to avoid dogmatic statements,' a 'philosophical liberty' which rejected authority in favour of a moderative and tentative mode of discussion.'[2] This 'philosophical style', as Sergei Zakin has recently suggested, found its most appropriate expression in the casual, open-ended

* An earlier version of this paper was given at the 1999 conference 'A Female Intellectual in her Milieu: Margaret Cavendish (1623–1673), or The Interior Exile' held at the Univerity of Paris VIII, St Denis.

and provisional form of the essay, and in a rhetoric which underlined this provisionality.[3] When viewed alongside other natural philosophers who cultivated an undogmatic and unsystematic approach, Margaret Cavendish's works seem less problematic than they might at first appear. When correctly contexualised (as Anna Battigelli has recently emphasised):

> the very characteristics that have caused scholars to dismiss Cavendish – her lack of method, her willingness to embrace contradictions, her confidence in deductive thinking, her eccentricity and self-absorption – become historically significant.[4]

While Battigelli here refers primarily to Cavendish's critique of Cartesian and Hobbesian philosophies of mind, the essayistic and probabilistic discourses of mid-century philosophers such as Boyle, Charleton and Glanvill can also help render Cavendish's apparent contradictions historically legible. If we compare, for example, Margaret Cavendish's *Grounds of Natural Philosophy*, published in 1668 with Robert Boyle's *The Origine of Formes and Qualities*, published in 1666, we find prefatory strategies which, in both cases, emphasise the peremptory and artless composition of their respective works. In Boyle's 'Prooemial Discourse to the Reader' his piece is described as an 'Attempt' compiled out of 'loose Sheets'.[5] These 'Expository Notes' were found, he says, as he 'rumag'd' among 'Loose papers' finding 'several Notes [...] under various heads, but yet all concerning the Origine of Forms and Qualities.' The papers were 'fairly copied out together by an 'Industrious person,' he says, but the 'Reader may not wonder to find the following Book not written uniformly in one continued tenor.'[6] Even given the incoherence of its compilation, Boyle suggests, his hurried notes are deemed superior to the 'precarious' and 'contradictious' writings of the 'Scholastical Philosophers,' because they are 'founded upon Experience, or the nature of the Things under debate,' rather than 'Metaphysical or Logical Subtleties.'[7] In his *Free Enquiry Into the Vulgarly Receiv'd Notion of Nature*, written in the same year, but not published until 1685/6, Boyle apologises for the disorderliness of his work. He brazenly alludes to the 'preposterous [...] Order' of his papers, where things are 'unduly plac'd.'[8] 'I [...] desire, to have this Rhapsody of my own loose Papers, look'd upon but as an *Apparatus*, or Collection of Materials, in order to make [what I well know this maim'd and confus'd Essay is not,] a compleat and regular Discourse.'[9] 'I hope it will be thought but a venial Fault, if the Contexture of the whole Discourse do not appear Uniform,' he says, 'nor all the Connections of its Parts so apt and close, as, if no Papers had been lost and supply'd, might reasonably be look'd for.' As the papers were 'not written in one continued *Series* of Times' he has been 'oblig'd' by friends to 'tack them together.'[10] There is more to these protestations than conventional modesty tropes, however, and behind these insistences on the casual and provisional status of his papers is a desire to construct a discourse which 'pretends not to *Dogmatize*, but *only* to make an *Enquiry*.' A discourse which equally rejects 'raising Superstructures' of dogmatic theory or slavishly 'relying on those of Others.'[11] His readers should not, therefore, expect 'Demonstrative arguements' but an 'Attempt', a 'heap of bare Probabilities.'[12] In the *Origine of Formes*, Boyle adopts the narrative device of speaking about his earlier work as if it were written by somebody else. This writing about himself 'as of a third person,' he says, allows him to 'play the Corpuscularian,' giving him 'the more Freedome and Conveniency [to] Adde, Explain, Alter, and even Retract, as I should see cause,' reserving 'the Freedom of questioning, and Correcting' his earlier theories. His intention, he says, is to provide 'Experiments and Queries' rather than to make 'hasty Assertions' or to 'Dogmatize'.[13] Boyle's casual essayistic style is then, the perfect vehicle for a mode of natural philosophy which seeks to authorise its own principles of investigation, paradoxically, by denying the authoritative nature of its statements. By emphasising the probable, hypothetical and provisional nature of its empirical findings, it avoids counter-arguments which sought to oppose it on the grounds of its lack of theoretical superstructures. Boyle's strategy attempts to authorise inquiry, experiment and investigation, rather than dogma, theory and over-elaborate argument.

In many of her works, Cavendish alludes to the unmethodical design of her writings. In her epistle 'To all the Universities in Europe', in the *Grounds of Natural Philosophy*, for example, she warns her academic readers:

> If you expect fair Proportions in the Parts, and a Beautiful Symmetry in the Whole, having never been taught at all, and having read but little; I acknowledg my self too illiterate to afford it, and too impatient to labour much for Method. But, if you will be contented with *pure Wit*, and the Effects of *meer Contemplation*; I hope, that somewhat of that kind may be found in this Book, and in my other *Philosophical*, *Poetical*, and *Oratorical Works*.[14]

Elsewhere she criticised the verbosity of scholastic philosophy as:

> very obstructive to the rational part of mans minde; for it imployes the mind with such busy, and unprofitable maters [*sic*], as all method is run out of breath, and gives not contemplation leave to search, and enquire after truth, nor understanding leave to examine what is truth [...] nor imagination leave to be ingenious, nor ingenuity leave to finde invention, nor wit leave to spin out the fine and curious threed of fancy, but onely to play with words on the tongue, as balls with rackets.[15]

Like Boyle, Cavendish's stress on the 'artlessness' of her style determines the terms of debate by rejecting in advance the authority of scholastic argument, although in her case the 'ingenious and free' discourse of wit and fancy, or rational contemplation notionally unguided by reliance on empirical data, is promoted rather than experimental investigation.[16]

In his *Free Enquiry*, Boyle observed that the 'Novelty of divers of the Sentiments and Reasonings, propos'd in the following Discourse, will be surprising, and encline many to look upon the Author as a bold Man, and much addicted to *Paradoxes*,' and Boyle contrasts his own '*Singular*' opinions with those which are '*commonly Receiv'd.*'[17] Those who are familiar with Margaret Cavendish's writings will find this statement eeriely familar – echoing as it does her claims to be daring, contradictory and singular. Boyle's insistence on his work as nothing more than a 'heap of bare Probabilities,' was not untypical of a number of mid-century critiques of peripatetic discourse, as the works of Barbara Shapiro and Henry Van Leeuwen have shown,[18] and it is not insignificant that two of Cavendish's most appreciative intellectual friends, Walter Charleton and Joseph Glanvill, were amongst the most outspoken probabilists of their day. In his *Physiologia Epicuro–Gassendo–Charltoniana* (1654), Charleton began by stating that his work was 'at most but ingenious Conjecture,' and repeatedly draws attention to the provisional nature of his discourse.[19] At the opening of Book 3, for example, he says:

> we have [...] præsented you no sparing account of our Conjectural opinion: which we desire may be candidly accepted in the latitude of *Probability* only, or how it *may* be, rather then how *it is*, or *must* be; i.e. that it is, though most *possible* and *verisimilous* [...] yet not absolutely *necessary*.[20]

For Charleton the 'true Idea of Nature' belongs to God alone, and it is madness to believe that man can 'prætend to an exact or adæquate comprehension thereof.' The 'Zenith' of his ambition is only 'plausibly satisfactory' explanations of phenomena.[21] In the final sentences of his work, Charleton returns to this theme, refusing to arrogate any authority to his statements:

> so far from being Magisterial in any of the Opinions I præsented; that considering my own Humor of Indifferency, and constant Dubiosity [...] it hath somewhat of wonder in it, that I ever proposed them to Others: nor, indeed, can any thing solve that wonder, but my Hopes, thereby secretly to undermine that lofty Confidence of yonger Heads, in the Certitude of Positions and Axioms Physiological; and by my declared Scepticism even in such Notions, as my self have laboured to assert, by the firmest Grounds, and strongest Inducements of Belief, to reduce them to the safer level of *Quo magis quaerimus, magis dubiamus*.[22]

For Charleton, all human knowledge is limited by the '*Obscurity of Nature*, the *Dimness and imperfection of our Understanding*, [and] the *Irregularity of our Curiosity*.'[23] Charleton's arguments regarding the 'erroneous judicature' of man's intellect are fundamentally religious, and revolve around the post-lapserian degradation of the reason and the other intellectual faculties, although Ciceronian probabilism could well have been a particular influence, and he claims to sympathise with the Academicks and Pyrrhonicks who claim that 'all things are Incomprehensible.'[24]

Joseph Glanvill, another of Cavendish's philosophical correspondents, whose defensive replies to her queries suggest a vigorous intellectual exchange, was also sceptical about certainty in natural philosophy. In a letter to Cavendish, dated 13 October 1667, Glanvill wrote:

> the manner of the most obvious sensible things is to us unknown; And by this we can only prove, that we have no certain Theory of Nature: And, in good earnest, Madam, all we can hope for, as yet, is but the History of Things as they are, but to say how they are, to raise general *Axioms*, and to make *Hypotheses*, must, I think, be the happy priviledge of succeeding Ages.[25]

Cavendish's own position on natural philosophy is close in spirit to both Charleton and Glanvill, and while she evidently had particular differences with them, she shared their views on the issue of certainty. While she rejects outright scepticism, as a doctrine which 'strive[s] to strangle, not only all opinions, but all knowledge,' she persistently rejected the possibility of absolute knowledge.[26] In her 'Epistle to the Unbelieving Readers in Natural Philosophy' in the *Worlds Olio*, for example, she argues against the radical scepticism of those who claim 'That in Natural Philosophy nothing is to be known, not the Cause of any one thing,' but takes up a compromise position, arguing that we can learn a great deal from 'Effects', which can help us 'produce more Effects thereby,' even if we do not entirely understand the causes. It is impossible, she said, 'that Nature should perfectly understand, and absolutely know her self, because she is Infinite, much less can any of her Works know her: yet it doth not follow, that nothing can be known [...].'[27] Given Cavendish's rejection of absolute knowledge it seems curious that when Charleton passed judgement on her natural philosophy in 1667, he criticises her not just for her obscurity, but for a paucity of convincing demonstrations:

> For your NATURAL Philosophy; it is ingenious and free, and may be, for ought I know, Excellent: but give me leave, Madam, to confess, I have not yet been so happy, as to discover much therein that's *Apodictical*, or wherein I think my self much obliged to acquiesce. But, that may be the fault of my own dull Brain: and Oracles have been after found true, that were at first Dark and *Enigmatical*. Again I am somewhat slow of belief also; a continual seeker: as conceiving, I have too much cause to be of *Seneca*'s opinion, that *Men may, indeed enquire and determine what is most probable, but God alone knows what's true, in the things of Nature*. Nor am I single in this Sceptical Iudgement. The ROYAL SOCIETY it self (the Tribunal of Philosophical Doctrines) is of a constitution exceedingly strict and rigid in the examination of Theories concerning Nature.

Charleton sugars the pill of his criticisms with assurances that his doubt extends to the accepted authorities of both the ancient and the new philosophies:

> This *Madam*, can be no discredit to your Philosophy in particular, because common to all others : and he is a bold man, who dares to exempt the *Physics* of *Aristotle* himself, or of *Democritus*, or *Epicurus*, or *Des Cartes*, or Mr *Hobbs*, or any other hitherto known. For my part, Seriously, I should be loath to affirm, that they are any

other but ingenious Comments of Mens Wits upon the dark and inexplicable Text of the World; plausible Conjectures at best.[28]

Ironically, however, while Charleton contrasts what he sees as Cavendish's 'Apodicticall' truth-claims with his own sceptical probabilism, her writings are at pains to deny their apodictical or axiomatic certainty, and are not incongruent with Charleton's own denials of absolute certainty in natural philosophy. In the *Worlds Olio*, for example, Cavendish stresses the provisional nature of human knowledge:

There have been of all Nations, that have troubled their Heads, and spent the whole time of their Lives, in study of Philosophy, as Natural and Moral, the first is of little or no use, onely to exercise their Opinions at the guessing at the Causes of Things, for know them they cannot; the last is a Rule to a strict Life, which is soon learned, but not so soon practiced, as they have made it [...].[29]

Her insistence on 'Guessing at the Causes of things' suggests a much less dogmatic position than Charleton's criticism implies, although it is true that in her exposition Cavendish can lose sight of her probablistic perspective, and lapse into moments of veridical insistence, but like Boyle in his experimental essays, she rejects in advance any claims to absolute discursive authority. In her *Philosophical Letters* of 1664, Cavendish declared her intention to 'to find out a Truth, [or] at least a Probability in Natural Philosophy by a new and different way from other Writers,'[30] a 'Probability' which she regarded as radically open to revision and correction:

I would rather praise, then contradict any Person or Persons that are ingenious; but by reason Opinion is free, and may pass without a pass-port, I took the liberty to declare my own opinions as other Philosophers do [...] [and] have done that, which I would have done unto me; for I am as willing to have my opinions contradicted, as I do contradict others: for I love Reason so well, that whosoever can bring most rational and probable arguments, shall have my vote, although against my own opinion.[31]

In the 'Epistle to Condemning Readers', in her *Philosophical and Physical Opinions* of 1655 she characterises her theories of material figures and motions as pure speculations: 'I guess by [...] the figures, or shapes,' she says, 'what the motion may be to produce them,'[32] but insists that these speculations have 'as much probability' as the opinions of the ancients:

For though in natural Philosophy there may be many touches found out by experiences, and experiments, yet the Study is onely conjecturally, and built upon probabilities, and until probablities be condemned by absolute and known truth, let them have a place amongst the rest of probabilities, and be not so partial [as] to contradict [them] [...] because young.[33]

It is this absolutely conjectural and probable nature of natural philosophical knowledge which becomes Cavendish's strongest claim to philosophical liberty. Her husband William in his 'Epistle to justifie the Lady Newcastle,' prefixed to the same work, uses a similar argument in defending her from charges of being a paradoxical writer:

> Why then all these are new opinions, and grounded upon Reason, I say some, but they are Paradoxes, what then? I hope a Paradox may be as true as an old opinion, and an old opinion as false as a Paradox, for neither the one nor the other makes a truth, either the new or the old, for what is most reason & reasonable; for in natural Philosophy, one opinion may be as true as another, since no body knows the first cause in nature of any thing. Then this Ladies Philosophy is excellent, and will be thought so hereafter [...].[34]

What sets Cavendish's probabilism and limited scepticism apart from that of other mid-century philosophers, however, is its derivation from her physical theories. Whereas Charleton emphasised man's fallen nature, and Boyle's essayistic probabilism developed out of his commitment to open-ended experimental investigation, Cavendish's beliefs regarding the limits of knowledge relate directly to her conception of nature as infinitely various. In *The Grounds of Philosophy*, for example, the 'variousness, or variety of Actions' between parts in nature, are seen as the cause of the 'varieties of Lives and Knowledges', as the 'Self-moving parts alter' so knowledge alters, and 'there cannot be an Infinite particular Knowledg.' she says, because 'Matter is divisible and compoundable,' and so 'particular Creatures' are restricted to 'finite Perceptions, or perceptive Knowledge,' and therefore knowledge consists of 'Suppositions' or 'Conjectures' rather than absolute truths.[35] 'To treat of Infinite Effects, produced from an Infinite Cause, is an endless Work, and impossible to be performed, or effected [...].'[36] The infinitely various motions and alterations of nature, precisely because of their infinite variation, cannot be known by any particular and limited individual in the universe, whose thoughts themselves are simply a limited and particular set of patterned motions and variations of parts. Thus for Cavendish every theory – or momentary configuration of rational parts in the brain – must necessarily be contingent.

In her 'essay' on 'The strength of erroneous Opinions' in the *Worlds Olio*, for example, she argues that:

> Nature is too various to be known, and her Curiosities too subtil to be understood; but men are so strangely delighted with what is new, that those men that have found a new Opinion are absolute to judge and rule over all others; such Reputation Singularity begets.[37]

It is significant here that Cavendish invokes the same aesthetic categories of conceited wit – variety, curiosity, novelty, delight and singularity – to explain the persistence of mistaken ideas as she uses to advance her own discursive tactics. If one reads the last passage against its counterpart 'The strength of Opinions', where she argues that 'an Opinion is but a guesse of what may be a Truth; but men should be as free to Opinions as Opinions to them, to let them come and go at pleasure.'[38] It seems clear that she sees the intellective process as identical whether it is veridical or sophistical, the crucial difference rests in the refusal of self-granted discursive authority. Her refusal to attempt to 'rule over all others' and to freely entertain ideas without insistence on their absolute truthfulness mounts a critique of axiomatic or dogmatic natural philosophy, and posits a delightful and various discourse of the fancy or wit in its place. But if, as Cavendish suggests, her philosophy consists only in 'probable opinions, wittie ingenuities ... [and] harmlesse phancies,'[39] what is the status or the objective of these unauthorised and unauthorisable statements? Infinite nature, she says in the *Philosophical Opinions* is uncontainable within discourse:

> Because the figures and motions of the infinite Spirits which they move and make are infinite, I cannot give a final description: besides, their motion is so subtle, curious, and intricate, as they are past finding out.[40]

As inexhaustible occasion for discourse, nature thus becomes the pretext for an interminable series of descriptive acts, it becomes, in fact, the foundation of a copious rhetorical discourse, in the Erasmian sense. For Erasmus, as for Cavendish, it is the infinite variety of nature itself which founds the infinite variety of speech:

> Variety has everywhere such great force that there is nothing at all, however polished it may be, which does not seem uncouth without its support. Nature herself rejoices particularly in variety, for there is nothing anywhere in the immense mulitude of things which she has left unpainted with the wonderful art of variety (*varietatis artificio*).[41]

Erasmus considered repetition without variation to be a 'great evil', and suggests that the perfect orator will acquire 'the facility of changing the same thought into more forms than Proteus himself is said to have transformed himself.'[42] Terence Cave argued that this Protean principle was, for Erasmus, 'not simply a pedagogical marker, but a generative principle.'[43] Cavendish too rejoiced in the Protean variety of her discourse, arguing in the *Worlds Olio*, that 'The variety of Wit' is 'like *Proteus* in several Forms'[44] – 'Wit is copious,' she says, 'and busies its self in all things, and humours and accidents [...].'[45] Natural philosophy for Cavendish becomes the occasion for her empowerment within speech itself, she cannot, and does not desire to 'give a final description,' but yearns instead for infinite descriptions, each as subtle and as various as the figures and motions of innated matter itself, a 'perpetual motion, with continual changes and varieties.'[46] Natural philosophy, Cavendish says in her *Philosophical and Physical Opinions*, is:

> Above all [...] a great delight, and pleases the curiosity of mens minds, it carries their thoughts above vulgar and common Objects, it elevates their spirits to an aspiring pitch; It gives room for the untired appetites of man [...] [and] gives pleasure in varieties, for infinite wayes are sirawed [*sic*] with infinite varieties, neither doth it binde up man to those strickt rules as other Sciances [*sic*] do, it gives them an honest liberty, and proves temperance is the greatest pleasure in nature.[47]

Cavendish's defence of philosophical liberty against 'strickt rules' recalls the polemical classification of her friend and correpondent Walter Charleton, who in his *Physiologia* characterised a new, and more open-minded, breed of philosophers (epitomised, in his view, by Descartes) which had emerged during the modern age in the following terms:

> Others there are (and those too few) whose brests being filled with True Promethean fire, and their minds of a more generous temper, scorn to submit to the dishonourable tyranny of that Usurper, Autority, and will admit of no Monarchy in Philosophy, besides that of Truth [...] This Order well deserves the Epithete, βεβαιωτικος, and therefore we shall Christen it, The Order of the ASSERTORS OF PHILOSOPHICAL LIBERTY, in regard they vindicate the native privilege of our Intellectuals, from the base Villenage of Præscription.[48]

While the confirmation of certain, factual knowledge (βεβαιωσις) was not high on Cavendish's agenda, claiming the 'native privilege of the Intellectuals' was. As a woman philosopher, Cavendish was bound by a double exigency – she needed to assert her liberty as a woman first, and then as a philosopher. Her championing of the infinite fecundity of natural wit or fancy rests on a thirst for liberty rather than truth, and in the sense that she seeks an unfettered freedom to apply her reason to natural phenomena in spite of the dictates of 'Autority' (whether it be scholastic, theological or experimental), Cavendish is a matchless representative of some of the most forward-thinking philosophy of her day. In her witty defenses of the 'honest liberty' of philosophical discourse Cavendish is not only perhaps seventeenth-century England's first significant woman natural philosopher, but also its first woman libertine philosopher.

Notes

[1] Sylvia Bowerbank, 'The Spider's Delight: Margaret Cavendish and the "Female" Imagination', *English Literary Renaissance*, 14 (1984), 392–408 (p. 407).

[2] Barbara J. Shapiro, *Probability and Certainty in Seventeenth Century England: A Study of the relationships between Natural Science, Religion, History, Law and Literature* (Princeton: Princeton University Press, 1983), p. 72.

[3] Sergei Zakin, 'Inside Books of the World: Issues of Textual Interpretation in Mid-Seventeenth Century Discourse on Knowledge', (unpublished doctoral thesis, University of Cambridge, 1997).

[4] Anna Battigelli, *Margaret Cavendish and the Exiles of the Mind* (Lexington: The University Press of Kentucky, 1998), p. 10.

[5] Robert Boyle, *The Origine of Formes and Qualities (According to the Corpuscular Philosophy,) Illustrated by Considerations and Experiments, Written formerly by way of Notes upon an Essay about Nitre* (Oxford, 1666), sig. a6 recto–verso.

[6] Boyle, *Origine*, sig. a7 recto–verso.

[7] Boyle, *Origine*, sig. a8 verso.

[8] Robert Boyle, *A Free Enquiry Into the Vulgarly Receiv'd Notion of Nature; Made in an Essay, Address'd to a Friend* (London, 1685/6), sig. a4 recto.

[9] Boyle, *Free Enquiry*, sig. a4 recto–verso. The square brackets in this quotation are Boyle's own.

[10] Boyle, *Free Enquiry*, sig. A5 verso, A8 verso.

[11] Boyle, *Free Enquiry*, 'The Preface', sig. A4 recto–verso. For the date of composition see sig. A8 recto.

[12] Boyle, *Free Enquiry*, sig. a2 verso–a3 recto.

[13] Boyle, *Origine*, sig. A2 recto–verso.

[14] *Grounds* (1668), sig. A2 verso–A3 recto.

[15] *Worlds Olio* (1655), 'Epistle', sig. E3 recto.

[16] I say 'notional' here because at various moments Cavendish defends the idea of the natural wit acting directly on empirical data in her philosophy. See, for example, *Worlds Olio* (1655), 'Epistle', sig. E2 recto: 'though nature is specious to be known, yet she is free to teach, for every straw, or grain of dust, is a natural tutor, to instruct my sense and reason, and every particular rational creature, is a sufficient School to study in [...].'

[17] Boyle, *Free Enquiry*, sig. A6 recto.

[18] On 'philosophical probabilism' see Barbara Shapiro, *Probability and Certainty*, pp. 37–61 and Henry G. Van Leeuwen, *The problem of certainty in English thought, 1630–1690* (The Hague: Martinus Nijhoff, 1963), *passim*.

[19] Walter Charleton, *Physiologia Epicuro–Gassendo–Charltoniana: or A Fabrick of Science Natural, Upon the Hypothesis of Atoms, Founded by Epicurus, Repaired by Petrus Gassendus, Augmented by Walter Charleton, Dr. in Medicine, and Physician to the late Charles, Monarch of Great-Britain* (London, 1654), p. 6.

[20] Charleton, *Physiologia*, p. 128.

[21] Charleton, *Physiologia*, p. 128.

[22] Charleton, *Physiologia*, sig. P4 recto.

[23] Charleton, *Physiologia*, p. 5.

[24] Charleton, *Physiologia*, p. 5. For Cicero's probabilism see, for example, *Tusculan Orations*, II, ii, 5: 'we, however, whose guide is probability and who are unable to advance

further than the point at which the likelihood of truth has presented itself, are prepared both to refute without obstinacy and be refuted without anger.' (*nos, qui sequimur probabilia nec ultra quam ad id, quod veri simile occurrit, progredi possumus, et refellere sine pertinacia et refelli sine iracundia parati sumus*), Cicero, *Tusculan Disputations*, trans. J. E. King, (Cambridge, Mass. and London: Loeb Classical Library / Harvard University Press, 1996), pp. 150–53.

[25] *Letters and Poems* (1676), p. 124.

[26] *Worlds Olio* (1655), 'Of several writings', p. 4.

[27] *Worlds Olio* (1655), 'An Epistle to the Unbelieving Readers in Natural Philosophy', sig. Y2 recto.

[28] Walter Charleton to Margaret Cavendish, May 7 1667, *Letters and Poems* (1676), pp. 111–12.

[29] *Worlds Olio* (1655), p. 158.

[30] *Philosophical Letters* (1664), 'To his excellency The Lord Marquis of Newcastle', sig. a verso.

[31] *Philosophical Letters* (1664), 'Preface to the Reader', sig. b recto–verso.

[32] *Physical Opinions* (1655), p. 26.

[33] *Physical Opinions* (1655), p. 27.

[34] *Physical Opinions* (1655),'An Epistle to justifie the Lady Newcastle, and Truth against falshood, laying those false, and malicious aspersions of her, that she was not Authour of her Books', sig. A2 verso.

[35] *Grounds* (1668), pp. 6–7, 24.

[36] *Grounds* (1668), p. 15.

[37] *Worlds Olio* (1655), p. 116.

[38] *Worlds Olio* (1655), p. 117.

[39] *Physical Opinions* (1655), sig. B verso.

[40] *Physical Opinions* (1655), p. 16.

[41] Desiderius Erasmus, *De Copia*, I,viii, cit. Terence Cave, *The Cornucopian Text: problems of writing in the French renaissance* (Oxford: Clarendon, 1979), p. 22.

[42] Erasmus, *De Copia*, I,viii, cit. Cave, *Cornucopian Text*, p. 23.

[43] Cave, *Cornucopian Text*, p. 23.

[44] *Worlds Olio* (1655), p. 119.

[45] *Worlds Olio* (1655), p. 23.

[46] *Worlds Olio* (1655), p. 11.

[47] *Physical Opinions* (1655), sig. a verso.

[48] Charleton, *Physiologia*, p. 3.

14

Margaret Cavendish, the Doctors of Physick and Advice to the Sick

Susan Fitzmaurice

> In short, private medical practice is governed not by science but by supply and demand; and however scientific a treatment may be, it cannot hold its place in the market if there is no demand for it, nor can the grossest quackery be kept off the market if there is a demand for it. A demand, however, can be inculcated. (George Bernard Shaw)[1]

> [...] yet she desires she may have the best Doctors Advice for her Health, wherefore she Intreats you to send her the most Renowned Doctors of Physick that are in your City, she will not spare Cost, if they have Skill, but Pay them for their Advice; for Doctors sell their Knowledge, and Patients Buy Healths, and their Knowledge is a Staple-Commodity, for the more Knowledg Doctors of Physick sell, the more Knowledg they get for Experience of Diseases; and so all things come in more by Practice than by Study, and Health gains more by Temperance, Exercise, and Air, than by Physick.[2]

Introduction

Thus in *CCXI Sociable Letters* Margaret Cavendish characterises as an expensive commodity the advice that 'Doctors of Physick' sell to the sick. Common sense advice about lifestyle and diet, she seems to say, are more likely to be beneficial to one's health and well-being than the expensive recipes for remedies sold by doctors in their counsels to the sick who are able to pay for them. And Shaw's acerbic comment underlines the fact that where there is a demand for medical remedies, services and advice, there is a ready supply of practitioners, licensed and unlicensed, professional and charlatan, to do the job.[3] The paying public included the ordinary as well as the socially elevated. In a buyers' market, cloth-workers' wives, servants and preachers sought medical advice and treatment. Men and women of Cavendish's circle and station made ample use of the physician's counsel, if we are to believe the physicians' accounts of their cases. Anne, Viscountess of Conway, was, Sarah Hutton observes, as a 'high-class patient treated by the top doctors of her age', among them Theodore Turquet de Mayerne, Thomas Willis, Luke Ridsley, the Warwickshire physician John Ward, as well as

Francis van Helmont, the unorthodox son of the controversial physician and chemist Jan-Baptista van Helmont.[4] Physicians like Thomas Willis and Thomas Sydenham record case histories of various patients, remarking on whether their advice and the treatment prescribed once sought were taken, and whether they were successful. Medical men like Mayerne wrote letters of advice to their noble patients and their attending physicians, and these counsels were subsequently made more publicly accessible, by translation as treatises for a wider lay readership.[5] Much of the medical literature produced in English in the course of the seventeenth century was directed at ordinary people. There were medical guides for those who lived in remote areas, or who could not afford the services of physicians and surgeons, 'regiments of health' instructing the reader how to establish healthy living habits, and more general works such as almanacs, cookery books and gardening manuals, which included medical advice and recipes among other information.[6] The writing of such guides was not restricted to the most educated and professional practitioners, but included ordinary practitioners trained by apprenticeship to physicians.[7] Frequently the books of advice printed by these practitioners were vehicles for advertising their services, so that descriptions of treatments and directions for their administration tended to be followed by assurances that special medicines not mentioned could be purchased from the writer's place of practice.[8] One sage old physician writes to a young colleague, remarking on the treatises 'being written for the Use of the Gentlewomen and Country Divines,' and complains, 'it has been too much in Use for some of much Leisure or little Business, to single out a popular Distemper, on which to harangue, no Matter how, in Expectation that the Sick of such Disease may be thereby allur'd to consult them; the Title Page of which often advertis'd, supplies the Place of a *Quack-Bill*.'[9]

But sick people in seventeenth-century England did not always rely upon the advice sold to them by physicians. As purveyors of a commodity in a marketplace populated by the mountebank, the apothecary and the surgeon, as well as the licensed doctor of physic, they were forced to compete among themselves for clients. Frequently, women undertook the routine care of their families and servants, and their relations were as likely to apply to them for advice regarding care in pregnancy, remedies for colds and minor injuries as consult a physician.[10] Since physicians were rarely able to guarantee success in the procedures and treatments they prescribed, and because their counsel was costly, patients often sought the advice given by friends and family for free. Family letters and personal diaries of the period thus tend to be full of the discussion of family ailments and their treatment; the writers frequently seek and offer or report advice about illness. Dorothy Osborne's letters to William Temple, the letters of John and Mary Evelyn, and the correspondence of Henry More and Lady Anne Conway and their circle convey a vivid sense of the nature of familiar discussion about health in the period, and the personal diaries of Lady Margaret Hoby and Ralph Josselin provide ample illustration of the kind of medical practice and advice available at the time, both lay and professional.

In this essay, I am interested in examining the functions and effects of medical advice of a particular kind: that offered in the sociable letter we encounter in Margaret Cavendish's *CCXI Sociable Letters* (1664). In this compendium of opinion, advice and gossip, Cavendish seems to borrow as much from the convention of the medical counsel as from the familiar letter to frame her own disquisitions and speculations about disease and remedies. Thus she herself offers advice and opinion about everything from the dangers of cordials (Letter 149), the benefits of milk over cream (Letter 154), remedies for poor digestion (Letter 140), to the conduct of pregnancy (Letter 47) and cures for fatigue and weakness (Letter 156). In addition to her homiletic epistles to her (fictional) woman correspondent, she offers advice and opinion to a physician on the condition of an individual afflicted with a complicated medical condition (Letters 208, 209). Cavendish's practice is worthy of scrutiny, for she turns a sociable but essentially private practice – offering advice to friends – into a public one through the publication of her opinions. To situate her practice textually and stylistically, I will consider the lay advice and support offered in the correspondence of her contemporaries as well as the medical counsels that were offered and reported by physicians of the time and subsequently translated and published for a wider readership.

The Gift of Friendly Advice

Cavendish goes about dispensing advice in different ways in her *CCXI Sociable Letters*. Occasionally she enters into a contract with her addressee, offering her advice which she grounds in her own knowledge by virtue of her experience; at other times she draws attention to the nature of advice, good and bad, by offering her own experience of it. In addition, she offers her opinion of the best and most appropriate advice that another person outside the correspondence ought to take; in these instances, she narrates the condition of an apparently mutual acquaintance, and then after analysing it, suggests a solution. This manner of dispensing advice is perhaps more professional and concerned with the substance or content of the opinion offered, and less sociable and interested in the response of her addressee than the process involved in both giving and receiving advice in a dyadic relationship.

In Letter 156, Cavendish sympathises with her correspondent's stiffness of the limbs, reassuring her that despite her discomfort 'there is no Danger of Death, for to be Weary when you Stand still, so as to be near Fainting, and to find Rest and Ease by Walking, is a Natural Effect of a Natural Cause.'[11] She does two things in this letter; first she describes in fine detail the natural source of the weakness or tiredness experienced by her addressee, and then she admits that she too is 'Troubled with the same Tenderness, insomuch as it is Tiresom to my Life.'[12] Her reference to her own comparable affliction authorises her to dispense advice; her own experience of the condition is sufficient education for her to assume a knowledgeable yet empathetic stance. With this qualification, she does not have to be a licensed physician in order to offer a good diagnosis and suggestion for a cure:

> [...] certainly the best Remedy will be to endeavour to Strengthen our Sinews and Nerves, only the Mischief will be, that what is good to Strengthen the Sinews and Nerves, is Hurtful, and apt to Obstruct the Liver, Splene, and Veins, so as the Remedy may prove worse than the Disease, for Gluttonous Meats are Good for the Sinews and Nerves, but Nought for Obstructions. But Physicians perchance can tell Remedies, for I that am none may be Mistaken in the Cause, and Ignorant of the Cure, wherefore I will leave you to the Advice of the Learned Practicers [...].[13]

Moreover, she is not selling her counsel but offering it as a gift, and so she does not depend on her correspondent's acceptance of it. Indeed, she allies herself with her addressee in considering what will be best for both of them and their bodies ('our Sinews and Nerves'). She cannot resist the dig, albeit humorous, at the apparent eagerness with which doctors dispense advice and of course peddle remedies. At the same time as professing her own ignorance of the efficacy of particular remedies, as well as indicating her possible error in identifying the cause of her correspondent's condition, she points out that the remedies prescribed by physicians might have side-effects that turn out to be more seriously injurious to health than the stiffness in the limbs and muscles that occurs when the body rests after exercise. One effect of this juxtaposition is to compare the authority of her stance with the authority commanded by doctors among their patients. She appears to persuade her addressee that because she is able to provide a coherent and plausible diagnosis of the condition being discussed, the counsel she offers must perforce be informed. It follows that if she is able to point out the defects as well as the benefits of particular attitudes to treatment, her advice must be worth heeding. But she ends by deferring to those 'Learned Practicers' whose advice must be paid for, not without a rueful sense that in leaving her addressee to the advice of the experts she is also leaving her to their devices.

Cavendish plays light-heartedly with the notion of advice as beneficial to the recipient in her *Sociable Letters*. In Letter 106 she teases her correspondent about the harm potentially posed to her by an ostensibly kind gift of fruit. In this letter Cavendish compares the contradiction of a harmful gift with the issuing of advice. To execute the comparison she constructs a medical scenario in which she deploys language with echoes of Genesis:

> I Know not whether I shall give you Thanks for the Present of Fruits you sent me; By which Present, give me Leave to Tell you, you did Tempt me to Eat a Forbidden fruit, as the Serpent in Paradise did our great Grandmother Eve, for though I was not Forbidden to Eat of that Fruit by God, yet Nature did Forbid me, saying, I should be cast from Health into Sickness, and be Condemned to the Painfull labour of Physick; but it hath given me Knowledge as to Know and Perceive my own Weakness, both for Constitution of Body, and Reason of Mind, that it could not Govern my Appetite with Temperance, and I must have suffer'd the Torments of a Hot burning Feaver, had not Letting Blood Saved and Redeemed me there from.[14]

The receiver announces the dilemma that the giver has placed her in. Although the fruit is a gift and therefore a mark of friendship, it is a harmful and thus forbidden one. Instead of being a blessing, therefore, the present is a temptation. Cavendish jocularly uses the allusion to the fruit God forbids Adam and Eve to consume and somewhat mischievously casts her correspondent as the serpent. But as she does so she mocks herself since we infer from the knowledge she gains that she did succumb to the temptation and indeed eat the fruit. She imitates the biblical cadences of the narrative of the Fall, putting words into Nature's mouth, intoning the consequences; in short, she makes use of the opportunity to have fun with the image. Amidst this joking she makes a serious point about health, somewhat shocking in its simplicity. She comments that to avoid 'the Painfull labour of Physick,' which she believed would eventually result from a fever induced by overindulgence, she had her blood let. The seriousness of this prophylactic procedure seems to accuse her correspondent more strongly than any biblical analogy could. Yet it is slipped in almost as an aside amidst the detail of the Fall image that now becomes all-consuming with a comparison between the correspondent's 'Kind Friendship' and the Devil, but without the malice and 'desire Hurtfull to Deceive' expected.[15] And so she concludes with an injunction to her friend to send in future with any present the appropriate advice to guide the recipient: 'But, pray Madam, if you send me any more Fruit, send me Good Advice with it, as to Advise me not to Eat so much as to make my self Sick.'[16] The continued comparison of spiritual temptation and bodily danger allows Cavendish to exploit to the full her view that health and medicine are topics important to one's social as well as corporeal well-being. Here Cavendish uses the medical scenario and parodies the drama of the fall in order to tease the good-natured gesture of giving a tempting present. Advice assumes in this context the status and importance of an antidote, a remedy all its own.

It is possible that Cavendish takes a cue for her approach in *Sociable Letters* to offering friendly advice on medical matters from the common practice of seventeenth-century correspondents to discourse at length about health matters, their own as well as that of their friends and families. Anne Conway's habitual ill health exercised her friends and family and at length exhausted their capacity for giving her sound and effective advice. Her brother, John Finch, who studied medicine at Padua and was a sometime professor of anatomy at Pisa, and thus a source of expert medical advice within the family, admits to being baffled by the persistence of Anne's illnesses and the failure of all attempts to cure her headaches.[17] But as his role is to offer advice he must do so:

> My Dear I know not what to say to your headache at this distance for I protest I am so amazed that neither hott things nor cold encrease your distemper, so that I cannot guesse at any other cause then what I formerly told you, unlesse it should come from the closenesse of the sutures in your head which may hinder the perspiring of vapours; but in regard few of your sex have that inconvenience, I do rather (considering likewise it use to ease you much to have your head rub'd and held hard

> which closes the suture) conclude that it is sprung from some what your sexe is onely incident unto which none living but your selfe can resolve me, though your inclination to vomitt in your grievous fitts of the headache makes me still inclin'd to my former opinion so much that I can scarce alter it. In the mean time I must advize you [not] onely to abstain from things or hot but rather very cold, for I am afraid you will overcoole your stomack which is when at best never hott enough. Certainly it were good against any putrefaction and to prohibit vapours to eat after your meales conserve of Rosesold about the bignesse of a Nutmeg or Walnutt. If you find any inconvenience in it, leave it. I protest I thinke you had best let Nature alone a little while and see how you are, if there be worse symptoms.[18]

John Finch professes his amazement at the lack of any effect on his sister's condition of 'hott' or cold things, and his somewhat bewildered conclusion that her illness stems from 'some what your sexe is onely incident unto which none living but your selfe can resolve me' leaves him with little option but to reiterate old advice already given. It is striking that he should feel obliged to offer his sister advice even if he has no idea of the cause of her ailments. The function of advice here appears to be more to assure the correspondent of her addressee's continued sympathy and understanding than to have a precisely calculated effect on her behaviour. The substance of the advice he proffers does not differ from other everyday advice. Finch recommends caution in diet, a common sense suggestion that finds echoes in Cavendish's discussion of the possibly deleterious effects on Lady G.D.'s digestive system of her regimen of 'Cooling Julips in the Morning, and Cordials when she goes to Bed' (Letter 140).[19] But while Finch's reference to a dose of 'conserve of Rosesold' at mealtime appears a gesture of helplessness rather than any assertion of authority, Cavendish's discussion of the dangers of cordials is altogether more confident and pointed. She is concerned with the subject of cooling and heating remedies rather than whether her addressee is likely to pass on her pronouncements to Lady G. D. She focuses on the subject at hand and dismisses from further consideration the individual whose practice provides the occasion for comment. The oblique advice she offers therefore serves to highlight her own opinions and draws attention to her own general knowledge at the expense of the well-being of Lady G.D.:

> The Bodies of Mankind, they are easier Cooled, when Inflamed, Applying Cooling Liquors, as Julips, Ptisan, Barly Water, and the like, than to Heat them with Cordials, when they are full of Raw, Crude, and Waterish Humours; for Fevers, although Violent, if they Proceed from no other Cause but a Supernatural Heat, are Sooner, and Easier Cured, than Cold Palsies, and other Cold Diseases; wherefore it is better to take Hot things first, and Cooling after, than to take Hot things after Cooling, for Hot things after Cooling do rather make a Smothering Heat, than a Concocting, Digesting, or Expelling Heat, so as it only fills the Body full of Vapors, like as Wet, or Green Fuel fills a Room with Smoak, but a Healthful Body must neither be too Hot, nor too Cold, nor too Dry, nor too Moist.[20]

Cavendish here deals in generalities, making assertions about the best treatments involving heating remedies like cordials and cooling ones like juleps, which gather authority from the assurance with which they are declared. While Finch cautions his sister against taking cooling things because he notes she tends to have a system which 'is when at best never hott enough', Cavendish's pronouncements on cordials are not directed to any particular person and do not depend on the specific constitution of any identifiable individual. Her introduction of Lady D.G. is merely a pretext for her to dispense her opinion, which masquerades as sociable advice. She makes use of the same stylistic strategies of analogy and comparison that she does in her gently scolding letter to her fruit-giving friend. However, instead of the biblical image she deploys the more homely one of burning wet and dry wood. The image itself is perfectly comprehensible, but its effectiveness as an analogy depends on the reader's apprehending the internal logic of the event she narrates. Actually, the event is reported as a prediction rather than an experiment; Cavendish is certain about the fact that wet wood takes longer to burn than dry wood, and moreover that wet wood will put flames out by virtue of its moistness (rather than that its wetness will resist kindling):

> [...] although there should be put much Fire to the Green, or Wet Wood, it will not hastily Burn, nay, such Wood doth oftener put Out the Fire, than the Fire doth Inkindle the Wood, for the moist Vapors that Issue, or are Drawn forth by the Heat of the Fire, do Destroy that Heat that Drew those Vapors out, whereas on the other side, Dry, or Sear Wood, when Kindled, and all of a Firy Flame, fling but a little Water on it, and it will Quench out the Flaming Fire.[21]

Cavendish recommends taking heating remedies before cooling ones, relying on the reader's comparison of the cool body smothered by the heat supplied by cordials with the wet wood which will not light but issues smoke, in order to understand the nature of the benefit asserted. It is noteworthy that Cavendish situates her narrative in the third person, and her addressee virtually disappears in the face of the general pronouncement. However, the frame Cavendish supplies – a friendly bit of gossip about a mutual friend – provides an essentially sociable context for the advice offered. It might seem, in its lack of orientation in the familiar dyadic situation with reference to her addressee and her feelings, her state of mind and health, that Cavendish's advice has more to do with the physician's account of individual cases and their treatments than the personal letter. However, it is because she is interested in the applicability of the general statement to common experiences that her sociable audience of women readers would recognise that her approach is very different from that of the physician's case book.[22] The complexities and history of an individual's symptoms, and the treatment tailored for her condition, which we encounter in the medical casebook, are too narrow to fulfil the function of advice in Cavendish's *Sociable Letters*. The sociability of the advice she uses her letters to frame lies in its attractiveness and relevance to a general readership, rather than to a single identifiable individual. To illustrate how different Cavendish's advice is from the physician's casebook, consider the opening of Thomas Willis's detailed account of the history of Anne Conway's headaches:

> Some few years since, I was called to see a Lady of Quality, troubl'd for above twenty years with a Head-ach, which at first was intermittent, but of late is almost continual. She was endowed with admirable gifts both of body and mind, so that she was excellently skill'd in the Liberal Sciences, and all Learning, above the condition of her Sex; but (as though Nature thought it too much for her to enjoy so great endowments, without some affliction) she has suffered very sorely from this Disease.[23]

Willis is evidently just as interested in Anne Conway's background, accomplishments and profile as in her illness. He roots his narrative of her case history in his own experience; he identifies himself as only a recent witness of her debilitating headaches. Curiously, in remarking her talents and learning, he slips in the wry bon mot – she should not be so 'endowed' without some 'affliction'. This observation is somewhat anticipated by Anne Conway's friend, Henry More, who offers her his own advice:

> I could wish your body was in as good a plight as your minde [...]. The best is I took your Ladiships part when I wrote to Dr Ridsley and told him that your malady was, as I conceived, mainly complexionall, not contracted by meditation and over much study. I do not at all mislike your resolution in giving over Physick if there be no better effect of it. Ease of minde, fresh ayr and diet, may leasurely do that, which Physick could not effect so suddenly. And you must absteine not onely from reading but from thinking too intensely.[24]

While appearing to agree with Lady Conway that her illness is not the result of intellectual strain, he then advises her to avoid activities like reading and thinking which might, he implies, result in further discomfort. He advises her overtly that the effects of 'fresh ayr and diet' and 'ease of minde' might well benefit her more than the medicine prescribed by physicians like Willis. The problem with More's apparently perfectly sane solution to Anne's ailments is that it is hard to guarantee the beneficial effects of remedies as nebulous as fresh air and diet. Cavendish's comments on the dangers of gluttonous meats (Letter 156) and cordials (Letter 140) alone indicate that diet is a vexed and complicated issue. More surprising in view of More's concession that Conway's illness is not a result of intellectual stress is his injunction to her to take a break from reading and thinking. These, ironically, constitute precisely those activities for which Willis admires her so greatly.[25] More's comments also underline the difficulty in pinning down the causes of the illness, and Finch's frustration at not being able to offer any new information or comfort to his sister becomes very comprehensible. Willis is painstaking in his record of Anne Conway's ailment and its history, offering a much clearer clinical picture of her illnesses than anybody else. However, before embarking on a technical description of the symptoms, he records a patient's narrative. That is, the history he narrates is in the ordinary experiential terms of the sufferer:

> Before she was eight years of age, upon her recovery from a dangerous Fever, she became obnoxious to pains of her Head, which were wont to arise sometimes of their own accord, but oftner on some light occasion offered; the Disease being not limited to one place or part of the Head; sometimes infested the right side, sometimes the left, and often its whole circuit. During the access (which seldom ending within the space of twenty four hours, often infested her for two, three, or four days) she could not endure light, speech, sound, or any motion; but sitting upright in her Bed in a darkened room; she was able to speak with none, nor to take any rest, or food: at length, as the Fit declined, she used to fall into a deep and troubled sleep; from which awaking she was wont to be better, and then by degrees to recover; and during the time of intermission, to be indifferently well. Formerly the Fit being raised only occasionally, seldom returned within twenty days, or a month, and then afterwards much more frequently; but of late she is seldom free from them. Moreover, through many occasions, or rather evident causes (such as are the changes of the Year, and of the Air, the great Aspects of the Sun and Moon, violent passions, and errours in Diet) she is sorely tormented with them. Now though this affect having sorely afflicted this noble Lady (when I went to see her) above twenty years, and pitching its Camp near the Confines of the Brain, had so long besieged its Royal Fort, however it had not yet gotten posession of it: But the diseased being free from a *vertigo, Scotomia,* Convulsive affects and any sleepy symptom, had still the chief Faculties of her Soul, whole and normal.[26]

The physician's role in this case history appears to be mere recorder. We are offered the point of view of the patient, and we are told her reactions to the headache episodes and her behaviour in coping with the pain from their onset at the tender age of eight. The patient is fore-grounded as the experiencing subject of the narrative and her history is as partial as the history we can assume was narrated to the doctor. His choice of language is notably empathetic with the victim as he animates and invests with a sense of volition the disease and its physical agents. Thus the pains in her head 'were wont to arise sometimes of their own accord' and the 'Disease' 'infested' her head for days at a time, the 'Fit' declines but also once 'raised' returns to torment its enemy. Throughout this war the patient remains passive, enduring. Willis takes Anne's perspective as he reports her reactions to the headaches: 'she could not endure light, speech, sound, or any motion; but sitting upright in her Bed in a darkened room; she was able to speak with none, nor to take any rest, or food.' This psychological profile warrants the inference that Willis pays considerable attention to his patient's own account of her experience. When Willis feels his part in her story ready to start, he brings the reader up to date; briefing us on the increasing frequency and intensity of her headaches, he turns to the technical account. Having raised the spectre of the Disease and animated it for his reader, it should not surprise that he marks the transition from patient's history to physician's diagnosis with a metaphor. He characterises the virtual permanence of the pain as a battlefield – an invader pitching camp on the confines of the 'Royal Fort', her brain. With this dramatic flourish he expresses surprise that his patient's faculties have not been impaired by the persistence of such pain. The historical portrait Willis provides is striking for its breadth and scope, as though he believes that in order to offer a proper historical perspective of the condition he must give not only the story of Anne's life experience of it, but also some sense of the continual danger in which the headaches place her.

When Willis turns to the history of the treatment of Anne's condition, he changes both his focus and his narrative strategy. He details the progress of the treatment by offering a general statement, before shifting to the detail of the different kinds of cures sought for her condition. It is striking that he lists everything from hot baths, spa waters and fresh air to experimental and dangerous substances (mercury treatments)[27] and all sorts of medicines (antiscorbutical, cephalic, hysteric)[28] to the most invasive procedures (bleeding, issues) in the attempt to demonstrate the resistance of her condition to effective treatment:

> In order to the obtaining, or rather endeavouring a Cure, throughout the whole progress of the Disease, a great many Remedies, prescribed by most skilful Physicians, as well as of our Country, as Foreigners; were used without any success, or ease: She tryed all the Great Remedies of every kind and form, but always in vain: a great many years since, she underwent a long-continued and most troublesome Salivation, by a Mercury Oyntment, so that she incurred a great danger of Life. Afterward, a Cure was twice undertaken by a Flux, though to no effect, by a mercury Powder, (which the famous Empirick *Charles Huis* generally gave): She try'd hot Baths, and drank Spaw-waters, almost of every Country and Nature, with the like success as the rest: She was frequently Blooded, and once in an Artery; she went with many Issues, made sometimes in the Sinciput, sometimes in the hinder part of the Head: She took the Air in divers Countries, *viz.* besides her Native, that of *Ireland* and *France*: She took Medicines of all kinds whatsoever; to wit, Cephalicks, Antiscorbuticks, Hystericks, all famous Specificks, nay, and Empirical Remedies, given both by the learn'd and unlearn'd, by Mountebanks and old Women.[29]

Anne appears the subject in this process: she is active in pursuit of her cure, she 'tried' all manner of remedies, 'underwent' a 'salivation' (incurring danger), was 'blooded', 'took' the air and all sorts of medicines. She is at the same time the patient (in grammatical as well as medical terms), acted upon by physicians and their physick. This strategy enables Willis to place his subject in focus to conclude for herself and in her own words the lack of effectiveness of all the remedies and treatments applied: 'yet she declared, that she had not receiv'd any where from any remedy, or method of Cure, the least help or relief.' Willis then adds a coda: 'But the refractory and obstinate Disease, being deaf to all inchantments of Medicines, would not be master'd,' which draws attention away from the suffering patient to the attacking disease. He thus readies himself for the remainder of his account, which is brief and inconclusive, since he too fails to cure her:

> Moreover, having possess'd so long the precincts of the Brain, though it could not enter its recesses; yet when I went to see her, extending its limits into certain other parts of the *genus Nervosum*, it began to raise violent pains in the Limbs, also in the loyns and *Abdomen*, such as are usual in a Rheumatism, and in a Scorbutick Colick.[30]

Given Willis's inability to discover any cure guaranteed to relieve this patient, it is no wonder that Anne's brother and friends should have been frustrated in their attempts to give useful advice.

Perhaps the function of advice between intimates has less to do with the transmission and exchange of knowledge, which is designed to benefit the recipient – should she choose to accept it – and more to do with demonstrating empathy and understanding by turning what is essentially a passive state (sympathy) into something which might actually have some tangible effect, just in case the recipient does something with it. Thus by labelling as 'advice' the piece of information or knowledge offered, the giver distinguishes it from the other aspects of the communicative act, investing it with illocutionary force, which, once apprehended, may be acknowledged and acted upon. By the same token, the advice may remain potential and devoid of any effect other than the meaning invested in the gesture as a speech act. It seems that Henry More's advice to Anne Conway was as significant in cementing their friendship as her discussion and critique of his work was in building their correspondence. For them, the sympathy and understanding engendered by the act of inquiring after each other's well-being helps to equalise and continue the correspondence. It is not clear that knowledgeable (or even empathetic) advice is an important ingredient of their association so much as sharing with one another their experience of illness.

Advice to a Physician

The act of giving advice directly to an addressee might have real consequences if the addressee accepts and acts upon the advice, whether or not the correspondents are equally qualified or licensed to do so. It is possible in such cases for the act of offering advice to be isolated from other aspects of communication, identified and valued in its own right. In this section I turn to the matter of professional advice or counsel, that which being recognised as expert and authoritative has perlocutionary rather than merely illocutionary force. That is, while the intimate advice we have been considering has a function that is principally communicative in force as it conveys empathy, understanding and friendship, the professional mode of advice to which we now turn has the potential for effecting a change in the state of the subject who accepts and acts upon the advice. In other words, the force consists in the promise of transformation, which, in the best situation, is a cure. Let us examine the ways in which Margaret Cavendish handles this mode of advice in her *Sociable Letters* in comparison with the professional counsels sold by contemporary physicians.

Although Margaret Cavendish discusses the different medical conditions of a variety of characters in her *CCXI Sociable Letters*, she does so for the most part as an exercise in the narrative of the condition she is concerned with. But in two of the very last letters in the collection, she addresses her diagnosis, not narrative, to a physician, whose analysis of the condition afflicting Mrs T. she challenges with her own opinion. In the first letter, Letter 208, Cavendish starts out with a polite apology to her correspondent for seeming to interfere in a domain which is not her own, namely the care of Mrs T.'s health. Despite the courtesy, Cavendish proclaims she is quite emphatic in the matter of offering her own opinion of the cause of her friend's malady:

> You may think it a Presumption and an Incroachment upon your Profession, to give my Opinion of Mrs. Ts. Disease, but it is neither Presumption, nor Confidence of my Judgment, that causes this Writing to you, but an Affection to your Patient, who deserves my Concernment concerning her Malady, which Forces me to write to you my Opinion, which is, that I do believe her Pain and that which Accompanies it, is Caused through an Inward Heat, which Rarifies the Humors into a Fluent Distillation, also it Rarifies the Blood, making it to Flow, or Overflow, for Cold is not so Active, but Congeals & Thickens, as we shall see when any Body is let Blood, the Blood whilst it is Hot, runs Freely forth of the Veins, and remains Thin and Fluid when it is out, but when it hath stood some Time, and begins to be Cold, it Thickens, and Congeals to a Cake; so when any hath used Exercise, which Heats, and Thins the Blood, the Colour appears in the Skin, Caused by the Flowing to the Outward Parts; the like in Hot Weather, whereas in Cold Weather, or when the Blood is not Heated, the Skin appears Pale and Lank.[31]

She writes with the assumption that her correspondent is entirely familiar with the subject's symptoms, and so there is little need for her to describe them, except to mention the pains that the patient is suffering. She is swift to move to identify what she believes is causing the discomfort: namely 'an Inward Heat'. Because she relies on layman's language rather than the terminology of the physician, she is at pains to make very clear what she understands by 'Heat'. And so she embarks on a careful explanation of her opinion. She grounds her explanation in an analogy that might well have been familiar to physician and layperson alike: what happens to blood when it cools. She refers obliquely to be sure to the movement of the blood and to this movement's effects on the body's appearance. So heat or rapid movement thins the blood and causes it to colour the skin, while cold slows the blood and drains the skin of its colour. This analogy is rooted in everyday experience and she alludes to the heating effects of exercise and hot weather. These two conditions recur commonly in treatises of the time providing apparently optimum conditions for rheumatic fever[32] and gout.[33] Cavendish situates her everyday references in a medical scenario – letting blood, or phlebotomy – a practice she evidently believed was effective treatment of feverish dispositions, as suggested in her Letter 106 above. At the same time, she does not appear to include this practice under the general heading of 'physick', but sees it rather as a prophylactic measure, thus differing quite markedly with contemporary medical opinion.[34] Having established the basis of her distinction between the primary qualities of heat and cold as internal manifestations which might affect the circulation of the blood, Cavendish turns to the business of associating different kinds of pain with the inflammation that signals heat. She does this by analogy too, rooting her categorisation of pain in the domain of illness by using the generic names of particular, common ailments:

> Wherefore my Opinion is, that her Pain Proceeds from Heat, for it is to be Observed, that all Inflamations are Painful, as all Sores or Swellings that are Inflamed, whereas those Sores that are not Inflamed, or those Swellings we call White Swellings, are not Painful, also for the Gout, the Pain is caused through the Inflamation; but mistake me not, I mean all Pulsive Pains, for there be many other Pains, as some which are caused through Wind, and those Pains are Painful Stitches, and most commonly caused from Hot Humours, as Bilious Choler, or some Salt Flegm, also Headaches are caused for the most part from Hot Vapours, or Rheums, the Stone in the Kidnies and Bladder is caused through Heat, so that most Pains are caused through Heat, unless it be Child-bearing Pains, and such like.[35]

Instead of displaying an orderly list of ailments, Cavendish trots out a series of common though distinct afflictions which contemporary physicians would almost certainly have treated separately. However, her point is that Mrs T.'s symptoms (not yet offered) are consistent with those ailments that involve inflammation of the joints, like gout (and rheumatism), but not with those that do not involve inflammation or hot swelling, like stitches, headaches or kidney stones. It is only after Cavendish has rehearsed aspects of her own humoral theory that she gets to the heart of the matter, incidentally referring to the site of Mrs T.'s pain: '[...] these Considerations make me believe that Mrs T.'s. Pain in her Back is Produced from Heat; for although it be an Intermitting Pain, and not Constant, yet it may nevertheless be Produced from Heat; as for Example, the Gout is not a Continual Pain, but it is only Painful when the Inflamed Humor falls on the Joynt, yet for the most part it alwayes Falls or Resorts to one and the same Place.'[36] While she is not prepared to commit herself to the unequivocal identification of the problem and thus lay herself open to correction by her more qualified and therefore authoritative correspondent, Cavendish is sufficiently confident of her diagnosis to compare Mrs T.'s back-ache with other ailments that involve continual or intermittent pain in the joints. In fact, we find her making the common mistake of confusing the symptoms presented, which suggest rheumatic joints, with some of those consistent with gout and scurvy, as described by both Willis[37] and Sydenham.[38] As Cavendish avoids precise diagnosis she moves swiftly to the problem of treatment. In keeping with her humoral pathology, she refers to remedies that are designed to have a cooling rather than a heating effect on the patient's constitution. She reminds the attentive reader of her disquisition on cordials and their harmful heating effects as she advises the administration of cooling medicines: 'wherefore I believe Cooling Medicines must be her Cure, for I do not perceive that Purging, Sweating, and Dry Dieting, which are all Heating, do her any Good, but she seems rather the Worse.'[39] Here, the essence of Cavendish's advice to the physician attending Mrs T. is indirectly presented; instead of framing it as a directive or imperative, she makes a statement, which in its subjectivity resists challenge. She embeds the proposition in belief, a non-factive assertion that will not admit contradiction, and further avoids the simple indicative that characterises factual statement by using the ambiguous modal 'must'. Thus Cavendish's advice to the physician amounts to a strong commitment to the belief that the application of cooling medicines (like juleps) is necessary in order to effect Mrs T.'s cure. Cavendish's lack of certainty in the matter of a cure surfaces in her added justification, 'and Trial is the True Touchstone of Experience.'[40] Thus she gives the impression, not that she has herself experimented with the remedy she prescribes, but that she is sufficiently confident in her belief that she recommends the attempt. This suggestion appears to go against the authoritative tenor of the letter so far; her utterance has been couched in the gnomic present tense, presenting tendencies and facts and truth. With the act of advice over, Cavendish anticipates her addressee's reaction, which she constructs as one that is off the point though telling: 'But you may use the Old Saying to me, which is, Physician Cure thy self.'[41] This aphorism is off the point because it is not manifest that the writer of the letter is herself ill (with the same complaint as Mrs T., in which case she may be masquerading as Mrs T.), but it is telling in the choice of the term of address, 'Physician'. Certainly, the writer of the letter is masquerading as a physician in diagnosing the problem, weighing up the evidence, reviewing the effects of current treatment and prescribing a new course of treatment. However, her injunction to try out the treatment contradicts her own speculative method; she is a consultant who observes, rather than a practitioner who acts or experiments.[42] It is important however to note that Cavendish's prescription is based on her perception (which we might justifiably construe as observation) that the usually favoured procedures of 'Purging, Sweating, and Dry Dieting' have not proved effective. Having put a direct response into the mouth of her addressee, she provides an answer which appears at first as unaccountable as the imperative that occasions it:

> I answer, that all Preachers do not Practise what they Preach, and some may give better Counsel than take Good Counsel, also Solomon sayes, that a Wise Saying may pass through a Fool's Mouth, and the best Physicians when they are Sick, Rely not upon their own Skill for themselves, but will send for other Physicians, for no man can Judg well of himself, either for Health, Sickness, or any other thing, by

reason Partial Self-love, Fearful Doubts, Flattering Hopes, Bribe, Corrupt, or Terrifie the Judgment.[43]

Cavendish again relies on the performative verb to characterise her response as such – 'I answer'. And then she offers not one 'Old Saying' but a string of three. First she counters the Physician figure with the proverbial Preacher refusing to 'practise'. Then she appeals to the old adage that to give is better than to receive in the case of advice offered and advice taken. Finally, she appeals to an unassailable authority, Solomon, in claiming that it is feasible for the ignorant to dispense wisdom. Her conjunction 'and' connecting this string to her attention to the imagined imperative of her physician correspondent is not additive in function but causal or consequential. She appears to be using a 'look and see' logic that finally allows her to absolve herself from the responsibility of having to account for her advice. If her judgement is indeed weak, as she assumes the role of non-practising preacher and foolish giver of good advice, she argues that her correspondent would do well to accept the advice and act on it as he sees fit. So she finally throws the ball firmly into her correspondent's court: 'but setting aside my own Judgment as Weak, either for my self or others, and Relying on yours in Case of your Patient, I rest.'[44]

Cavendish plays with the figure of the physician giving counsel, but physicians who were practising at the same time she was writing sold and indeed profited by their advice. It is instructive to compare Cavendish's somewhat wry acts of advice in her *Sociable Letters* with the advice doctors dispensed and collected payment for. Physicians like Sir Theodore Mayerne wrote letters of advice directly to their patients, but they also wrote advising other physicians on the treatment of particular patients. In 1677, Thomas Sherley, himself a physician in Ordinary to King Charles II, translated *Medicinal Councels, or Advices*, a set of fifteen letters, twelve of them written by Mayerne for different patients between 1621 and 1645. In his preface to the reader, Sherley singles out for praise among physicians who write about their subject:

> those *Authors* which have writ *Consultations* and *Councels* [...]. For by this singular *Artifice*, (or way of writing) we are taught to effect that which is the most difficult thing in the *Art of Physick*, viz. The Application of general *precepts*, to particular *Subjects* and *Persons*: For the *Art of Physick is long by precepts, but is rendred short and efficacious by Examples.* And by this means we have the *Knowledge, Learning,* and *Experience* of industrious able *Physicians*, (which they have labour'd all their life to acquire) convey'd to us in *Epitomy*.

Of course, one of the chief attractions of this work is that it presents 'so many *Testimonies* of his *worth* and *skill* amongst the *Nobility* and *Gentry* of this *Kingdom*,' which is why Sherley thinks the book worth offering in English to a wide audience.[45] Mayerne advised his patients on all kinds of conditions, from consumption and plague to kidney infections and ulcers. In his seventh counsel, he presents first a letter describing the symptoms of a 'Noble Patient' from the man's physician and then his own answer. The physician's letter details the history of the disease (a gangrenous ulcer and urinary infection), his treatment of it, together with the recipes for the various medicines prescribed and administered, and the outcome. His conclusion appears positive: 'Now God be prais'd, this Gentleman enjoys a perfect health, nor doth perceive any inconveniency of these great Griefs.' But this good news seems undercut by the actual current physical state of the patient, which the physician is obliged to give to the great authority, Mayerne, before indicating the reason for the letter – a request for further advice: 'he makes water freely, there being left only this impediment, that he is sensible of a certain painful itching in the place where the Ulcer was formerly; moreover, many times there appeareth a Branny substance in his Urine, and as often as he makes water, there appeareth one drop of a white, viscous, glutinous matter at the top of the Urinary passage, before the making of his water.'[46] So it turns out that the patient is not completely cured, and there is something for Mayerne to do. The inquiring physician writes his request as if it were on behalf of his patient. The effect of this indirect approach is to take attention away from the attending physician's role in the case and in so doing diminish his responsibility for the patient's health and his influence on the patient's actions. The second opinion becomes all-important, the source of the first acting now as the patient's agent or spokesman:

> This Gentleman desires to know of you what kind of matter this is, and from whence it cometh? I suppose this matter to proceed from the weaken'd, and not sufficiently strengthen'd *Prostatas*, and that it is as it were an Excrement of the *Seed*, by the benefit of Nature thrust out to the extremity of the Yard. He also inquires, why that painful itching when he makes water, should only happen after Supper, when he is about to go to bed, and is not perceived in the morning, or day time? I judge Nature doth in the night time (which is the time she performs her chief Operations in) furnish that part which wants its Membrain, with a certain viscous, glutinous matter, to the intent to defend it from the acrimony of the Urine, that it be not hurt by it; but in the day time, by reason of making Urine often, that matter is washt away, and the part being yet weak, is vellicated and gnawn; if this be not probable, it seems so to me.[47]

Thus the patient's attending physician asks for a second opinion on a number of matters, offering his own for scrutiny and assessment in each case. The request has a clear structure, as the physician asks a question on behalf of the paying patient before providing evidence of his own consideration of the problem and his consequent advice. It is appropriate for the patient to be identified explicitly as the person seeking advice, for he will be the one to pay for whatever opinion is sent in response and for following such advice. However, the writer of the letter is not merely a secretary who will have no more to do with the case once the inquiry is despatched – it will be his task to interpret the response to the patient and to administer or oversee the ensuing treatment should the patient decide to accept it. It is striking that apart from offering his own opinion the physician does not explicitly ask his colleague for confirmation of his interpretation of the patient's condition.

Mayerne is quick to observe the niceties governing such a communication, applying some delicacy in the observation of his correspondent's part in the case with a formal salutation and congratulation on the physician's effectiveness thus far. But he shifts quite rapidly to a brief summary of the case and thence on to the opinion sought:

> [...] which Friendship I extremely desire may be improved by our personal Converse: The great God allow me and mine a long and quiet Lot, and grant we may enjoy your wishes: [...] In the mean time I most affectionately return you my love for yours; and know that I am yours. Behold how propitious Heaven is to us wretched men, which as with one hand it afflicted our Generous *Patient* with almost incurable Diseases, so with the other it raised him up again by the help and Operation of Remedies, by which (if ever) seasonable presence of yours, this excellent man was restored to life, and snatched out of the Jaws of death, and emerg'd from an *Iliad* of Diseases: The great and good God, the Author of health, perform your desires, to whom be praise; and let there be dedicated to your self *Æsculapius* his *Cock*, the *Hieroglyphick* of Vigilance.[48]

The elaborate encomium Mayerne delivers to the other doctor appears designed principally for the eyes of their 'Generous patient'. Yet he is careful to attenuate this praise by allowing God some part in letting the attending physician treat their afflicted patient so successfully lest he risk undermining the importance of his own role in finding a cure for the patient. But, bearing in mind that referrals such as this might be quite profitable and that to submit to the temptation to denigrate his predecessor's care in order to puff his own opinion might easily result in an end to the business of second opinions, Mayerne arguably exaggerates the life-saving actions of the correspondent (with the help of whose treatment, the patient was 'snatched from the Jaws of death') and the seriousness of the patient's condition ('almost incurable'). The exhortation to God to 'perform your desires,' and the wish for dedication as reward, establish this brotherhood of physicians who act together in the service of their patient. In dealing with the medical scenario Mayerne takes care to continue praising his colleague's good work: 'by the Divine goodness these mischiefs have already been removed by you, the curing of which I certainly attribute to your *Tranmatic Decoction*, with which I am well acquainted, and have approved by manifold experiments.'[49] This continual flattery has the double effect of making the two men appear united in their equal and serious concern for the patient, and of presenting a panel of opinion which is removed from the lay-person. In this latter effect, the collusion of these doctors differs strikingly from Cavendish's attempt to advise Mrs T.'s physician to influence the course of treatment prescribed. In that letter, Cavendish assumes the position of opponent or disputant rather than colleague; after all, she also positions herself as the patient's friend rather than her attending physician. Mayerne despatches his advice when he gets to it with efficiency and comparative brevity:

> For the first, I do with you attribute it [painful itching] to the yet tenderness, and rawness of the part, which is scarce yet covered with a *Cicatrix*; and is of that tender and exquisite sense, that (being by the reiterated excretion of *Urine* in the day time, cleansed and washed from that *mucus* substance with which the whole passage in the time of sleep was moistned, and as it were lined) this nervous body is easily hurt by the acrimony of the Urine, and is moreover irritated by the frequent solicitation of the expulsive faculty.[50]

In fact, Mayerne continues to feel it necessary to concur with his correspondent, which move appears to obviate the need for separate or independent advice. To overcome this apparent fault in the process of advice he suggests a course of treatment: 'To avoid this inconveniency, let the *Cicatrix* be confirmed by drying medicines: make *vulnerary Injections* into the *Urethra*, adding to them the insipid *Ocher* of *Vitriol* thorowly calcin'd, and also *Sugar* of *Lead*: let the *Perinæum* be fumed (in a Chair with a hole in it) with *Frankincense, Mastick, Sanderack, Amber, Aloes, Myrhh,* adding crude *Antimony*, and also the *Cinabar* of *Antimony*, in small quantity.'[51] Here, Mayerne directs the attending physician to facilitate a practical course of treatment, but he does it in such a way as to avoid laying entire responsibility for the treatment on his correspondent. Instead of assuming a directive, imperative voice, which might jeopardise the collegiality developed in the preamble to the matter at hand, he chooses an optative tone and syntax. This strategy also allows the subject of the communication (the patient) a choice in accepting or rejecting the treatment, which involves ointment to heal the scar, injections to help restore the urethra's lining, and a fuming-treatment, presumably to help cleanse the infected area. Mayerne finds he is not able to offer a conclusive answer to the second question, and so suggests two possibilities: 'Tis questionable whether the Branny substance proceed from the Kidneys, or, which often happens, by the length of the disease, it hath drawn the *Prostratas* into consent; or whether the *Bladder* (by reason of the long distemperature, *tumour*, and *solution* of the *continuity* of the adjacent parts) be not afflicted with a kind of Scabbiness.'[52] In other words, the bran-like substance in the patient's urine might be scab fragments from the bladder or even, more fundamentally, the kidneys. It is in the matter of the third question that Mayerne is able to provide a different, more definite opinion:

> As for the white viscous matter, it appears to be of the nature of [...] *Pus,* or corruption, and I suppose it to sweat out [...] thorow the thin *membrane* of the *Ulcer*; or to proceed from the ulcerated *Prostratas*, grown hard at the bottom: which *Glandules* since they naturally contain an excrementitious slime very different from *Seed*, (which matter is design'd to line the urinary passage, that the Seed and Urine may be excreated easily, and without pain) if they be weakned, the quantity of this humour will then exceed more then usually, and it doth commonly impose upon many under the *species* of a *Gonorrhæa*: This *Symptom* will be cured by the

> foresaid *injections*, and *fume*, to which if there be joyn'd the Artificial use of *Medicinal Waters*, and at length we exhibit for a month or two, *Pills* compos'd of *Turpentine*, and *Mastick*, I hope we shall have done all that is necessary for a perfect Cure.[53]

He is quite clear that the white mucus observed by both patient and physician is not semen but pus. He finds it necessary to elaborate on his identification of the secretion, which his colleague compares with semen, as markedly different by comparing it with the properties of the secretion discovered in gonorrhoea. Given the polite and rather public forum of the advice articulated he is quite delicate in applying this comparison, making the connection as oblique as possible: 'it doth commonly impose upon many under the *species*.' The question is why he chooses a symptom of venereal disease to illustrate the matter he describes rather than a condition or substance less likely to offend or shock. One reason must be that he needs to justify his authority and expertise as the source of a second opinion by highlighting the ignorance of a physician who could identify semen with such a radically different substance as pus, though he cannot take the risk of seriously insulting his correspondent by asserting the complete absence of any connection between them, however notional. Another might be that he is concerned that his diagnosis be taken sufficiently seriously for the attending physician to persuade the patient to permit him to implement the course of treatment prescribed. Finally, his diagnosis provides an opportunity to confirm the predicted benefits of the treatments, the injection and the fume procedure, which he suggests at the outset.

At the end of this advice, all that there remains to do is urge his correspondent not to hesitate in applying to him if need be, underlining the new situation in which the two physicians share responsibility (and a fee) for the 'Generous Patient': 'The history of this Disease is long, which God grant I may see an end of when I come to you; if any thing remain to be done more, let it be perform'd by mutual service; in the mean time, proceed to afford your assisting hands to this generous man.'[54] Thus Mayerne's advice is carefully laid out to satisfy several requirements of the counsel. Firstly, as a medical expert who is paid for his service he satisfies the request for a second opinion of a diagnosis already given together with a plan of treatment. Secondly, given the nature of the contract between a team of two colleagues treating a patient he ensures that he does not damage the face of his colleague by pointing out his failure to cure the client himself. Thirdly, he attends to the disposition and face needs of the client–patient for whom the advice is written as evidence of service rendered by paying proper attention to his treatment.

Margaret Cavendish's second letter to the physician regarding Mrs T.'s illness does not appear to be as elaborately attentive to the disposition and standing of her correspondent as Mayerne's letters of advice routinely are. Her advice seems almost peremptory by comparison as she seizes the opportunity to rehearse her views of an aspect of the ailment suffered by the patient quite different from that considered in her first letter. She does not enter into any debate or argument about the previous letter to elaborate or change her view, but takes her leave to begin her disquisition:

> I Received your Letter, and Glad to see you write, that you doubt not of Curing Mrs. T. of her Painful Disease; as for the Numbness in her Hand, Thigh, Leg, and Foot, give me leave to tell you my Opinion, which is, that it Proceeds not from a Coldness but a Dryness, for if it were only a Stupifying Cold, her Sweating would have Rarified and Evaporated that Congeal'd Cold, or her Purging would have Carried or Driven out that Gross, Cold Humor, or her Dry, Strict Diet would have Consumed that Obstructed Cold, or Cold Obstruction, but she hath felt that Numb Disease since she hath used those Remedies.[55]

At first glance Cavendish appears to be talking about a completely new ailment: a numbness that has not been mentioned before. But, in fact, she alludes to the failure of several methods of treatment to disperse and destroy the previous ailment, apparently diagnosed as a 'cold'. She observes that sweating, purging, and diet have not affected this so-called cold condition in the ways that might have been expected had the condition actually amounted to a cold. Cavendish thus underlines both the singular lack of success of the previous treatment and its misdiagnosis in her description of this supposed 'Cold' through lexical variation: 'Stupifying', 'Congeal'd' and 'Obstructed' are all terms which she implies may be associated with numbing as well as cold. The treatment's evident failure impels her to offer an alternative course of treatment, but not before she has extensively argued for its basis in theory. This involves a series of moves that first lists possible sources of different kinds of numbness and then eliminates them:

> at least, it is more Apparent, which shews, it Proceeds not from Cold, but Dryness, which Inward Heat and Dryness causes a Cold outward Effect, for Numbness and Deadness of Parts Proceed from Divers, and Different Causes, as from Cold, either Outwardly taken, by the Cold Weather, or Climat, or Clothing, or the like, or by Inward Cold, as by Overcooling Meats, or Drinks, or Cold Obstructing, or want of Blood, or too much Watry Humors, which Quench out the Natural Heat, and this Numbness is easily Cured. Another Numbness Proceeds from Obstructions of the Inward Parts, or Veins, either by Clammy Humors, or by Burnt and Adust Humors. Another Numbness Proceeds from a Driness of some Particular Parts, which being Insipid, cannot be Active, or Move according to their Functions, or Faculties, or Proprieties, and a Ceasing of Motion is Death. Another Numbness Proceeds from some Cold, or Thick Gross Humors that fall upon the Sinews or Muscles. Another Numbness is caused through Excessive Heat, which hath Burnt out the Natural Heat. Another Numbness Proceeds from a Decay of some Noble Parts, and this Numbness is Incurable.[56]

Because she fails to label these various numbnesses for her reader, it is the physician's job to make sense of precisely what illnesses and conditions she is referring to. Thus the anonymous physician who authored *Discourse of the Nature, Cause and Cure of Melancholy and Vapours*, offers a summary of precisely the symptoms pointed out by Cavendish, but he labels them as common to the vapours or 'Hysterick Passion in Women.'[57] In some respects Cavendish here presents a version of a patient's self history, but it is one which lacks the detailed description and context of the physical symptoms that a patient might be able to provide. Instead we are offered a set of abstract causes of particular though undefined numbnesses – one might be the effect of external or 'outward' cold factors like climate or clothing, or indeed a consequence of internal cold, induced by particular foods, humours and state of the blood. Other altogether less easily treated numbnesses are the effects of internal imbalances of humours, moist ('clammy'), dry ('insipid'), cold ('thick, gross') and hot ('excessive'). Thus Cavendish rehearses her inventory of different causes of what appears to be the same physical condition and so demonstrates her own knowledge to the expert reader she assumes to be familiar with Galenic principles.[58] To be sure, she avoids labelling and differentiating between the numbnesses and so also avoids laying open her interpretation to challenge. Having outlined her understanding of the causes of the condition Cavendish then turns to 'the Reason why I think Mrs. Ts. Numbness Proceeds from Dryness', which turns out to be 'that she hath been of a very Spare Diet three or four Years, Eating and Drinking but once a Day, and that not Much, her Meat being for the most part Rost Mutton, and when she was with Child, she did Eat so Little, & Seldom, as sometimes not in two or three Dayes, as I have often wondred how she could Live, and Nourish her Child within her, which Excessive Fasting must needs Dry, and so consequently Heat her.'[59] If we stop here, it is possible to begin to match Cavendish's description of Mrs T.'s dietary habits and the numbness she suffers with Willis's description of the symptoms and causes of various scorbutical conditions, including gout, selective paralysis, rheumatism, dropsy and 'Crackling of the Bones'.[60] Willis does not provide in 'Some Stories and rare Cases of Persons troubled with the Scurvy' the Baconian analysis that Cavendish does.[61] Instead, his advice to the public by way of ostensive definition relies upon making the symptoms and treatment provided as transparent as possible:

> A woman of Renown, tall and graceful, about the twenty fifth year of her Age, had contracted a Scorbutick Taint, by reason of various errours committed in Diet. The signs of which were a Spontaneous Lassitude, a difficult Breathing, Pains and Spots in the Legs, and her Gums likewise swoll'n, and full of Blood; in the Spring time after an Abortion, falling into a Tertian Ague, she soon became in a languishing and weak condition, from which Disease nevertheless, first being methodically proceeded with in Physick, she had soon recovered, but that indulging her self to eat Flesh and other improper things, she soon had a Relaps; and then being a weary of Physick, she took only Empirical Remedies, with which sometimes the Fits of the Ague were driven away, but often presently return'd, mean while the Diseas'd being pale, unable for motion, and wanting Breath, continued swol'n and blown up about the Ventricle and Hypochondres. About the third Month of her being sick, she began to have Gripes and bitter Tortures in her Belly; with which shooting sometimes to the Back, sometimes to the Stomach she was afflicted almost

> continually day and night: Moreover she was affected by a frequent vertigo, and sometimes with Fits as it were, Hysterical: Also being troubled with a frequent Vomiting, she daily threw up a viscous and froathy Phlegm: Within a Months space this Disease pasing to its highest pitch, rais'd Pains in the Back and Loins, and so afterward in all the parts of the Body: Besides, at this time she complain'd of mighty straitness of her Brest, great contraction of the Viscera: Mean while the habit of the Body fell away to a mighty Leanness, so that the Bones being destitute of Flesh, scarce stuck to the Skin; the Urine was little and very ruddy; on the surface of which grew a little thin film garnish'd with various colours like the Tail of a Peacock: A short while after this, a Numness and Formication was perceiv'd sometimes in the Belly, sometimes in the Limbs, and afterward the Gripes and Pains began to remit; nevertheless in their stead, a Palsey succeeded, which within a weeks space so pervaded all the Members of the whole Body, that she was not able to bend, or any way to stir from its place either Hand or Foot, or any other part.[62]

Comparison of Cavendish's account of Mrs T. and Willis's description of his scorbutick patient is instructive. While Cavendish pays comparatively little attention to the presentation of Mrs T.'s symptoms and scant attention to the behaviour which might precede the onset of the numbness, she offers an elaborate analysis of her friend's condition in terms of the humoral pathology to which she subscribes. This seems surprising in a letter ostensibly set up as part of a correspondence about the question of efficacious and expert advice, but not surprising in one which is designed to offer her own opinion on a medical matter. By contrast, the physician Willis, whose task is to illustrate as clearly as possible the diverse nature and form of the symptoms associated with scurvy, is painstaking in his account of the lady's symptoms and history, leaving his interpretation of the symptoms until he is satisfied that he has presented a copious account of the illness. The description Cavendish furnishes of her friend's illness and history, compared with Willis's account of the condition of his lady patient, suggests that Mrs T might have a variety of scurvy. The stiffness and inflammation in the joints Cavendish discusses in her first letter about Mrs T., coupled with evidence of a sparse and inappropriate diet both before and during pregnancy, encourages the inference that the extreme numbness in the limbs observed might be the extenuation of the condition, although in the absence of detail it is difficult to be categorical. Indeed, Cavendish avoids this pitfall altogether by relying on her humoral interpretation to take the place of any diagnosis or prognosis. Cavendish concludes her letter with further analysis of the effects of Mrs T.'s behaviour on her health before asking that the patient be treated in a particular way, with 'Cooling and Moistening Remedies', which, she argues, will cure not only the numbness at the heart of Mrs T.'s complaint, but also 'the Overflowing of her Natural Flux', which is itself caused by Heat.[63] In the process, Cavendish allows the focus to shift slightly from attention to her own opinion and interpretation to Mrs T.'s active engagement in the treatment of her disease. Having introduced the matter of her friend's odd diet and her pregnancy, Cavendish now attributes volition and intentionality to her in seeking to

'Strengthen or Ease' her weak stomach:

> for though Fasting may Cool after Excess, Wasting the Superfluities, which would otherwise cause too many Vapors, or Corruption, which Corruption, or Vapors, might cause an Unusual, or Unnatural Heat, yet in Scarcity, or where there be no Superfluities, Fasting doth Heat, the like doth Sweating; and thus Mrs. T. finding her Stomack Weak, or rather Ill Digesting, to Strengthen or Ease it, hath Over-heated, or Dried the other Parts of her Body, and hath fill'd her Body, or rather her Thread-Veins, with Thin, Sharp, Salt, Bitter Humor, which Humor Proceeds from Heat, and Heat and Dryness many times Proceed from those Humors; where-fore there should be Applyed such Remedies as to Draw out those Pernicious Humors which are Corroding, Burning, and Drying.[64]

Mrs T.'s course of action in seeking relief fails to restore balance to the humors, and further overheats and dries out her body. Unlike physicians like Mayerne, who sells his clients detailed recipes for remedies along with his advice for administering them, Cavendish does not identify or describe in any helpful way the nature of Mrs T.'s treatment. Her interest and preoccupation with common remedies like cordials and juleps allows (but does not oblige) us to infer that Mrs T. probably took a cordial, a heating rather than cooling remedy. Willis's description of the treatment he offered his scorbutical patient follows his account of the history of the treatments sought and followed by her: 'This Lady living far hence, by the advice of a Neighbouring Physitian took Medicines usual against the Collick; which doing no good, and the Disease growing worse, the Patient being brought to *Oxford*, tryed a great many Remedies both Antiscorbutick and Antiparyliticks almost of every kind and form, though without any benefit.'[65] Apparently, Willis casts his patient as the agent of her own treatment by making her the active subject here just as Cavendish does, but there is a difference. He takes care to identify as the authority in the matter of the procedure a 'Neighbouring Physitian' who causes the woman to take the anti-colic remedy. Although the patient agrees to try the medicine, she does not originate the action herself but acts on the advice of a doctor. This is quite different from Cavendish's account of Mrs. T. There is a brief interlude in Willis's account in which he refers neither to the physician already mentioned nor to himself as the second opinion. In fact, his account is objectified and passive, the diagnosis rather than the originator of the diagnosis fore-grounded: 'Since therefore any ordinary Method of healing seem'd not sufficient for this Disease, it was thought good to proceed to great Remedies, and truly such as were not wholly void of danger.'[66] Having reported the opinion, Willis proceeds to the matter of treatment. Here, he does not refer to himself as the sole administrator of treatment, but assumes the less personal, first person plural voice of a panel: 'Wherefore we gave this sick person, weak and worn away as she was, a Mercurial Medicine for raising a Salivation, which effect ensued according to our desire, for a Flux arising within two days, and gently continuing for many days without any ill Symptoms, gave a very great relief to the noble Lady.'[67] The attending physicians, if we believe that Willis is not alone in treating the woman, administer a mercury treatment, which succeeds in relieving the patient's pain. Once the act of treatment and its effects have been reported, Willis returns the woman to active and experiencing subject from her stance as passive recipient of the procedure.[68]

One question raised by comparison of Margaret Cavendish's *Sociable Letters* with Willis's work in the *London Practice of Physick* is whether the latter might properly be considered under the general rubric of advice. In the preface to the volume, Willis's translator claims that people will find very useful 'this Practical part by itself, as a Portative Manual to direct them in Practice on all occasions,' and is careful to point out for the readers precisely what they may expect to find in the work, namely 'all the Definitions or Descriptions which Dr. Willis gives of Diseases and Symptoms,' 'his Method of Curing in any Disease, containing all his Physical Indications and Intents of Curing,' and he finally emphasises that 'There is not a Recipe in order to the Cure of any Disease in any of his Tracts, but it is here inserted.'[69] In being presented as a practical guide to the identification and treatment of a range of common diseases, Willis's *London Practice of Physick* does indeed provide an authoritative source of medical advice. The case studies offered in meticulous detail provide vivid examples of the diseases covered and which the reader might confidently expect to encounter in his or her society. Cavendish's letters of advice to her physician correspondent, we might argue, are less informative than the advice offered by Mayerne's or Willis's descriptions, but they do indicate the extent of the engagement of a layperson with illness and its many causes. Thus, despite being addressed to an expert, her Letters 208 and 209 are not out of place in the body of *Sociable Letters*.

It is rare to encounter the explicit rejection of advice, whether the friendly, free counsel offered by a friend, or the professional service sought from an expert. Anne Conway's constant ill health, together with a solemn regard for those who inquired after her and tried to relieve her suffering, prevent her from dismissing advice, however hopeless it seems. While our physicians occasionally indicate when treatments prescribed have not improved the condition of their patients, they do not very often report on whether their medical counsels are rejected by patients. In a competitive medical marketplace, it is clear that in addition to seeking further opinions from qualified physicians and testing the efficacy of different kinds of medicine from different sources, as Willis reports Anne Conway to have done, it was possible for patients to reject outright the treatments prescribed them. In some respects, Cavendish's challenge to her physician correspondent over the case of Mrs T., in Letters 208 and 209 in *Sociable Letters*, does precisely this. As a friend of the patient and an informed observer of the case, she undertakes to disagree with a professional diagnosis, providing her own as an alternative. In this act, Cavendish demonstrates that disagreement is possible, that there is a place for the rejection of advice as well as for its acceptance.

The Nature of Advice

As a postscript to this discussion of medical advice and its reception by patients and doctors, it is worth looking briefly at a slightly different kind of medical counsel. This is an epistolary counsel 'written to a young Physician, who had desir'd the Author's Thoughts about this Subject of Fevers', which deals in addition with the 'young Gentleman's Mind, as to his moral Conversation' and the matter of appropriate behaviour in 'a sick Man's Chamber'.[70] The advice in this text is more concerned with the conduct of physic than the substance or content of it, and its author adds to the familiar issue of a cure for an affliction an apparently new concern for the patient's experience of medical care. The writer tells his student 'as you ever expect to be a successful Practitioner, not a *talking Physician*, you must have a constant and careful Eye to Practice,'[71] where 'practice' does not solely signify observation of symptoms and practical problem solving, but includes the sense of behaviour or conduct. His language is exhortatory, relying on the force of the modal *must* to carry through the sense of obligation he is placing on the addressee. This tone continues throughout the text, as the wise old physician enjoins his young colleague to be 'very careful how you give too much Encouragement; for it is always best that your Patient and his Friends should be rather surpriz'd at his doing well, than his Decease.'[72] He attends to the appropriate way for the good physician to deal with what he terms the 'Glorious Office' of tending the poor, and to the correct conduct of the physician among 'those who are your Patients, or make use of you when they are Sick, where I would never have you over familiar', and those 'who instead of feeing you handsomely, will be apt to place your Visits to the Account of their Civilities, and treat you rather as their *Friend* than *Physician*': 'Be affable with them and sociable as you will, but cautious how you dip your Finger in their Dish, or take a Bottle at their Cost.'[73] This seeming paragon finally produces his recipe for the character of a good Physician, directing his correspondent to pay careful attention to it. This physician's advice encompasses directions about the proper deportment and conduct befitting a member of the profession of physicians, as well as opinion and argument about the appropriate and most effective ways of diagnosing and treating fevers. The breadth of advice dispensed in this epistolary text addressed to a physician has some affinity with Cavendish's advice to Mrs T.'s physician, with its range of opinion, theory and personal interest.

The advice issued by the doctors of physic which I have examined in this essay also shares something with our age, namely, interest and concern in the counsel to a patient or a physician regarding the correct diagnosis, prognosis and treatment of a set of symptoms. Having dispensed their advice, the physicians leave their patients and colleagues with the option of accepting or rejecting it, as well as the responsibility for acting upon it. By contrast, once the physician has committed his counsel to record, whether it takes the form of a letter or a practical guide, it gains substance as an identifiable entity that might be designated a monetary value. And although the counsel might have been designed for and directed to a specific individual, there is nothing preventing the consultant from marketing his counsel and selling it as one might any other commodity. Therefore the medical counsel has substance as a saleable entity which might be sought, marketed and dispensed as a product for a consumer.

The advice dispensed to ill people by friends and family in the form of the familiar letter is not authoritative in the way that the professional counsel of the day is, nor can it be identified as a commodity. Instead, as advice given (rather than sold) and as an expression of the writer's opinion about the particular set of circumstances and conditions which define the addressee as a unique individual, it is a gesture marking the relationship between advisor and advisee. To acknowledge and act upon such advice is to understand and acknowledge it as a mark of empathy and understanding, and hence intimacy.

Margaret Cavendish's dispensing advice in *Sociable Letters* amounts to a slightly different project from both of these. She does not provide recipes or regimens that her advisees might take up and act upon, but she does offer pieces of knowledge or opinion that they might choose to acknowledge. She leaves the reader–advisee with the option of pursuing whatever action is implied by the opinion if they happen to agree it. Indeed, Cavendish's advice is less a clearly instantiated commodity which can be implemented wholeheartedly than a set of arguments supporting one approach to the treatment of particular symptoms. One stylistic consequence of the contrast between counsel and opinion is that Cavendish is not directive in the way that the physicians practising in her period are, but is more oblique and allusive in persuading her addressees of the rightness of her position. Her advice differs from that which friends offer and accept from one another in being generalised and abstract, not tailored to the individual to whom it is directed. Finally, her advice differs from the guide to the proper conduct of physicians in their treatment of patients. While Cavendish was interested in the behaviour and conduct of men and women in society and the place of physicians, clergymen and politicians in it, she separated her sociology and ethics from her physic and science, thus distinguishing between medical practice and treatment and the conduct of physicians.

Notes

[1] George Bernard Shaw, 'Preface on Doctors', *The Works of Bernard Shaw*, 33 vols (London: Constable, 1930–1938), XII, p. 61.

[2] *Sociable Letters* (1664), Letter 132, p. 270.

[3] See Harold J. Cook, *The Decline of the Old Medical Regime in Stuart London*, (Ithaca and London: Cornell University Press, 1986).

[4] Sarah Hutton, 'Of Physic and Philosophy: Anne Conway, F. M. van Helmont and seventeenth-century Medicine' in Ole Peter Grell & Andrew Cunningham (eds.) *Religio Medici: Medicine and Religion in Seventeenth-century England* (Brookfield,Vermont and

Aldershot: Ashgate and Scolar Press, 1996), pp. 228–246 (p. 231).

[5] Theodor Turquet de Mayerne, *Medicinal Councels, or Advices: by Dr Theodor Turquet de Mayerne Baron of Aubonne, Counsellor and Chief Physician to the late King and Queen of England. Englished by Tho. Sherley, MD, Physician in Ordinary to his present Majesty.* (London: Printed for N. Ponder, at the Peacock in the Poultry near Cornhill, and in Chancery-lane near Fleetstreet, 1677).

[6] Lucinda Beier, *Sufferers and Healers: The experience of illness in seventeenth-century England* (London and New York: Routledge and Kegan Paul, 1987), p. 166.

[7] Thus licensed physicians like Robert Wittie complained that ordinary practitioners, of whom many claimed to be related to or to have learned from 'some eminent physician' were multiplying rapidly. See preface 'To the Reader', in James Primrose, *Popular Errours, or the Errours of the People in Physick,* trans. by Robert Wittie (London, 1651).

[8] See Cook, *Decline*, p. 43. He quotes the examples of Nicholas Sudell's *Mulierum Amicus: Or, The Woman's Friend* (1666), and William Sermon's *The Ladies Companion, or, The English Midwife* (1671) as examples of this practice. A later example is the advertisement at the end of the anonymous pamphlet, *A Treatise of Diseases of the Head, Brain and Nerves* (London, 1711), which declares 'All the Medicines prescrib'd in this Treatise, may be had of the Author's own preparing, at the *Hatch* with *blue Spikes* near the *Square* in *Haydon-yard* in the *Minories, London*, where only he has allow'd them to be dispos'd of, at the following Prices; which are much cheaper than any one else can rightly prepare them, with the best Ingredients, in small Quantities.' Prices range from 3^{s} 6^{d} for a bottle of 'Emetick Pouder' or a bottle of 'Volatile Essence', to 7^{s} 6^{d} for a parcel of *Hypochondriacum Digestivum* or one of *Pulvis Corroborans*.

[9] Anonymous, *A Discourse Concerning Fevers. In Two Letters to a young Physician. The First, Dissuading from all Hypotheses and Theories, whether Physical or Mechanical, as vain and delusive. The second, Directing his Regimen for the Cure, and his Conduct to the sick Person.* (London, 1727). pp. 286–287.

[10] See Alice Clark, *The Working Life of Women in the Seventeenth Century* (New York: A. M. Kelley, 1968), pp. 254–259.

[11] *Sociable Letters* (1664), p. 326.

[12] *Sociable Letters* (1664), p. 328.

[13] *Sociable Letters* (1664), p. 328.

[14] *Sociable Letters* (1664), p. 212.

[15] And so she continues, 'Thus, Madam, your Kind Friendship hath been a Devil to me, only you wanted a Devils Design, which is a Desire Hurtfull to Deceive, and you wanted the Malice, though not the Evil Effect. But some may think, this is a strange Style, or Conversation of Friendship, as to call my Friend a Devil, but my Friend being of a Divine Nature and a God-like Wisdome, knows that an Evill Effect may Proceed from a Good Intention as her Present shews; also she Knows that I her Friend Love and Honour her Intention, though I Rail and Exclame against the Effect, so that in the Effect and Intention of Friendship, we are as Intire and Loving Friends as ever we were, neither do true Friends take Exceptions at Words, knowing their Souls are so United, as not to be Divided neither in Life nor Death [...].' (*Sociable Letters* (1664), pp. 212–213).

[16] *Sociable Letters* (1664), p. 213.

[17] Hutton, 'Of Physic and Philosophy', p. 232.

[18] *The Conway Letters: The Correspondence of Anne, Viscountess Conway, Henry More, and their Friends, 1642–1684*, ed. by Marjorie Hope Nicholson, revised by Sarah Hutton (Oxford: Clarendon, 1992), Letter 37, April 9 1653 (NS), p. 79.

[19] *Sociable Letters* (1664), p. 290.

[20] *Sociable Letters* (1664), Letter 140, p. 290. Cavendish discourses in an essay on cordials in her *Grounds* (1668), pp. 157–158, where she asserts, apparently somewhat contradictorily, '[...] all such Applications as are named *Cordials*, are not hot: for, some are cool, at least, of a temperate degree.' It is striking that unlike her learned contemporaries, Cavendish does not offer any recipes as such for cooling remedies like juleps or heating ones like cordials. In his *London Practice of Physick*, Willis has a section entitled *Pharmaceutice Rationalis*, in which he provides instructions and recipes for emetic and anti-emetic medicines, diuretic and anti-diuretics, diaphoretics and anti-diaphoretics as well as cordials and opiates (pp. 1–69).

[21] *Sociable Letters* (1664), p. 290.

[22] Thomas Willis, in his treatise on fevers, in *The Remaining Works of that Famous and Renowned Physican Dr Thomas Willis*, trans. S. Pordage (London: Printed for T. Dring, C. Harper and J. Leigh, 1681), echoes Cavendish's caution in the prescription of cordials: 'which, if administred in the Feaverish fit, do too much strengthen, the former violent motion of the Heart, and oftentimes break its strength, (as when a small flame is troubled with a more strong blast of wind) life is easily extinguished; wherefore tis a vulgar observation, that Cordials often accelerate death, for that by too much troubling the Blood, they sooner beat down strength.' (p. 106).

[23] Thomas Willis, *The London Practice of Physick: Or the whole Practical Part of Physick Contained in the Works of Dr Willis. Faithfully made English, and Printed together for the Publick Good* (London: Printed for T. Bassett, 1689). *Tract of the Diseases that regard the Corporeal Soul, and its subjects, viz. the Brain and Genus Nervosum*, Chapter 1, 'Instructions and Prescripts for the Cure of the Head-ache', p. 394.

[24] *Conway Letters*, Letter 39, April 18 1653 (NS), p. 80.

[25] Her reputation as a disputant and critic in the scientific circle of which Henry More was a member was immense, and to point to those talents as possibly contributory to her illness was tantamount to allying her lack of fitness for tough intellectual endeavour with her sex. See Hilda L. Smith, *Reason's Disciples: Seventeenth-Century English Feminists*. (Urbana: University of Illinois Press, 1982), p. 61n.

[26] Willis, *London Practice*, pp. 394–395.

[27] Willis, *London Practice*, p. 390, comments on the use of such remedies to treat headaches, but which were used typically in the treatment of venereal disease thus: 'I confess the examples of certain persons have scared me from trying that method. [...] A certain Lady of great Quality [Anne Conway] for curing a violent and long continued Headache, has undergone three copious Salivations, *viz.* first by a Mercury Ointment directed by Sir *Theodore Mayern*, and afterward twice by taking the late famous Powder of *Charles Huis*, and this without any relief, (and I wish it were not with some detriment to her) for since for many years, even to this day, she has given ground to the cruel Tyranny of this Distemper growing by degrees upon her. It fell out somewhat worse than this with that excellent man, *D.G.D.* for the cure of whose ancient Head-ach, when a Mercury Ointment was applied to his Head pained, the Salivation raised thereby, made him blind, without curing the Disease.

Truly every man, duly considering the Operation of mercury in the Body of Man, ought to dread these kinds of effects from the rash giving of it.'

[28] Willis, *London Practice*, pp. 384 *et seq.*, deals with the appropriateness of prescribing for different kinds of headaches antiscorbutical (or chalybeat medicines) 'which restore the Crasis of the Blood' (p. 385) and cephalics, 'the Medicines that render the nervous Liquor more friendly and benign to the Membranes of the Head, which are wont to be offended by it.' (p. 386). He goes on to assess the effectiveness of surgical procedures in treating headaches, such as plasters (p. 388), the 'burning or cutting of *Issues* in several parts of the Body' (p. 389), trepanning (p. 390) and 'the opening of an Artery' (p. 392). He does not discuss hysteric remedies.

[29] Willis, *London Practice*, p. 395.

[30] Willis, *London Practice*, p. 395.

[31] *Sociable Letters* (1664), p. 444.

[32] Thomas Sydenham, *The Whole Works of that Excellent Practical Physician, Dr Thomas Sydenham*, third edition, ed. by John Pechey (London: Printed for Richard Wellington and Edward Castle, 1701), p. 200.

[33] Willis, *London Practice*, p. 505: 'Immoderate or unseasonable exercise of the Body, violent Passions, immoderate Venery, and a disorderly Diet, and likewise whatsoever things greatly trouble or exagitate the Spirits and Humors, and consequently raise fluxions of the nervous Juice, or of the Recrements cause Arthritick pains.'

[34] Willis, *London Practice*, p. 179–180 differentiates between the 'Spontaneous Eruption' which might occur as symptoms of disease in fevers like the plague, measles, small-pox or as 'Critical', that is, advantageous to health, as in the 'Menses of Women, and in some the Flux of the Hæmorrhoides, and in others yearly bleedings at the Nose,' (p. 177) and Phlebotomy, supplied in case spontaneous eruption fails, by 'Physick the Handmaid of nature.' (p. 179) He goes on to discuss its 'use and effects both good and evil in the Practice of Physick.' (pp. 180 *et seq.*).

[35] *Sociable Letters* (1664), p. 445.

[36] *Sociable Letters* (1664), p. 445.

[37] Willis, *London Practice*, p. 365. Willis deals with rheumatism under the general chapter heading of scurvy, in his tract of the Scurvy, pp. 326–379. In fact, two of his case histories seem usefully comparable with the condition of Mrs. T. (pp. 374–376).

[38] Sydenham, *Works*, pp. 203–205. He comments in his section 'Of a Rheumatism', 'various Symptoms appear in those Bodies, in which some matter is newly generated, fit to produce the *Gout*, but not yet cast upon the Joynts, which seems to be Scorbutical, till the *Gout* is formed, and actually exerts it self, and then it plainly appears what the Disease is: Neither are we ignorant that as many Symptoms resembling the *Scurvy*, afflict gouty People after the Fit is over; [...] And this may be said not only of the *Gout*, but also of an *Incipient Dropsie*; though it is commonly said, where a *Scurvy* ends, there a *Dropsie* begins, yet most commonly this Rule is to be understood no otherwise than that when a *Dropsie* is apparent, the pre-conceived Opinion of the *Scurvy* vanishes: and the same may be affirmed of very many other chronical Diseases, as yet growing in the Body, and having not yet assumed any Type, or of those which are partly subdued, yet not totally vanquished and expelled [...].'

[39] *Sociable Letters* (1664), p. 445.

[40] *Sociable Letters* (1664), p. 445.

[41] *Sociable Letters* (1664), p. 445.

[42] I explore Cavendish's characterisation and justification of her speculative method elsewhere. Interestingly, Willis deals with speculation, glossed as 'a seeing or discovering a thing by contemplation,' in his Preface to his tract on 'Feavers', in *Remaining Works*, p. 54, in the following terms: 'But that the Light, clearly inkindled by the Antients, did so suddenly shut up, and darkned the Eyes of Posterity, it was, the preposterous study of those, who too hastily framed, almost out of their own Brain, Physick into a general Method, after the manner of some Speculative Science: for by this means, before they had laid a firm Foundation, a sufficiently specious, and deceitful Pile of unstable Doctrine, was erected. That therefore in the Cure of Feavers, some Indications being more antiently received, remain yet unconfirmed, and are to be perpetually observed, is to be ascribed wholly to Experience, the first Mistress of this Art, and not to the Precepts of Scholars.'

[43] *Sociable Letters* (1664), pp. 445–6.

[44] *Sociable Letters* (1664), p. 446.

[45] Mayerne, *Medicinal Councels*, sig. B2 recto–verso.

[46] Mayerne, *Medicinal Councels*, p. 62.

[47] Mayerne, *Medicinal Councels*, pp. 62–3.

[48] Mayerne, *Medicinal Councels*, p. 64.

[49] Mayerne, *Medicinal Councels*, p. 65.

[50] Mayerne, *Medicinal Councels*, p. 66.

[51] Mayerne, *Medicinal Councels*, p. 66.

[52] Mayerne, *Medicinal Councels*, p. 67.

[53] Mayerne, *Medicinal Councels*, p. 67.

[54] Mayerne, *Medicinal Councels*, pp. 66–68.

[55] *Sociable Letters* (1664), p. 446.

[56] *Sociable Letters* (1664), p. 447.

[57] Discourse attached to the anonymous *Treatise* (see note 8), p. 114. The author's summary is as follows: 'But among all the Torments of this Disease, there is none so common as a Pain in the Back, which most certainly all Women feel how little soever they are afflicted with the Vapours. It is also common, that after the Pains are gone off, there is such a Stiffness of the Parts, or Numbness or Soreness, as if beaten, so that the Patient cannot bear to have the places touch'd; but this Tenderness goes off by degrees. And this among the rest is worth observing, That all Hysterick Women complain of a Dejection and Sinking of the Spirits, who when they would shew the place where the sinking of the Spirits is, point to the Region of the Lungs. Yet of all the Symptoms that attend this Disease, nothing is more common or inseperable, and more shews the Patient to be troubled with Vapours, than that their Urine is as clear as Rock-water, and comes away when they make it in a plentiful Quantity, especially when they have just before found themselves faint, ill, or sickish. Moreover, Women much troubled with Vapours belch up ill Fumes as often as they eat, tho' they only eat moderately, and as they have an Appetite. Also they sometimes in their Fits laugh exceedingly, and sometimes cry as much, without any real Cause for either.' (pp. 116–117).

[58] The writings of two seventeenth-century physicians, Daniel Sennert (1572–1637) and Lazar Riverius (1589–1655), who adhered to Galenic teachings, were made available to the general English reader through translations. Sennert's *Epitomes institutionum medicinae* was

translated as *Institutions or Fundamentals of the Whole Art, Both of Physick and Chirurgery* (London, 1656), and Riverius's *Institutiones medici* was translated as *The Universal Body of Physick* (London, 1657). See Lester S. King, 'The Transformation of Galenism', in Allen G. Debus (ed.) *Medicine in Seventeenth Century England. A Symposium Held at UCLA in Honor of C. D. O'Malley* (Berkeley: University of California Press, 1974), pp. 7–31.

[59] *Sociable Letters* (1664), p. 447.

[60] Willis, *London Practice*, p. 361 *et seq.*

[61] Francis Bacon, *History Natural and Experimental of Life and Death: or, Of the Prolongation of Life* (London: Printed for William Lee, 1669). I have labelled Cavendish's mode of analysis 'Baconian' after Bacon's method of combining the philosophical and abstract with the corporeal and clinical in discussing a range of topics which might be construed as belonging under different heads, but which Bacon deals with together, for example the ways in which the human body might 'remain youthful, and renew their Vigour.' (p. 28) Each paragraph treats of a slightly different topic, the combination of which Bacon argues puts the 'Spirits [...] into such a temperament and degree of activity, that they should not drink and guzzle the juices of the Body, but sip them onely.' (p. 28).

[62] Willis, *London Practice*, pp. 373–374. Willis continues: 'It is obvious that those severe Symptoms proceeded from a Corbutick Root, for by reason of the taint principally fixt on the Blood, the Spontaneous Lassitude, the difficult Breathing, nay, and the intermitting Fever hapning at random, and often returning, and the Bickerings of other Symptoms previous, as it were, and light, were caus'd: Again the Lixivial Urine, and that diversified colour of it plainly shew'd the Blood to be seis'd with a Sulphureo-saline Discrasie; which kind of Urine I have observ'd to be so mark't in many others, affected with the like Disease: Moreover when in this sick Lady, the Morbid Seminal Root being increast in its store, and flowing into the Mass of Blood, came to spread it self on the Confines of the Brain and *Genus Nervosum*, the other more violent affects arose.'

[63] *Sociable Letters* (1664), p. 448: 'and there-fore I pray Use Cooling and Moistening Remedies, lest in striving to Cure one Disease, a Worse be Produced, but Cooling and Moistening will not only Cure her Numbness, but the Overflowing of her Natural Flux, which is caused through Heat, which Over Rarifies the Blood, and makes it Flow when it should Ebb, like as a Double Tide; But I leave all to your Better Judgment, Skill, Practice, Observation, and Wisdom, and rest.'

[64] *Sociable Letters* (1664), p. 448.

[65] Willis, *London Practice*, p. 374.

[66] Willis, *London Practice*, p. 374.

[67] Willis, *London Practice*, p. 374.

[68] Willis, *London Practice*, p. 374. He continues, 'For the Pains being mitigated, she began in some measure to move her Limbs, to have a better Stomach, and to digest her Food better, and to enjoy a quiet Sleep: The Salivation being over, she took a Decoction of Sarza and China, with Antiparylitick Ingredients for a few days: Afterward being carried to *Bathe* and having there us'd the temperate hot Baths, for some time she recover'd an indifferent state of Health. The whole Winter she constantly took Medicines against the Scurvy and the Palsey: And upon her renewing the use of the hot Baths the year following, she grew perfectly well; and since is become the joyful Mother of many Children.'

[69] Willis, *London Practice*, Preface, sig. A1 recto, sig. A2 verso. The translator,

Eugenius Philiatros, identifies the sort of reader at which this digest is targeted: 'I have been induc'd to believe on several Grounds that the Practical part of Dr. Willis's *Works*, set forth after this manner, would be acceptable to many. For, in truth, besides the cheapness and portableness of the Volum, if any Persons unacquainted with the Latin Tongue buy Dr. Willis, it cannot be thought that they will have the patience to peruse a deal of Theory, consisting of large Anatomical and Physiological Discourses, and the like, which though never so clearly delivered in English, cannot be comprehended by them under some years study.'(sig. A3 recto). Alfred White Franklin suggests that Willis resorted to 'fabrications and to dreams' in his failed attempt to correct the errors of Aristotle's theories and Galen's practice by setting up an alternative system. And he claims that Philiatros 'considered it necessary to strip him of his theorizing to make him more readable and better understood.' See Alfred White Franklin, 'Clinical Medicine', in Debus, *Medicine*, pp. 113–145 (p. 128).

[70] Anon., *Discourse*, 'Adverstisement', sig. A2 recto–verso; A3 recto (see note 9).

[71] Anon., *Discourse*, p. 163 [153].

[72] Anon., *Discourse*, p. 342.

[73] Anon., *Discourse*, pp. 345–346.

15

Paradigms and Politics: Hobbes and Cavendish Contrasted

Neil Ankers

In his account of the rise of 'chaos theory', James Gleick describes how its converts often view themselves as evangelists of a new paradigm, allowing them to 'speculate about determinism and free will, about evolution, about the nature of conscious intelligence. They feel they are turning back the trend in science towards reductionism [...], they believe they are looking for the whole.'[1] I would like to argue that Margaret Cavendish's natural philosophy betrays a similar kind of evangelism. Indeed, as part of the umbrella movement termed 'new philosophy', Cavendish's philosophy should be evaluated in relation to the acceptance of the laws of mechanics as the fundamental laws of nature. Yet, just as Gleick's 'chaos theorists' felt empowered to speculate about a future science of 'the whole', I would like to argue that Cavendish's natural philosophy implicitly engages with more than the physics of the new philosophy to address its most controversial political off-shoot, Thomas Hobbes's *Leviathan*. Cavendish's ideas concerning matter and motion, I argue, can best be understood as a counter to the attempt by Hobbes to produce a unified theory of nature, man and society. To this end, Cavendish appropriates the central analogy of the *Leviathan*, the 'artificial man', in order to oppose Hobbes's conclusions concerning subjectivity and a brutal and competitive 'state of nature'. To simplify matters I will hereafter use the term 'paradigm' to designate my understanding of the assumptions underlying Hobbes's and Cavendish's philosophical projects.[2]

While much has been made of the ambiguity and apparent incoherence of Margaret Cavendish's natural philosophy,[3] relatively little has been said of its close resemblance to certain key features of Thomas Hobbes's natural and political philosophies.[4] Yet this is undoubtedly the most important factor leading to her philosophy. Recent research has begun to acknowledge her intellectual debt to Hobbes, but as yet an adequate evaluation of her philosophy lacks precision because it has not been recognised that while ostensibly concerned with the laws of nature, Cavendish's conception of these laws acts to oppose the unified vision of Hobbes's philosophical project.[5] Accordingly, despite the fact that they were in close contact during the period of Cavendish's intellectual development (the most significant period for Cavendish being 1645 to 1652, when Hobbes was composing the *Leviathan* and Margaret Cavendish the ideas published in her *Poems and Fancies* (1653), *Philosophical Fancies* (1653), and *Philosophical and Physical Opinions* (1655)), commentators tend to interpret Cavendish's philosophical ideas in isolation. Thus they ignore the correspondences between Cavendish and Hobbes, and the fact that Hobbes viewed the political, psychological and natural elements of his philosophy as unified.[6] Given that Hobbes himself promoted this view, it is entirely likely, I argue, that Margaret Cavendish should engage, if 'covertly', with the totality of Hobbes's thought.

Margaret Cavendish (then Lucas) arrived in Paris as a maid-in-waiting to the Queen in June 1644. The defeated royalist William Cavendish arrived soon after, and in 1645 the two were married.[7] Together with his brother Charles, William Cavendish was a noted patron of the arts and sciences. In particular, William Cavendish was on close terms with Thomas Hobbes. As is evident from the published letters of Charles Cavendish, it is clear that the Cavendish household retained its interest in Hobbes's ideas throughout his career;[8] a fact that Margaret Cavendish herself acknowledges in a preface to her *Philosophical and Physical Opinions*.[9]

Given this proximity, the question of Hobbes's influence upon Margaret Cavendish arises and, in broad terms, this influence is clear enough. Firstly, there is a shared allegiance to a thoroughgoing materialism. For both Hobbes and Cavendish there can be no valid natural philosophy that does not begin and end with matter.[10] In addition, though less obvious, there is a shared approach to philosophical method, which breaks things down into essential component parts before analysing their essential relationship. As Hobbes puts it in the *De Corpore*, the 'subject of philosophy' is:

> Every body of which we can conceive any generation, and which we may, by any consideration thereof, compare with other bodies, or which is capable of composition and resolution.[11]

With this typically concise statement Hobbes indicates that to be properly available to systematic analysis a subject must be both material and 'capable of composition and resolution'. It is significant that these criteria lend themselves to a holistic approach, which bridges the divide between a physical 'body' and a 'body politic'. The material 'body' and the 'body politic', Hobbes suggests, are approachable using the same method and principles. This further suggests, not only that the prestige attached to the proofs of science should exclude anything not properly conceived to be a 'body', but equally that science can extend its proofs to complex forms of the material body. As we shall see, it is the close attention Hobbes pays to the rules of precise definition that allows him to make an equivalence between different forms of body. In addition, the new philosophy encouraged more accurate forms of representation by enforcing a strict demarcation between poetic and scientific analogy.[12] As David Johnston argues, Hobbes intends nothing less than a 'cultural transformation' of society by this means, by reason that 'both theology and metaphysics were of direct political importance,'[13] and 'that political consequences flowed from the widespread adoption of certain theological and even metaphysical views.'[14] As political stability is arguably the chief aim of Hobbes's philosophical project, nothing less than a unified paradigm encompassing culture, society and nature will suffice to bring about a new social cohesion.

Hobbes was concerned, therefore, to extend to the motivations of human nature the scientific certainty that the new philosophy demonstrated with regard to simple forms of matter in motion. To do so he proposed a unified three-fold philosophy beginning with the laws of nature, thereafter a psychology of man, and finally arriving at a political philosophy with genuine scientific validity. To be successful Hobbes needed to indicate an equivalence between the mechanical principles of matter and motion and the motive forces propelling human desire. In this way Hobbes, more than any other philosopher (excepting perhaps Spinoza), paved the way for what Carolyn Merchant sees as the cultural dominance of the mechanico–materialist paradigm.[15]

In a preface to her *Philosophical and Physical Opinions* (first edition, 1655) Margaret Cavendish appears to echo Hobbes's method and intent; stating bluntly that, 'the first cause is matter/ the second is motion/ the third is figure/ which produceth all natural effects'. To this she adds:

> Nature is matter, form and motion, all these being, as it were, one thing; matter is the body of nature, form is the shape of nature, and motion the spirits of nature, which is the life of nature.[16]

Not only is matter the 'first cause', it is matter in its various forms and characteristic motions which results in every 'effect' of nature; therefore Cavendish appears to echo not only the materialism but also the holistic approach of Hobbes. Furthermore, she echoes Hobbes's form of the 'resolutive–composite' method by suggesting that the fundamental basis for explanation and interpretation rests with matter, form and motion alone. Cavendish, though, appears to go a step further in explicitly identifying motion with the 'spirit of nature' and the 'life of nature'. This implies that motion is identical to life, and that the laws of motion also apply to life, leaving religion little to do with respect to the 'motions' and 'motivations' of the human individual. This is clearly an implication taken from Hobbes, but it is less equivocal in its conflation of the two terms. In later versions of her philosophy, Cavendish altered this stance by admitting a non-material soul alongside the material; by this time, though, the damage was done, and she was branded a brazen atheist by Ralph Cudworth.[17] As one recent commentator has noted, the bold conflation of motion with life led even her sympathisers (Joseph Glanvill and Walter Charleton among them) to distance themselves from her views.[18] Along with Hobbes and Spinoza, Margaret Cavendish is therefore among the most outspoken and explicit materialists of the period.

From this it is clear that it is the question of motion and its relationship to life and human 'motivations' which forms the crucial point of comparison between Hobbes and Cavendish. In particular, the role played by the mechanical philosophy in the politics adopted by Cavendish and Hobbes. To this end I will pay particular attention to the role given to systematic analogy by Hobbes to promote an equivalence between the laws of inertial motion and the motivations of the human individual. I will argue that Margaret Cavendish attempts to undermine the mechanical basis for Hobbes's analogies, especially those promoting a competitive 'state of nature'. As a direct contrast to Hobbes's attempt to create a unified paradigm for science and culture, I argue that Cavendish offers an alternative, where willing compliance replaces competitive struggle as the fundamental 'motivation' in nature.

There are, as Tom Sorell has re-emphasised, well grounded reasons for denying a causal link between the three elements of Hobbes's philosophy.[19] The question is therefore not beyond dispute, but has been re-appraised in a fruitful way by Thomas Spragens and Michel Verdon.[20] Spragens's and Verdon's thesis, in brief, is that influenced by the inertial mechanics of Galileo and Descartes, Hobbes came to believe that the laws of inertial motion provided a scientific model which could be extended to include human 'motion'. Spragens and Verdon do not argue that Hobbes saw no distinctions between the two, but rather that they were analogous to a very high degree. This is important, as it is the role played by systematic analogy in Hobbes's political philosophy that allows him to infer that, at root, human nature is governed by the same mechanical principles as those governing inert matter. By promoting the idea that language and definitions can be universally precise when guided by these laws, Hobbes is able to suggest that his physiological political analogies are fundamentally correct and not subject to the influence of culture.

Following Galileo, Descartes had significantly extended the implications of rectilinear inertial motion for matter.[21] Descartes overturned the Aristotelian theory of cosmology, where bodies in motion strove to find their 'natural' positions and thereafter remained at rest. After Descartes, the natural state of bodies, once moved, was to remain in motion until impacted upon by another body. Solving the problem of changes of direction, Descartes argued for collisions resulting in impact-induced transfers of motion. In removing the need for any active principles, Descartes instituted a fully mechanised system, which in theory could account for all moving matter.[22] Hobbes removed Descartes insistence on a mind–body division, and thus removed the remaining obstacle to transferring these laws to human behaviour. With the mechanical philosophy analogically transposed to human psychology, Hobbes has a theoretical framework for a political science.[23] For Hobbes, therefore, the theory of continual inertial motion resulting in impacts and chance collisions becomes a political and psychological paradigm for human behaviour and motivation.

As Cartesian and Hobbesian physics are generally convergent, for Hobbes's political philosophy the problem was to demonstrate that this political science was properly correspondent with the ego-psychology, and this in turn with the laws of matter and motion. In Verdon's eyes, the process is complete in *De Cive*, where Hobbes reveals the essence of human motion to be an instinct or *universal motion* for security leading to an unending desire for all things at all times.[24] From this premise Hobbes is able to construct his materialist psychology predicated upon the universal and endless movement of desire.[25] As inert matter is subject to the play of force, so too is human 'motion', leading to 'collisions' and conflict, and as the motion of inert matter is essentially arbitrary, so are the motions of individual desire, unless restrained by lawful power.

Hobbes's most extensive treatment of this theory is in the *Leviathan*, and it is here that systematic analogy takes on its full importance. In the introduction, Hobbes outlines a model of civil society via the analogy of the 'artificial man': a new version of the 'body politic', but premised upon his egoistic psychology. Analogy is the key to Hobbes's analysis. The term 'art' in this context acts as shorthand for reason, and Hobbes's intention to make definitions adhere to scientific laws. Rather than the poetic or intuitive analogies used by the divine or mystic, art can now proceed unhindered to construct political structures precisely derived from nature.[26] This makes possible for the first time a truly scientific solution to the problem of order and restraint by imitating nature's order:

> NATURE (the Art whereby God hath made and governes the World) is by the *Art* of man, as in many other things, so in this also imitated, that it can make an Artificial Animal. For seeing life is but a motion of Limbs, the begining whereof is in some principall part within; why may we not say, that all *Automata* (Engines that move themselves by springs and wheeles as doth a watch) have an artificiall life?[27]

Hobbes intends his example to be more than a literary conceit. The 'artificial man' analogy is derived from the 'art' of nature and thus has a legitimacy beyond the merely figurative. For Hobbes, the philosopher's task is to indicate the mimetic logic of his models, acting as mere conduit and not as a creator. Hobbes intends, of course, merely to refer to the already familiar analogy between the 'artificial life' of any mechanical device (a clock, for example) and the 'workings' of a society of human individuals. In doing so he intends to suggest that the mathematical laws which govern the workings of the universe may also, ultimately, be responsible for human interactions. This, however, comes close to identifying life with motion, just as Cavendish more openly does in her text (issued shortly after the *Leviathan*). If motion is in some way equivalent to life, it suggests that the rules governing motion must in some fashion be applicable to life also. As Hobbes indicates, the thread that unites the two is the mechanical hypothesis, so that: '*Art* goes yet further, imitating that Rationall and most excellent worke of Nature, *Man*. For by Art is created that great LEVIATHAN called a COMMON-WEALTH, or STATE, [...] which is but an Artificiall Man.'[28] While leaving no doubt that it is 'artful', Hobbes suggests that his analogy is appropriate because it is governed by the same mathematical laws which determine all of nature's phenomena.

Thus Hobbes can proceed to a civil system correspondent with the imagery of the mechanised body to 'flesh out' this imitative 'artificial man':

> *Soveraignty* is an Artificiall *Soul*, as giving life and motion to the whole body; The *Magistrates*, and other *Officers* of Judicature and Execution, artificiall *Joynts*; *Reward* and *Punishment* [...] are the *Nerves*, that do the same in the Body Naturall

[...] *Equity*, and *Lawes*, an artificiall *Reason* and *Will*; *Concord*, *Health*; *Sedition*, *Sicknesse*, and *Civill War*, *Death*.[29]

The self-consciously artful analogy illustrates the point that the artificial rules of a society are here imitative of nature's rules. And while the correspondence may appear loose to the modern eye, it is worth remembering that Hobbes placed great importance upon the simplicity and clarity of his philosophy and hoped for the greatest dissemination possible. Equally, Hobbes indicates that self-evidence is the means by which lawful restraint can be both imposed and willingly accepted. Hobbes therefore aims to instil a unified perception of the mechanical universe in order to make his political system a material reality. The overlapping of the political and the mechanical registers will in circular fashion serve to reinforce the rightness of the doctrine and thereby help to ensure the assent of the many. Creating a constituency for a new unified paradigm is Hobbes's implicit aim with the *Leviathan*. The meshing of analogies, simultaneously both poetic and scientific, helps to foster the security of perception that underpins Hobbes's didactic intent. In Hobbes's system obedience to authority is seen as equivalent to obedience to the immutable laws of nature, and obedience to the laws of nature as conformity to an immutable logic.

Margaret Cavendish, like Hobbes, seeks to construct a natural philosophy which unifies nature, the individual and society. Yet, as we shall see, Cavendish appropriates Hobbes's 'artificial man' analogy and applies it to nature rather than to the nation state or 'commonwealth'. Nature, however, for Cavendish, is analogous to a fully-autonomous, non-mechanical, human individual; in effect, then, she reverses the analogy so that, as an individual, nature displays all of the 'variousness' and caprices associated with a non-mechanical view of the human individual. Rather than conforming to the mathematical laws which underpin the mechanical philosophy, Cavendish suggests that nature (and human desire) is naturally 'non-conformist', which of course means that the problem of obedience and conformity become, once again, a question of the individual and subjective perceptions of poetic analogies. More than this, though, Cavendish suggests, as we have already seen with her conception of motion, that analogy is not merely equivalent, but self-identical. For Cavendish, if nature is a machine, then such a machine is a living being whose motives are a mystery. This means that nature is once more fully autonomous in terms of motives and motivations. The result for Cavendish is nature restored to a pristine mystery, without impacts or collisions and, as such, very different to Hobbes's competitive model, which produces autonomous individuals whose impacts and collisions can only be restrained by the state.

Cavendish begins this re-appropriation by dividing nature into two primary degrees of matter: the 'animate' (or 'innated') and the inanimate (also 'dull'). As this suggests, the distinction equates to an animate, which is 'self-moving', and an inanimate moved by the animate. The degrees are governed by the rarity of matter, so that as matter becomes more subtle it at some distinct point becomes animate of itself. Within the animate degree there is a further division between the 'sensitive' and the 'rational', which together order and govern nature:

> First, that Nature is Infinite, and the Eternal Servant of God: Next that She is Corporeal, and partly self-moving, dividable and compoundable; that all and every particular creature, as also all perception and variety in Nature, is made by Corporeal self-motion, which I name sensitive and rational matter, which is life and knowledge, sense and reason. That these sensitive and rational parts of matter are the purest and subtlest parts of Nature, as the active parts, the knowing, understanding and prudent parts, the designing, architectonical and working parts, nay the Life and Soul of nature.[30]

Cavendish's model of nature upon close inspection approximates to the Hobbesian human individual, just as Hobbes's post-Harveian 'artificial man' relies upon the laws of mechanics for its coherence. However, as Cavendish's analogy implies that nature itself is equivalent to the human individual, she can suggest that it has 'rational' and 'sensitive' attributes, which are not governed or determined by scientific laws. Furthermore, as an inseparable part of that primary individual, for the human there is permitted only a probabilistic and limited perception of its unfathomable motives and motivations. Cavendish the natural philosopher thus, in effect, moves to restore the mystery of nature central to religious belief while remaining within the ambit of science. Cavendish instigates a kind of secular or scientific religion which will re-establish submission to an unfathomable whole as its central message. Nature is thus the only true individual, and while its parts, in microscopic resemblance, appear autonomous they are mimicking rather than fully possessing nature's attributes, as full autonomy belongs only to the whole. Thus 'sense' and 'reason', which are the 'knowing, understanding and prudent parts, the designing, architectonical and working parts,' while working to a greater design and purpose, do not of themselves supply the part with a means to fathom the motives of the whole.

Unlike Hobbes, therefore, Cavendish is not required to equate motion with a desire for all things at all times, but rather nature's 'architectonical and working parts,' which, as the 'life and soul of nature,' are the servants of a greater yet unknowable design. This requires her to undermine inertial motion, as this would not allow nature to operate according to a self-willed design. For Cavendish, life and motion are interchangeable terms and do not require mechanist and determinist laws of motion to account for motivation and behaviour. This conception of autonomy is thus also linked to a non-determinist human autonomy, and this makes possible the elevation of the subjective as reference point for hints to general motivation. As Cavendish often points out, the only self it is possible to know reliably is the authorial, self-fashioning self; in effect, then, nature and individual self become interchangeable, as well as life and motion. Thus nature can be a canvas upon which personal motives and desires can be portrayed as general principles. As Jay Stevenson, amongst others, has observed, Cavendish often represents or stages the drama and conflicts of the self as though these were interchangeable with the hidden motives and passions of nature.[31] Quite literally, for Cavendish, the autonomous individual and the autonomy of nature are essentially the same thing.

In order to make her analogies work, though, Cavendish is required to provide a detailed account of the microcosmic and macrocosmic individual with regard to agency. Cavendish addresses this question via the model of the 'artificial man' of the *Leviathan*. While Hobbes's 'artificial man' upholds the primacy of the new philosophy, Cavendish suggests that a 'self moving' nature is not constrained by the laws of inertial motion, and is therefore not determined in any way. So Hobbes's emphasis upon the mechanics of desire, entailing collisions and impacts at a human scale, is denied in Cavendish's model. As a 'part' of that greater individual, the human, or any other 'part', is required only to perceive its proper role and function via analogies of identity between the two forms of individual. The motivation for the 'part' is thus to align oneself with nature.

For this to happen, though, agency must find an equivalence with the motive forces animating nature. If the 'parts' transfer motion in some manner they would be mechanical, therefore authorising Hobbesian competitive struggle. Cavendish must avoid this trap without distancing her model from the authority of the new philosophy. This Cavendish attempts by arguing for a 'double perception' of parts as 'individual' in themselves while remaining integrated within a dynamic whole. 'Parts', Cavendish argues, are not distinct agents determined by inertial motion, but are integrated with each other in ways determined by the unspecified motivation of nature as infinite individual. Making this point in relation to the composition of any 'creature', Cavendish echoes mechanist language, but with her 'parts' moving to a different purpose, so that:

> when they move regularly, then they move to one and the same Design, or one and the same united action. So, although a Creature is composed of Several Sorts of Corporeal Motions; yet these Several Sorts, being properly united in one Creature, move all agreeably to the Property and Nature of the whole Creature.[32]

Cavendish effectively removes power and force and instead emphasises the role of relationship. She indicates that the operation and function of motion is not inertial but teleological. With Cavendish, the microcosmic creature functions in a fashion identical to all creatures and thus the infinite individual. To be 'healthy', a creature's parts must function 'agreeably to the Property and Nature of the whole Creature'. Whereas for Hobbes, the priority for a political philosophy is to proscribe limits upon freedom, for Cavendish limits arise naturally from a perception of relationship of parts to parts. Her conception of a non-coercive nature remains redolent of Hobbes's determinist political project. Her philosophical explanations resonate with signification concerning freedom and autonomy, so that:

> though every self-moving Part, or Corporeal Motion, have free-will to move after what manner they please; yet, by reason there can be no Single Parts, Several Parts unite in one Action [...] at the same point of time of division [...] is there uniting or joining.[33]

With Cavendish, the materialist framework is used to address the critical question of agency and autonomy, and suggests that the danger of fully autonomous parts, such as atoms or human individuals, is negated by a relational imperative. Cavendish argues not that there are not 'single parts' in nature, but that they cannot exist singly and must always be functioning as parts of the greater individual, so that some form of uniting must accompany division. This, if true for all matter, must also be true for human beings and the 'body politic'. As Hobbes argues in the *Leviathan* that perception mediated by scientific analogy provides against wilful self-fashioning, Cavendish argues that perception is the key to the proper functioning of parts and that this is the proper role for natural philosophy. Within Cavendish's nature new forms arise spontaneously from the dissolution of the old. Division, with Cavendish, is countered by 'uniting or joining', because the parts work harmoniously when perceiving the needs of the greater body. Free will exists for the parts, but as parts they can only prosper when moving to the needs of the whole; only then will they be in accord with the will and design of the 'several parts' which 'unite in one action'.

A consequence of Cavendish's argument is that as the 'parts' of nature cannot for themselves perceive the motives of the whole, they must infer the nature of their role via analogies of harmony and order. Although nature is 'but one body', with 'no sharer or co-partner' having 'but one Infinite natural knowledg and wisdom,' it is also 'divided into infinite several parts' that are 'ignorant of the others knowledg and perception,' which 'causes ignorance as well as knowledg amongst Natures Creatures,'[34] while 'a whole creature has both a general knowledg, and a knowledg of parts.'[35] In Cavendish's 'state of nature', the 'parts' of her body politic can be unaware of this, and thus unaware of the dimensions of their ignorance and prerogative. Her philosophy, though, attempts to affirm the positive attributes of perspectivism belonging to a limited perception. Cavendish therefore argues that any new paradigm must, paradoxically, be aware of its limited and provisional status:

> for reason being dividable, because material, cannot move in all parts alike; and since there is but one truth in nature, all those that hit not this truth, do err, some more some less [...] nevertheless, all do ground there opinions upon reason; that is, upon rational probabilities, at least, they think they do.[36]

For Cavendish, a doctrine such as Hobbes proposes, including its attempt to unify via systematic analogy, is especially open to error if it does not recognise that reason itself is 'dividable'. Thus Cavendish implies that her own self-conscious system, which does not finally rely upon reason alone but instead embraces the relativism of reason, is more likely to succeed in the attempt to describe the 'one truth in nature'. Her philosophy creates nature as an infinite version of the individual and the self, and thus Cavendish can infer that truth and fidelity to the self can be extrapolated as the truth of nature; fidelity to honest self-searching is fidelity to the universal truths of nature. When applied to the problems of society and government it will provide equally truthful answers.

The question of the nature of governance and our perception of it is addressed in a more explicit way in the *Philosophical Letters*. Here Cavendish argues that 'Nature hath but one wise law, viz. to keep infinite matter in order, and to keep so much peace as not to disturb the foundation of her Government.'[37] Evoking the question of order and disorder in human society, she returns to the analogy of the physical, microcosmic body:

> for example, some corporeal motions in the body turning Rebels, by moving contrary to the health of the animal Creature, it must become sick; for not every creature hath an absolute power, the power being in the infinite whole, and not in the divided parts.[38]

To be harmonious a body must act in unison and not as factious 'rebels', and to do this is to act with regularity; and for action to be regular implies that it has the right perception of the relationship of parts to the whole. With Cavendish, therefore, there is a fundamental qualification to Hobbesian philosophy. Cavendish does not finally support submission to an arbitrary 'absolute power' which exists within the community of parts, as this would encroach upon the fidelity to the self, which is the only means to the truth of nature. We can be reasonably sure that this is the motive behind her opposition to the mechanical materialism of her mentor. It seems evident that Cavendish could not support the attempt to promote order as an imposed counter-balance to the willed autonomy of the individual. Paradoxically, Cavendish argues for the right to remain the author of her own self-fashioning, not submitting to any conformist system, while equally wanting to promote unity and order for society. Squaring this circle is the underlying aim of her philosophy. Hobbes's mechanist psychology and prescriptive political philosophy, with its rigid codification of a competitive 'state of nature', produces a vision of nature in sharp contrast to the willing conformity Cavendish wishes to promote to balance the needs of self-fashioning with social order.

As a philosopher, Cavendish, unlike Hobbes, is preoccupied with nature's potential for variety and non-competitive freedom of action, thus:

> Nature delights in variety; Nevertheless she is more wise than any Particular Creature or part can conceive which is the cause that Man thinks Nature's wise, subtil and lively actions are as his own gross actions, conceiving them to be constrained and turbulent, not free and easie, as well as wise and knowing; Whereas Nature's Creating, Generating and Producing actions are by an easie connection of parts to parts, without Counterbuffs, Joggs and Jolts.[39]

As coded political commentary, it is clear Cavendish views the mechanist perception of nature as enshrining a combative model of continual conflict and forced restraint. The mechanical paradigm reproduces its 'state of nature' as a reflection of the violent imagery of competition, which disallows an 'easie connection of parts to parts, without Counterbuffs, Joggs and Jolts.' The new paradigm, while seemingly objective, is, for Cavendish, not superior or antecedent to a poetic vision of nature as harmonious and orderly. Cavendish thus creates a division between art as the masculine mode requiring conformity and nature as the feminine mode that embraces variety. A new natural and social philosophy must by implication be aware of these modes in order to embrace the truth of nature's self-generating order and 'infinite varieties'. And Cavendish it seems was happy to acknowledge herself one of these varieties.

Notes

[1] James Gleick, 'Chaos', in Timothy Ferris (ed.) *The World Treasury of Physics, Astronomy and Mathematics* (Boston and London: Back Bay, 1991), pp. 456–473 (p. 460).

[2] My usage of the term 'paradigm' derives from Thomas S. Kuhn, *The Structure of Scientific Revolutions*, (Chicago and London: Chicago University Press, 1962). For a discussion of this expanded usage see Fritjof Capra, *The Web of Life: a New Synthesis of Mind and Matter* (London: Harper Collins, 1996), pp. 5–6.

[3] See, for example, Lisa T. Sarasohn, 'A Science Turned Upside Down: Feminism and the Natural Philosophy of Margaret Cavendish', *Huntington Library Quarterly*, 47 (1984), 289–307.

[4] The similarity of outlook has been referred to in Sophia B. Blaydes, 'Nature is a Woman: The Duchess of Newcastle and Seventeenth-Century Philosophy', in Donald C. Mell, Theodore E. D. Braun and Lucia M. Palmer (eds.) *Man, God, and Nature in the Enlightenment*, Studies in Literature, 1500–1800, 2 (Woodbridge and East Lansing: Boydell and Brewer and Colleagues Press, 1988), *passim*. See also Sarasohn, 'Science Turned Upside Down', *passim*.

[5] Sarah Hutton has provided the best discussion so far of the relationship between Hobbes's philosophy and Cavendish's, in Sarah Hutton, 'In Dialogue with Thomas Hobbes: Margaret Cavendish's natural philosophy', *Women's Writing*, 4 (1997), 421–432.

[6] See, for example, Thomas Hobbes, *The Elements of Law Natural and Politic, part one, Human Nature, part two, and De Corpore Politico, with Three Lives*, ed. by J. C. A. Gaskin, (Oxford: Oxford University Press, 1994), p. xvi.

[7] See *Glorious Fame*, Chapter 4.

[8] For an interesting discussion of Hobbes in relation to William Cavendish and Interregnum politics see Timothy Raylor and James R. Jacob, 'Opera and Obedience: Thomas Hobbes and *A Proposition for Advancement of Moralitie* by Sir William Davenant', *The Seventeenth Century*, 2 (1991), 205–250. For further information on the esteem held by both William and Charles Cavendish toward Hobbes, see Frithiof Brandt, *Denmekaniske Naturopfattelse hos Thomas Hobbes* (Copenhagen: Levin & Munksgaard: 1928), trans. Vaughan Maxwell and Annie I. Fausbøll, *Thomas Hobbes' Mechanical Conception of Nature* (Hachette: London, 1928), pp. 163–165. Also, Jean Jacquot, 'Sir Charles Cavendish

and his Learned Friends: a Contribution to the History of Scientific Relations Between England and the Continent in the Earlier Part of the Seventeenth Century', *Annals of Science*, 8 (1952), 175–191.

[9] See Helen Hervey, 'Hobbes and Descartes in the Light of some Unpublished Letters of the Correspondence between Sir Charles Cavendish and Dr. John Pell', *Osiris*, 10 (1952), 67–91. See also 'An Epiloge to my Physical Opinions', in *Physical Opinions* (1655), sig. B3 verso, where she says, 'And for Master *Hobbes*, it is true I have had the like good fortune to see him, and that very often with my Lord at dinner [...] I cannot say I did not ask him a question, for when I was in *London* I met him, and told as truly I was very glad to see him, and asked him if he would please do me that honour to stay at dinner, but he with great civility refused me, as having some businesse, which I suppose required his absence.'

[10] For a discussion of the implications of Hobbes's materialism, see Samuel I. Mintz, *The Hunting of Leviathan: Seventeenth Century Reactions to the Materialism and Moral Philosophy of Thomas Hobbes* (Cambridge: Cambridge University Press, 1962).

[11] Hobbes, *De Corpore*, p. 191.

[12] Brian Vickers, 'Analogy Versus Identity: the Rejection of Occult Symbolism, 1580–1680', in Brian Vickers (ed.) *Occult and Scientific Mentalities in the Renaissance* (Cambridge: Cambridge University Press, 1984), pp. 95–163.

[13] David Johnston, *The Rhetoric of Leviathan: Thomas Hobbes and the Politics of Cultural Transformation*, (Princeton: Princeton University Press, 1986), Introduction, p. xx.

[14] Johnston, *Rhetoric*, p. xix.

[15] Carolyn Merchant, *The Death of Nature: Women, Ecology and the Scientific Revolution*, (San Francisco and London: Harper and Row, 1979).

[16] *Physical Opinions* (1655), 'The Text to my Natural Sermon', sig. a4 verso.

[17] Stephen Clucas, 'The Duchess and the Viscountess: negotiations between mechanism and vitalism in the natural philosophies of Margaret Cavendish and Anne Conway', *In Between*, 9:1 (2000), 125-136 (pp. 125–29).

[18] Douglas Grant, *Margaret the First: A Biography of Margaret Cavendish, Duchess of Newcastle, 1623–1673* (London: Rupert Hart-Davis, 1957), p. 212.

[19] See Tom Sorrell, 'The Science in Hobbes's Politics', in G. A. J. Rogers and Alan Ryan (eds.) *Perspectives on Thomas Hobbes* (Oxford: Clarendon Press, 1988), pp. 67–81.

[20] Michel Verdon, 'On the Laws of Physical and Human Nature: Hobbes's Physical and Social Cosmologies', *The Journal of the History of Ideas*, 43 (1982), 653–665, and Thomas A. Spragens, *The Politics of Motion: the world of Thomas Hobbes* (Lexington: University Press of Kentucky, 1973).

[21] Verdon, 'Hobbes's Physical and Social Cosmologies', 654–655. See also John Roche, 'Theories of Matter in the Seventeenth Century', in Rom Harré (ed.) *The Physical Sciences Since Antiquity* (London: Croom Helm, 1986), pp. 29–41.

[22] See John Henry, 'Occult Qualities and the Experimental Philosophy: Active Principles In Pre-Newtonian Matter Theory', *History of Science*, 24 (1986), 335–381.

[23] Famously, Descartes viewed the mind, or soul, as non-material, thus 'saving the phenomena' of religious experience from the clutches of mechanical–materialism. The compromise was, nonetheless, sufficiently disturbing to the majority of English natural philosophers and divines to lead them toward theories which maintained a greater role for active principles. Hobbes and Cavendish, by contrast, both deny the distinction, insisting that the mind, and by implication the soul, are material and liable to scientific explanation.

[24] Verdon, 'Hobbes's Physical and Social Cosmologies', p. 656.

[25] See Frederic S. McNeilly, *The Anatomy of Leviathan* (London: Macmillan, 1968).

[26] See Vickers, 'Occult Qualities'.

[27] Thomas Hobbes, *The Leviathan*, ed. by Richard Tuck, (Cambridge: Cambridge University Press, 1991), p. 9.

[28] Hobbes, *Leviathan*, p. 9.

[29] Hobbes, *Leviathan*, p. 9.

[30] *Philosophical Letters* (1664), sig. b2.

[31] Jay Stevenson, 'The Mechanist–Vitalist Soul of Margaret Cavendish', *Studies in English Literature, 1500–1900*, 36 (1996), 527–545.

[32] *Observations* (1666), p. 4.

[33] Margaret Cavendish, 'Of Perception of Parts, and United Perceptions', in *Grounds* (1668), p. 19.

[34] *Observations* (1666), pp. 3–4.

[35] *Grounds* (1668), p. 19.

[36] *Writings* (1994), p. 123.

[37] *Philosophical Letters* (1664), p. 146.

[38] *Philosophical Letters* (1664), p. 151.

[39] *Philosophical Letters* (1664), pp. 152–153.

Bibliography

Algarotti, Francesco, *Il Newtonianismo per le dame, ovvero, dialoghi sopra la luce e i colori* (Naples, 1737) trans. Elizabeth Carter, *Sir Isaac Newton's Philosophy Explained for the Use of Ladies*, 2 vols (London: E. Cave, 1739).

Anonymous, *A Treatise of Diseases of the Head, Brain and Nerves* (London, 1711).

Anonymous, *A Discourse Concerning Fevers. In Two Letters to a young Physician. The First, Dissuading from all Hypotheses and Theories, whether Physical or Mechanical, as vain and delusive. The second, Directing his Regimen for the Cure, and his Conduct to the sick Person* (London, 1727).

Ariès, Philippe, and Duby, Georges (eds.), *A History of Private Life*, trans. Arthur Goldhammer, 3 vols (Cambridge, Mass. and London: Harvard University Press, 1987–1989).

Armstrong, Nancy and Tennenhouse, Leonard (eds.), *The Ideology of Conduct: Essays on Literature and the History of Sexuality* (London: Methuen, 1987).Backscheider, Paula R., *Spectacular Politics: Theatrical Power and Mass Culturein Early Modern England* (London: Johns Hopkins University Press, 1993).

Bacon, Francis, *History Natural and Experimental of Life and Death: or, Of the Prolongation of Life* (London: Printed for William Lee, 1669).

Bacon, Francis, *The Advancement of Learning*, ed. by G. W. Kitchin (London: J. M. Dent & Sons Ltd., 1973).

Ballaster, Ros, 'Seizing the means of seduction: Fiction and feminine identity in Aphra Behn and Delarivier Manley' in *Women, Writing, History*, pp. 93–108.

Barbour, Reid, 'The Early Stuart Epicure', *English Literary Renaissance*, 23 (1993), 170–100.

Barker, Francis, *The Tremulous Private Body: Essays on Subjection* (London: Methuen, 1984).

Barroll, Leeds, 'The Court of the First Stuart Queen', in Linda Levy Peck (ed.), *The Mental World of the Jacobean Court* (Cambridge: Cambridge University Press, 1991).

Battigelli, Anna, *Margaret Cavendish and the Exiles of the Mind* (Lexington: The University Press of Kentucky, 1998).

——, 'Between the Glass and the Hand: the Eye in Margaret Cavendish's Blazing World, 1650–1850', *Ideas, Aesthetics, and Inquiries in the Early Modern Era*, 2 (1996), 25–38.

Bazeley, Deborah Taylor, 'An early challenge to the precepts and practice of modern science: The fusion of fact, fiction, and feminism in the works of Margaret

Cavendish, Duchess of Newcastle, 1623–1673' (unpublished doctoral thesis, University of California, San Diego, 1990).

Behn, Aphra, *Sir Patient Fancy: A Comedy As it is Acted at the Duke's Theatre.* (London, 1678).

——, *The Dutch Lover,a Comedy acted at the Dukes Theatre* (London,1673).

——, *The Widow Ranter or, The History of Bacon in Virginia. A Tragi-Comedy, Acted by their Majesties Servants* (London, 1690).

——, *The False Count, or, A New Way to play an Old Game. As it is Acted at the Dukes Theatre.* (London, 1682).

——, *The Amorous Prince, or the Curious Husband. A Comedy, As it is Acted at his Royal Highness, the Duke of York's Theatre* (London, 1671).

——, *The Rover, or, the Banish't Cavaliers. As it is Acted at His Royal Highness the Duke's Theatre* (London, 1677).

——, *The Town-Fopp: or Sir Timothy Tawdrey. A Comedy* (London, 1677).

——, *The Luckey Chance, or An Alderman's Bargain. A Comedy. As it is Acted by their Majesty's Servants. Written by Mrs. A. Behn* (London, 1687).

Beier, Lucinda, *Sufferers and Healers: The experience of illness in seventeenth-century England* (London and New York: Routledge and Kegan Paul, 1987).

Blaydes, Sophia B., 'Nature is a Woman: The Duchess of Newcastle and Seventeenth-Century Philosophy', in Donald C. Mell, Theodore E. D. Braun and Lucia M. Palmer (ed.), *Man, God, and Nature in the Enlightenment*, Studies in Literature, 1500–1800, 2 (Woodbridge and East Lansing: Boydell and Brewer and Colleagues Press, 1988).

Boesky, Amy Diane, 'The Rhetoric of Reform: English Utopian Narrative, 1516–1667' (unpublished doctoral thesis, Harvard University, 1989).

——, *Founding Fictions: Utopias in Early Modern England* (Athens: University of Georgia Press, 1996).

Bowerbank, Sylvia, 'The Spider's Delight: Margaret Cavendish and the "Female" Imagination', *English Literary Renaissance*, 14 (1984) 392–408.

Boyle, Robert, *The Origine of Formes and Qualities (According to the Corpuscular Philosophy,) Illustrated by Considerations and Experiments, Written formerly by way of Notes upon an Essay about Nitre* (Oxford, 1666).

——, *A Free Enquiry Into the Vulgarly Receiv'd Notion of Nature; Made in an Essay, Address'd to a Friend* (London, 1685/6).

——, *The Christian Virtuoso, shewing that by being addicted to experimental philosophy a man is rather assisted than indisposed to be a good christian,* (London: Edward Jones, 1690).

Brandt, Frithiof, *Denmekaniske Naturopfattelse hos Thomas Hobbes* (Copenhagen: Levin & Munksgaard, 1928) trans. Vaughan Maxwell and Annie I. Fausbøll, *Thomas Hobbes' Mechanical Conception of Nature* (Hachette: London, 1928).

Brant, Clare and Purkiss, Diane, (eds.), *Women, Texts and Histories 1575–1700* (London: Routledge, 1992).

Brink, Jean R., Horowitz, Maryanne C. and Coudert, Allison P. (eds.), *Playing with Gender: A Renaissance Pursuit* (Urbana: University of Illinois Press, 1991).

Brown, Sylvia, 'Margaret Cavendish: Strategies Rhetorical and Philosophical Against the Charge of Wantonness, Or her Excuses for Writing So Much', in *Critical Matrix: Princeton Working Papers in Women's Studies*, 6 (1991), 20–45.

Bunyan, John, *Pilgrim's Progress*, ed. by Roger Sharrock (Harmondsworth: Penguin Books, 1987).

Butler, Judith, *Gender Trouble: Feminism and the Subversion of Identity* (London: Routledge, 1990).

Butler, Martin, *Theatre and Crisis 1632–1642* (Cambridge: Cambridge University Press, 1984).

Capra, Fritjof, *The Web of Life: a New Synthesis of Mind and Matter* (London: Harper Collins, 1996).

Casaubon, Meric, *A Treatise Concerning Enthusiasm as it is an effect of nature but is mistaken by many for either divine inspiration or diabolical possession* (London: Roger Daniel, 1655) repr. with an introduction by Paul J. Korshin (Gainesville, Florida: Scholar's Facsimile and Reprints, 1970).

Case, Sue-Ellen (ed.), *Performing Feminism: Feminist Critical Theory and Theatre* (London: Johns Hopkins University Press, 1990).

Castle, Terry, *Masquerade and Civilization: The Carnivalesque in Eighteenth-Century English Culture and Fiction* (London: Methuen, 1986).

Cave, Terence, *The Cornucopian Text: problems of writing in the French Renaissance* (Oxford: Clarendon, 1979).

Cavendish, Jane and Brackley, Elizabeth, *The Concealed Fancies* in S. P.

Cerasano and Marion Wynne-Davies (eds.), *Renaissance Drama by Women: Texts and Documents* (London: Routledge, 1996), pp. 127–54.

Cavendish, Margaret, *Poems, and Fancies: Written by the Right Honourable, the Lady Margaret Countesse of Newcastle*, (London: Printed by T[homas] R[oycroft] for J. Martin and J. Allestrye at the Bell in Saint Pauls Church Yard, 1653, facsimile reprint: Menston: Scolar Press, 1972).

——, *Philosophicall Fancies. Written By the Right Honourable, The Lady Newcastle* (London: Printed by Tho[mas] Roycroft, for J. Martin, and J. Allestrye, at the Bell in St Pauls Churchyard, 1653).

——, *The Philosophical and Physical Opinions, Written by her Excellency, the Lady Marchionesse of Newcastle* (London: Printed for J. Martin and J. Allestrye at the Bell in St Pauls Church-Yard, 1655).

——, *Philosophical and Physical Opinions. Written By the Thrice Noble, Illustrious, and Excellent Princess, the Lady Marchioness of Newcastle* (London: William Wilson, 1663).

——, *The Worlds Olio. Written By the Right Honorable, the Lady Margaret Newcastle* (London: J. Martin and J. Allestrye at the Bell in St Pauls Church-Yard, 1655).

——, *Natures Pictures drawn by Fancies Pencil to the Life. Written by the thrice Noble, Illustrious, and Excellent Princess, the Lady Marchioness of Newcastle. In this Volume there are several feigned Stories of Natural Descriptions, as Comical, Tragical, and Tragi-Comical, Poetical, Romancical, Philosophical, and Historical, both in Prose and Verse, some all Verse, some all Prose, some mixt, partly Prose, and partly Verse. Also, there are some Morals, and some Dialogues; but they are as the Advantage Loaves of Bread to a Bakers dozen; and a true Story at the latter end, wherein there is no Feignings* (London: J. Martin and T. Allestrye, 1656).

——, *Natures Picture Drawn by Fancies Pencil To the Life. Being several Feigned Stories, Comical, Tragical, Tragi-comical, Poetical, Romancical, Philosophical, Historical, and Moral: some in Verse, some in Prose; some Mixt, and some by Dialogues. Written by the Thrice Noble, Illustrious, and most Excellent Princess, The Duchess of Newcastle. The Second Edition* (London: A. Maxwell, 1671).

——, *Orations of Divers Sorts, Accommodated to Divers Places. Written by the thrice Noble, Illustrious and excelent Princess, the Lady Marchioness of Newcastle* (London: [n. pub.], 1662).

——, *Playes Written by the Thrice Noble, Illustrious and Excellent Princess, the Lady Marchioness of Newcastle* (London: Printed by A. Warren for John Martyn, James Allestry and Tho[mas] Dicas, at the Bell in Saint Pauls Church Yard, 1662).

——, *Philosophical Letters: or Modest Reflections Upon some Opinions in Natural Philosophy, maintained By several Famous and Learned Authors of this Age, Expressed by way of Letters: By the Thrice Noble, Illustrious, and Excellent Princess, The Lady Marchioness of Newcastle* (London: [no pub.], 1664).

——, *CCXI Sociable Letters, Written by the Thrice Noble, Illustrious and Excellent Princess, the Lady Marchioness of Newcastle* (London: William Wilson, 1664).

——, *Margaret Cavendish: Sociable Letters*, ed. by James Fitzmaurice (NewYork: Garland, 1997).

——, *Observations upon Experimental Philosophy. To which is added, the Description of a New Blazing World. Written By the Thrice Noble, Illustrious, and Excellent Princesse, the Duchess of Newcastle* (London: A. Maxwell, 1666).

——, *Observations upon Experimental Philosophy: to which is added, The Description of a New Blazing World. Written by the Thrice Noble, Illustrious, and Excellent Princesse, the Duchess of Newcastle. The second Edition.* (London: A. Maxwell, 1668).

——, *Grounds of Natural Philosophy: Divided into thirteen parts: with an Appendix containing five parts. The Second Edition, much altered from the First, which went under the Name of Philosophical and Physical Opinions.*

Written by the Thrice Noble, Illustrious, and Excellent Princess, the Duchess of Newcastle (London: A. Maxwell, 1668).

——, *Plays, Never Before Printed. Written by the Thrice Noble, Illustrious, and Excellent Princesse, the Duchess of Newcastle* (London: A. Maxwell, 1668).

——, *Poems, or, Several Fancies in Verse: With the Animal Parliament, in Prose. Written By the Thrice Noble, Illustrious, and Excellent Princess, The Duchess of Newcastle. The Third Edition* (London: A.Maxwell, 1668).

——, *A True Relation of the Birth, Breeding, and Life, of Margaret Cavendish, Duchess of Newcastle*, ed. by Sir Egerton Brydges (Kent: Private Press of Lee Priory, 1814).

——, *The Life of the Thrice Noble, High and Puissant Prince William Cavendishe, Duke, Marquess, and Earl of Newcastle; Earl of Ogle; Viscount Mansfield; and Baron of Bolsover, of Ogle, Bothal and Hepple: Gentleman of His Majesties Bed-chamber; one of His Majesties most Honourable Privy-Councel; Knight of the most Noble Order of the Garter; His Majesties Justice in Ayre Trent-North: Who had the honour to be Governour to our most Glorious King, and Gracious Soveraign, in his Youth, when He was Prince of Wales; and soon after was made Captain General of all the Provinces beyond the River of Trent, and other Parts of the Kingdom of England, with Power, by a Special Commission, to make Knights. Written by the Thrice Noble, Illustrious, and Excellent Princess, Margaret, Duchess of Newcastle, His Wife* (London: A. Maxwell, 1667).

——, *The Life of William Cavendish, Duke of Newcastle, To which is added the True Relation of my Birth Breeding and Life By Margaret, Duchess of Newcastle*, ed. by C. H. Firth (London: George Routledge & Sons Ltd., 1906).

——, *The Description of a New World Called the Blazing World and Other Writings*, ed. by Kate Lilley, (London: Pickering & Chatto, 1992; Penguin Classics, 1994).

——, *Sociable Letters*, ed. by James Fitzmaurice (New York: Garland, 1997).

——, *The Convent of Pleasure*, ed. by Jennifer Rowsell (Oxford: Seventeenth Century Press, 1995).

Cavendish, William, *The Phanseys of William Cavendish, Marquis of Newcastle, Addressed to Margaret Lucas* ed. by Douglas Grant (London: Nonesuch, 1956).

——, *Letters and Poems In Honour of the Incomparable Princess, Margaret, Dutchess of Newcastle* (London: Thomas Newcombe, 1676).

Chalmers, Hero, 'Dismantling the Myth of "Mad Madge": The cultural context of Margaret Cavendish's authorial self-presentation', *Women's Writing*, 4 (1997), 323–39.

——, Hero, 'The Politics of Feminine Retreat in Margaret Cavendish's *The Female Academy* and *The Convent of Pleasure*', *Women's Writing*, 6 (1999), 81–94.

Chapman, George, *Chapman's Homer: The Iliad, The Odyssey and the Lesser Homerica*, ed. by Allardyce Nicoll, 2 vols (London: Routledge and Kegan Paul, 1957).

Charleton, Walter, *Physiologia Epicuro–Gassendo–Charltoniana: or A Fabrick of Science Natural, Upon the Hypothesis of Atoms, Founded by Epicurus, Repaired by Petrus Gassendus, Augmented by Walter Charleton, Dr. in Medicine, and Physician to the late Charles, Monarch of Great-Britain* (London, 1654).

——, *The Immortality of the human soul, demonstrated by the light of nature in two dialogues* (London: William Wilson, 1657).

Chedgzoy, Kate, Osborne, Melanie and Trill, Suzanne (eds.), *'Lay By Your Needles, Ladies Take the Pen': Writing Women in England, 1500–1700* (London: Arnold, 1997).

Chernaik, Warren, *Sexual Freedom in Restoration Literature*, (Cambridge University Press, Cambridge, 1995).

Cicero, Marcus Tullius, *Tusculan Disputations*, trans. J. E. King, (Cambridge, Mass. and London: Loeb Classical Library and Harvard University Press, 1996).

Cixous, Hélène, 'The Laugh of the Medusa', trans. Keith Cohen and Paula Cohen, in Elaine Marks and Isabelle de Courtivron (eds.), *New French Feminisms: An Anthology* (New York: Schocken Books, 1981), pp. 245–64.

Clark, Alice, *The Working Life of Women in the Seventeenth Century* (New York: A. M. Kelley, 1968).

Clément, Catherine, 'The Guilty One', in *The Newly Born Woman*, Hélène Cixous and Catherine Clément, trans. by. Betsy Wing (Manchester: Manchester University Press, 1986), pp. 1–59.

Clifford, Anne, *The Diaries of Lady Anne Clifford*, ed. by D. J. H. Clifford (Stroud: Alan Sutton, 1990).

Clucas, Stephen, 'The atomism of the Cavendish Circle: A Reappraisal', *The Seventeenth Century*, 9 (1994), 247–273.

——, Stephen, 'The Duchess and the Viscountess: negotiations between mechanism and vitalism in the natural philosophies of Margaret Cavendish and Anne Conway', *In Between*, 9:1 (2000), 125–136.

Colie, Rosalie, *Light and Englightenment: A Study of the Cambridge Platonists and Dutch Arminians* (Cambridge: Cambridge University Press, 1957).

Conway, Anne, *The Conway Letters: The Correspondence of Anne, Viscountess Conway, Henry More, and their Friends, 1642–1684*, ed. by Marjorie Hope Nicholson, rev. by Sarah Hutton (Oxford: Clarendon, 1992).

Cook, Harold J., *The Decline of the Old Medical Regime in Stuart London*, (Ithaca and London: Cornell University Press, 1986).

Cotton, Nancy, *Women Playwrights in England c. 1363–1750*, (New Jersey: Associated University Press, 1980).

Craig, E. H. (ed.), *Ben Jonson: The Critical Heritage* (London: Routledge, 1990).

Cudworth, Ralph, *The True Intellectual System of the Universe* (London: Richard Royston, 1678).

Daele, Wolfgang van de, 'The Social Construction of Science: Institutionalisation and Definition of Positive Science in the Latter Half of the Seventeenth Century', in Everett Mendelsohn, Peter Weingart and Richard Whitley (eds.), *The Social Production of Scientific Knowledge* (Dordrecht: Reidel, 1977), pp. 27–54.

Daly, Peter M., *Literature in the Light of the Emblem: Structural Parallels between the Emblem and Literature in the Sixteenth and Seventeenth Centuries* (Toronto: University of Toronto Press, 1979).

Davis, Lennard J., *Factual Fictions: The Origins of the English Novel* (New York: Columbia University Press, 1983).

Deleuze, Gilles, *The Fold: Leibniz and the Baroque*, trans. Tom Conley (London: The Athlone Press, 1993).

Deleuze, Gilles, and Guattari, Félix, *What is Philosophy?*, trans. Hugh Tomlinson and Graham Burchill (London and New York: Verso, 1994).

De Mayerne, Theodor Turquet, *Medicinal Councels, or Advices: by Dr Theodor Turquet de Mayerne Baron of Aubonne, Counsellor and Chief Physician to the late King and Queen of England. Englished by Tho. Sherley, MD, Physician in Ordinary to his present Majesty.* (London: Printed for N. Ponder, at the Peacock in the Poultry near Cornhill, and in Chancery Lane near Fleet Street, 1677).

De Santis, Maria, 'Projecting a New Science: Restoration and Eighteenth-Century Scientific Method' (unpublished doctoral thesis, Columbia University, 1992).

Descartes, René, *Discours de la méthode pour bien conduire sa raison et chercher la verité dans les sciences. Plus la dioptrique, les meteores et la géometrie, qui sont des essais de cette méthode* (Leyden, 1637).

Descartes, René, *Discours de la Methode*, ed. by Etienne Gilson (Paris: Vrin, 1947).

Digby, Kenelm, *Observations vpon Religio Medici. Occasionally written by Sir Kenelome* [sic] *Digby, Knight* (London, 1643).

D'Monté, Rebecca, 'Re-Presenting the Female Body in Seventeenth-Century Drama: The Plays of Margaret Cavendish, Duchess of Newcastle, and Aphra Behn' (unpublished doctoral thesis, University of London, 2000).

Donoghue, Emma, *Passions between Women: British Lesbian Culture 1668–1801* (London: Scarlet Press, 1993).

Dryden, John, *The Poems and Fables of John Dryden*, ed. James Kingsley (Oxford: Oxford University Press, 1970).

Dusinberre, Juliet, *Shakespeare and the Nature of Women* (Basingstoke: Macmillan, 1975).

Evelyn, John, *Diary and Correspondence of John Evelyn*, ed. by William Bray, 4 vols (London: Henry Colburn, 1857).

Ezell, Margaret J. M., '"To Be Your Daughter in Your Pen": The Social Functions of Literature in the Writings of Lady Elizabeth Brackley and Lady Jane Cavendish', *Huntington Library Quarterly*, 51 (1988), 281–296.

Farmer, Richard D. (ed.), *Collection of Letters and Poems, Written by Several Persons of Honour and Learning, Upon Divers Important Subjects to the late Duke and Duchess of Newcastle* (London, 1678).

Farrington, Benjamin, '*Temporis Partus Masculus*: An Untranslated Writing of Francis Bacon', *Centaurus*, 1 (1951), 193–205.

Ferguson, Margaret W., 'Renaissance Concepts of the Woman Writer', in Helen Wilcox (ed.), *Women and Literature in Britain, 1500–1700* (Cambridge: Cambridge Univeristy Press, 1996), pp. 146–152.

Fitzmaurice, James, 'Fancy and the Family: Self-characterisations of Margaret Cavendish', *Huntingdon Library Quarterly*, 53 (1990), 198–209.

Foucault, Michel, *The History of Sexuality*, 2 vols (London: Allen Lane, 1979).

Fowler, Alistair, *The Country House Poem: A Cabinet of Seventeenth-Century Estate Poems and Related Items* (Edinburgh: Edinburgh University Press, 1994).

Fumerton, Patricia, *Cultural Aesthetics: Renaissance Literature and the Practice of Social Ornament* (Chicago and London: University of Chicago Press, 1991).

Gabbey, Alan, '*Philosophia cartesiana triumphata*: Henry More (1646–1671)' in Thomas M. Lennon et al. (eds.), *Problems of Cartesianism* (Kingston and Montreal: Queen's McGill University Press, 1982), pp. 171–250.

Gabbey, Alan, 'Henry More and the Limits of Mechanism', in Sarah Hutton (ed.), *Henry More: Tercentenary Studies*, pp. 19–35.

Gagen, Jean, 'Honor and Fame in the Works of the Duchess of Newcastle', *Studies in Philology*, 56 (1959), 519–538.

Gallagher, Catherine, 'Embracing the Absolute: the Politics of the Female Subject in Seventeenth-Century England', *Genders*, 1 (1988) 24–89.

——, 'Who was That Masked Woman? The Prostitute and the Playwright in the Comedies of Aphra Behn', in Janet Todd (ed.), *Aphra Behn, New Casebooks* (Basingstoke: Macmillan Press, 1999).

Gatti, Hilary, *The Renaissance Drama of Knowledge: Giordano Bruno in England*, (London: Routledge, 1989).

Gilbert, Ruth, '"Probleme of Sexes": Representing the Renaissance Hermaphrodite' (unpublished doctoral thesis, University of Southampton, 1996).

Girouard, Mark, *Life in the English Country House: A Social and Architectural History* (Harmondsworth: Penguin, 1980).

Glanvill, Joseph, *Essays on Several Important Subjects in Philosophy and Religion* (London: John Baker, 1676).

——, *Philosophia Pia, or, a discourse of the religious temper and tendencies of the experimental philosophy which is expressed by the Royal Society* (London: J. Macock, 1671).

Gleick, James, 'Chaos', in *The World Treasury of Physics, Astronomy and Mathematics*, ed. by Timothy Ferris (Boston and London: Back Bay, 1991), pp. 456–473.

Gouge, William, *Of Domesticall Duties: Eight Treatises* (London: William Bladen, 1622).

Graham, Elspeth et al. (eds.), *Her Own Life: Autobiographical Writings by Seventeenth-century Englishwomen*, (London and New York: Routledge, 1989).

Grant, Douglas, *Margaret the First: A Biography of Margaret Cavendish, Duchess of Newcastle, 1623–1673* (London: Rupert Hart-Davis, 1957).

Grean, Stanley, *Shaftesbury's Philosophy of Religion and Ethics: A Study in Enthusiasm* (Athens: Ohio University Press, 1967).

Greene, Thomas M., *The Light in Troy: imitation and discovery in Renaissance poetry* (New Haven: Yale University Press, 1982).

Greer, Germaine, (ed.), *Kissing The Rod: An Anthology of Seventeenth-Century Women's Verse* (London: Virago, 1988).

Gregory, Elizabeth, 'Unravelling Penelope: The Construction of the Faithful Wife in Homer's Heroines', *Helios*, 23 (1996), 3–20.

Grundy, Isobel and Wiseman, Susan (eds.), *Women, Writing, History 1640–1740* (London: Batsford, 1992).

Hackett, Helen, '"Yet Tell Me Some Such Fiction": Lady Mary Wroth's *Urania* and the "Femininity" of Romance', in Brant and Purkiss (eds.), *Women, Texts & Histories*, pp. 39–68.

Hall, A. Rupert, *Henry More: Magic, Religion and Experiment* (Oxford: Blackwell, 1990).

Harding, Sandra, 'Women look at science', *Women: A Cultural Review*, 1:1 (1990), 99–105.

Harth, Philip, *Swift and Anglican Rationalism: The Religious Background of A Tale of a Tub* (Chicago: University of Chicago Press, 1961).

Helgerson, Richard, in *Self-Crowned Laureates. Spenser, Jonson, Milton and the Literary System*, (Berkeley and London: University of California Press, 1983).

Henry, John, 'Thomas Harriot and Atomism: A Reappraisal', *The History of Science*, 20 (1982), 255–96.

Herbert, George, *The English Poems of George Herbert*, ed. by C. A. Patrides (London: J. M. Dent and Sons, Everyman's Library, 1974).

Herdt, Gilbert, (ed.) *Third Sex, Third Gender: Beyond Sexual Dimorphism in Culture and History*, (New York: Zone Books, 1994).

Hervey, Helen, 'Hobbes and Descartes in the Light of some Unpublished Letters of the Correspondence between Sir Charles Cavendish and Dr. John Pell', *Osiris*, 10 (1952), 67–91.

Hester, Marianne, *Lewd Women and Wicked Witches: A Study of the Dynamics of Male Domination* (London: Routledge, 1992).

Hillis Miller, J., *Ariadne's Thread: Story Lines* (New Haven: Yale University Press, 1992).

Hobbes, Thomas, *The Elements of Law Natural and Politic, part one, Human Nature, part two, and De Corpore Politico, with Three Lives*, ed. by J. C. A. Gaskin, (Oxford: Oxford University Press, 1994).

Hobby, Elaine, *Virtue of Necessity: English Women's Writing 1649–88* (London, Virago Press, 1988).

Hotson, Leslie, *The Commonwealth and Restoration Stage* (Cambridge Mass.: Harvard University Press, 1928).

Houghton Jr., Walter E., 'The English Virtuoso in the Seventeenth Century', *Journal of the History of Ideas*, 3 (1942) 51–73 and 190–219.

Huebert, Ronald, 'Privacy: The Early Social History of a Word', *The Sewanee Review*, 105 (1997), 21–38

Hughes, Derek, 'The Masked Woman Revealed; or, the prostitute and the playwright in Aphra Behn criticism', *Womens Writing*, 7:2 (2000), 149–164.

Hume, Robert D., *The Rakish Stage. Studies in English Drama 1660-1800*, (Carbondale and Edwardsville: Southern Illinois University Press, 1983).

Hunter, Lynette, 'Women and Domestic Medicine: Lady Experimenters 1570–1620', in Lynette Hunter and Sarah Hutton (eds.), *Women, Science and Medicine 1500–1700. Mothers and Sisters of the Royal Society* (Stroud: Alan Sutton, 1997), pp. 89–107.

Hutton, Sarah, 'In Dialogue with Thomas Hobbes: Margaret Cavendish's natural philosophy', *Women's Writing*, 4 (1997), 421–432.

——, 'Anne Conway, Margaret Cavendish and Seventeenth-Century Scientific Thought', in Lynette Hunter and Sarah Hutton (eds.), *Women, Science and Medicine 1500–1700. Mothers and Sisters of the Royal Society* (Stroud: Alan Sutton, 1997), pp. 218–234.

——, (ed.), *Henry More: Tercentenary Studies* (Dordrecht: Kluwer, 1990).

——, 'Lord Herbert and the Cambridge Platonists', in *Routledge History of Philosophy*, 10 vols (London and New York: Routledge, 1993–1999), V: *British Philosophy in the Age of Enlightenment*, ed. by Stuart Brown, (London and New York: Routledge, 1996), pp. 20–42.

——, 'Damaris Cudworth, Lady Masham: Between Platonism and Enlightenment', *British Journal for the History of Philosophy*, 1:1 (1993), 29–54.

——, 'Of Physic and Philosophy: Anne Conway, F. M. van Helmont and seventeenth-century Medicine', in Ole Peter Grell and Andrew Cunningham (eds.), *Religio Medici: Medicine and Religion in Seventeenth-century England* (Aldershot and Brookfield: Ashgate and Scolar Press, 1996), pp. 228–246.

Jacquot, Jean, 'Sir Charles Cavendish and his Learned Friends: a Contribution to the History of Scientific Relations Between England and the Continent in the Earlier Part of the Seventeenth Century', *Annals of Science*, 8 (1952), 13–27 and 175–191.

——, 'Un Amateur de Science, Ami de Hobbes et de Descartes, Sir Charles Cavendish', *Thales*, 6 (1949–1950), 81–88.

James, Susan, 'The Philosophical Innovations of Margaret Cavendish', *British Journal for the History of Philosophy*, 7:2 (1999), 219–244.

Jardine, Lisa, *Reading Shakespeare Historically* (London: Routledge, 1996).Johnston, David, *The Rhetoric of Leviathan: Thomas Hobbes and the Politics of Cultural Transformation*, (Princeton: Princeton University Press, 1986).Jones, Ann Rosalind, 'Nets and Bridles: Early Modern Conduct Books and Sixteenth Century Women's Lyrics', in Nancy Armstrong and Leonard Tennenhouse (eds.), *The Ideology of Conduct: Essays on Literature and the History of Sexuality* (London: Methuen, 1987), pp. 39–72.

Jones, Kathleen, *A Glorious Fame: The Life of Margaret Cavendish, Duchess of Newcastle, 1623–1673* (London: Bloomsbury, 1988).

Jonson, Ben, *Ben Jonson*, edited by C. H. Herford and Percy and Evelyn Simpson, 11 vols (Oxford: Clarendon Press, 1925–1963).

Jowitt, Claire, 'Imperial Dreams? Margaret Cavendish and the Cult of Elizabeth', *Women's Writing*, 4.3 (1997), 383–99.

Kahn, Victoria, 'Margaret Cavendish and the Romance of Contract', *Renaissance Quarterly*, 50 (1997), 526–566.

Kaplan, E. Ann, 'Is the Gaze Male?', in *Powers of Desire: The Poliics of Sexuality*, ed. by Ann Snitow, Christine Stansell and Sharon Thompson (London: Virago, 1984), pp. 321–38.

Kargon, Robert Hugh, *Atomism in England from Harriot to Newton*, (Oxford: Clarendon Press, 1966).

Keeble, N. H. (ed.), *The Cultural Identity of Seventeenth-Century Woman. A Reader* (London: Routledge, 1994).

——, 'Obedient subjects? The loyal self in some later seventeenth-century Royalist women's memoirs', in Gerald Maclean (ed.), *Culture and Society in the Stuart Restoration: Literature, Drama, History* (Cambridge: Cambridge University Press, 1995).

Keller, Eve, 'Producing Petty Gods: Margaret Cavendish's Critique of Experimental Science', *English Literary History*, 64 (1997), 447–471.

Khanna, Lee Cullen, 'The Subject of Utopia: Margaret Cavendish and Her Blazing World', in Jane L. Donawerth and Carol A. Kolmerten (eds.), *Utopian and Science Fiction by Women: Worlds of Difference*, (New York: Syracuse University Press, 1994), pp. 15–34.

King, Lester, *The Philosophy of Medicine: The early Eighteenth Century* (Cambridge, Mass.: Harvard University Press, 1978).

Kline, Morris, *Mathematical Thought from Ancient to Modern Times* (New York: Oxford University Press, 1971).

Kuhn, Thomas S., *The Structure of scientific Revolutions* (Chicago and London: Chicago University Press, 1962).

Kundera, Milan, *Slowness*, trans. Linda Ash (New York: Harper Collins, 1996).Kunzle, David, 'World Upside Down: The Iconography of a European Broadsheet Type', in Barbara A. Babcock (ed.), *The Reversible*

World. Symbolic Inversion in Art and Society (Ithaca: Cornell University Press, 1978), pp. 39–94.

Lamb, Charles, *Elia and the Last Essays of Elia*, ed. by E.V. Lucas (London: Methuen, 1912).

Lamb, Mary Ellen, *Gender and Authorship in the Sidney Circle* (Madison: University of Wisconsin Press, 1990).

Langbaine, Gerard, in *An Account of the English Dramatick Poets. Or, Some Observations and Remarks On the Lives and Writings, of all those that have Publish'd either Comedies, Tragedies, Tragi-Comedies, Pastorals, Masques, Interludes, Farces, or Opera's in the English Tongue* (Oxford, 1691).

Langhans, Edward A., *Restoration Promptbooks*, (Carbondale and Edwardsville: Southern Illinois University Press, 1981).

——, *Eighteenth Century British and Irish Promptbooks. A Descriptive Bibliography* (Connecticut: Greenwood Press, 1987).

Laurence, Ann, *Women in England, 1500–1700: A Social History* (London: Weidenfeld and Nicolson, 1994).

——, 'The Ambiguous Privacy of the Closet: How Private Was Women's Space in the Early Modern Period?' (unpublished conference paper, 1995).

Lauretis, Teresa de, (ed.), *Feminist Studies, Critical Studies* (Bloomington: Indiana University Press, 1986).

——, 'Sexual Indifference and Lesbian Representation', in Sue-Ellen Case (ed.), *Performing Feminism: Feminist Critical Theory and Theatre* (London: Johns Hopkins University Press, 1990), pp. 17–39.

Lawrence, Karen R., *Penelope Voyages: women and travel in the British literary tradition* (Ithaca: Cornell University Press, 1992).

Leslie, Marina, 'Gender, Genre and the Utopian Body in Margaret Cavendish's Blazing World', *Utopian Studies*, 7 (1996), 6–24.

Lewalski, Barbara, *Writing Women in Jacobean England* (Cambridge, Mass.: Harvard University Press, 1993).

Lewcock, Dawn, 'More for Seeing than for Hearing: Behn and the use of Theatre', in Janet Todd (ed.), *Aphra Behn Studies* (Cambridge: Cambridge University Press, 1996), pp. 66–83.

Lichtenstein, Aharon, *Henry More: The rational theology of a Cambridge Platonist* (Cambridge, Mass.: Harvard University Press, 1962).

Lieb, Laurie Yager, '"The Works of Women are Symbolical": Needlework in the Eighteenth Century', *Eighteenth-Century Life*, 10 (1986), 28–44.

Lilley, Kate (ed.), *The Description of a New World Called the Blazing World and Other Writings* (London: William Pickering, 1992).

——, 'Blazing Worlds: Seventeenth-Century Women's Utopian Writing', in Brant and Purkiss (eds.), *Women, Texts and Histories 1575–1760*, pp. 102–133.

McAfee, Helen, (ed.), *Pepys on the Restoration Stage*, (Newhaven: Yale University Press, 1919)

Macfarlane, Alan, *Marriage and Love in England: Modes of Reproduction 1300–1840* (Oxford: Basil Blackwell, 1986).

McKeon, Michael, *Origins of the English Novel 1600–1740* (Baltimore and London: Johns Hopkins University Press, 1987).

Maclean, Ian, *The Renaissance Notion of Woman* (Cambridge: Cambridge University Press, 1980).

Macheski, Cecilia, 'Penelope's Daughters. Images of Needlework in Eighteenth-Century Literature', in Mary Anne Schofield and Cecilia Macheski (eds.), *Fetter'd or Free? British Women Novelists, 1670–1815* (Athens: Ohio University Press, 1986), pp. 85–100.

Malet, Antoni, 'Barrow, Wallis, and the Remaking of Seventeenth-Century Indivisibles', *Centaurus*, 39 (1997), 67–92.

Mancosu, Paolo, *Philosophy of Mathematics and Mathematical Practice in the Seventeenth Century*, (Oxford: Oxford University Press, 1996).

Marks, Elaine and Courtivron, Isabelle de (eds.), *New French Feminisms: An Anthology* (New York: Schocken Books, 1981).

Masten, Jeffrey, *Textual Intercourse: Collaboration, Authorship, and Sexualities in Renaissance Drama* (Cambridge: Cambridge University Press, 1997).

Mendelson, Sara Heller, *The Mental World of Stuart Women. Three Studies* (Brighton: Harvester, 1987).

Merchant, Carolyn, *The Death of Nature: Women, Ecology and the Scientific Revolution*, (San Francisco and London: Harper and Row, 1979).

Meyer, Gerald Dennis, *The Scientific Lady in England, 1650–1760* (Berkeley: University of California Press, 1955).

Milhous, Judith, and Robert D. Hume (eds.), *A Register of English Theatre Documents 1660–1737*, 2 Vols (Carbondale: Southern Illinois University Press, 1991).

Milling, Jane, 'Lady Contemplation's Philosophical Fancies: The Closet Drama of Margaret Cavendish' (unpublished conference paper, 1995).

Mintz, Samuel I., *The Hunting of Leviathan: Seventeenth-Century Reactions to the Materialism and Moral Philosophy of Thomas Hobbes* (Cambridge: Cambridge University Press, 1962).

——, 'The Duchess of Newcastle's Visit to the Royal Society', *Journal of English and Germanic Philology*, 51 (1952), 168–176.

Mittag, Martina, 'Soma, Sema, Sexus: Territorialisierung der Körper im frühneuzeitlichen Diskurs', in Heide Wunder (ed.), *Geschlechter-perspektiven: Forschungen zur Frühen Neuzeit* (Königstein: Ulrike Helmer Verlag, 1998), pp. 395–407.

Moi, Toril, *Sexual–Textual Politics. Feminist Literary Theory* (London and New York: Routledge, 1988).

More, Henry, *Psychodia Platonica; or a platonicall song of the soul* (Cambridge, 1642).

——, *Philosophical Poems* (Cambridge, 1647).

——, *The immortality of the soul so farre forth as is demonstrable from the knowledge of nature and the light of reason* (London: J. Flesher, 1659).

——, *A Collection of Several Philosophical Writings* (London, 1662).

——, *Enthusiasmus Triumphatus, or a brief discourse of the nature, causes, kinds and cure of enthusiasm* (London, 1662), repr. with an introduction by Michael V. Da Porte, Augustan Reprint Society, 118 (Los Angeles: William Andrews Clark Memorial Library, 1966).

Mulvey, Laura, *Visual and Other Pleasures* (Basingstoke: Macmillan, 1989).Needham, Francis (ed.), 'A Collection of Poems by Several Hands', *Welbeck*

Miscellany, 2 (Bungay: Richard Clay and Sons, 1934).

Nerlich, Michael, *The Ideology of Adventure. Studies in modern consciousness, 1100–1750*, trans. by Ruth Cowley, 2 vols, Theory and History of Literature, 42–3 (Minneapolis: University of Minnesota Press, 1987).

Nicolson, Marjorie Hope, *Pepys' Diary and the New Science* (Charlottesville: University Press of Virginia, 1965).

——, *Voyages to the Moon* (New York: MacMillan, 1948).O'Connor, Barry, 'Late Seventeenth-Century Royal Portraiture and Restoration Staging', *Theatre Notebook*, 49:3 (1995), 152–64.

Olejniczak, Verena, 'Unendliche Welten. Margaret Cavendishs imaginative Konstruktion der Wirklichkeit zwischen Skepsis und Platonismus', *Mitteilungen des Zentrums zur Erforschung der frühen Neuzeit*, 1 (1994), 222–259.

Osborne, Dorothy, *Letters to Sir William Temple*, ed. by Kenneth Parker (Harmondsworth: Penguin, 1987).

Pagel, Walter, *Jan Baptista van Helmont, Reformer of Science and Medicine* (Cambridge: Cambridge University Press, 1982).

Parker, Patricia, *Literary Fat Ladies: Rhetoric, Gender, Property* (London: Methuen, 1987).

Parker, Rozsika, *The Subversive Stitch: Embroidery and the Making of the Feminine* (London: The Women's Press, 1984).

Partridge, Eric, (ed.), *The Penguin Dictionary of Historical Slang*, sixth edition, abridged by Jacqueline Simpson (Harmondsworth: Penguin, 1988).

Patterson, Annabel, *Censorship and Interpretation: The Conditions of Writing and Reading in Early Modern England* (Madison: University of Wisconsin Press, 1984).

Payne, Linda R., 'Dramatic Dreamscape: Women's Dreams and Utopian Vision in the Works of Margaret Cavendish, Duchess of Newcastle', in Mary Anne Schofield and Cecilia Macheski (eds.), *Curtain Calls: British and American Women and the Theater 1660–1820* (Athens: Ohio University Press, 1991), pp. 18–33.

Pearson, Jacqueline, '"Women May Discourse ... as Well as Men": Speaking and Silent Women in the Plays of Margaret Cavendish, Duchess of Newcastle', *Tulsa Studies in Women's Literature*, 4 (1985), 33–45.

——, *The Prostituted Muse: Images of Women & Women Dramatists, 1642–1737* (New York and London: Harvester–Wheatsheaf, 1988).

Pepper, Jon V., 'Harriot's Calculation of the Meridional Parts as Logarithmic Tangents', *Archive for History of Exact Sciences*, 4 (1968), 359–413.

Pepys, Samuel, *The Diary of Samuel Pepys*, ed. by Robert Latham and William Matthews, 11 vols. (London: Bell and Hyman, 1970).

Primrose, James, *Popular Errours, or the Errours of the People in Physick*, trans. by Robert Wittie (London, 1651).

Raehs, Andrea, *Zur Ikonographie des Hermaphroditen. Begriff und Problem von Hermaphroditismus und Androgynie in der Kunst* (Frankfurt: Peter Lang, 1987).

Randall, Dale B. J., *Winter Fruit: English Drama, 1642–1660* (Lexington: University Press of Kentucky, 1995).

Raylor, Timothy J., '"Pleasure Reconciled to Virtue": William Cavendish, Ben Jonson, and the Decorative Scheme of Bolsover Castle', *Renaissance Quarterly*, 52 (1999), 402–39.

Raylor, Timothy J., and Jacob, James R., 'Opera and Obedience: Thomas Hobbes and *A Proposition for Advancement of Moralitie* by Sir William Davenant', *The Seventeenth Century*, 2 (1991), 205–250.

Read, John, *Prelude to Chemistry: An outline of alchemy, its literature and relationships* (London: G. Bells & Sons, 1936).

Reynolds, Myra, *The Learned Lady in England 1650–1760* (Boston: Houghton Mifflin Co., 1920).

Riverius, Lazar, *The Universal Body of Physick* (London, 1657).

Roberts, Josephine A.,'An Unpublished Literary Quarrel Concerning the Suppression of Mary Wroth's "Urania" (1621)', *Notes and Queries*, 222 (1977), 532–535.

Robinson, David, 'What's a Nice Muse Like You Doing in a Text Like This?, or: (Pro) Lesbian Readings of Margaret Cavendish's Works' (unpublished conference paper, Margaret Cavendish Conference, University of East Anglia, 1996).

Rogers, John, *The Matter of Revolution: Science, Poetry and Politics in the Age of Milton* (Ithaca: Cornell University Press, 1996).

Rosenthal, Laura J., *Playwrights and Plagiarists in Early Modern England*, (Ithaca: Cornell University Press, 1996).

Ross, Alexander, *The Philosophical Touchstone: or Observations upon Kenelm Digby's Discourses of the nature of Bodies and of the reasonable Soule* (London: James Ross, 1645).

Rous, Francis, *The Mysticall Marriage; or, Experimentall Discoveries of the Heavenly Marriage Between a Soule and her Saviour* (London: Printed by W. I. and T. P. for I. Emery, 1635).

Ruggiero, Guido, 'Marriage, Love, Sex, and Renaissance Civil Morality', in James Grantham Turner (ed.), *Sexuality and Gender in Early Modern Europe: Institutions, Texts, Images* (Cambridge: Cambridge University Press, 1993), pp. 10–30.

Russo, Mary, 'Female Grotesques: Carnival and Theory', in Teresa de Lauretis (ed.), *Feminist Studies, Critical Studies* (Bloomington: Indiana University Press, 1986), pp. 213–29.

Salzman, Paul (ed.), *An Anthology of Seventeenth-Century Fiction*, (Oxford: Oxford University Press, 1991).

Sanders, Julie, '"A Woman Write a Play!": Jonsonian Strategies in the drama of Margaret Cavendish, or Did the Duchess Feel the Anxiety of Influence', in S. P. Cerasano and Marion Wynne-Davies (eds.), *Readings in Renaissance Drama by Women* (London: Routledge 1998), pp. 293–305.

Sarasohn, Lisa T., 'A Science Turned Upside Down: Feminism and the Natural Philosophy of Margaret Cavendish', *Huntington Library Quarterly*, 47 (1984), 289–307.

——, 'Thomas Hobbes and the Duke of Newcastle: A Study in the Mutuality of Patronage before the Establishment of the Royal Society', *Isis*, 90 (1999), 715–737.

Saunders, John Whiteside, *The Profession of English Letters* (London and Toronto: Routledge and Toronto University Press, 1964).

Schiebinger, Londa, *The Mind has no Sex? Women in the Origins of Modern Science* (Cambridge, Mass.: Harvard University Press, 1989).

Schofield, Mary Anne and Cecilia Macheski, (eds.), *Curtain Calls: British and American Women and the Theater 1660–1820* (Athens: Ohio University Press, 1991).

Sellers, Susan, *Language and Sexual Difference. Feminist Writing in France* (Basingstoke: Macmillan, 1991).

Sennert, Daniel, *Institutions or Fundamentals of the Whole Art, Both of Physick and Chirurgery* trans. 'N. D. B. P., late of Trinity Colledge in Cambridge', (London, 1656).

Shapin, Steven and Schaffer, Simon, *Leviathan and the Airpump: Hobbes, Boyle, and the Experimental Life* (Princeton: Princeton University Press, 1985).

Shapiro, Barbara J., *Probability and Certainty in Seventeenth-Century England: A Study of the relationships between Natural Science, Religion, History, Law and Literature* (Princeton: Princeton University Press, 1983).

Sherman, Sandra, 'Trembling Texts: Margaret Cavendish and the Dialectic of Authorship, *English Literary Renaissance*, 24 (1994), 184–210.

Shirley, James, *The Maides Revenge. A Tragedy. As it hath beene acted with good Applause at the private house in Dury Lane, by her Majesties servants* (London, 1639).

Slaughter, Thomas P., *Ideology and Politics on the Eve of the Restoration: Newcastle's Advice to Charles II* (Philadelphia: American Philosophical Society, 1984).

Smith, Hilda L., *Reason's Disciples: Seventeenth Century English Feminists*, (Urbana: University of Illinois Press, 1982).

Smuts, R. Malcolm (ed.), *The Stuart Court and Europe: essays in politics and political culture*, (Cambridge: Cambridge University Press, 1996).

Snitow, Ann, Stansell, Christine and Thompson, Sharon (eds.), *Powers of Desire: The Politics of Sexuality* (London: Virago, 1984).

Sokol, B. J., 'Poet in the Atomic Age: Robert Frost's "That Millikan Mote" Expanded', *Annals of Science*, 53 (1996), 399–412.

——, 'Logic and Illogic in Marvell's "To His Coy Mistress"', *English Studies*, 71 (1990), 244–252.

——, 'Thomas Harriot – Sir Walter Ralegh's Tutor – on Population', *Annals of Science*, 31 (1974), 205–12.

——,, 'The Problem of Assessing Thomas Harriot's "A briefe and true report" of his Discoveries in North America', *Annals of Science*, 51 (1994), 1–16.

Sorrell, Tom, 'The Science in Hobbes's Politics', in G. A. J. Rogers and Alan Ryan (eds.), *Perspectives on Thomas Hobbes* (Oxford: Clarendon Press, 1988).

Sprat, Thomas, *History of the Royal Society*, ed. by Jackson J. Cope and Harold Whitmore Jones (London: Routledge & Kegan Paul, 1958).

——, 'An Account of the Life and Writings of Mr.Abraham Cowley Written to Mr. M. Clifford', in *The Works of Mr Abraham Cowley. Consisting of Those which were formerly Printed: And Those which he Design'd for the Press, Now Published out of the Author's Original Copies* (London: Printed by J. M. for Henry Herringman, 1668).

Stanton, Domna C., 'Recuperating Women and the Man behind the Screen', in James Grantham Turner (ed.), *Sexuality and Gender in Early Modern Europe: Institutions, Texts, Images* (Cambridge: Cambridge University Press, 1993), pp. 247–265.

Staves, Susan, *Players' Sceptres. Fictions of Authority in the Restoration.* (Lincoln and London: University of Nebraska Press, 1979).

Stevenson, Jay, 'The Mechanist–Vitalist Soul of Margaret Cavendish,' *Studies in English Literature 1500–1900*, 36 (1996), 527–543.

Stewart, Alan, *Close Readers: Humanism and Sodomy in Early Modern England* (Princeton: Princeton University Press, 1997).

——, 'The Early Modern Closet Discovered', *Representations,* 50 (1995), 76–100.

Stewart, Stanley, *The Enclosed Garden: The Tradition and the Image in Seventeenth-Century Poetry* (London: University of Wisconsin Press, 1966).

Stone, Lawrence, *Road to Divorce, England 1530-1987* (Oxford: Oxford University Press, 1990).

Straznicky, Marta, 'Reading the stage: Margaret Cavendish and Commonwealth closet drama', *Criticism*, 37 (1995), 355–390.

Stuart, Arbella, *The Letters of Lady Arbella Stuart*, ed. by Sara Jayne Steen (Oxford: Oxford University Press, 1994).

Suleiman, Susan Rubin, (ed.), *The Female Body in Western Culture: Contemporary Perspectives* (Cambridge, MA: Harvard University Press, 1986).

Suzuki, Mihoko, 'The Essay Form as Critique: Reading Cavendish's *The World's Olio* through Montaigne and Bacon (and Adorno), in *Prose Studies*, 22:3 (1999), 1–16.

Swift, Jonathan, *A Tale of a Tub with Other Early Works*, ed. by Herbert Davis (Oxford: Blackwell, 1965).

Sydenham, Thomas, *The Whole Works of that Excellent Practical Physician, Dr Thomas Sydenham*, third edition, ed. by John Pechey (London: Printed for Richard Wellington and Edward Castle, 1701).

Todd, Janet, *The Sign of Angellica: Women, Writing and Fiction, 1660–1800* (London: Virago, 1989).

Tomlinson, Sophie, '"My Brain the Stage": Margaret Cavendish and the Fantasy of Female Performance', in Brant and Purkiss (eds.), *Women, Texts and Histories 1575–1700*, pp. 134–63.

——, 'She That Plays the King: Henrietta Maria and the Threat of the Actress in Caroline Culture', in Gordon McMullan and Jonathan Hope (eds.), *The Politics of Tragicomedy: Shakespeare and After* (London: Routledge, 1992), pp. 189–207.

Trease, Geoffrey, *Portrait of a Cavalier: William Cavendish, First Duke of Newcastle* (London: Macmillan, 1979).

Trussler, Simon (ed.), *An adaptation of The Rover (The Banished Cavaliers) by Aphra Behn. A programme/text with commentary by Simon Trussler* (London: Methuen, by arrangement with the Royal Shakespeare Company, 1986).

Turner, James Grantham, (ed.), *Sexuality and Gender in Early Modern Europe: Institutions, Texts, Images* (Cambridge: Cambridge University Press, 1993).

Van Lennep, William B., (ed.), *The London Stage 1660-1800, Part I, 1660-1700* (Carbondale: Southern Illinois University Press, 1965).

Verdon, Michel, 'On the Laws of Physical and Human Nature: Hobbes's Physical and Social Cosmologies', *Journal of the History of Ideas*, 43 (1982), 653–665.

Vickers, Brian, 'Analogy Versus Identity: the Rejection of Occult Symbolism, 1580–1680', in Brian Vickers (ed.), *Occult and Scientific Mentalities in the Renaissance* (Cambridge: Cambridge University Press, 1984), pp. 95–163.

Vickers, Nancy J., 'This Heraldry in Lucrece' Face', in Susan Rubin Suleiman (ed.), *The Female Body in Western Culture: Contemporary Perspectives* (Cambridge, Mass.: Harvard University Press, 1986), pp. 209–22.

Ward, Richard, *The Life of Henry More, Parts 1 and 2*, ed. by Sarah Hutton et al., Archives internationales d'histoire des idées, 167 (Dordrecht and Boston: Kluwer Academic, 2000).

Watkins, J. W. N., *Hobbes' System of Ideas: A Study in the Political Significance of Philosophical Theories* (London: Hutchinson University Library, 1965).

Weber, Ingeborg, (ed.), *Weiblichkeit und weibliches Schreiben* (Darmstadt: Wissenschaftliche Buchgesellschaft, 1994).

Wiesner, Merry, *Women and Gender in Early Modern Europe* (Cambridge: Cambridge University Press, 1993).

Wilcox, Helen,'Private Writing and Public Functions: Autobiographical Texts by Renaissance Englishwoman', in S. P. Cerasano and Marion Wynne-Davies (eds.), *Gloriana's Face: Women, Public and Private in the English Renaissance* (London: Harvester Wheatsheaf, 1992), pp. 47–62.

Williams, Gweno, '"Why may not a Lady write a good play?" : Plays by Early Modern women reassessed as performance texts' in S. P. Cerasano and Marion Wynne-Davies (eds.), *Readings in Renaissance Women's Drama Criticism, history and performance 1594–1998* (London: Routledge, 1998), pp. 95–107.

Willis, Thomas, *The Remaining Works of that Famous and Renowned Physican Dr Thomas Willis*, trans. S. Pordage (London: Printed for T. Dring, C. Harper and J. Leigh, 1681).

——, *The London Practice of Physick: Or the whole Practical Part of Physick Contained in the Works of Dr Willis. Faithfully made English, and Printed together for the Publick Good* (London: Printed for T. Bassett, 1689).

Wilmot, John, Earl of Rochester, *The Letters of John Wilmot, Earl of Rochester*, ed. by Jeremy Treglown (Oxford: Blackwell, 1980).

Wilputte, Earla W., 'Margaret Cavendish's Imaginary Voyage to The Blazing World: Mapping a Feminine Discourse', in Donald W. Nicol (ed.), *Transatlantic Crossings: Eighteenth-Century Explorations* (St.Johns: Memorial University of Newfoundland, 1995), pp. 109–111.

Wiseman, Susan, *Drama and Politics in the English Civil War* (Cambridge: Cambridge University Press, 1998).

Wiseman, Susan, 'Gender and Status in Dramatic Discourse: Margaret Cavendish, Duchess of Newcastle', in Grundy and Wiseman (eds.), *Women, Writing, History 1640–1740*, pp. 159–77.

Woodbridge, Linda, 'Patchwork: Piecing the Early Modern Mind in England's First Century of Print Culture', *English Literary Renaissance*, 23 (1993), 5–45.

Woolf, Virginia, *A Room of One's Own* (London: The Hogarth Press, 1929).

——, *The Common Reader. First Series* (London: Hogarth Press, 1925).

Wroth, Mary, *The First Part of the Countess of Montgomery's Urania*, ed. by Josephine A. Roberts (Binghampton, New York: Medieval and Renaissance Texts and Studies, 1995).

Yolton, John, *Thinking Matter: Materialism in Eighteenth-century Britain* (Minneapolis: University of Minnesota Press, 1983).

Zakin, Sergei, 'Inside Books of the World: Issues of Textual Interpretation in Mid-Seventeenth Century Discourse on Knowledge' (unpublished doctoral thesis, University of Cambridge, 1997).

Zimbardo, Rose, *A Mirror To Nature: Transformations in Drama and Aesthetics 1660–1732* (Kentucky: University of Kentucky Press, 1986).

Index